A MURDER IN CEYLON

THE SATHASIVAM CASE

Vijitha Yapa Publications
Unity Plaza, 2 Galle Road, Colombo 4, Sri Lanka
Tel. (94 11) 2596960   Fax (94 11) 2584801
e-mail: vijiyapa@gmail.com
www.srilankanbooks.com
www.vijithayapa.com

Copyright © Professor Ravindra Fernando

Paperback ISBN 978-955-1266-20-2
Hardback ISBN 978-955-1266-33-2

All rights reserved. No part of this book may be reproduced, stored in a retrieval system or transmitted by any means, electronic, mechanical, photocopying, recording or otherwise, without written permission from the author.

First Edition June 2006
First Reprint May 2007

Printed by Tharanjee Prints, Sri Lanka

A MURDER IN CEYLON

THE SATHASIVAM CASE

Professor Ravindra Fernando
MBBS, MD, FCCP, FCGP, FRCP (Lond)
FRCP(Glasgow), FRCP(Edin), FRCPath(UK), DMJ(Lond)

Senior Professor of Forensic Medicine and Toxicology
Faculty of Medicine
University of Colombo

Vijitha Yapa Publications
Sri Lanka

FROM THE AUTHOR

Newspaper articles on the murder investigation of Mrs. Sathasivam fascinated me even before I became a medical student. Its complex medico-legal issues created a great interest when I studied Forensic Medicine in the Faculty of Medicine, University of Colombo, in the third and fourth years of medical studies.

When I was a third year medical student, I had an opportunity to read the chapter 'A Murder in Ceylon' in Professor Sydney Smith's autobiography "Mostly Murder", which I borrowed from the medical library. It stimulated me to study further the research conducted by Professor G. S. W. de Saram, the first Professor of Forensic Medicine in Ceylon, to determine the time of death of Mrs. Sathasivam. But then I never thought I would be writing this book as the Professor of Forensic Medicine of the same University.

After finding the limited number of documents relating to the case in Sri Lanka, I wanted to peruse more documents that should be available in the Department of Forensic Medicine in the University of Edinburgh, where Professor Sydney Smith worked. When I contacted the Department, I was informed that all his papers and documents were given to the library of the Royal College of Physicians of Edinburgh.

When I contacted the library, I was overjoyed to be informed that Professor Smith's documents on the Sathasivam case are well preserved and available.

Ms Joy Pitman, the Archivist wrote to me, "Since our last telephone conversation, I have been going through the papers we have on this case to see how much material there is...I am afraid that the answer is a great deal!"

Initially, I got photocopies of some documents and later I visited the library to see the historic collection. There were photographs, handwritten notes of Professor Sydney Smith, and copies of some medical evidence given, that helped me to complete this book.

Hon. Lakshman Kadirgamar, who was the private secretary to Justice E. F. N. Gratiaen when the Sathasivam murder trial was on, reviewed the last Chapter of the book. He agreed to write the foreword for the book, in spite of his extremely busy schedule as the Minister of Foreign Affairs. It is with deep regret that I have to mention that he was assassinated the day before he was to write the foreword.

I thank former Supreme Court Judge Hon. A. R. B. Amarasinghe for granting permission to publish the photograph of Justice E. F. N. Gratiaen from his book "Supreme Court of Ceylon", and Dr. Nihal Jayawickrama for providing me with a photograph of Mr. T. S. Fernando.

A word of gratitude to my first English tutor, Mr. L. Mahen Fernando, who patiently read through the script and advised me how I could improve the same.

I am grateful to Professor Sharya Scharenguivel for her advice.

I thank Ms. Joy Pitman, the then Archivist and Ms. Estella Dukan presently working in the library of the Royal College of Physicians of Edinburgh for their assistance and Mrs Dharma Diyasena, former librarian at the Attorney-General's Department for her co-operation.

I am grateful to Reverend Angunabadulle Gnanadassi, and attorneys-at-law Ms. Melani Palihakkara and Mr. Sunil Jayarathna for helping to trace William, the pardoned Crown Witness in the murder case, and Dr. K. D. G. Wimalaratna, the former Director, National Archives and his staff for their co-operation.

I thank Dr. Kishani Abeywardana, Dr. Ranil Jayawardena, Dr. Thilini Jayasooriya, Dr. Medhani Hewagama, Ms Ruwandika Ariyathilake, attorney-at-law and Ms Subashini Senanayake for their assistance in finalising this publication.

All the assistance given to prepare this publication by Ms Chandrani Wijegoonewardane, Ms. Ramya Ennos, Ms. Shirani Wijewickrama, Ms. Apsara Liyanage, Ms. Swarna Premaratne, Ms. Sasala Senaratne, Ms. Mahesha Abeywickrama, Ms Gayani Nilanduwage, Ms Chandani Surandika Liyanage and Ms. Kumudu Rathnamalala is gratefully acknowledged.

Finally, I thank Mr. Vijitha Yapa, the Publisher, and his staff and Tharanjee Prints for the co-operation extended to me.

Professor Ravindra Fernando

CONTENTS

		Pages
1.	Body in Garage	1-3
2.	Life and Times of Mr. and Mrs. Sathasivam	4-17
3.	The Inquest and the Post-mortem Examination	18-28
4.	In Search of William	29-34
5.	Case for the Prosecution	35-135
6.	Evidence of the Professor of Forensic Medicine	136-182
7.	Conflicting Medical Evidence	183-220
8.	Cross-Examination of the Professor of Forensic Medicine	221-225
9.	Sir Sydney Smith's Evidence for the Defence	226-254
10.	Evidence of the Radiologist	255-257
11.	Evidence of the Forensic Scientists	258-270
12.	Evidence of the Inspector-General of Police	271-277
13.	Case for the Defence	278-301
14.	Counsel's Address to the Jury	302-317
15.	Judge's Summing up and the Verdict	318-445
16.	In Search of William – Again	446-451
17.	Postscript	452-464
	Figures	467-479

CHAPTER 1

BODY IN GARAGE

The 9th of October 1951 was a humid, sunny day in Colombo, the capital city of the beautiful Indian Ocean Island Ceylon, as it was known then, with temperatures hovering in the region of 84 degrees Fahrenheit (29 degrees Centigrade).

It was another routine day for Austin, a 24-year-old laundryman from Meegoda, a sleepy village in the suburbs of Colombo. Austin's occupation was to remove soiled laundry from residences in Colombo and its suburbs for washing and ironing, and return them in a few days. In the era before washing machines, this was a common practice in some upper as well as middle class families, living in cities in Ceylon.

At about 3 in the afternoon, after delivering some clothes at Wellawatte, a town in the city of Colombo, Austin proceeded to 'Jayamangalam', the house at No. 7, St. Alban's Place, in the adjoining town Bambalapitiya.

St. Alban's Place was a gravel road on the seaside of the main Colombo-Galle Road, leading to the south of the Island. It was about 20 feet wide sloping gently towards the sea. The house No. 7 was situated approximately 90 yards from the main road.

It was the residence of Mr. and Mrs. Sathasivam and their four daughters.

As the front door of the house was open, Austin went into the house and peeped into the lady's bedroom upstairs. The room was open. He did not find the lady or anyone else. Then he came downstairs and saw Mrs. Sathasivam's two-younger children, Manjubashini and Rajendrani, aged 4 and 3 years respectively, and asked them where their mother was. The children murmured something that could not be clearly understood.

But as they mentioned the word 'garage', he went through the kitchen up to the garage. What Austin saw shocked him!

Mrs. Sathasivam, the lady of the house, was lying on the floor of the garage face upwards with a wooden mortar placed on her neck. (See Figure 1. Page 467)

Austin was alarmed and ran into the adjoining house and informed Carolinahamy, the domestic servant there that Mrs. Sathasivam was sleeping flat on her back with a mortar against her neck!

Carolinahamy accompanied Austin to the garage. Seeing the body she realised that the lady was dead. Austin took the bundle of clothes and went away. He made a statement to the Police about 4 days later.

Carolinahamy told Manjubashini, the elder child, to speak to their mother. She tugged at the saree of her mother saying "Mummy, mummy".

There was no reply.

Carolinahamy then told her landlady, Mrs. Foenander, the sad news. Mrs. Foenander, a 28-year-old wife of a doctor, immediately rushed to the garage with the two children and having seen the body realised that Mrs. Sathasivam was dead. She immediately came out of the garage.

Mrs. Foenander heard the two children shouting "Daddy", "Mummy" and "Hora" (meaning 'thief') and a mixture of Sinhalese and English words. It was not clear whether the three words "Daddy, "Mummy" and "Hora" were used in three separate sentences or in one sentence. These three words were used in quick succession and Mrs. Foenander could not make any sense of what the two children were saying because they were speaking simultaneously and in a medley of languages. It was mainly the older child who used these three words.

At the same time, the domestic servant of the house Podihamy came in a rickshaw with the two school going elder children of Mrs.

Sathasivam. Podihamy went upstairs to get some money to pay the rickshawman. When she came down Mrs. Foenander informed her what she saw in the garage.

Mrs. Foenander, Podihamy and all four children then went to the garage. Seeing Mrs. Sathasivam's body, Podihamy started shouting and crying and the four children also cried.

Podihamy while crying took the mortar off the neck of Mrs. Sathasivam and put it aside.

Mrs. Foenander used to visit Mrs. Sathasivam's house occasionally to take calls from the telephone downstairs. As this telephone was locked, Podihamy told her to use the telephone upstairs. Mrs. Foenander telephoned the Bambalapitiya Police and said that Mrs. Sathasivam was dead. As the Police Station was a few yards away, when she came downstairs after phoning, Mr. Siriwardana, a Police Constable, was standing at the front door. The time was 3.23 p.m.

A team of Police Officers, lead by Mr. Richard Aluvihare, the Inspector-General of Police, visited the scene soon after.

As the news of the mysterious tragedy spread, curious crowds gathered at the scene and the entire road was congested with vehicular and pedestrian traffic till far into the night. The Police had to stand guard outside the house to keep the crowds away from its immediate vicinity.

CHAPTER 2

LIFE AND TIMES OF
MR. AND MRS. SATHASIVAM

Mahadeva Sathasivam was the only son of Mr. Tiruvalingam Sathasivam and Ambikai Sathasivam of "Swarna", Campbell Place, Maradana, in the city of Colombo.

He was one of the finest cricketers ever produced by Ceylon.

It is said that wherever the British planted their Union Jack, the cricket stumps followed suit not long after. They planted their National Flag in Ceylon after conquering the entire Island in 1815, and the Colombo Journal of 3rd November 1832 reported a cricket match between the newly formed Colombo Cricket Club (CCC), comprising entirely of expatriate members (a condition for membership that persisted until 1961!) and a team drawn from the 97th Regiment of the British Garrison. The match was played at the now defunct Sports Club grounds at picturesque Galle Face. The CCC was subjected to a trouncing by 10-wickets at the hands of the British Garrison team!

It was really the British militia that introduced the summer game to Ceylon. But early chroniclers have given most of the credit for the popularisation of cricket to Rev. Brooke Bailey who came to Ceylon as Assistant to the Head Master of the 'Colombo Academy', now known as Royal College, Colombo.

Mr. S. P. Foenander, local cricket chronicler, also known as the "Wisden" of the East, records in his authoritative "Sixty Years of Ceylon Cricket" the 'splendid pioneering work' done by the tea and coffee planters and of the early matches, beginning from 1870, played at the picturesque Darrawella ground nestling in the hills.

The first visiting representatives to play a match on local soil was Ivo Bligh's Marylebone Cricket Club (MCC) team bound for Australia in 1882, which was responsible for the birth of the Ashes on that tour.

Young Mahadeva Sathasivam first played cricket at the very tender age of 15 years for Wesley College. He produced several magnificent innings for the school. His last season for Wesley in 1936 was considered by far his best and most magnificent, when he terminated the season with a brilliant 145 against St. Thomas' College at Mount Lavinia. It is said that a schoolboy batsman rarely has had the privilege of notching up a century on the windswept grounds of Mount Lavinia.

Sathasivam was a stylish right-handed batsman and a maestro of the willow. He used to cut, drive, and pull with extreme power. His late cut with the flashing blade was considered his best shot.

Sathasivam was also a right arm bowler of no mean ability. When the better-known bowlers could not get a batsman out, it is said that captains always called upon Sathasivam to get rid of him, and he did.

After leaving school, Sathasivam represented and captained the 'Tamil Union Cricket and Athletic Club', the same club Muththiah Muralitharan, the world's leading off spinner represents today.

Sathasivam first played for Ceylon in 1945, scoring a glorious 111 runs against India.

In 1948, he captained Ceylon against Don Bradman's all conquering Australian team.

Sathasivam held the ground record at Chepauk, the home ground of the Madras Cricket Club, where several test matches were played. In 1947, playing against an Indian XI, which comprised of M.J. Gopalan, Ram Singh and fast bowler Rangachari, all of whom were test cricketers at the time, he made a brilliant 215, surpassing West Indian Jeff Stollmeyer's 211 to set the record.

Cricket fans in India described Sathasivam's innings as the best seen on this ground. Sathasivam's batting compared well with that of the late Everton Weekes and Frank Worrell of the West Indies.

Schoolboys and adults alike flocked to see Sathasivam batting, and even if he did not score many runs, they gave him a standing ovation, as his innings was full of class. Ingenuity was written all over it.

His 99 runs against the West Indies team comprising of Frank Worrell, John Goddard and the two trundlers Prior Jones and John Trim, was considered to be a gem of an innings. At the end of his masterly innings West Indian skipper Goddard had said that he had never seen such a commanding innings in any of the countries he had played Test Cricket!

Sathasivam was, by all accounts, a genius of a batsman. Frank Worrell, the former West Indian captain, had publicly announced that if he were to pick a World XI, the first batsman he would pick would be "Sathasivam from Ceylon!"

Mahadeva Sathasivam, whose occupation was mentioned as a broker in the marriage certificate, married Ms. Paripooranam Anandan Rajendra, the younger daughter of Mr. and Mrs. Ramanathan Rajendra of "Sukhasthan", Horton Place, Colombo 07.

Mrs. Sathasivam was a grand-daughter of Sir Ponnambalam Ramanathan, who was one of the greatest freedom fighters among the patriotic Tamil Community in Ceylon. He studied law in the Presidency College, Madras, India, under A.G. Richard Morgan and was called to the Bar in 1876. He was the Solicitor-General of Ceylon from 1892-1906 and was knighted in 1921. Sir Ponnambalam Ramanathan was an active politician and was elected to the Legislative Council of Ceylon.

The civil or legal registration of the marriage of Mr. Mahadeva Sathasivam and Miss Anandan Rajendra, both Ceylon Tamils, was held on 9th February 1940. The wedding ceremony according to Hindu customs and rites was held in 1941. This signified the consummation of the marriage.

Their eldest daughter, Jothiswary was born in March 1942.

In October 1944, Mr. Sathasivam instituted a divorce action. Through the intervention of relatives, differences that existed relating to the action for divorce were smoothened and the couple agreed to live with each other again. In December 1944, the action was withdrawn.

Mrs. Sathasivam had been gifted with two immovable properties as part of the dowry, in addition to the jewellery, which is generally worn by many women of their class of society. Of these properties, one was outside Colombo and the other was a half share of her parents' house located in Horton Place, an exclusive area of the more affluent in the city of Colombo.

In December 1944, soon after the reconciliation following the withdrawal of the divorce action, Mrs. Sathasivam sold her property outside Colombo.

The second daughter of the Sathasivam's, Yajnaroopa, was born in September 1945. The third daughter Manjubashini was born in July 1947 and the youngest Rajendrani was born in November 1948.

In 1949, Mrs. Sathasivam sold the half-share of her parents' house in Horton Place, which she received as dowry, to her sister, who held the other half-share. With the proceeds of that sale, Mrs. Sathasivam bought No. 7, St. Alban's Place, Bambalapitiya, the house named 'Jayamangalam'.

It was in this house that she had to face a tragic death two years later.

In 1950, Mr. Sathasivam's mother took residence in her daughter-in-law's house. She had a telephone installed in the drawing room downstairs while Mrs. Sathasivam had a telephone installed in her bedroom upstairs.

The same year, Mahadeva Sathasivam appeared to have formed an attachment with Miss Yvonne Stevenson, a pretty young lady born to a Dutch mother and a Polish father. When Yvonne's mother remarried one Mr. Stevenson, Yvonne took his surname. (See Figure 2. Page 468)

Yvonne was employed for a few months in a private firm in Colombo, named "Bogstra and de Wildt".

Mr. Sathasivam met Yvonne at various places. Sometimes he visited her at her flat. One morning in late 1950, Mr. Sathasivam visited her flat and found it empty. Then he went to her office, "Ismail and Sons", and found to his amazement that she had left to India!

Mr. Sathasivam immediately went to meet his friend Mr. Bogstra, who had employed Yvonne for a few months earlier, and asked for 500 rupees to go to India to look for her! Mr. Bogstra refused to give him the money.

Mr. Sathasivam had said that he would get the money from somewhere and would bring Yvonne back to Ceylon, "Even if she had to be handcuffed!"

As promised, a few days later Mr. Sathasivam came back with Miss. Stevenson to Mr. Bogstra's office! He had met her in Madras and she had decided to come back to Ceylon. Mr. Sathasivam told Mr. Bogstra that they were leaving for England together in a short time.

He said that he was to be sent to England by "Cargills", a leading departmental store in Colombo, which was established in 1844, to be trained in 'Sports lines' and that he would then come back to Ceylon and take up the management of the Sports Department at "Cargills". Miss Stevenson was to come back with him. Mr. Sathasivam had said that he would make arrangements to marry her.

In early November 1950, Mr. and Mrs. Sathasivam left on a trip to England, on board the ship "Himalaya".

Miss. Stevenson also went to England in November 1950.

Mrs. Sathasivam returned to Ceylon alone on 8th February 1951. While returning to Ceylon by ship, on 2nd February 1951 she wrote a letter to her husband, who was then at 5, Queen's Gate Gardens, Gloucester Road, London. It was posted at Aden.

"Dearest,

I regret having to write this letter to you, but through sheer desperation and bitterness I put my pen to paper before you fall between two stools.

Even on this boat I am not spared the scandal of my husband having another woman. I was told that you were seen very often in Colombo with a woman of about 6 feet tall and hefty, big made, by the name of Yvonne. She is thought to be of Dutch origin. As you know, this was aroused before too by quite different people to me. I definitely now know that you did take a woman about. Of course you can do what you like. You are not going to be 'henpecked' but why torture me?

I will release you from the bond of this unhappy marriage. It is because you want something better than me to take about, that you leave me at home, and take another woman out with you. We are just not made for each other. I can never tolerate another woman to be seen with you, so why should we quarrel over this? You must do as you like, and as long as I am married to you, I will not allow this kind of taking women out 'behind my back'.

The real aim of this letter is to let you know that it is absolutely useless our trying to make a happy home together. You want gaiety and variety of which I am not in favour.

Silver Fawn, dancing, playing cards, "giving lifts", drinking at clubs, playing mixed games, I cannot bear.

So why attempt the impossible. Either you must give up your woman and ways, which I know only too well you will not or I must put up with everything you do which I cannot. Any way the past has gone never to come back, so let us look forward to a brighter future, more suited to our entirely different temperaments.

There is nothing to be angry about, in your opinion, I suppose, you think there is "no harm" in taking this woman out with you, but I consider you have misused the trust I had in you and disgraced me. Any way all is well that ends well so let us part as FRIENDS. Wish you all the best.

Yours no longer,

Ananda"

This letter indicated that Mrs. Sathasivam had now realized that their marriage could not be salvaged.

Mr. Sathasivam replied to her letter on the 8th of February 1951.

Five days after Mrs. Sathasivam arrived in Ceylon, she replied to her husband's letter.

Addressing Mr. Sathasivam "Dearest", she said, "I do not wish to worry you over and over again. The whole trouble with us is that you think that as long as you do not sleep with another woman everything is all right, and you can go out and be seen openly everywhere with her with or without other people, and talk and laugh with her is O.K.

But it is definitely not all right with a "narrow-minded" woman that I am. Your bachelor friends may do the same but you are married, and a sensible married man who really loves his wife has a deep obligation to his wife and he has to respect her wishes if he wants to be happy with her and have a loving HOME".

"Four walls and money will certainly build a house but you will find it needs a loving and happy wife to make a home. You may find happiness with the woman you take out but never again with me. Now you have made me understand that you do not care a pin for me, my wishes, or my welfare. I, to you, is just the refuse of the coconut, which after extracting of the juice and all good, is thrown into the dustbin. That is what I feel you have done to me. Had you cared a pin for me, this would never have happened. If your love to me was sincere and true as you try to make me believe, you cannot possibly so much as talk to another woman leave alone taking her out and being seen with her. You just tolerate me, as I happen to be the mother of your children - nothing more - I do not want that kind of tolerance from you even though I have not got a cent for my upkeep or to call my own."

"I would much rather beg from door to door. Anyway your life and money is yours not mine. I have been very foolish and was misguided. But Repentance comes too late and it has come to me, and as surely will come to you later. I do not believe in so called "Friendship" with the opposite sex. We have been married for 10 years then why is it only now and with this particular woman - your "acquaintance" - that your name is scandalized. I, for one, will never call her a lady, as a lady will never break a man's home especially when there are 4 innocent children in it, she can only be called a low woman in my opinion, but most certainly your mind fix differs from mine."

"You will realize in your later life the actual TRUTH of all this. We have had quarrels and quarrels and each and every time we have made up but this time I have an overflowing bitterness and disgust in my heart, just the thought of being treated like this."

Mrs. Sathasivam was then at "Sukhasthan", her parent's house and she stated in her letter that she was very uncomfortable there.

"I managed to get a room elsewhere and hope to leave on the 17th.

Your mother had given my mother Rs.60/- for February and she also paid the milk bill of Rs. 57/- making Rs. 117/- in all. She gave me Rs. 175/-, 20 coconuts, 16 measures of rice. She asked me when I am coming to "Jayamangalam". I asked her what she is going to do and she said she is not leaving as you had written to her not to shift, and I said I am not coming to live there. I think I made all this perfectly clear to you before I left you."

"I have always been perfectly candid, honest and frank with you and trusted you implicitly both in money as well as character and all else. I have never lied to you, believe it or not, and that is why I feel so hurt and bitter now. But I suppose these things had to happen so I can only say Thy Will Be Done."

Mrs. Sathasivam then wrote about their children.

"Ranjitha is very fair and these 3 months has made her talk and walk well. She has lovely long hair and has turned out to be a beautiful child. There is not much change in the others kids. All are quite well."

Mrs. Sathasivam, a dog lover, did not forget to write to her husband about her pet dogs.

"Thakin Nu, the Pekingese is a perfect beauty. He is full white and has a beautiful coat and is really a wonderful specimen, very much better than what you see there. Only his eye is inflamed and Chinnaiya is treating. Poor Jock and Yasha are dead. I got back Badger, but he is intolerable. He chases Lovekin's daughter when she rides a bike and she fell down many times. Jessica is very thin and small but keeping well."

Mrs. Sathasivam informed her husband that her sister, who is affectionately called "Baba", had no driver and that it was costly to go by 'Quickshaws' cabs.

In spite of serious financial and marital difficulties, Mrs. Sathasivam did not forget to write on various people they knew and even on trivial issues.

She continued, "Herewith your vaccination card and suitcase key. Please thank Raja for all he did to me and tell him I am very sorry I could not meet him at Tilbury to bid him goodbye. Also tell Weerakoon and Visvanathan that all their things were delivered safely. I had a very pleasant voyage and all the dolls and other toys were in perfect condition. Now Jothi wants a bed for her doll and I suppose all the rest also will want the same. I lost my wristlet watch on the "Chusan", while I was at lunch it was left in the cabin, when I went up after lunch it was missing. Gunasekera's house is still in the making. Mrs. Visa and her mother called personally for their parcel and Weerakoon's sisters came for theirs. Amarasekera came with a big story about your mother, and I told him to write to you a detailed account of the whole story and that I know nothing of it. He said that you do not reply to him. I suggest that you reply to his letter direct to him. How is Stephen's dog, Rani? These dogs never forget a person. You should have seen how Badger, Shandy and Jessica greeted me, only the Peke was too proud to greet me much. He only wagged his tail and snorted. Have you returned my Ration card to the authorities?"

Mrs. Sathasivam told her husband that she wanted a new pen.

"A Parker pen with the new filling device and gold cap was Rs. 85/- in Ceylon. It was only 3 - 15sh. at the Chusan. I did not know the difference was so great. All told it is not a good pen. A Sheaffer Lifetime is better. No more news," Mrs. Sathasivam concluded her letter and signed "Ananda".

'Raja' mentioned in the letter was Raja Ratnagopal, the landlord with whom the Sathasivams were living in London. 'Lo' was a tenant at 'Sukhasthan' and 'Chinnaiya' was a veterinary surgeon.

Mr. Sathasivam returned to Ceylon on the 19th of March 1951, but left again to England sometime in May. His mother joined him in England.

In September, Mr. Sathasivam and his mother set sail from London to Ceylon in the "Himalaya", curiously enough in the same ship that took Mr. and Mrs. Sathasivam to London in November 1950.

On 6th September, about a month before her death, Mrs. Sathasivam took a step, which she appears to have been determined to go through with.

That is the institution of an action for a divorce. This time, she was the plaintiff!

She contacted her proctor, Mr. P. D. A. Mack, and insisted upon seeing him that day. A consultation was arranged with an advocate. He was called upon to prepare, that night itself, papers for a divorce; and true to his undertaking, he prepared the necessary papers the same night! Mr. Mack filed the petition for divorce on the 7th of September in the District Court, Colombo.

The petition was as follows:

"No. 2592 Divorce
Paripooranam Anandan Sathasivam (nee Rajendra)
of No. 7, St. Alban's Place, Bambalapitiya,
Colombo.

Plaintiff.
Vs.

Mahadeva Sathasivam of 75, Tottenham Lane,
Hornsey, London, England.
Defendant.

On this 7th day of September 1951.

This plaint of the plaintiff above named, appearing by Peter Daniel Anthonisz Mack and Orton Peter Mack, both Proctors of the Honourable Supreme Court of the Island of Ceylon practising together in partnership as such under the name style and firm of "P. D. A. Mack & Sons" her Proctors, states as follows: -
 1. The Plaintiff resides within the jurisdiction of this Court and the cause of action set out below, arose within the said jurisdiction. The Defendant although presently resident in England, is a Ceylonese with Ceylonese domicile.
 2. The Plaintiff and the Defendant were married at Colombo on or about the 9th February 1940. A certified copy of the Registration of the said marriage is filed herewith marked "A" and pleaded as part and parcel of this plaint.
 3. There are four children of the marriage, to wit: -

Jothiswary born on 8th March 1942
Yajnaroopa born on 15th September 1945
Manjubashini born on 2nd July 1947 and
Rajendrani born on 15th November 1948.

The said four children are all girls, and are presently living with the Plaintiff, their mother.

4. Since the 9th of May 1951, the Defendant maliciously deserted the Plaintiff, and a cause of action has accrued to the Plaintiff to sue the Defendant for a decree of divorce a vinculo matrimonii on the ground of malicious desertion.

5. The Plaintiff asks for the custody of the four children of the marriage.

6. The Plaintiff also asks for permanent alimony in a sum of Rupees Three Hundred (Rs.300/=) per mensem, and for maintenance in respect of all four children at the rate of Rupees two hundred (200/=) per mensem.

Therefore the Plaintiff prays:-
 (a) for a decree of divorce a vinculo matrimonii against the defendant,
 (b) for the custody of the four children of the marriage,
 (c) for permanent alimony at the rate of Rs.300/= per mensem,
 (d) for maintenance of the children at the rate of Rs.200/= per mensem, and
 (e) for costs and all such relief as to this Court shall seem meet.

Proctors for Plaintiff.

Settled by Kingsley Herat, Advocate, and a certified copy of the marriage certificate was also filed."

Mrs. Sathasivam met with her death on the 9th October 1951, one month and two days after the institution of this action for a divorce.

The Court ordered summons to be issued on the 21st of September 1951. An effort had been made to have the summons served in England but it did not happen.

The same day the action was filed, that is on 7th September 1951, curiously enough, Mrs. Sathasivam received a cablegram from "Himalaya". The one line message was "Arriving twenty first Himalaya - Sathasivam".

Mrs. Sathasivam was concerned about the arrival of her husband and was worried that he may turn violent. She phoned Mr. C. C. Dissanayake, Superintendent of Police and discussed this with him. He asked her to write to him.

On 17th September, she wrote the following letter to Mr. C. C. Dissanayake.

"Dear Sir,

I am writing to you, as requested over the telephone, to inform you that I have filed an action in the Colombo District Court asking for a divorce from my husband Mr. M. Sathasivam on the ground of desertion. He has been away in England and the summons though issued has not yet been served. He will be arriving in Colombo per SS Himalaya on the 21st instant, and I understand from his Attorney that he intends to come to this house (which is mine) with his mother and reside here. In view of the pending divorce action this cannot be allowed, and I have been advised to refuse him admittance.

But, from my knowledge and experience of my husband, I have reason to fear that he may attempt to force his way into the house and use violence and cause a breach of the peace.

In this situation I need protection and I therefore request that you will instruct the Bambalapitiya Police to afford me the same if I telephone to them. I have a telephone in the house and the Police Station is close by.

I may mention that I have my four young children in the house with me and I am also apprehensive on their account.

Yours faithfully,
Ananda Sathasivam"

Mr. Dissanayake asked Mr. Thiedeman, the Inspector of Police, Bambalapitiya, to meet with her. After the meeting he recorded that he saw Mrs. Sathasivam on 20th September at her house and explained that "Police had no right of intervention unless there was a breach of peace and that her husband yet had a legal right of entrance."

"She wanted Police to refrain from seeing Mr. Sathasivam. Unless anything serious takes place, I advised her to treat him carefully in view of the pending action. She did not wish me to contact him and said she would telephone Police if necessary. I have a feeling that the parties may make up for the sake of their children. It was never a love match, but arranged and temperaments appear different," recorded Mr. Thiedeman.

On the 22nd of September, Mr. Sathasivam and his mother arrived in Ceylon, and in the same ship travelled a friend of his, Mr. Haniffa, who also had a house in Horton Place. Mr. Sathasivam received intimation at the jetty itself that he was not welcome back at Mrs. Sathasivam's house.

Therefore, he asked Mr. Haniffa whether he could come along and stay with him. Mr. Haniffa replied, "Well, till some other arrangements are made, you can stay with me."

He agreed to take Mr. Sathasivam's bags to his house. From the jetty, both went to the Grand Oriental Hotel, just next to the jetty.

Grand Oriental Hotel, popularly known as GOH, is among the renowned hotels in the East such as Raffles of Singapore and Taj Mahal in Mumbai. The GOH building, which was originally British Army barracks, was converted to a British Colonial Hotel in the year 1875 and was named Grand Oriental Hotel. It has played host to several celebrities including the world famous writer Anton Chekhov and Philippine's national hero Jose Rizal. Two suites have been dedicated to them to commemorate their visits to the Hotel.

Mr. Sathasivam contacted Mrs. Sathasivam's sister, Mrs. Pathmanathan, from the GOH and went over to her house. From there, he called his wife. Surprisingly, she came along with the children!

Meanwhile, Dosihamy, an 80-year-old widow known to the families of Mr. and Mrs. Pathmanathan and Mr. and Mrs. Sathasivam for a long time, had met a young boy called "William" close to the house of Mrs. Pathmanathan on 29th September 1951. When she spoke to him she found out that he was looking for a job in Colombo.

Remembering that Mrs. Pathmanathan wanted her to look for a servant boy, she took William to the house of Mrs. Pathmanathan. After speaking to William, Mrs. Pathmanathan sent Dosihamy and William with her driver to the house of her sister Mrs. Sathasivam. Dosihamy entrusted William to Mrs. Sathasivam and she was given 50 cents as bus fare. She heard Mrs. Sathasivam discussing the salary with William when she was leaving the house.

On 3rd October, Mrs. Sathasivam's lawyers who filed the divorce suit, applied to the District Court for special service of summons. Apparently, they were insistent on getting summons served and commencing the case.

Summons was actually served on Mr. Sathasivam, who was living in the Horton Place house of Mr. Haniffa, at 8 o'clock in the morning of 8th October. The Fiscal's Process Server went there and was successful in serving the summons on Mr. Sathasivam. At the same time another summons in a case involving financial matters was also served on him.

This was a day before Mrs. Sathasivam's death.

Sathasivam's two elder children, Jothiswary and Yajnarupa, attended St. Bridget's Convent and Mr. Sathasivam and Mr. Haniffa on their way from the Orient Club came across these two girls travelling in a rickshaw with Podihamy.

Mr. Sathasivam saw them, stopped the car, and asked the children and Podihamy to get in. They got into the car and proceeded to No. 7, St. Alban's Place. There Mr. Haniffa got hold of Mrs. Sathasivam's hand and asked her to give up the divorce case. Mrs. Sathasivam smiled and said nothing. After some little conversation they left.

That night Mr. Sathasivam had dinner with his proctor at his cricket club, 'Tamil Union', and made his way home by a lift being given by his proctor, back to No. 7, St. Alban's Place, at about 1 o'clock. That is on the night of the 8th, the morning of the 9th October.

Podihamy was awakened by the noise of the car coming and she saw Mrs. Sathasivam coming down and opening the door. Mr. Sathasivam went upstairs with her.

That was the last day of Mrs. Sathasivam's life.

CHAPTER 3

THE INQUEST AND THE POST-MORTEM EXAMINATION

As soon as Sir Richard Aluvihare, the Inspector-General of Police, received information about Mrs. Sathasivam's death, he visited the scene with Mr. J.A.P. Cherubim, a Crown Counsel of the Attorney-General's Department.

He decided to request Professor G.S.W. de Saram to perform the post-mortem examination because he thought that the case was going to be intricate and expert evidence was necessary. (See Figure 3. Page 468)

Professor G.S.W. de Saram was the Judicial Medical Officer of Colombo for 4 years and he was appointed the first Professor of Forensic Medicine in the University of Colombo in 1951.

He had his training with Professor Sydney Smith for 10 or 11 months at the University of Edinburgh. He had worked in London in the Scotland Yard Laboratories and also attended some post-mortem examinations with Dr. Keith Simpson, who became the Professor of Forensic Medicine at Guy's Hospital, London. Professor de Saram has also worked in the Medico-Legal Institute in Cairo, Egypt, for about six months.

Professor de Saram visited the scene and examined the body and the scene with Police Officers, the Government Analyst and other scientists.

The body was removed to the General Hospital mortuary and Professor de Saram conducted the post-mortem examination the next day.

An inquest on Mrs. Sathasivam's death by Mr. J.N.C. Tiruchelvam, the City Coroner, commenced on the 10th of October 1951. An inquest must be held for all suspicious and homicidal deaths according to the Criminal Procedure Code of Ceylon

At the inquest, Mr. J.A.P. Cherubim, Crown Counsel assisted by Messrs. L. N. Pieris, Deputy Inspector-General of Police, J.W.L. Attygalle, Assistant Superintendent of Police, Colombo South, and Mr. M.W.B. Thiedeman, Inspector of Police, Bambalapitya, led evidence.

Mr. R.L. Pereira, King's Counsel, with Messrs. M.L. Abeywardena and K.C. Nadarajah instructed by Messrs. L.B. and L.M. Fernando watched the interests of the suspect Mr. Sathasivam, who was produced from custody.

The first witness was 77-year-old Podihamy, from the village of Pitipana, who was a domestic servant of Mrs. Sathasivam. She had been with Mrs. Sathasivam's family for the last 44 years.

Mrs. Rajendra, Mrs. Sathasivam's mother, initially employed Podihamy. She was with her when Mrs. Sathasivam was born and looked after her as a baby.

Young Mrs. Sathasivam and her husband from the time of their marriage employed Podihamy.

Giving evidence, she said that Mr. and Mrs. Sathasivam were married for 11 years and had four children. They were Jothiswary aged 10 years, Yajnaroopa aged 6 years, Manjula 4 years and Rajendrani aged 3 years.

Podihamy said that Mr. and Mrs. Sathasivam lived happily during the early part of their marriage but in the last 3 years they did not live happily.

Podihamy further said, "They used to have disputes and quarrels off and on. The trouble was about Mr. Sathasivam's drinking habits. He used to promise to give up drinking habits. He did abstain for sometime. He used to come home in a drunken state late at night."

Podihamy said that she knew the suspect as a well-known

cricketer.

"He recently went to England and returned only three weeks ago. He said that he was taking part in cricket while he was away in the United Kingdom. He was away from home for about 16 weeks. During his absence in England Mrs. Sathasivam used to complain to me about her husband's drinking and gambling habits and that the children were not provided for while he was away."

Podihamy said that she remembered the return of Mr. Sathasivam from England.

"He did not come home but went to a hotel. He sent a cable before his return regarding his arrival but Mrs. Sathasivam did not go to the jetty. Mr. Sathasivam had phoned Mrs. Sathasivam's sister Mrs. Pathmanathan. He requested Mrs. Pathmanathan to send her car and Mr. Sathasivam went to Mrs. Pathmanathan's house. Then he telephoned Mrs. Sathasivam to come up there. She went to see him with all her children. They all came back to the house with Mr. Sathasivam. He stayed there for three days. There was no quarrel during those three days."

Podihamy was aware that Mrs. Sathasivam asked Mr. Sathasivam to leave the house as she has filed a divorce case. He went to live with one Haniffa. Podihamy knew Haniffa as a good friend of Mr. Sathasivam. After he went to live with Haniffa up to the day of death he paid three visits to Mrs. Sathasivam's house. He visited her about three or four days after he went to live with Haniffa.

Continuing her evidence Podihamy said, "On one occasion he came at about 2 a.m. and slept in Mrs. Sathasivam's room. He was there till I left with the children at about 8.15 a.m. that day. When I returned with the children at about 3 p.m. Mr. Sathasivam was not at home. During these visits there were no quarrels but Mrs. Sathasivam told me that she did not want him to come owing to the pending case."

Relating an incident that took place on the 8th October, Podihamy said, "I remember bringing both the children from school on that day in a rickshaw. On the way near the racecourse, I saw Mr. Haniffa, Mr. Abbas and Mr. Sathasivam coming in a car and pulled up by the side of our rickshaw. Mr. Sathasivam asked us to get into the car and we did. We proceeded towards home."

"On the way, Mr. Sathasivam asked me to tell Mrs. Sathasivam that he had been served with summons in the divorce case. All of us, including Mr. Sathasivam and his two friends went into the house. All three sat in the hall and had a conversation. Mrs. Sathasivam went up on being called by Mr. Sathasivam. All of them were fully drunk. They went away in the same car half an hour later. After they left, Mrs. Sathasivam told me that Haniffa and Abbas both asked her to withdraw the divorce case. She told me that she refused to withdraw the case."

Podihamy said that on 8th October night, when she was sleeping she heard a car come and halt at about 1 a.m. in front of the house. Mrs. Sathasivam went down and opened the door. Both Mr. and Mrs. Sathasivam went to the bedroom upstairs. She looked out of the window and saw the car leaving. It was a 'Quickshaws' cab. She heard Mr. and Mrs. Sathasivam having a conversation.

Podihamy said as usual she got up at 6 a.m. on the 9th. She prepared and gave the children their milk. She found the door of the bedroom where Mr. and Mrs. Sathasivam slept, locked. This was about 7 a.m. She then knocked at the door because she wanted money to buy some plantains. Mrs. Sathasivam came out and Podihamy saw Mr. Sathasivam sleeping in the bed. Mrs. Sathasivam then called William, the servant boy, and gave money to buy some plantains. He was asked to bring the paper and string-hoppers also.

In the meantime, Podihamy dressed the children. Mrs. Sathasivam telephoned for a 'Quickshaws' cab. When she left for school with the two children Mr. Sathasivam was still sleeping. He was wearing a sarong and he had nothing on the upper part of his body.

Podihamy told the Coroner, "Before I left for school Mrs. Sathasivam told me that her husband had come last night. I said I saw it and she further asked me not to permit the children to disturb his sleep. I left by 'Quickshaws' with the children."

Sadly, this was the last time the two elder children saw their mother.

Podihamy left the school with the children in a rickshaw by about 2.30 p.m. reaching home about 3 p.m. She saw Mrs. Foenander who used to visit the house for the purpose of taking telephone calls there. As she got to the entrance to the house the two younger children came crying.

Podihamy narrated what happened then.

"Manjula spoke to me and said that her mother had been killed and a mortar had been placed on her neck. She told me further that her mother was lying in the garage. The eldest child Jothiswary worried me to go and see the mother. I went up to the garage with the four children."

"I saw Mrs. Sathasivam lying on the floor and a mortar placed on her neck. I raised the mortar off her neck and felt her neck. It was icy cold. Then I held her arm and felt her pulse and found it has ceased. I asked Mrs. Foenander to phone the Police immediately, which she did from the phone upstairs."

Then the children started crying loud. Manjula told her that daddy had carried her mother and placed her in the garage. Manjula also told her that she saw daddy beating her with a broom in her room upstairs. She said that daddy had placed the mortar on the neck. She then got the eldest girl to telephone Mrs. Rajendra, Mrs. Sathasivam's mother and Mrs. Pathmanathan, her only sister.

Podihamy said that the wooden mortar was usually left in the garage and it was a light one which could easily be lifted.

Podihamy recalled that when she went to school in the morning, Mrs. Sathasivam was wearing the 'thalikody' and she always wore that and a ring with three brilliants. The ring was given to her by her father.

Podihamy informed the Coroner that the garage was permanently locked with a padlock from outside from the time Mr. Sathasivam left for England. The key was always with Mrs. Sathasivam.

She said, "I gave the key to the Inspector. There is a small entrance from inside and that was always open. I went in by the small entrance. When I went there I saw the front entrance as usual locked up. There is a small door for the inside entrance but it is always kept open. Besides William and myself there are no other servants in the house. William does the cooking. When I returned William was not there. I asked Manjula where William was. She told me that he had put his shirt on and went away. Manjula told me that daddy telephoned for a car and went in it. She further told me that William went away after Mr. Sathasivam left."

At this stage Mr. Cherubim, Crown Counsel, requested that the evidence of the four-year-old daughter of Mr. and Mrs. Sathasivam, Manjula, be recorded.

Mr. R.L Pereira objected on the grounds that her evidence was not admissible. But the Coroner allowed the child to be brought in. Repeated attempts however, to get even the child's name failed. She was reluctant to speak. In fact, the child was restive and was seen struggling with the old domestic servant Podihamy.

The Crown Counsel asked that the child be produced later.

After completing the post-mortem examination, Professor de Saram attended the inquest.

He informed the Coroner that he has just completed his post-mortem examination and that he needs sometime to prepare his report. The Magistrate decided that it was convenient to record his evidence on the 14th.

Then the inquiry was adjourned for the 14th October.

Professor G.S.W. de Saram, who performed Mrs. Sathasivam's post-mortem examination, gave evidence on the 14th.

He said, "On 9th October at 5.55 p.m. I visited No. 7, St. Alban's Place, Bambalapitiya, the residence of Mr. and Mrs. Sathasivam. I saw the body of Mrs. Sathasivam lying on its back in the garage with feet towards the inner wall separated from each other by about 16 inches. The face was turned toward the outer door of the garage and slightly upwards. The right arm lay fully extended by the right side of the body. The hand was slightly bent at the wrist with the palm 9 inches away from the right thigh. The left arm was bent at the elbow and the hand lay over the middle of the abdomen and the fingers stretched out and the palm downwards. The chin was five inches away from the inner end of the collar bone and showed the front of the neck and the under surface of the chin".

Professor de Saram said that the rectal temperature of the body taken at 6.55 p.m. was 93.2 degrees Fahrenheit. The room temperature was 81.5 degrees Fahrenheit. Rigor mortis was present in the face, neck, jaws and extremities and was setting in the fingers and toes.

He said that he examined the vagina and took a vaginal swab, which showed non-motile spermatozoa, large squamous epithelial cells and bacteria.

"Other specimens I have not yet examined," said Professor de Saram.

He said he held the post-mortem examination at 7 a.m. the next day at the General Hospital mortuary.

Mr. S. Pathmanathan, her brother-in-law, and Mr. K. Sathasivam, uncle of Mr. Sathasivam, identified Mrs. Sathasivam's body.

Professor de Saram said Mrs. Sathasivam was a fairly built but poorly nourished person.

After stating the number of external and internal injuries, he said that in his opinion, death was due to asphyxia from manual strangulation.

He said, "I mean by manual strangulation, strangulation by hands. I definitely rule out suicide. I will also rule out accidental death."

He said the strangulation was by an external agency, done deliberately.

"It is difficult to say the height of the assailant but if Mrs. Sathasivam was standing when she was strangled, the assailant must have been a taller person. Considerable force has been used in strangling. Strangulation must have taken place between 10 a.m. and 11.30 a.m. I base this conclusion on my observations such as cooling and other conditions, such as the degree of rigor mortis and the quantity of food in the stomach. It was three hours after she had taken the last meal," Professor de Saram said.

Mr. Pereira asked, "Has Podihamy influenced your decisions?"

"Who is Podihamy?" Professor de Saram queried!

The Coroner commented, "That is the best answer the Professor could have given," implying that Professor de Saram's opinion was independent, and not influenced by Podihamy.

The Coroner asked, "From which side had the strangulation taken place?"

"From behind."

He further said that all the injuries were ante-mortem injuries and they were abrasions and contusions. 'Ante-mortem' means before death.

Professor de Saram informed the Coroner that the rest of the evidence pertaining to the post-mortem findings would be typed and submitted later.

After Professor de Saram's evidence, Manjula was brought to give evidence again.

The Coroner said that they were making a preliminary inquiry and quoted an authority on the competency of witnesses which said, "While it is admittedly undesirable to cause any child or young person to attend at a Coroner's Court if his presence can be dispensed with, there may be occasions when it is required to take evidence from such. The competence of a child depends not upon age, but upon the degree of knowledge and understanding that appears to be possessed by him. To arrive at a decision on this, the Coroner should examine the child in a preliminary manner."

The Coroner said that it further provided with regard to a criminal trial, that a person accused of a crime should not be convicted upon such evidence, unless it is corroborated by material evidence implicating the accused person.

Continuing he said, "A Coroner will be well advised to adopt a similar safeguard in any case in which a child of tender years has to be called as a witness. For it has been well said that children as a class are untrustworthy witnesses. They mistake 'dreams for reality', repeat as of their knowledge what they have heard from others, and are greatly influenced by fear of punishment, by hope of reward and by desire for notoriety."

Mr. R.L. Pereira requested the Coroner to record that when Manjula was brought on the previous day, she struggled with Podihamy and refused to make a statement.

Podihamy was then given a seat and Manjula was allowed to stand by her. Podihamy was warned not to interfere with Manjula's evidence. The City Coroner and the Crown Counsel questioned Manjula on general matters to see if the child was able to talk intelligently.

Mr. Cherubim, the Crown Counsel, by way of a preliminary leading question to acclimatize the child to the crowded inquest room and the many grave faces, including that of her father, asked where her mother was. Little Manjula wriggled a bit and gaining confidence looked up with quiet intelligent eyes and replied "Mummy went abroad!"

He asked her whether she remembered Police Officers coming to her house. Manjula said she did not remember.

Manjula gave all her evidence in Sinhalese and Mr. Pereira asked the Court to record the replies of the child.

Pointing to Mr. Thiedemen, the Crown Counsel asked, "Did this gentleman come to your house?"

Manjula – "I know him, he came to our house."

Crown Counsel – "Do you remember Mr. Thiedemen coming to your house one evening?"

Manjula – "I remember."

Crown Counsel – "On this day when Mr. Thiedemen came to your house did you drink your milk?"

Manjula – "Podihamy gave me the milk to drink. My sisters also had their milk. I cannot remember where my mummy was when she gave us milk. I do not know what I had that day for morning tea. That day my sisters went to school with Podihamy. They ate bread before going to school. I also had bread. After sisters went to school mummy was in the garage".

Crown Counsel – "How did your mummy go to the garage?"

Manjula – "Mummy had fever and when I have fever I can also go to the garage."

Crown Counsel – "Where was daddy?"

Manjula – "Daddy went away."

Crown Counsel – "Where was daddy?"

Manjula – "He was near the wall."

Crown Counsel – "What is this wall?"

Manjula – "Wall is in mummy's room."

Crown Counsel – "Did you see daddy dressing up?"

Manjula – "I did not see."

Crown Counsel – "Did you see daddy doing anything that morning?"

Manjula – "No."

Crown Counsel – "Did you see daddy going away?"
Manjula – "I did not see him going away."
City Coroner – "What did you have that noon?"
Manjula – "We did not have anything to eat because the boy was not there to cook."
Crown Counsel – "Why did you not ask mummy to have something to eat?"
Manjula – "Mummy was having fever."
City Coroner – "You must have been very hungry?"
Manjula – "I did not feel hungry. I did not go to the garage and ask mummy because I was feeling shy. She was sleeping in the garage".
Crown Counsel – "How did she go to the garage?"
Manjula – "When I have fever I could walk to the garage."
Crown Counsel – "Did any thief come there?"
Manjula – "No thief came there that day."

After the conclusion of Manjula's evidence, Mr. Sathasivam's counsel Mr. Pereira wanted the evidence of the 'Quickshaws' driver recorded.

He said it was only fair that the driver's evidence should be recorded, especially as the medical evidence showed that Mrs. Sathasivam had died between 10 a.m. and 11.30 a.m.

He also added that when the Police questioned the 'Quickshaws' driver, he had stated that Mrs. Sathasivam bade good-bye to Mr. Sathasivam and the Police had checked Mr. Sathasivam's movements from that hour.

However, after Manjula's evidence, Mr. Tiruchelvam recorded his finding of the inquest as "I am of opinion that death was due to asphyxia by manual strangulation – Homicide".

On 15th October 1951, Mr. M.W.B. Thiedeman, Inspector of Police, Bambalapitiya, reported to the Magistrate, Colombo South, that he is inquiring into the murder of Mrs. Sathasivam and he mentioned the following:

"a. Professor G.S.W. de Saram held a post-mortem and was of the opinion that death was due to manual strangulation.

b. Mrs. Foenander stated that at 3.15 p.m. on 9th October she went to the house of the deceased and the child Manjula took her to the garage saying something in Sinhalese and words "Daddy" "Hora (meaning thief)" and "Mummy".

    c. A domestic aid, Podihamy, has stated that when she returned from school with the elder children, the younger child Manjula told her that daddy assaulted mummy and carried her downstairs to the garage and placed the mortar on her neck.

    d. Manjula, 4 years and 3 months old at the time, stated that daddy assaulted mummy with a broomstick and hands and carried her downstairs to the garage and took the gold chain from her neck and placed the mortar on her neck.

    e. Inspector Grenier stated that on 11th October 1951 at 3.30 p.m. one D. R. Weerasinghe who was released from remand prison the previous day informed Mr. Grenier that he met Mr. Sathasivam in the remand prison and that he told him that he squeezed his wife's neck and finding her dead carried her to the garage and that he had no intention of killing her."

Meanwhile the missing servant boy William was arrested on 18th October. At 6 p.m. on 19th October, the Inspector-General of Police, Mr. Richard Aluvihare recorded a statement of William (See Chapter 4).

On the 20th of October, Mr. Thiedeman produced Mr. Sathasivam at the Magistrate's Court and moved that he be remanded till 24th October. The Magistrate allowed this. Crown Counsel Mr. Cherubim appeared for the prosecution to assist the Police. Advocates Mr. Abeygunawardane and Mr. K.C. Nadarajah instructed by Mr. L. M. Fernando appeared for Mr. Sathasivam.

Mr. Thiedeman then produced Hewa Marambage William, and moved that his statement be recorded under the provision of section 134 of the Criminal Procedure Code. Mr. N.M.J. Rajendram, the Magistrate, recorded his statement and William was also remanded till 24th October.

CHAPTER 4

IN SEARCH OF WILLIAM

When the body of Mrs. Sathasivam was found, both males who were at her residence, her husband and the servant boy William, were missing.

Mr. Sathasivam was arrested the same evening at a friend's house.

Then it was quite clear to the police that the missing servant boy William had to be arrested to solve the mystery of Mrs. Sathasivam's murder. All Police Stations were alerted about William and a description given. The Police offered a reward of 1000 rupees for any information leading to William's arrest.

The hunt for William continued for over a week and special Police Officers had been sent to areas in the south of Ceylon like Walasmulla, Yakkalamulla and Galle, in search of him. (See inner back cover)

No relation of William contacted the Police. The Police had also found it difficult to contact any relative either as even the address of William's parents was not known.

While the Police were searching for William, a young man's body was found in the Mahaweli river in Kandy, a historical and picturesque town, 116 kilometres away from Colombo.

Professor G. S. W. de Saram was requested to perform a post-mortem examination on this body. On 14th October, he went to Kandy to perform the post-mortem examination of this unidentified body, believed to be that of William.

Joseph George Ragal, a driver employed by Mrs. Pathmanathan, Mrs. Sathasivam's sister, until four days prior to her death and who had seen William, identified the body as that of William's!

However, the Police decided that the body was not that of William because Professor de Saram described the body as that of a well-nourished man, between 25 and 30 years of age. Furthermore, the height of the body was 5 feet 6 inches whereas William's height was determined to be about 5 feet 2 inches.

Professor de Saram said that there were no injuries on the body and the cause of death was 'Asphyxia from drowning'.

While the search for William was on, an official spokesman remarked that it would have been considerably easier to locate William if he had been registered as a servant at the nearest Police Station. He added that it was unwise of householders, pressed by the shortage of servants, to employ servants 'whose antecedents were unknown'.

The Police had in the past campaigned for the registration of servants by employers for which all the necessary facilities were provided at every Police Station.

During the search for William, numerous informants came forward with "clues" to locate William, especially after the reward of 1,000 rupees was offered. None of them were dismissed lightly.

The 'Ceylon Daily News' of 19th October reported, "After William left the Sathasivam home, he is believed to have travelled down to his village, Kamburupitiya, near Matara. On hearing that the Police were looking for him, he left Kamburupitiya for Hungama, where some of his relatives lived. Work was found for him easily as it was the harvesting season. William was only two days at his new job when it leaked out that the Police were looking for him."

In the meantime, William's father and his brother came to Colombo and informed the Police authorities that they were prepared to co-operate with the Police and assist them to locate William.

Meanwhile, on certain information that William was likely to be in the Southern Province, a police officer had been sent to track him down and he was successful in finding him on the 18th.

Inspector H. Wickremaratne, disguised as a cultivator, traced William at Kalametiya, a village 11 kilometres from Hungama in the Tangalle district, in the deep south of Ceylon. He was informed that William was at a threshing floor. Workers at the floor in turn said that William had gone out to get some water, but would soon be back. When William returned, Inspector Wickremaratne arrested him.

William was brought to the Matara Police Station, a town situated about 160 kilometres from Colombo, sometime in the morning and the Assistant Superintendent of the Police (ASP), Matara informed Colombo about the arrest by a radio message.

"Events in the Sathasivam homicide inquiry took a dramatic turn yesterday when William, the servant employed at the Sathasivam's house made a statement to the Police exculpating Mr. Sathasivam," reported the next morning's newspapers.

"William, the servant boy who was missing from the date of Mrs. M. Sathasivam's death, was found by the Police yesterday morning. William was taken to the Matara Police Station for preliminary questioning by Mr. F.J.M. de Saram, ASP, and Mr. F. Adihetty, ASP."

"As soon as the Police established William's identity, messages were relayed to all Police Stations that the boy had been found. In the afternoon, William was handed over to Mr. M. Albert de Silva, Superintendent of Police (Crimes) and Mr. John Attygalle, ASP (Crimes) who went to Matara. William was brought to Colombo last night."

"They questioned William about the murder and the sale of the articles and brought him to Panadura and recovered certain articles - the stones from the ring as well as a gold bar - from a man who admitted he bought them from William. They also recovered the dirty sarong and shirt William left behind in a boutique at Panadura."

"It is learnt that William made three statements to the Police at various times during the examination. On a statement made by him, the Police were able to recover the gold 'thali' and bangles of Mrs. Sathasivam. According to this statement, on the morning of Mrs. Sathasivam's death, William had sold the 'thali' at a pawnbroker's shop in Wellawatte before 11 a.m.," reported the newspapers.

"News of Mrs. Sathasivam's death was unknown to him," said one report!

William's arrest brought to a close one week's intense searching for a man whose description had to be built up by the Police on carefully sifted shreds of information and who could have been anywhere in Ceylon.

William was brought to Colombo and not taken to the Bambalapitiya Police Station, which was directly concerned with the investigation of this crime, but was taken to the Police Station at Modera. He was questioned again there.

William was then taken to the Inspector-General of Police, Sir Richard Aluvihare's office and he recorded a statement from William. This statement, reproduced below, was an important and controversial document at the trial.

"I.G.'s Office
6 p.m. 19.10.1951
DIG Range 1, Mr. L. N. Peiris, the Legal Adviser, Mr. Cherubim, Mr. M. Albert de Silva, SP Crimes, Colombo, Mr. E.A. Koelmeyer, SP CID, and Inspector M.W.B. Thiedeman of Bambalapitiya are present in my office together with the boy named Hewa Marambage William who was taken into Police custody at Hungama on the 18th.

I read the statement made by him to Mr. E.A. Koelmeyer, SP of the CID. After reading his statement I ask William whether the statement he made to SP CID Mr. Koelmeyer was a voluntary statement, not subjected to any inducement or on the promise of a reward.

'I have made a true statement. I have described the incident, which occurred on the day of the murder. I have spoken the truth. Yesterday I made a statement as instructed by an Inspector whose name I am not certain of. He was the gentleman who arrested me near Hungama. He took me to a place close to the Matara Police Office. I can point out to you the spot. He asked me to make the statement that when the deceased lady came into the kitchen while I was scraping coconut, I released the coconut, got up and held her throat with both hands from behind took her to the garage and killed her. Thereafter, the Inspector brought me to the office and I made that statement to this gentleman (he points to Mr. M. Albert de Silva).'

'The same Inspector asked me to make the following statement after I was arrested near Hungama. He asked me to state that the master came to the kitchen after the lady was killed, gave me eight ten rupee notes and asked me to leave the place. I made that statement too to Mr. M. Albert de Silva at the Police Office in Matara.'

I ask him if he has any further statement to make.

'The Inspector told me that if I made the statements that I have already referred to that he would employ me in his bungalow as a servant.'

He states at this stage that he wanted to come out with something, which the Inspector told him but he cannot recall it just now. He now states that the Inspector told him that he would be given 1,000 rupees if he made the statement that the Inspector desired him to make. He states that there is nothing further to state.

Signed William

Read over and explained to him in Sinhalese, and admitted to be correct.

Made in my presence
Richard Aluvihare, I.G.P."

William was then produced before Mr. N.M.J. Rajendram, the Magistrate, and a detailed statement was recorded.

At 8.30 am on the 19th of October, William was produced before Professor G.S.W. de Saram for a medical examination.

He noted that his height was 5 feet and 4 inches.

Professor de Saram also noted that William had 8 injuries on the body. (See Figure 4.19 and 20. Pages 468 and 477). His fingernails of both hands were short and the nails of left hand appeared cut while the nails of right hand appeared bitten. There was no discharge from tip of penis and his prepuce (foreskin) could not be withdrawn.

After Professor de Saram's examination, William was remanded.

An identification parade was held at the Hulftsdorp prison the following day to enable Podihamy and Jothiswary to identify William, the person who worked as a servant. Twelve persons of about same age and about the same height as William were lined up for the parade. Podihamy and Jothiswary identified William without any hesitation.

On the 20th of October, the Inspector-General of Police, Sir

Richard Aluvihare met Professor de Saram with Mr. Cherubim and Mr. Thamotheram, the Crown Counsel. They had a long discussion about the post-mortem findings and the statement that William had made to Mr. Koelmeyer, the Superintendent of Police, Criminal Investigation Department, that William assisted Mr. Sathasivam to kill his wife.

Professor de Saram said that story was highly improbable!

He said he thought that the statement he had made to Inspector Wickremaratne at the Matara Police Station that he personally strangled Mrs. Sathasivam in the kitchen without anybody else's assistance was more consistent with the post-mortem findings.

CHAPTER 5

THE CASE FOR THE PROSECUTION

According to the law of Ceylon, a magisterial inquiry had to be held on the murder of Mrs. Sathasivam, before trial in a higher court. This inquiry began on 2nd November 1951.

Over one hundred witnesses, which included several Police Officers, medical experts, the Government Analyst, family members of Mr. and Mrs. Sathasivam, 'Quickshaws' cab drivers, Podihamy, Austin and Mrs. Foenander gave evidence at this inquiry.

Several witnesses including Sir Richard Aluvihare, the Inspector-General of Police, Police Officers Messrs. M. Albert de Silva, F.J.N. de Saram and P.H. Wickremaratne and the first accused Mr. Sathasivam were called by Dr. Colvin R. de Silva, the senior defence counsel of Mr. Sathasivam, to give evidence for the defence.

The inquiry lasted from 2nd November 1951 to 3rd April 1952. It ended with Mr. Sathasivam and William both being committed to the Supreme Court for trial.

A unique and unusual event that changed the whole course of the Sathasivam murder trial took place on 16th October 1952, almost one year after the death of Mrs. Sathasivam.

On that day, a warrant of pardon for the second accused William was received from the Attorney-General.

The fiscal officers produced William on 31st October before Mr. N.M.J. Rajendram, the Magistrate.

Mr. Rajendram informed William that he was authorised by the

Attorney-General, in terms of section 284 of the Criminal Procedure Code, to tender him a pardon, "On condition that William making a full and true disclosure of the whole of the circumstances within his knowledge of the murder and abetment of a murder and relative to every other person concerned, whether as principal or abettor in the commissioning of the said offence."

Mr. Rajendram then read out and interpreted the conditions of the pardon to William. Then he asked William a few questions to enable him to find out whether he had understood the implications of the condition on which the pardon is offered to him, and the nature and effect of his understanding.

"Do you understand the condition under which the pardon is tendered?" asked Mr. Rajendram.

"Yes."

"Do you understand the nature of the undertaking given by you?"

"Yes," replied William.

The Magistrate then informed William that if by concealing anything essential or by giving false evidence he has not complied with the condition on which the tender of the pardon is made, he may be tried for the offence in respect of which the pardon is tendered, or for any other offence of which he appears to have been guilty in connection with the same offence.

He asked William whether his acceptance was free and unqualified.

William answered, "Yes."

Then the Magistrate tendered the pardon and asked whether he accepted the pardon.

William answered the Court that he accepted the pardon on the conditions read out and explained to him. The Magistrate recorded that he was satisfied with the answers of William.

Then William was taken out of the dock meant for suspects. William's attorney-at-law, Mr. Seneviratne made an application, under section 283 of the Criminal Procedure Code, to keep William in custody till the termination of the trial. He said that William himself decided that he be detained in Police custody. The Magistrate ordered accordingly.

On 5th November 1952, Mr. Sathasivam was produced before the Magistrate and he was informed that William has been tendered a pardon.

Crown Counsel Mr. Cherubim appeared for the prosecution with Mr. V.T. Thamotheram. Dr. Colvin R. de Silva instructed by Mr L.D.S. Gunasekera appeared for the only accused now, Mr. Sathasivam.

Dr. de Silva in his submissions said that the present inquiry would seem to be supplementary in terms of Section 389 of the Criminal Procedure Code. Consequently the case would appear to stand committed for trial in the Supreme Court and this inquiry is only for the purpose of rounding off the evidence for the purpose of an indictment already determined upon.

He said, "In terms of the Code and in response to the legal query of Mr. Sathasivam, his proctor has already filed in this court a list of witnesses Mr. Sathasivam would require at the trial, and one of the witnesses therein was Mr. Cherubim, who appears for the Crown. He is also one of the witnesses, when indicated, might be necessary for Mr. Sathasivam at the preliminary inquiry itself. On that occasion it was left for Mr. Cherubim to decide."

"Today," Dr de Silva said, "I have to object to Mr. Cherubim's presence at all when the pardoned second accused William's evidence is taken as that of a witness."

He referred to the volume of evidence that brought in Mr. Cherubim in direct relationship with William in the very material stages in the course of the investigation.

Dr. de Silva said, "In law, and in conscience anyhow, it is gravely objectionable that William should be in the witness box, being in the direct control of the very witness in respect of whose relations with William himself at every material and relevant stage of events will necessarily be the subject of investigation, both at this stage and at trial stage."

Mr. Cherubim disagreed with the submissions made by Dr. de Silva. He said that the Attorney-General has considered the fact that he has been cited as a witness by the defence, and the Court has no jurisdiction to entertain Dr. de Silva's application.

Dr. de Silva submitted that the application made on behalf of William on the day the pardon was tendered was calculated gravely to prejudice the interest of the accused, Mr. Sathasivam, and to create an adverse impression.

On 17th November 1952, Mr. N.M.J. Rajendram, the Magistrate, made the following order.

"Mr. Cherubim has not been called as a witness at this inquiry. There is no provision in law, which he could be called as a witness before me at this stage of the inquiry. In terms of section 392 (1) of the Criminal Procedure Code, Mr. Cherubim as Crown Counsel is conducting the prosecution. He is therefore entitled to conduct the prosecution and I permit him to do so."

Following this order, Crown Counsel Mr. Cherubim with Mr. Thamotheram, Crown Counsel, led the evidence of Hewa Marambage William.

William said he was a 19-year-old cultivator from the village Angunabadulla, situated about 5 miles (8 kilometres) from Matara. He said he had studied up to the second standard in Sinhalese and he was employed at Wellawatte for about 6 months as a domestic servant. During this period he got to know the Wellawatte area very well. After 6 months, he left the job and went home. Then he worked in Ambalantota, a town in the deep south of Ceylon as a salesman for a about a month and left that employment on 26th September.

The same day he left Matara to come to Colombo in search of employment. He arrived at Colombo the following day and went around Fort and Wellawatte looking for jobs. He slept that night on the verandah of a barber's shop in Wellawatte. Next day, on the 28th of September, he met Dosihamy, an old woman, near the Wellawatte bridge. She took him first to Mrs Pathmanathan, and then to her sister Mrs. Sathasivam.

Then William described in detail what happened on the day of the murder. He said he was called by Mr. Sathasivam to assist him to kill Mrs. Sathasivam. Subsequently, he was given the jewellery worn by her and asked to go.

After William's evidence, the proceedings in the Magistrate's

Court were concluded.

The Supreme Court trial commenced on 20th March 1953, almost one year after the magisterial inquiry, before Justice E. F. N. Gratiaen. (See Figure 5. Page 469)

The Acting Solicitor-General, Mr. T.S. Fernando, Queen's Counsel, led the prosecution with Crown Counsel Messrs. Douglas Jansze, Ananda Pereira and V.T. Thamotheram. (see Figure 6. Page 469)

Dr. Colvin R. de Silva with Messrs. T.W. Rajaratnam and H.A.G. de Silva, instructed by Merrill Pereira and Gunasekera, appeared for the defence.

Mr. Sathasivam alone was charged with the murder of his wife this time under section 296 of the Ceylon Penal Code. He entered a plea of 'Not guilty'.

The second accused in the Magistrate's Court, William, who was given a conditional pardon by the Attorney-General, became the chief witness for the prosecution.

Justice Gratiaen making a few preliminary observations to the jury stated that they have been empanelled to try a case, which has attracted a considerable amount of publicity during the past eighteen months.

"It is more than probable that all of you have read or heard a good deal about this unfortunate affair. You may have read or heard a good deal which you will find does not form part of the case which is being presented by the Crown against the prisoner. I want you all, as far as it is humanly possible to do so, banish from your minds, from your recollection, anything that you have previously heard by way of rumour or idle talk regarding the case," he said.

"You have taken a solemn oath and it will be your duty to give a verdict, upon the evidence placed before you. I am sure all of you are conscientious enough to appreciate that fact," continued Justice Gratiaen.

He warned the jury at the outset that the case was going to take a considerable amount of time.

He also reminded the jury that at the end of each day's work each one of them would take an oath of separation prescribed by the law.

"The purpose of that oath is really to remind you of what you already know, that is from now till the end of this case, you must have no communication with anybody other than with each other regarding the facts of this case. If any outsider tries to communicate with you regarding this case, he will be guilty of contempt of court and I am sure you will bring such impropriety to my notice," said Justice Gratiaen.

Mr. T.S. Fernando, the Acting Solicitor-General prosecuting, alleged that Mr. Sathasivam, between 9.00 and 9.30 a.m. on the 9th of October 1951 strangled his wife in the bedroom upstairs with the help of William, and then brought the body down to the garage and kept it there, to show that William committed the murder.

The motive he said was the pending divorce case filed by Mrs. Sathasivam because of Mr. Sathasivam's alleged affair with Miss Yvonne Stevenson.

"If the divorce action went through, Mr. Sathasivam would have to pay alimony to his wife and also bear the expenses of the children and he would have to support Miss Stevenson," said Mr. Fernando.

The defence position was that Mrs. Sathasivam victim was strangled by William in the kitchen and/or garage after Mr. Sathasivam has left the house at 10.30 a.m.

The almost entire first day of the trial was spent on legal arguments on admissibility of certain documents and statements.

Just before the adjournment, Dr. Colvin R. de Silva, the counsel for the defence made an application to have a specimen of blood from the witness William to be examined. The Acting Solicitor-General did not object.

William consented to give a sample of blood. Justice Gratiaen then made an order directing the prison authorities that Professor G.S.W. de Saram should be permitted to take William's blood.

Legal arguments continued on the 23rd also.

Only on the 24th of March, Mr. T. S. Fernando, the Acting Solicitor-General commenced his opening address to the jury.

In his address, Mr. Fernando also stressed the importance of the function of the jury.

He said, "His Lordship already told you this case has attracted a lot of publicity in this Island, and it is probable, perhaps inevitable, that all of you or at least some of you, may have, at some stage or other, read the newspapers and discussed the matter in your clubs. On behalf of the Crown, I wish most respectfully to endorse his Lordship's remarks regarding what may have happened in this case, that you are to try this case on the evidence placed before you."

"This is a trial by jury. Not a trial by newspaper or trial by rumour or a trial by report. Perhaps it is hardly necessary for me to impress on you that fact, but it is out of abundance of caution that one is constrained to tell the jury to bear this in mind. I have no doubt that you will hear this case without any prejudice in your minds."

Then Mr. Fernando traced the life and times of Mr. and Mrs. Sathasivam referring to their marriage, children, turbulent family life, and the two divorce cases filed.

Mr. Fernando then referred to Mr. Sathasivam's affair with Miss Yvonne Stevenson and letters sent by her after Mr. Sathasivam came to Sri Lanka in September.

Mr. Fernando said, "By August 1950, Mr. Sathasivam had formed a strong attachment to that other woman whom I mentioned to you earlier, which appears to have been so strong that one witness, who will give evidence in the case, a Mr. Bogstra, a Dutchman, says that the accused came to see him some time in August 1950, at a time when he was aware that this lady, Miss Stevenson, had left Ceylon and gone to India."

"Mr. Sathasivam wanted to know her whereabouts and he had told him that he wanted to bring back this lady, even if he had to bring her back handcuffed. He appeared again at the office of Mr. Bogstra - this time with Miss Yvonne Stevenson - indicating that he had brought the girl back to Ceylon. Events moved thereafter, took a certain shape, which did not make for a happy marriage."

Referring to the letters written by Mrs. Sathasivam, Mr. Fernando said, "Well gentleman, those appear to have been the sentiments of Mrs. Sathasivam at the time she returned to the Island without him. In a way she was aware that her married life was floundering."

Mr. Fernando said that there was evidence that Mr. and Mrs. Sathasivam were seen, in one or two places and they paid a visit together to her sister's husband's house.

"There is also evidence that notwithstanding the request that had been made to Mr. Sathasivam or the suggestion that he was not welcome in Mrs. Sathasivam's house, that he stayed in the house off and on, till about the 2nd of October; and, according to Mr. Sathasivam's own admission, she threatened to leave her house and take up residence in the Y.W.C.A. unless he left; and he did leave the house on the 2nd of October."

Mr. Fernando continued, "A special Process Server was asked to serve the summons at No. 79, Horton Place, the address of Haniffa, Mr. Sathasivam's friend, and we come very near the fateful day!"

"We have also evidence, gentlemen, that on that day, sometime in the course of the day, Mr. Sathasivam's mother came to No. 7, St. Alban's Place and placed a padlock on her telephone. The result of padlocking a telephone is that one is able to receive calls but cannot make a call," explained Mr. Fernando.

"Meanwhile gentlemen, Mr. Sathasivam was receiving communications from Miss Stevenson, who was then in England. She wrote a letter on 27th September from England, about 5 days after Mr. Sathasivam arrived in Ceylon."

"In that letter, Miss Stevenson stated, to begin at the beginning, 'I cannot come to you until you have the divorce started. I have no objection to being the co-respondent, but there must be the certainty that we do get married. As things are, if I go to you, the family will be through with me. It is not worth it when you think we might never get married.' Then later on in the letter, 'I cannot live without you, and to be with you and Amma (Mr. Sathasivam's mother) is going to be hard, but I cannot believe you to say we are going to end like this.' Then she says later on, 'I was so happy when your letter came. The idea of going back was like a dream come true; but then, I realized that I could not get cracking on the divorce. Arrange my accommodation, job, and settle my debts. All the same, I love you and shall wait for you. I would give anything to be out of this country, anything to be with you, but for once, I am sitting tight. What will happen if I lose both you and my people? Can you see me wandering around, with no one, penniless?'"

Mr. Fernando said the next day she followed up with another letter, which stated that she had taken a new job.

"She indicates that she was only coming if she had a chance of getting married. Then, gentlemen, on the 29th she began another letter which she continued - she wrote by fits and starts - a few lines on the 29th and continued on the 30th."

Mr. Sathasivam has sent a cable on 2nd October to Miss Stevenson at 37C, Cornwall Gardens, London SW7, stating, "Why no letters. Action filed. Come at once. Passage Paid Cooks. Love – Satha." Mr. Sathasivam mentioned 79, Horton Place, the residence of Mr. Haniffa's as his address.

The same day she wrote a reply to this cable beginning, "Got your cable today."

Mr. Fernando referred to the serving of summons to Mr. Sathasivam on the divorce case filed by his wife on the 8th of October.

He said, "It would appear that on the night of the 8th, the morning of the 9th, near about one o'clock, Mr. Sathasivam came to his wife's house, was admitted by his wife opening the front door, thereafter, on the 9th at about 10.30 in the morning, he left that house."

Mr. Fernando then described what happened on the tragic day.

He said that on 9th morning the usual routine in this class of household apparently took place. At this time, the only servants in the household were the woman Podihamy and William.

"At about 7 o'clock, William was sent out to the boutique to buy string-hoppers, the morning newspaper and some betel. Meanwhile, Podihamy got the two elder children, ready for school. Podihamy gave milk to all four children and gave rice for the mid-day meal to William whose duty was to cook the rice. William came and questioned her about the vegetables to be prepared for the mid-day meal. Thereafter, she took the two elder children in a cab of 'Quickshaws' at about 8.15 a.m."

Mr. Fernando then related William's own account of what happened that morning.

"He says that he got up in the morning at about 6 o'clock and washed his face; he then swept the house and the compound. Some time after that Mrs. Sathasivam called him upstairs and gave him a rupee and fifteen cents and wanted him to bring some betel, the newspaper and twenty string-hoppers. William went up to the boutique in Galle Road and bought them. Then he took them up to her room and left them on a table, which was in the room. When he was about to come downstairs after leaving the things, Podihamy gave him some bread for his morning meal and told him to bring his cup upstairs so that she may pour out his portion of tea."

"When William took his cup upstairs, he, at the same time, took up the basket to bring the rice so that he may cook it for the mid-day meal. He says he got these and came down with the tea and the rice; he drank off the tea and kept the bread. He says, some little time thereafter he was called upstairs and Mrs. Sathasivam gave him some money and asked him to bring some plantains, eggs and a pound of sugar. He says before he went out to do that, he went to the kitchen to prepare a 'sambal' to eat with the string-hoppers."

'Sambal' is a mixture of scraped coconut with chilli and other spices.

"William said that he took this up with some bread and a spoon and some plates and left them on the same table in her room. Thereafter, he went out for the things and brought the eggs and plantains, but appears to have had some difficulty about the sugar. The boutique did not have a pound of sugar or something like that. He told Mrs. Sathasivam about this and ultimately he went back again to bring a pound of brown sugar. He says that he brought this sugar."

"He says that at the time he took it upstairs, Mr. Sathasivam was brushing his teeth. He came downstairs and began cleaning the rice. Rice has to be cleaned and washed before you boil it. William says he was called upstairs again. Podihamy asked him to take the vegetables for the mid-day meal. She asked him to make drumsticks and ash-plantains, which he was told was downstairs in the cupboard or shelf. And he also says that he remembers the children leaving with Podihamy when the car came."

Mr. Fernando then told the jury a crucial and a controversial fact, stated by William.

"After the children had left, he went upstairs to ask for some garlic. He also asked her on that occasion how many drum-sticks and ash plantains should be cooked for the mid-day meal, and having got instructions on these points, he got these two vegetables and put them in certain shallow pots to cook them."

"William said that he started to scrape a coconut to extract the milk to be used for the curry. (See figure 7. Page 469) He had not gone very far with the process when Mr. Sathasivam came down. He was dressed in a shirt, trousers and shoes. He held William by his hand and took him to the dining room. William said, 'Let go my hand, otherwise I will get late to prepare the meals.' Mr. Sathasivam then asked him whether he would agree to a suggestion that he was going to make. William asked what it was and said that if it was possible he would agree."

"Mr. Sathasivam told him, 'There is a divorce case against me and it is possible that I might lose this case; I must kill the lady, and you must help me.' William said, 'Let me go', but Mr. Sathasivam would not let him go. Mr. Sathasivam said that he would give William certain articles, which would fetch about three hundred to four hundred rupees."

Mr. Fernando then narrated William's story how Mrs. Sathasivam was killed.

"Holding me by his hand, Mr. Sathasivam took me up the stairs. Still holding me he entered Mrs. Sathasivam's bedroom. At that time, she was seated on the bed. Mr. Sathasivam with his right hand held Mrs. Sathasivam in the region of the throat. At that moment William's hand was released. As he held Mrs. Sathasivam, he jerked her down on the floor, still holding her throat, and at the time one knee of his was pinning one of the arms of Mrs. Sathasivam. She was waving her legs and her free hand about."

Mr. Sathasivam at that stage, shouted out calling William 'Hold, you devil!'

Continuing Mr. Fernando said, "William himself squatted and held Mrs. Sathasivam in the region of her hips on both sides. Her free arm gripped the upper portion of William's left forearm. William managed to wrest his arm free but with some difficulty. She would appear to have been making some feeble attempt to grab the person holding her by the waist. When his forearm was released, the free right arm of the Mrs. Sathasivam gripped his left cheek. It was again with difficulty that he managed to free his cheek from the grip of the her hand."

"William released himself from that grip and got up. Mr. Sathasivam also got up about that time, and he trampled in the region of her throat with his foot. At that moment the boy says that Mrs. Sathasivam's neck went to a side," said Mr. Fernando demonstrating the neck being pushed to a side.

"Thereafter, according to William, Mr. Sathasivam took off the 'thali' from the lady's neck."

" 'Thali' or 'thalikody' is a traditional necklace worn by Hindu ladies after marriage, and which, on no account, would be taken away by them," explained Mr. Fernando.

"Mr. Sathasivam, according to William then gave the 'thali', two gold bangles, which Mrs. Sathasivam had in her arm and a ring from one of the fingers. There was another gold bangle and some plastic bangles on her hands, but they were not taken. Then Mr. Sathasivam opened the lady's wardrobe and took out her handbag. He took three rupees from it and gave it to William and told him, 'There are only a few loose coppers left, do you want those?' He said, 'No'."

Continuing the story as William related, Mr. Fernando said then Mr. Sathasivam asked William to wait in the bedroom and went downstairs and closed the front door. Then he came up again and asked William to hold Mrs. Sathasivam in the region of the legs, while he himself held her body by her armpits, and Mrs. Sathasivam's body was brought down the stairway, taken through the dining room, through the kitchen and dumped in the garage.

"Once the body was put in the garage William turned to go, but as he got to the kitchen door, something prompted him to look back. He saw Mr. Sathasivam lifting a wooden mortar, which was lying in the garage. William did not wait to look any more but took a short cut through the dining room into the front verandah, opened the door and got on to the compound," said Mr. Fernando.

"He then saw the two children on the swing and told them that he was going and went to the bus stand. He got into a bus, which took him to the Wellawatte junction, and he went to a boutique of a jeweller. He saw the man who was normally in the boutique and asked him where the jeweller was. The jeweller was contacted and he sold the gold necklace to the Station Road jeweller for a mere 100 rupees. It was worth very much more."

Mr. Fernando said, "The jeweller is a witness in the case, gentlemen, and having regard to the nature of the whole transaction, it cannot be said that the jeweller was not unaware of the real nature of this gold article, because that gold necklace was melted down that very next day!"

Mr. Fernando said, "William then had some tea and took a bus which went no further than Panadura, a town about 26 kilometres from Colombo. There he went into a shop and bought himself a sarong and then went into another shop and bought a shirt. He made some inquiries whether a ring and bangles could be sold there and there again he found no difficulty because the man who sold him the shirt made contact with another jeweller who was able to get this boy to sell this ring and bangles for a paltry thirty rupees. With the proceeds of the articles he made a hundred and thirty rupees, but spent thirteen rupees on a sarong and a shirt."

Continuing his address, Mr. Fernando said that there was an independent witness, Sanmugam, who had no interest in this case, seeing a boy talking to the man in that shop in High Street, Wellawatte some little time before 10 o'clock.

Mr. Fernando said, "Sanmugam, this witness, wanted that day to take a girl Premawathie, to the General Hospital for treatment, and he wanted to go along with one Edmund in the shop in the High Street. At that time the girl was to be admitted to Hospital. There is the evidence of Sanmugam and the doctor who examined the girl whom Sanmugam took that day on the 9th of October to the General Hospital. The doctor has examined the girl at 10.20 in the morning."

"You are familiar, gentlemen, that at the General Hospital particularly, one would take a little time before one can contact a doctor for admission. There does not appear to have been much delay for Sanmugam and Edmund, to contact a doctor. Evidence will be led, gentlemen, of the doctor and of documents which support the doctor, the time he saw the girl and the time of admission of the girl into the ward. The doctor's examination precedes the admission to a ward. The admission took place at 10.30 and the examination was at 10.20 in the morning."

Mr. Fernando continued, "Let us now leave the boy for a moment and come back to the house. Mr. Sathasivam on his own admission left this house at 10.30 in the morning. He says he left by a 'Quickshaws' cab. He says from No. 7, St. Alban's Place, he made his way towards the Fort and got down at the Galle Face Hotel."

The Galle Face Hotel, founded in 1864, claims to be the oldest hotel east of the Suez. It is situated in the heart of the commercial capital of Sri Lanka. It regularly featured on the itineraries of royalty. Princess Alexandra of Denmark commented that 'the peacefulness and generosity encountered at the Galle Face Hotel cannot be matched'. Former guests include the first man in space, Yuri Gagarin, former British Prime Minister Edward Heath, Prince Sadruddin Aga Khan, Lord Louis Mountbatten and Marshal Tito. The Galle Face Hotel is considered an oasis of tranquility amidst the hustle and bustle of the city by the side of the Indian Ocean.

Mr. Fernando said that Mr. Sathasivam met some friends at the Galle Face Hotel. They were Mr. Haniffa and one Mr. Perera.

"From there, he was dropped at the Bank of Ceylon, while his friends Haniffa and Perera went to the Grand Oriental Hotel. Mr. Sathasivam joined his friends at the Hotel round about noon and after a couple of drinks there, and at about 2 o'clock in the afternoon they went to Mr. Haniffa's house."

Mr. Fernando then explained how Sanmugam came to be a witness in this case.

"Mrs. Sathasivam's death was reported the next day in the newspapers. Sanmugam learned that the Police wanted a boy, and at once it struck him to question Edmund about the boy to whom he spoke. He questioned Edmund and asked him whether the boy to whom he spoke had sold him any articles."

"Then Edmund contacted Dharmasena, a jeweller in Station Road. He informed Sanmugam that he had seen a description of the boy in the Sinhalese newspaper. This report had mentioned that the necklace was worth about four hundred rupees."

Mr. Fernando said Sanmugam then contacted no less a person than the Superintendent of Police, Mr. Albert de Silva. Sanmugam telephoned his residence and could not get at him. He then wrote the following letter on the 17th of October.

"At this time William had not been even arrested," said Mr. Fernando.

This was the letter sent by Sanmugam to Mr. Albert de Silva, on 17th October.

"*M.A. De Silva Esqr.*
Superintendent of Police (Crimes)
Colombo.

Sir,

I think the following information may be of some help to trace the missing servant boy William in the Sathasivam murder case.

On or about the 11th instant when I was at No. 37, High Street, Wellawatte, at the boutique of A.P. Edmund (a friend of mine) he told me a boy of the description given by the Police called at his premises on the 9th instant - time between 10 and 10.20 a.m. - enquiring for the jeweller next door, whose premises were closed at the time. The boy when questioned by Edmund told him that he had gold jewellery to sell. Edmund then directed him to a shop visible from his place in Station Road, Wellawatte, and owned by D.C.A. Sirisena, at No. 54. I further understood from Edmund that during the course of his conversation with Sirisena late one evening when Sirisena was going past his shop that on the 9th instant the boy had sold a gold necklace to him for 100 rupees and the article was worth 490 rupees, which he had melted down, and further he had entered in his book the boy's name and an address in Kirillapone. From the description given to me by Edmund, the boy was wearing a red striped poplin sarong and a half sleeve striped shirt and aged about 18 years.

Edmund was very anxious to report these facts to the Police but subsequently I found him reluctant through fear that he may be bodily harmed by Sirisena. I have my doubts if he has done so yet.

My request to you Sir is that you do not disclose my name or that of

Edmund at this stage.
I am, Sir
Your Obedient Servant,
V.S.N. Sanmugam"

Mr. Fernando said when Sanmugam was getting ready to post it on the night of the 17th of October, Mr. Albert de Silva came to his house along with Inspector Orr and some constables and asked him whether he had tried to contact him. He said, 'Yes' and handed over the letter, which was then in an envelope.

Albert de Silva read that letter and said, 'I will see about it' and went away.

Mr. Fernando, continuing his opening address said, "Now, gentlemen, Sanmugam, the witness who had originally written the letter dated the 17th of October, stated that as nothing had happened after the visit of Albert de Silva on the night of the 17th, although he was told that the matter would be attended to, decided to write another letter to Albert de Silva, and that was written on the 20th in which he made certain references to the visit he made to the Wellawatte Police Station and to the questions put to him by the Police on the 19th. He sent this letter by Registered Post to Albert de Silva's address at the Police Office, Colombo."

In this letter Mr. Sanmugam wrote, "With reference to my letter of the 17th instant, Messrs. Attygalle, Adihetty and Wickremaratne questioned me yesterday as to the exact time I engaged the 'Quickshaws' to go to the General Hospital with Edmund. To be precise, I called at their office yesterday in Station Road, Bambalapitiya, and enquired from them to tell me the time I had phoned for a 'Quickshaws'. I phoned them giving my name and address 37, High St. (Edmund's boutique). On referring to their book, they told me it was at 9.40 a.m. they got my message. I phoned them from General and Medical Stores, No.41, High Street, one door next to Edmund's."

Mr. Fernando continuing said, "Then, he followed it up with another letter; this time he wrote to the Inspector-General of Police. He was complaining that he had written two letters, but had not even received an acknowledgement, and that in spite of certain action taken by him, it was very discouraging that it did not even seem to have been appreciated."

When Mr. Fernando, the Acting Solicitor-General referred to letters written by Sanmugam, Dr. Colvin R. de Silva, the defence counsel objected because Sanmugam referred to Mr. Attygalle, a Police Officer, but the prosecution is not calling Mr. Attygalle as a witness.

"Since it is being said that Edmund and Sanmugam were asked by Attygalle and somebody else what time they had seen certain things, I take it that the Crown is calling Attygalle and the others," said Dr. de Silva.

"I am not calling Attygalle," said Mr. Fernando.

"That being the case, Your Lordship, I object to any statement being put into the mouth of anybody, who is not being called in this case. What anybody said to Attygalle, I have no objection. It is my respectful submission that one cannot, through the intervention of a letter, to introduce inadmissible evidence," said Dr. de Silva.

"I will observe the rules of evidence, My Lord," said Mr. Fernando and continued his address.

He said the Police questioned both Edmund and Sanmugam. Mr. Attygalle who was present also questioned them.

"And it is a significant fact that no statement of Edmund and no statement of Sanmugam was recorded by the Police on the 19th. Very Well. Sanmugam on the 20th, the following day, writes to Albert de Silva, 'With reference to my letter of the 17th instant, Messrs Attygalle, Adihetty and Wickremaratne questioned me yesterday as to the...'"

At this stage Dr. de Silva intervened.

"I must object, My Lord, to parts of that letter going in which refer to statements made by persons who are not being called as witnesses. It is my respectful submission that one cannot, through the intervention of a letter, introduce inadmissible evidence. I submit it is not permissible for anyone to say that anyone else who is not a witness in this case told him, asked him, or gave him directions; or to admit any statement of anyone who the Crown does not choose to call."

Mr. Fernando said, "The questioning by the Police Officers was at the very lowest, most surprising and not at all like that expected of Police Officers. It was evidence of some important factor in regard to time."

Justice Gratiaen queried, "Would it not be more convenient, Mr. Solicitor, to present the case for the Crown, in your opinion, against the prisoner; and, as the case proceeds, if the conduct of any Police Officer is attacked, that criticism could be more conveniently brought to the jury at the relevant stage of the case?"

"Very well, My Lord," replied Mr. Fernando.

Continuing he said that the importance of the evidence of this group of witnesses, Sanmugam, Edmund and the witnesses from the hospital, is that all indicated that Edmund and Sanmugam had seen William, before they left on their trip with the patient Premawathie to the Hospital.

"This would take us round about 10 o'clock, at a time when, according to Mr. Sathasivam's own admission, he was still inside the house; and at that time, the inference appears to be that William had the gold necklace on him," said Mr. Fernando.

He then described how William was arrested in Hungama, a village in the deep south of Ceylon, on 18th October and brought to Colombo.

"The Inspector-General, who had interested himself - and quite rightly if I may say so - in this case, kept in touch with Matara and he says he got a certain impression as to what the boy had stated at Matara. He got that impression by 18th night. On 19th morning, at the suggestion of certain Police Officers he went down to the Modera Police Station and there he listened to a statement which was read out to him which was said to be the statement of William."

"The Inspector-General said that the statement which was read out to him took him by surprise, in view of what he had heard from Matara, and he questioned the Police Officers who recorded this boy's statement, and he says, he was dissatisfied with the conduct of the Police officers and ordered, then and there, that the Crime Police, of which Albert de Silva and Attygalle were the head and assistant respectively, were to stop investigating this crime, and the Criminal Investigation Department was ordered to take over."

Dr. Colvin R. de Silva said that the taking over was made subsequently and certainly not at the Modera Police station.

Continuing Mr. Fernando said, "Sometime in the course of that day an order was made that the Criminal Investigation Department should record the boy's statement in the presence of Albert de Silva and one of the Deputy Inspectors General Mr. L.N. Peiris; and either that night or the following morning the Inspector-General made the order that the Criminal Investigation Department continue the investigation, and not the Colombo Crime Police."

Mr. Fernando informed the jury that Mr. Sathasivam has said that he left the house at 10.30 in the morning and appeared in the company of Haniffa and Perera at the Galle Face Hotel. He was back at Haniffa's house some time after 2 o'clock.

"Meanwhile, the two children Manjula and Rajendrani were apparently alone in the house, with a dead body in the garage. They were so there till nearly 3 o'clock in the afternoon. Austin, the family laundryman came there roughly about 3 o'clock or a little before that. As was apparently the custom, he took the bundle of clothes upstairs, and seeing nobody about, came out. His attention was attracted by the children, apparently saw the dead body, and in turn contacted somebody else, and the body was discovered by a neighbour, Mrs. Foenander, shortly after 3 o'clock."

"About the time that Mrs. Foenander had come out and seen the body in the garage, Podihamy returned to the house with the two elder children in a rickshaw. When she went upstairs to get some money to pay the rickshawman, she says she found the wardrobe open, the keys on the ground, and the fan working. She says the first thing she did was to put off the fan as it was working uselessly! Then she got some money and paid the rickshawman, and soon after that, apparently as a result of somebody telling her, she went and looked into the garage, saw what had happened and set up a wail. Her first instinct was to remove the mortar and keep it aside."

Mr. Fernando then told the jury that, Mrs. Foenander telephoned the Police Station at Bambalapitiya.

"She had to telephone from the telephone upstairs because the telephone downstairs was locked. The Police received the message at quarter past three in the afternoon, and the Reserve Constable there, asked Police Constable Siriwardena to investigate, and at 3.23 in the afternoon he arrived at No. 7, St. Alban's Place. Inspector Thiedeman, who was in charge of the Bambalapitiya Police Station, arrived soon after and took charge of the place. He contacted Mr. Adihetty, the Assistant Superintendent of Police, and, thereafter Albert de Silva and Attygalle, who were his superior officers in the Crime Branch."

"Mr. Nadarajah, advocate, a friend of Mr. Sathasivam, came there later in the evening. He accompanied the Police, that is, Albert de Silva and Attygalle, to No. 79, Horton Place, where Mr. Sathasivam was arrested in the evening at about 6 o'clock. From No. 79, Horton Place, Albert de Silva and Attygalle took Mr. Sathasivam to the Fort Police Station - not the Bambalapitiya Police Station. Inspector Thiedeman, who had made certain investigations and recorded certain statements himself, went to the Fort Police Station, at about midnight on the 9th of October and questioned Mr. Sathasivam."

"On the 18th William was arrested. On the 19th the Inspector-General was present when his statement was read. Sometime on the 19th or the 20th, there was a change of Police Officers investigating the case, and on the 19th night, the boy William, was taken before the Magistrate, Colombo South. William made a voluntary statement to the Magistrate, after due caution had been administered to him."

Commenting on the medical evidence, Mr. Fernando said, "Evidence will also be led in this case, gentlemen, expert medical testimony, based upon the post-mortem findings, that Mrs. Sathasivam was certainly dead within an hour of her morning meal, which certainly appears to have included string-hoppers."

"It is in that context that the prosecution places a lot of reliance upon the evidence of Sanmugam and Edmund, which indicates that the boy was there, trying to sell the jewellery at about 10 o'clock, when Mr. Sathasivam was still in the house. And I want to indicate to you at this stage, as I have already indicated, that the case for the prosecution is that at the time Mr. Sathasivam states he left No. 7, St. Alban's Place, Bambalapitiya, he left it with a dead body - the dead body of his wife - in the garage."

"It is the case for the Crown, gentlemen, that at the time he left that house, which we are going to see tomorrow, No. 7, St. Alban's Place, Bambalapitiya, Mrs. Sathasivam was a dead woman. It is the case for the Crown that she met with her death by manual strangulation, that is, to use a simple term, throttling; and the prosecution will contend that the throttler was no other than her own husband, the prisoner in the dock," said Mr. Fernando.

Mr. Fernando said that at this opening stage it was not necessary to acquaint the jury with facts in greater detail.

"You will now listen to the evidence that will be led in this case. Thank you, My Lord," he concluded.

On the 24th of March the Crown summoned the first witness. He was Mr. M.W. B. Thiedeman, now Inspector of Police, Fort.

Examined by Mr. Douglas Jansze, Crown Counsel, he said that as the Inspector of Police, Bambalapitiya, he went to No. 7, St. Alban's Place, at about 3.30 p.m. on the 9th October 1951 and found the dead body of Mrs. Sathasivam in the garage. He said the garage door, leading out on to the front compound, was padlocked.

He said he visited the house on several occasions thereafter.

He requested a draughtsman of the Public Works Department, Mr. B.D.J. Devapuraratne, to prepare the sketches of the house.

Mr. Thiedeman described in detail the sketch and described the furniture and items found in the house, in both the ground floor and upstairs. (See Figure 8 Page 470 and the description in page 471)

He said that one door of an almirah (a wardrobe or a movable cupboard) in the bedroom upstairs was open and the keys were on the ground.

Mr. Thiedeman found a finger bowl (used to wash hands after having a meal), a large plate with a spoon, string-hoppers, 'sambal' and a small aluminium plate.

"At the top of the stairs, as you enter the upstairs, just opposite the staircase, there is a window, and through that you can get a clear view of the Bambalapitiya Police Station," Mr. Thiedeman explained.

Cross-examined by Dr. Colvin R. de Silva, the senior defence counsel, Mr. Thiedeman said that the distance from the back verandah of No. 7, St. Alban's Place to the garden of the Bambalapitiya Police Station would not be more than 60 feet as the crow flies.

"If you look across from the highest step of the back verandah of No. 7, St Alban's Place, can you see the Police Station?" asked Dr. de Silva.

"Except for a hedge there would be no obstruction of the view," he replied.

Dr. de Silva asked whether any person standing on the landing upstairs and looking out through the window there would directly see the crime office building of the Police Station.

"You get a fairly straight view of the crime office," Mr. Thiedeman answered.

"If anybody stood at that window and yelled out 'Murder, Help, Police', it would be heard at the crime office of the Police Station?"

"Yes," he replied.

Next day, 25th March, Justice Gratiaen, in the company of counsel for the Crown and the defence, the jury, the accused Mr. Sathasivam and the Clerk of the Court visited No. 7, St. Alban's Place, arriving there at 9.45 a.m.

For Mr. Sathasivam this must have been a traumatic experience because he was now visiting the house, which he said he left at 10. 30 a.m. on 9th October 1951.

Justice Gratiaen had requested the clerk previous day to make arrangements so that the present occupants of the house will be away from the premises from 9.30 a.m. till the Court leaves the scene on the 25th of March.

Mr. Thiedeman was re-called and sworn in.

Justice Gratiaen told him, "I want you to take the Court and the gentlemen of the jury and point to us everything which is depicted in the sketch of the ground floor. I wish you also to indicate any differences which now exist as compared with what appears in the sketch."

As requested, Mr. Thiedeman went through the house with Justice Gratiaen and others pointing everything depicted in the sketch. Justice Gratiaen asked the Acting Solicitor-General, defence counsel and the jury to ask any questions from Mr. Thiedeman.

Answering a query from Dr. Colvin R. de Silva as to what one can see from upstairs window Mr. Thiedeman said, "From this window you can actually see the table in the crime office of the Police Station; it is the Inspector's table."

After further clarifications by Mr. Thiedeman to queries of the Acting Solicitor-General and the defence counsel, the party left the scene at 11.25 a.m.

Mr. S. Pathmanathan, Chairman of the Low Country Products Association, who was married to the elder sister of Mrs. Sathasivam, gave evidence next.

He described Mrs. Sathasivam as a "Very quiet, exemplary type of lady with very high ideas and very devoted to her home and children."

Mr. Pathmanathan mentioned about the dowry given to Mrs. Sathasivam, dates her children were born and the two divorce cases filed.

He said on the 24th of September 1951, Mr. and Mrs. Sathasivam visited him at his estate, where he was staying alone.

Next day, his wife and daughter, together with Mr. and Mrs. Sathasivam visited him.

"The object of the visits was to bring about reconciliation, as a result of a little unpleasantness between me and my wife. They stayed about half an hour and all of us then went back together," Mr. Pathmanathan said.

Answering further questions of Mr. Jansze, Crown Counsel, Mr. Pathmanathan said he heard of Mrs. Sathasivam's death at about 3.00 p.m. on 9th October.

"I was in my office and I received a telephone message from my wife. I immediately went and picked up my wife and went to No.7, St. Alban's Place. I saw the dead body of the Mrs. Sathasivam lying in the garage," he said.

At about 3.30 p.m. he telephoned Mr. Sathasivam's uncle and gave him the information.

Cross-examined by Dr. Colvin R. de Silva, Mr. Pathmanathan said Mr. Sathasivam's mother, who came with his uncle, left No.7, St. Alban's Place, the scene of murder, almost immediately.

"There was a little unpleasantness on her arrival at No. 7, St. Alban's Place?" Dr. de Silva asked.

"Yes. At that time as far as we were concerned Mr. Sathasivam's mother was not welcome in that house. She felt people in the house were cold or something like that and did not treat her well and therefore she left".

Podihamy, the trusted old servant of Mrs. Sathasivam was summoned next by the Crown to give evidence.

Podihamy answering questions of Mr. Fernando said, "I did not stay at the house at St. Alban's house with the children, during the time Mr. and Mrs Sathasivam were away in England. We went to Horton Place, the residence of Mrs. Sathasivam's mother. Mr. Sathasivam's mother stayed at St. Alban's Place, Bambalapitiya. Mrs. Sathasivam returned from England in about three months and she went to Horton Place."

"Mr. Sathasivam's mother was still at St. Alban's Place, Bambalapitiya. She left that house on the same day that Mrs. Sathasivam came there with the children from Horton Place."

Answering a query from Justice Gratiaen, Podihamy said that there was a telephone downstairs but not upstairs at this time. The telephone upstairs was installed about 2 months prior to the death of Mrs. Sathasivam.

Podihamy further said that after Mrs. Sathasivam employed William his duties were to wash the pots and pans.

"He carried out the duties I entrusted to him well, and he was respectful to the lady of the house. He did not at any time refuse to obey her, and from the time he came he appeared to me to be a good boy for those ten days," remarked Podihamy.

Referring to the divorce case, Podihamy said that Mrs. Sathasivam had told her that she had asked Mr. Sathasivam to leave the house and take up his residence elsewhere.

Podihamy explained how Mr Sathasivam met her and the children on the 8th October when they were returning from school.

"As I was going home with the children I met Mr. Sathasivam who came in a car. There were two other gentlemen in the car with him. I knew them. They were Mr. Haniffa and Mr. Abbas. The car was stopped and I was asked by Mr. Sathasivam to get in with the children and we did so."

"The car went to St. Alban's Place. Mr. Sathasivam spoke to me and said that he had received summons. I knew that it was summons in the divorce case. He did not say anything further."

"When we went home I did not tell Mrs. Sathasivam anything about the summons because Mr. Sathasivam also was there at the time. I went upstairs with the children. Mr. Sathasivam and the other two gentlemen entered the house downstairs and sat in the hall. Mrs. Sathasivam also came down. I was not there and I do not know what was said."

Podihamy said that when she came downstairs after changing clothes of the two elder girls, they had all left.

She also said that when Mr Sathasivam and his two friends came, she noticed that all three were after liquor!

Podihamy said that Mr. Sathasivam's mother came to the house that afternoon, after they left.

"She padlocked the telephone downstairs. I am unable to say at what time she did that. The telephone downstairs was Mr. Sathasivam's mother's telephone. She had some other things in the house but she had taken them away earlier."

Explaining the normal activities of the household, Podihamy said that the meal is kept warm for them in the gas stove till the children returned from school.

"Usually, the two younger children who are at home should be fed by Mrs. Sathasivam but I do not know at what time she did that," Podihamy said.

Podihamy said that when Mr. Sathasivam was living at St. Alban's Place after his return from England, his dinner was kept for him.

"He used to come so late that his dinner was not eaten. On the 8th night, I got up hearing the car he came home leaving. I got up and looked and I saw it going away. Then I heard Mrs. Sathasivam talking to him in the bedroom upstairs."

Mr. Fernando then asked Podihamy the events that happened on the day of the murder.

"I knocked at the door and put Mrs. Sathasivam up to get down some aerated waters such as 'Orange barley' and some plantains for the children," she said.

"Did you see William come up when Mrs. Sathasivam called him?"

"Yes."

"Did you hear what she told William?"

"She gave William money asking him to bring two bottles of 'Orange barley', plantains, eggs and string-hoppers."

"The direction to bring all those things was given at the same time?"

"Yes, he brought and gave me the plantains and the 'Orange barley'. And he brought the string-hoppers and eggs too. When William brought those goods from the boutique, I gave him the bread and the tea which was prepared."

She said William brought the newspaper upstairs also when it was delivered.

"Before I left she sent for the boy, took his account and noted them down in a book," Podihamy said.

"At what time did you leave?"

"8.15 a.m."

Then Podihamy was questioned about the eating habits of the Sathasivam household.

"You gave the two younger children the milk in the morning?"

"Yes."

"You did not give them anything else to eat or drink?"

"I did not."

"Who feeds them?"

"Mrs. Sathasivam."

"Did you see Mrs. Sathasivam eat anything at all that morning before you left?"

"No."

"Can you tell us roughly at what time Mrs. Sathasivam had this milk and coffee?"

"At about 7.00 a.m."

"Do you know whether she took that on this morning too?"

"Yes, she did."

On further questioning by Mr. Fernando, Podihamy said Mrs. Sathasivam was wearing a saree and a petticoat that morning.

"These two garments are the garments that were on her body when you saw her dead body too?"

"Yes."

"Did she come downstairs to the front door when you left with the children?"

"No, she was standing on the landing of the staircase."

"Is it her custom to come down when the children go in the morning?"

"No."

"When you left on that morning of the 9th did you see Mr. Sathasivam?"

"Yes, he was sleeping on the bed."

Podihamy said after she returned from school with the two children in the afternoon, she went straight upstairs because she did not have enough money to pay the rickshaw man.

"You went into Mrs. Sathasivam's bedroom?"

"Yes."

"In what condition was the room?"

"The fan was working; the almirah was open."

"Which section of the almirah?"

"The road side of the almirah."

Podihamy further said that the keys were on the ground and the plates on which the string-hoppers had been eaten were on the table.

"Was there anything surprising?" Mr. Fernando asked.

"It was not the normal way in which that house was kept."

"Did you get any money from the room on that occasion?"

"Yes. I took 80 cents from Mrs. Sathasivam's handbag, which was inside the almirah."

"On which side of the almirah was that handbag?"

"The middle shelf. It was on the left hand side, in the open portion of the almirah."

Answering questions about the garage of the house, where Mrs. Sathasivam's body was, Podihamy said that the front door of the garage was always kept padlocked from outside.

Continuing her answers Podihamy said, "I went up to the body of Mrs. Sathasivam and touched it and found it cold!"

"Did you see anything placed across the neck?"

"Yes, the mortar."

Shown the mortar to her, Podihamy said, "This is the mortar that was placed across her neck. This mortar is usually kept in the garage. It is a wooden mortar. When I saw this mortar across her neck I removed it and put it aside."

"And you cried?"

"I began weeping."

"Well, you cried and the children cried and you had the presence of mind to ask Jothiswary to telephone her grandmother and her aunt, that is Mrs. Sathasivam's mother and sister?"

"Yes."

"You know that Mrs. Foenander telephoned the Police?"

"Yes."

"Do you know from which telephone Mrs. Foenander telephoned?"

"The telephone upstairs."

"Why not the telephone downstairs?"

"Because it was padlocked."

Asked about the 'thalikody', Podihamy said that Mrs. Sathasivam never took it off.

"When you left with the children that morning she had the 'thali' on?"

"Yes."

Podihamy said Mrs Sathasivam normally had four gold bangles on her wrists and a ring with three stones.

"They were white stones but I cannot say what they were."

Shown three gem stones she said, "They were stones similar to this."

Questioned about the keys of the almirah, Podihamy said she could not remember anyone putting the keys on the dressing table.

Mr. Fernando showed the mirror found in the garage close to Mrs. Sathasivam's body and asked Podihamy, "Whose mirror was that?"

"Mrs. Sathasivam's."

"Where was that usually kept?"

"On the dressing table upstairs."

"Had you ever seen that downstairs?"
"Never."
"You had never certainly seen it in the garage?"
"Never."
"Do you remember this being taken from the garage by the Police?"
"Yes, the Police came and took it from the garage," replied Podihamy.

Shown the finger bowl that was in Mrs. Sathasivam's bedroom, Podihamy said it was always on the table in Mrs. Sathasivam's bedroom.

"On this day, was the finger bowl there when you came back from the school?"

"I noticed this on the table when I returned and it contained dirty water and pieces of string-hoppers."

Podihamy said when she came from the school William was not there. In the kitchen, the vegetables that were cut up were in two pots. William had started to scrape the coconuts and they were there.

"Did you find anything upset? The table upset or anything like that?"

"Nothing."

"The kitchen when you saw it that afternoon was exactly as you saw it when Inspector Thiedeman came there?"

"That is so."

She said the pot of rice was on the Dover stove in the kitchen. Dover stove was a type of stove commonly used at that time. It was fuelled by firewood.

"Did you handle that pot of rice at all after you came back?"
"I opened it, looked at it and closed it up."
"When you opened it what was the condition of the rice?"
"It was boiled. There was no water in the pot."

She said she could not say whether anybody else took it away from the Dover stove and placed it elsewhere.

Shown the sarong and the shirt worn by William from the day Mrs. Sathasivam employed him, Podihamy identified them.

She also identified the saree, the petticoat, the plastic bangle and the ear studs Mrs. Sathasivam wore on the day she was killed. In one ear stud the centre pearl was missing.

Cross-examined by Dr. Colvin R. de Silva, Podihamy said that in one kitchen there was a Dover stove, and in the room adjoining the kitchen there was a gas stove.

Questioned about items kept in the kitchen, she said condiments are kept in the gas stove kitchen and the curry stuffs for immediate use are kept in the cupboard in the Dover stove kitchen.

Dr. Colvin R. de Silva realised the importance of the smell of garlic in Mrs. Sathasivam's body, mentioned in the post-mortem report of Professor G.S.W. de Saram because William said in his evidence in the Magistrate's Court that garlic was found in the kitchen cupboard, as well as upstairs.

To clarify this Dr. de Silva asked Podihamy about the kitchen cupboard.

"If anything has to be taken out of that cupboard when you are at home you would take the key and open that cupboard?"

"Yes," replied Podihamy.

She also said, "I place them there and close it up and I issue them. I have the key of the cupboard that was in the gas stove kitchen."

"When you are not at home Mrs. Sathasivam has the key?"

"I leave the key with her. She does not understand the issue of these provisions and she has never done it!"

"By the provisions which are in that cupboard you mean such things as chillies, coriander, saffron, onions, garlic and so on?"

"That is so."

"Such things are not kept upstairs?"

"That is so," confirmed Podihamy.

This answer contradicted William's story that garlic was kept upstairs.

Dr. de Silva also questioned Podihamy about feeding of the younger two children who did not attend school.

"You have said already it is Mrs. Sathasivam who customarily fed those younger children?"

"Yes."

"She had that habit?"

"Only on days that I go to school, but on other days I feed them."

Podihamy said when she left for school at 8.15 a.m., the parcel of string-hoppers brought from the boutique was there in the room, still tied with a string.

"Now on this day when you went to ask Mrs. Sathasivam for money she was in the little room outside the bedroom of the children?"

"Yes."

"It was in that very room that the string-hopper parcel had been left by William?"

"Yes."

"And it was there when you went to speak to Mrs. Sathasivam?"

"Yes."

"She went into the bedroom and came with the money?"

"Yes."

"At that time did you see Mr. Sathasivam sleeping on that bed?"

"When I went to wake up Mrs. Sathasivam in the morning I saw him sleeping on that bed."

Podihamy said after Mrs. Sathasivam opened the bedroom door in the morning, it was not closed again and she could see into the bedroom through that door.

"So when you went up to the bedroom door and when she went in to bring the money, you could see him sleeping on the bed?"

"Yes, because once that door is opened the whole room is visible."

Dr. de Silva asked, "You were really not looked at as a servant in the family. You were long past that stage, is it not?"

"That is so."

Justice Gratiaen queried, "You had gradually come to be regarded as one of the family?"

"That is so."

Continuing his questioning Dr. de Silva asked, "Even though you were thus like one of the family, when the master was at home in the bedroom, would you go into that bedroom?"

"No."

"I mean, that was not expected of anybody in the house?"

"That is so."

"You yourself, Podihamy, if you were anywhere near the place you would not permit the male servant in the house to go into that bedroom when the master was there?"

"I would not allow it. If anybody or a new servant who had taken employment shortly before, did attempt that, I would remain with him until he finished his job and came out."

Podihamy further said that Mrs. Sathasivam would not allow keys of the cupboards to pass into the hands of anybody else except her.

"From what I gather, Mrs. Sathasivam seems to have been a very careful person?" asked Justice Gratiaen.

"That is so."

After the conclusion of the cross-examination of Podihamy, Mr. T.S. Fernando commenced his re-examination.

"Have you ever seen William massaging the legs of the master?"

"I do not see how you can get that evidence?" queried Justice Gratiaen.

"My learned friend put questions about the boy not being allowed to go into the bedroom of Mrs. Sathasivam."

Dr. de Silva remarked, "If it is an omission I do not object to it. I do not object to any matters the Solicitor-General wishes to ask the witness."

Mr. Fernando again asked, "Have you seen William massaging Mr. Sathasivam's feet?"

"I saw it one day and it took place upstairs when Mr. Sathasivam was lying on his bed. Yes, that took place in Mrs. Sathasivam's bedroom," Podihamy replied.

Mr. Fernando asked Podihamy whether the curry-stuffs in the tins in the Dover Stove kitchen were accessible to William without reference to Podihamy or to Mrs. Sathasivam.

Podihamy replied, "No."

Answering questions of Justice Gratiaen, Podihamy said massaging of the legs of Mr. Sathasivam took place one morning.

"It was not on a school day. It was either on a Saturday or on a Sunday. All the children were in the room at the time and Mrs. Sathasivam was in the room as well," replied Podihamy.

"When Mrs. Sathasivam was upstairs did she normally walk about bare-footed?"

"Yes, she did."

"Normally, before you take the children to school does she have occasion to go down?"

"She does not. She has no necessity to go downstairs."

"On this particular day, the 9th of October, did she come downstairs before you left?"

"No."

"If she wanted to give any instruction to William in connection with his work downstairs, normally the practice would be for her to send for him and give him those instructions somewhere at the top of the stairs. Is that so?"

"Yes."

"Mr. Sathasivam, as far as you knew, was sleeping on the bed. Is that right?"

"Yes."

"And where was Mrs. Sathasivam when you left?"

"She was in the little room adjoining the children's bedroom, reading the papers."

Answering questions of the jury, Podihamy said that after returning from England, Mr. Sathasivam spent the night at No. 7, St. Alban's Place on three occasions and he remained there till Podihamy left for school.

She further said he slept in the same bedroom as Mrs. Sathasivam.

"And on the same bed?" asked Justice Gratiaen.

"Yes," Podihamy replied.

The Crown next summoned Dr. J.H. Dible to give evidence, regarding the death of Dr. Taylor, who gave evidence in the Magistrate's Court.

Answering questions of Mr. T. S. Fernando he said, "I have come to Ceylon in connection with the holding of the primary examination for the Fellowship of the Royal College of Surgeons. I knew Dr. John Frank Taylor of St. George's Hospital. I am aware that he came to Ceylon last year. He also did so in connection with the holding of the primary examination early last year. Dr. Taylor died in England in June 1952."

Dr. de Silva did not ask him any questions.

On the 27th of March, William, the pardoned Crown witness, who was still in the remand jail, gave evidence.

Examined by Mr. T.S. Fernando, William said he was a 19-year-old cultivator from Angunabadulla, a village about 8 kilometres from Matara. He said he has studied up to the second standard in Sinhalese at the Thihagoda school, and he can write Sinhalese.

William said he was employed at the residence of Mr. Eric Rajapakse, an optician, at Wellawatte for about 6 months as a domestic servant. During this period he got to know the Wellawatte area very well.

After 6 months, he left the job and went home. He was employed at a textile shop as a salesman for about 10 days in Ambalantota, a town down south, and left the employment on 26th September.

At about 6 p.m. the same day, he left Matara to come to Colombo in search of employment. He arrived at Colombo the following day and went around Fort and Wellawatte looking for jobs. He slept that night on the verandah of a barber's shop in Wellawatte.

Next day he met an old woman, Dosihamy, near the Wellawatte bridge. William said he was looking for a job and she took him first to Mrs Pathmanathan's house. Then he was sent with her driver and Dosihamy to her sister Mrs. Sathasivam's residence.

Answering the queries from Mr. Fernando, William said that Mrs. Sathasivam asked her whether he had any cloths. He said that he had only the cloths he was wearing; those were the shirt and the sarong and nothing else.

She also asked whether he had his rice ration book.

'Rice ration book' was a document every citizen of Ceylon had, to get two measures of rice at a subsidised price from the Government, once in two weeks.

"I replied that I had no rice ration book. Then she asked me the salary I wanted. I told her that I wanted 25 rupees. She said I have to work as a servant boy and also do the cooking in the house. Finally, I agreed to work for 20 rupees a month," William said.

So William did the cooking that night at the house and Podihamy, the servant woman helped him on that first day.

William said he slept in the kitchen and Mrs. Sathasivam provided him with a pillow and a mat. He said in the morning he sweeps the whole dining room, back verandah, kitchen and all the rooms upstairs. He said he swept the room of Mrs. Sathasivam too whether she was in or not, as instructed by Podihamy.

William said he used to do the marketing in the morning. He bought string-hoppers for breakfast from a boutique at Bambalapitiya at 3 cents each.

William said that there were four girls in the house and they, as well as Mrs. Sathasivam, talked to him and Podihamy in Sinhalese. He knew that Mr. and Mrs. Sathasivam were Tamils but even the children talked amongst themselves in Sinhalese.

He said one night before dinner he was asked by Mr. Sathasivam to massage his legs in Mrs. Sathasivam's bedroom upstairs. Mr. and Mrs. Sathasivam, all four girls and Podihamy were there.

"Did you come to know of any case before you left that house?" asked Mr. Fernando.

"Yes."

"How is it that you came to know about any case?"

"The master and the lady were talking at the dining table to each other."

"In what language was that?"

"In Sinhalese."

"About how many days before this incident was that?"

"About 3 or 4 days prior to this incident."

Justice Gratiaen asked, "What were they talking about? What sort of a conversation was that?"

"Mr. Sathasivam asked the lady to withdraw a case."

"And what did she reply?"

"She refused."

"That was at dinner, was it?"

"No it was at about 2 p.m. It was after lunch. When Mrs. Sathasivam said 'No', he said 'All right' and left the house."

"How did you find out what kind of a case it was?"

"I do not know," replied William.

William said the day prior to the death of Mrs. Sathasivam, Mr. Haniffa and another gentleman came to the house and talked in English.

Answering further questions William told the Court that on the 8th Mr. Sathasivam came home late night, and he heard the couple talking to each other and going upstairs.

William said on the day of the murder he went to the market before he received his bread and tea.

"A child called me upstairs and I went up. Mrs. Sathasivam asked me to get some things from the boutique, the usual sort of things – string-hoppers, betel, paper, eggs and plantains. The money was given," William said.

In fact page 60 of Mrs. Sathasivam's notebook mentions what she bought that day. In rupees and cents they were as follows:

Paper	0.15
Betel	0.30
Plantains	0.32
Sugar	0.45
Hoppers	0.40
Eggs	1.14

Explaining what happened that morning after the children went to school, William said, "I remember going to the boutique and bringing the limes. After that I got ready to cook in the kitchen. I first cut up the drumsticks. Then I took the ash plantains. There was no garlic, so I obtained some from Mrs. Sathasivam upstairs. There was garlic upstairs. Then I prepared them to cook."

"I washed the rice about 15 minutes after Podihamy left. I washed the rice and then put the rice to boil in a saucepan on the Dover stove. Firewood is required for that stove. I lighted the fire. The firewood was stacked in the garage, but some of it was kept in the kitchen. I used to bring the firewood from the garage and place it in the kitchen, as and when I required it."

"After that I prepared the vegetables. Having cut the vegetables, I put them into the 'chatties' (clay pots). Thereafter, I went to the place where the coconuts are kept and took one. They are kept in the room adjoining the room the gas cooker is fixed. It was a husked coconut. I brought it and broke it into two using the blow-pipe."

"Then I started scraping the coconut. At that moment, Mr. Sathasivam came down. He was wearing long trousers, long-sleeved shirt and shoes," William said.

Answering a query from Justice Gratiaen, William said, "Up to this point of time Mrs. Sathasivam had not come downstairs for the whole morning."

Continuing William said, "Mr. Sathasivam came into the kitchen and held me by the hand. I was still sitting down on the coconut scraper. (See Figure 7. Page 469) He stooped and held me by the hand and took me into the dining room. All this time he did not speak a word. I asked him 'Why are you holding my hand? It is getting late for me to prepare the meals. Let me go.' He said, 'Boy, don't be afraid. Will you agree to what I propose I want you to do?' I said, "If it is a thing I can do I will, but otherwise I cannot.' He said, 'It is something that you can do. Come'."

William said they had this conversation in the dining room.

He asked Mr. Sathasivam, "What is it?" He replied, "The lady has filed a divorce case against me. There is the possibility of my losing the case. Therefore, come to kill her."

William said then he told Mr. Sathasivam, "I do not want any wages for the eleven days I have stayed here. Release me and let me go. But Mr. Sathasivam did not release me. He said, 'Boy, don't get frightened. I will give you sufficient articles to realize three to four hundred rupees.' I said, 'I do not want them, release me.' But he did not release me," said William.

"If he released me, I would have run away," William said replying to a question from Justice Gratiaen.

William demonstrated by holding the hand of a Court official how Mr. Sathasivam held him by the hand. He held the left hand of the official with his right hand at the wrist.

Continuing his evidence William said, "Mr. Sathasivam held my hand and took me upstairs. The front door of the house was then open. He held me by that grip till we went upstairs. We went up the stairs and came to the landing. He was still gripping my hand. I know Mrs. Sathasivam's bedroom. There are two doors to that room. One was the door opening on to the balcony and the other near the landing. The door near the landing was open. He and I went into the room through that door and he was still holding my hand. As I entered the room, I saw Mrs. Sathasivam seated on the bed doing nothing and looking in the direction from which we were coming."

"Mr. Sathasivam went up to her taking me with him. Then he released my hand and suddenly seized her by her neck and hair, which was tied in a knot. He gripped her neck with his right hand and her hair with the other," William said.

"Then he dragged her down to the floor. She fell on the ground face upwards. She was pulled down and pressed down by the neck. When she was thrown down, her head was towards the almirah and her feet were towards the doorway. I was on the other side of her. When she was on the floor Mr. Sathasivam was still holding her by the throat. From the time he gripped her throat when she was sitting on the bed up to the point of time he put on the ground he did not release his hold on her throat. When she was jerked on the floor he released his hold of her hair and squeezed her throat with both hands," explained William.

William said Mr. Sathasivam was on the left side of her. "He had one knee on the floor and the other knee was bent. I cannot say whether that knee was touching her body."

While describing the act of strangling, William demonstrated on a peon of the Court how Mr. Sathasivam strangled Mrs. Sathasivam, with both hands on her neck. Hands were either side of the neck, with the thumbs crossed at the centre of the neck. The right hand web between the thumb and fingers were at the front of the throat. The left thumb was on the left side of the throat and the right thumb on the right side of the throat. The fingers of the left hand were on the right side of the throat and the fingers of the right hand on the left side.

The peon was lying on his back on the floor with William kneeling on his left side by his head. William's right knee was on the ground and the left knee over the left arm of the peon, which is bent across his body. William's both hands were round the throat, the left hand on the peon's right side of the throat and the right hand on the left side of the throat.

William said that with Mr. Sathasivam's left knee he was preventing the lady from moving her left arm by pressing it down on her body. Her right arm was free. "I cannot say exactly in what manner the left arm of the lady was pinned down but he pinned it down in some way."

The peon was asked when William pressed down his left arm with his knee, whether he was able to move it. He stated that he could not.

William said, "I was standing 8 feet away from Mrs. Sathasivam towards the window in a line with her knees. Mr. Sathasivam did not at any time get on her body. When he held her as I have shown, she was struggling with her legs by moving them about, and with her free arm. I cannot say whether she struggled to free her left arm. Then Mr. Sathasivam said, 'Seize her you devil.' I bent down and held her legs."

William demonstrated on the peon the manner in which he held Mrs. Sathasivam. He pressed on the right thigh of the peon with his right knee and with his right hand he pressed the peon's left thigh. With his left hand he pressed down the right thigh. His left knee was on the ground.

William said while Mr. Sathasivam was so holding her, he was looking at her face.

"I continued to hold her in that way for about five minutes. While I was holding her she held my face with her right hand and I got a scratch on my cheek. I released my hold of her thigh with my left hand and took her hand away from my face. Again I held her by the thigh with my left hand as before. She then caught my left forearm with her right hand. Then I released her hold with my right hand and stood up."

Answering a query from Justice Gratiaen William said, "Mr. Sathasivam had been holding her throat for four or five minutes before I held her legs. Then I got up releasing her legs. Mr. Sathasivam also got up. At that time she was unable to speak but she was alive. She was breathing heavily. Then Mr. Sathasivam gave her a kick on the neck."

William then demonstrated how Mr. Sathasivam stamped on her neck on the peon, by raising his right leg to a height of about 18 inches, and bringing it down on the front of the throat with the instep on the centre of the throat.

He said after Mr. Sathasivam took his foot off from her neck, her head fell to the right side and her heavy breathing stopped, but there was still life.

Mr. Fernando then asked William to demonstrate the manner Mr. Sathasivam dragged Mrs. Sathasivam from the bed and put her on the ground.

A bench was placed to indicate the bed and the peon was made to sit on it in the way Mrs. Sathasivam was sitting on the bed, with her body facing the door of the bedroom, as Mr. Sathasivam and William came into the room. William seized the throat of the peon by his right hand, and with his left held the hair and jerked him to the ground.

Continuing his evidence on the act of strangling, William said, "Mrs. Sathasivam was jerked down and there was a thud when she fell on the ground. Her hair was still being held when she fell on the floor. Then Mr. Sathasivam released his grip of her hair and seized her throat with both hands. When Mr. Sathasivam held her first, he was on her right, but after she fell he got on to her left."

William said thereafter Mr. Sathasivam took off her gold chain, 'thalikody', pair of bangles and a ring and gave those to him. He said he put them under his banian.

Mr. Fernando, continuing his questioning asked, "And that 'thali' was the first article removed off her body?"

"Yes."

"Was that a short chain or a long one?"

"It was a long one."

"How was that removed?"

"It was taken off her head."

William further said that two gold bangles were taken off one hand of Mrs. Sathasivam.

"Apart from those two gold bangles on that arm were there any other bangles – coloured bangles?"

"She had some other bangles. I do not remember what they were."

"There were some other bangles on the other arm as well?"

"Yes."

"None of those bangles were removed?"

"None were removed. Apart from the chain, the bangles and a ring set with stones was also removed by him."

"All that was given to you?"

"Yes."

"Was the taking off of the bangles and the ring also done by Mr. Sathasivam?"

"Yes."

William said after those articles were removed, Mr. Sathasivam opened the almirah using the key that was on the dressing table.

"Which portion – do you remember?" asked Mr. Fernando.

"I cannot remember. After opening the almirah with the keys, he took Mrs. Sathasivam's handbag and took 3 rupees out of it and gave it to me. Then he said, 'There are some loose coins in it. Do you want them as well?' and I said, 'I do not want the loose coins.' I took the 3 rupees and put it inside my banian with the gold articles. Then he said, 'You wait there' and went downstairs. He said he was going downstairs to close the front door."

"What did you do?"

"I remained inside the room."

Justice Gratiaen asked, "With this woman who was either dead or dying?"

"Yes."

William said Mr. Sathasivam was away from the room for about three or four minutes, and he heard Mr. Sathasivam closing the door.

"After he came what happened?" asked Mr. Fernando.

"Then he asked me to help him to hold Mrs. Sathasivam to be taken to the garage. Mr. Sathasivam held her from the direction of the neck and I held the legs."

"And she was brought down the stairs in that fashion?"

"Yes."

Justice Gratiaen asked, "Who went first?"

"Mr. Sathasivam went down first and I was following carrying her legs."

William said he saw the front door closed at that time.

"What was the route the two of you took?" asked Mr. Fernando.

"We went through the dining room passing two or three doors. They were the entrance to the hall, and the door leading from the dining room to the back verandah. We passed through these two doors, through the verandah and the room where the gas cooker was and then through the kitchen, also holding her in the same fashion."

Answering a query from Justice Gratiaen, William said, "We never put her body down all the way to the garage."

Mr. Fernando asked whether they were able to take Mrs. Sathasivam through that narrow passage without much difficulty.

"Mr. Sathasivam had to move at an angle to get through that doorway."

"Did Mrs. Sathasivam's legs come into contact with the ground as you were going through the kitchen at any stage?"

"No."

"And they never dropped?"

"No."

This was an answer very favourable to the defence.

Mr. Fernando asked, "Then what happened in the garage?"

"She was placed in the garage with her legs towards the kitchen, and with the head towards the wall. Then I left the garage."

"From the garage where did you get to?"

"I went across the kitchen and took my shirt which was in the firewood room."

"Before you left the garage did you see anything?"

"Yes."

"What?"

"There was a mortar placed in the garage close to the kitchen door. I saw Mr. Sathasivam lifting that mortar."

"Do you know what he did with that?"
"No."
"You did not wait there?"
"No. I did not."
"Then what did you do?"
"I took my shirt and went to open the front door. Then I stood at the door and I saw the two younger children playing on the swing and I said 'Baby I am going' and I left."
"Have you any idea of the time at which you left the house?"
"About 9.30 or 10 a.m."
William said he saw the two younger children on the swing as he was going out of the house that day.
"Where had you seen the two younger children in the house before that? In which part?"
"About a quarter of an hour before Mrs. Sathasivam was killed, the two children came out of the house to play."
William said after leaving the house he decided to go to his village and went to the bus halt near the market. He then went to Wellawatte, the adjoining town by bus, after waiting for about ten to fifteen minutes for one.
"I decided to go home to my village. When I was at Bambalapitiya bus halt, two or three buses going to Galle passed that way but they did not stop. Therefore, I decided to go to Wellawatte and take a bus from there," said William.
Answering further questions of Mr. Fernando, he said, "I do not know where the bus in which I travelled from Bambalapitiya to Wellawatte was going to. I got down at Wellawatte and went to High Street in Wellawatte. I do not know anyone in High Street. I went to a little boutique there in High Street intending to sell the chain. I did not know that boutique before."
"What made you go to that particular boutique?"
"I was on my way to where my cousin was, so I thought I would step into this boutique."
"Where was your cousin living?"
"He was working about half a mile from there in High Street."
"Had you seen the boutique which you went to, before that?"

"Yes."

"Had you been along this road, High Street, before this?"

"Yes."

William said he went and spoke to a man in that boutique.

"I have since seen this man when he came to give evidence. He is called Edmund."

"What did you tell him?"

"I said, 'I have got a chain, will you buy it?'"

William said he put his hand inside his banian, took the chain out and showed it to Edmund. He had the other articles wrapped up in the fold of his sarong in his waist.

"Edmund took the chain and went into the shop asking me to wait there a while. A man went past that boutique and Edmund spoke to him saying, 'Ask the elder brother to come.' He returned and said that the elder brother would be coming shortly, as he was taking a shave. I waited there and so did Edmund. Then the man came. I saw him come to give evidence in this case. I do not know his name."

"Did you show the 'thali' to the man who came?"

"Yes."

"Where was it shown? On the road, the boutique or where?"

"Inside that boutique."

"What did that man say?"

"He said, 'Do you want 100 rupees for this?' I did not know the value of it and I said 'All right.' At this time, Edmund was in the boutique and the whole transaction took place in the same boutique. I agreed to take 100 rupees and I was given 60 rupees and he said, 'I will bring you the balance 40 rupees.'"

Mr. Fernando then showed a certain witness and asked, "Who is this man? Do you know him?"

"I do not know him."

William insisted he had never seen him.

Mr. Fernando then said that witness was D.C.A. Dharmasena.

Shown another witness by Mr. Fernando, William identified him as the person who bought the chain. Mr. Fernando then said his name was Sirisena.

"Is it this man Sirisena, whom you have just been shown, the man who had the transaction about the sale of the chain. He offered you 100 rupees for it?"

"Yes," William replied.

Shown another witness by Mr. Fernando, William identified him. He was Edmund.

William said, "He is the man in the boutique at High Street to whom I first spoke about the chain. He was preparing to close up the boutique as soon as I was leaving. I stayed in that boutique for about 20 or 25 minutes as far as I can judge. Then I went to the 'Ariyasinhala Hotel' to have a cup of tea. I ate a bun and drank a cup of tea."

Answering a question from Justice Gratiaen, William admitted, "Yes, I was never so rich in my life!"

William said he stayed in the 'Ariyasinhala Hotel' for about ten or fifteen minutes and then went again to the bus stand opposite the Wellawatte market.

"I was waiting there for about 20 to 25 minutes for a Galle bus, when one bound to 'Panadura' came and I went in that bus up to Panadura."

Having alighted from the bus at Panadura, William said he made inquiries for the time of the bus leaving for Galle. He was told it was at 2 or 3 p.m. He could not quite recollect which time it was.

William said then he went to the Panadura bazaar and bought a sarong.

"I paid rupees 7.50 or 8.50 for the sarong. I got it stitched in the shop in which I purchased it. From a different shop, which was about 100 yards away, I bought a shirt. It was roughly about fifteen minutes after I bought the sarong. I spent about 15 minutes buying the sarong, and sometime in getting it stitched."

Mr. Fernando asked whether he attempted to sell the bangles anywhere.

"Yes, at the boutique where I bought the shirt. I offered to sell the bangles to the man from whom I bought the shirt."

"Did you show the two bangles and the ring to that man?"

"Yes."

Mr. Fernando showed a witness and William identified him as the person from whom he bought the shirt. He was Arlishamy.

"What did he say?"

"He took those articles and went to another boutique, a jeweller's shop, which was within sight of the shop I bought the shirt. I had to wait for about ten minutes till the jeweller was free. While waiting I said 'Hurry up, I must go home before dark.'"

William said Arlishamy came again and said, "They said it is not worth very much." He asked William, "How much do you want for the three articles?"

William said, "Give me 60 rupees." He again went to the boutique and returned and said, " I will give you 30 rupees."

He ultimately accepted 30 rupees given by Arlishamy. William said he did not see the man to whom the pair of bangles and the ring were sold.

Justice Gratiaen asked, "Did they ask you, either the man at Wellawatte or at Panadura, where you got these articles from?"

"At Panadura, the man from whom I bought the shirt asked me from where I got the articles and I said I stole them. The man at Wellawatte did not ask me where I got the 'thali' from."

Continuing his evidence William said, "At the boutique I changed my clothes and wrapped up my old clothes in a piece of paper. I went to another boutique to drink a glass of cool water and left the parcel there and then went to the Panadura bus stand."

"At about 3.00 p.m., a Galle bus turned up and I went to Galle. I reached Galle at about 7.00 p.m. and my intention first was to go to my village. As soon as I got out of the bus in Galle, I went to a boutique opposite the bus stand and had a meal and then travelled to Matara by bus again. I reached Matara at about 9.00 p.m. and went to the boutique of 'Matara Mudalali' and slept there."

Galle is situated 116 kilo metres from Colombo on the south coast and Matara is 45 kilo metres from Galle.

"Next morning, I had my tea and went to my village. I was at home till the 17th. On the 17th I went to Hungama. I heard that the Police had come in search of me," William said.

"Is that then why you left home?" asked Mr. Fernando.

"I wanted to go to the Police Station, but my parents were against it and they sent me to Hungama. I went to Hungama on the 17th with two other boys and a grand uncle of mine. On the 18th morning, I was arrested by the Police at Hungama," replied William.

"Have you told your parents what had happened?" asked Justice Gratiaen.

"Yes," he replied.

William said after his arrest the Police Officers brought him to the Hungama Police Station and then to the Tangalle Police Station. Later, he was taken to the Matara Police station at about ten or eleven in the morning where he was questioned by Police Officers.

"I was taken behind a latrine by a Police Officer and told what I should say. But I did not say what I was asked to say," William said.

"Though they tried to make you say something different you stuck to your story consistently which is what you have told us today?" asked Mr. Fernando.

"That is so."

William further said that the Police Officer who told him to say something else behind the latrine was Inspector Wickremaratne.

He said that he demonstrated at the Matara Police Station how Mr. Sathasivam strangled Mrs. Sathasivam.

"You said you were questioned by more than one Officer at the Matara Police Station. Did you make the same statement to them?" queried Justice Gratiaen.

"I made the same statement to all of them but they did not record all that I told them."

"Before you set out in the car from the Matara Police Station did you demonstrate at the Matara Police Station how this strangulation took place?"

William said he did not demonstrate at Matara, but in some office he demonstrated.

This contradicted what he said a few minutes ago.

William said on his way to Colombo from Matara they stopped at Panadura. They went to the boutique where he sold the bangles and the ring and also to the place where he kept his old sarong and the shirt. The Police recovered all these.

At about 2.00 a.m. next day, William was brought to the Modera Police Station. He said he was very sleepy and could not remember whether he signed anything.

Mr. Fernando further questioning asked William, "Do you remember being taken to a bungalow that day to be examined by a doctor?"

"Yes."

"From there do you remember being taken to Station Road, Wellawatte where you showed a boutique?"

"Yes."

"Which boutique did you show?"

"At the time I sold the chain, the man there told me to show another boutique in Station Road and I did so."

"Who is the man who asked you to show that boutique?"

"The owner of the boutique in High Street, Wellawatte, that is Edmund. He told me, 'We do not know whether this is a stolen article. If by any chance something happens you better point out the boutique in Station Road and not my boutique', and showed me the boutique, which I should point out. Therefore, I showed it to the Police."

Justice Gratiaen asked, "Ultimately, when the Police took you there, in deference to Edmund's wishes you pointed out the boutique in the Station Road, Wellawatte?"

"Yes."

William said he did not know whose boutique that was.

"From there you were taken to an office in Colombo and you made a statement?" asked Mr. Fernando.

"Yes."

"Was a demonstration of this incident given there?"

"Yes."

"Do you remember some Police Officers coming and questioning you at the Matara Police Station that afternoon after your arrest?"

"Yes."

"One was a lean tall gentleman?"

"Yes."

"Do you know Mr. Albert de Silva now?"

"Yes."

"Was he one of the gentlemen who came to the Matara Police Station?"

"Yes."

Justice Gratiaen asked, "Was one of those who told you to tell lies?"

"He was not present on that occasion. It was that other gentleman who had arrested me who took me near the latrine and told me what I should say," William replied.

He said when he was questioned at the Criminal Investigation Department Office in Colombo on the 19th afternoon, the Inspector-General of Police and Mr. Albert de Silva were present. That night he remembered being taken to the Magistrate's bungalow.

"Did you know that you were being taken there to make a statement to the Magistrate?"

"No."

"Did the Magistrate ask you whether you wished to make a statement and tell you that you need not make a statement if you did not wish to?"

"Yes."

"But you said you wanted to make a statement and the Magistrate recorded it?"

"Yes."

At this stage, Mr. Fernando asked William to demonstrate again how Mr. Sathasivam held Mrs. Sathasivam's neck during strangling. Two peons of the court took the places of Mr. and Mrs. Sathasivam.

With that demonstration Mr. Fernando concluded his examination-in-chief.

Dr. Colvin R. de Silva then began his lengthy cross-examination of William by asking what happened after his arrest.

Referring to William's statement that Mr. Albert de Silva questioned him at Matara, Dr. de Silva asked, "On that occasion, is it a fact, is it not, that you told Mr. Albert de Silva as follows: When the deceased lady came into the kitchen while I was scraping coconut, I released the coconut, got up and held her both hands from behind and took her to the garage and killed her?"

"I did not say that. That is what the Inspector taught me to say," replied William.

Dr. de Silva questioned at length about the statements William had made to Police. William said except Mr. Wickremaratne, nobody else asked him to say anything.

Justice Gratiaen queried, "Did the Inspector-General of Police (IGP) ask you whether you told Mr. Albert de Silva what the Inspector had asked you to say?"

"Yes."

"What was your answer?"

"I told the IGP that I said nothing, but that they were telling me, 'We will take you to big people in Fort and you must tell them what we asked you to say.'"

Dr. de Silva continuing his cross-examination asked, "So your position is this: The Inspector of Police told you, say this when you are asked, and when you are taken to higher officers say the same thing?"

"Yes."

"Therefore, you take up the position today in this Court that the IGP himself has made a record, in your presence, of a statement you never made?"

"I do not know."

"Mr. Wickremaratne arrested you at Hungama?

"Yes."

"Mr. Wickremaratne brought you from Hungama along with other officers to Matara?"

"Yes."

"Including a village headman?"

"Yes."

"The only time Wickremaratne told you anything was behind that latrine?"

"Yes."

William said that he was taken behind the latrine when Mr. Albert de Silva and his team from Colombo was present. It was after the mid day meal.

"I want to ask you about what you told the IGP. The IGP has

recorded as your having told him on that same occasion, after you pointed out Mr. Albert de Silva to the IGP, as follows: 'The same Inspector asked me to make the following statement after I was arrested near Hungama. He asked me to state that Mr. Sathasivam came to the kitchen after the lady was killed, gave me eight ten rupee notes and asked me to leave the place.' Did you say that to the IGP?"

"I did not say that. I was asked 'Did you say this?' and I said I did not."

Repeating the question Dr. de Silva asked, "You never told the IGP on the evening of the 19th October at 6 p.m. that 'The same Inspector asked you to say that Mr. Sathasivam came to the kitchen after Mrs. Sathasivam was killed, gave me eight ten rupee notes and asked me to leave the place'?"

"I did not."

"Then did you say this to the IGP: 'I made that statement to Mr. M. A. De Silva at the Police Station in Matara'?"

"I did not."

"So, when the IGP recorded you are saying this and took your signature too, he did record something you never said?"

"I do not know."

William was then shown the signature on the document in which his statement was recorded. He said, "This is my signature. I have written my name in Sinhalese."

Questioning further Dr. de Silva asked, "You say only one of these suggestions was made to you by Inspector Wickremaratne?"

"Yes. Inspector Wickremaratne taught me to say what I had already admitted, but they had noted down various other things and I had denied to the IGP that I ever told that to them."

"The only statement that Mr. Wickremaratne asked you to make was a statement admitting that in the kitchen you grabbed the lady by the neck, killed her and put her into the garage. And that you alone were the killer?"

"That is so."

Dr. de Silva then questioned William about what he told Mr. de Saram, Assistant Superintendent of Police, Matara.

"Then to come to what you told Mr. de Saram, did you tell him you were scraping coconuts in the kitchen?"

"Yes."

"Then Mr. Sathasivam, the master, came in to the kitchen?"

"Yes."

"Then did you say that the master who came into the kitchen caught you by the ear, scolded you for not washing the upstairs bathroom, gave you 5 rupees and told you to go home – did you say that to Mr. de Saram?"

"I did not."

During the cross-examination, Justice Gratiaen informed Mr. Fernando, the Acting Solicitor-General that though he criticized the decision of the Police Officers to take William to Modera Police Station, by-passing the Bambalapitiya Police Station, it was the decision of the IGP.

Mr. Fernando said that the suggestion came from certain Police Officers.

As Dr. de Silva continued to question William about the statements he made, Justice Gratiaen told William, "Tell us in your own words what you told the Inspector General of Police that morning, one, with regard to what the Inspector instructed you to say and two, what you in fact said when questioned by Mr. Albert de Silva."

"The Inspector-General of Police read out two or three statements, which he had before him. I cannot remember what those statements were. He asked me, 'Is it true you made these statements?' I said 'No'. I said, in the office of the Assistant Superintendent of Police, Matara, the Inspector took me to the latrine and asked me to make a statement in certain terms. I said 'All right' but made no statement. There was one statement, which contained the allegation that Mrs. Sathasivam came into the kitchen and I killed her. That is what the Inspector asked me to say. I told the Inspector-General of Police that I did not make the statement but that the Inspector recorded what he wanted me to say at Matara in the presence of Mr. Albert de Silva. I agreed to make those statements, intending to come to Colombo and speak the truth. The statement, which the Inspector wanted me to make, was written in the book. I cannot remember whether I signed it or not. My signature was not obtained there. That is the gist of what I told the Inspector- General of Police in his Office," explained William.

Dr. de Silva then questioned William in detail about the act of strangulation and asked, "When you were brought upstairs by Mr. Sathasivam you had to pass the front door?"

"Yes."

"When you passed that door you saw that it was wide open?"

"Yes."

"You say that in the dining room Mr. Sathasivam told you that he was taking you to upstairs to get your assistance to kill Mrs. Sathasivam?"

"Yes."

"Did you take the slightest step to even to yell?"

"I did not."

"Why?"

"Because I was frightened!"

"You passed that window on the landing, which looked out in to the Police Station?"

"Yes."

"Of course you were too frightened to shout through that window?"

"I was frightened to cry out not knowing what would be done to me."

Referring to the struggle in the bedroom, Dr. de Silva asked, "Now, you had Mr. Sathasivam with both hands occupied on the floor?"

"Yes."

"You did not try to run out of that room yelling?"

"I did not try to run away. If it was downstairs I might have run but not in upstairs, because if I ran downstairs I would have tripped and fallen and injured myself and the master could have got hold of me too."

"But to get hold of you Mr. Sathasivam would have had to let go the lady?"

"Yes."

"So, if he started holding you, Mrs. Sathasivam could have

yelled?"

"Yes."

"His whole attention was concentrated on Mrs. Sathasivam?" asked Justice Gratiaen.

"Yes."

William said he did not attempt to run away. "Through fear I stayed there."

"That is, you thought that if you tried to run away, Mr. Sathasivam would do you harm?" Dr. de Silva asked.

"Yes."

"That is to say, you thought that so long as you were in the house, you dared to do nothing about this murder?"

"I did not know what he would do with me and therefore I did whatever he told me to do."

"That was why, with both his hands occupied when Mr. Sathasivam said 'Hold you devil' you held the lady?"

"Yes."

"He had no means of compelling you then because both his hands were occupied?"

"If I did not obey his orders I did not know what he would have done to me. Therefore, I meekly obeyed him."

"How did you understand what he meant by the words 'Hold you devil'?"

"When he said that, I thought he meant that I should hold the lady so that she may not struggle."

"Unfortunately, you held Mrs. Sathasivam at a place where she could injure you?"

"Yes."

"If you held her by the ankles, she could not have injured you?"

"That is so."

"Then Mr. Sathasivam went downstairs to close the door?"

"Yes."

"He took care to leave the door open to the wide world while he committed the murder, and then after the murder he went to close the door?"

"He closed the door in order to take the body downstairs."

"If she had uttered one little cry, anyone passing the road could have come in?"

"That is so."

"He was away for 2 or 3 minutes closing the door?"

"Yes."

"You were still in the room looking at Mrs. Sathasivam who still was not dead?"

"I remained there."

"Behind you there was a wide window, looking on to St. Alban's Place?"

"Yes."

"A window, through which you could have yelled to the houses on either side of St. Alban's Place, although of course you did not?"

"I did not cry out."

"You know the word 'murder'?"

"Yes."

"You did not use that word?"

"I did not."

"If you get through the passage to the balcony you could have yelled to the Police Station?"

"Yes."

"But you were too frightened to do that?"

"Yes."

"So for three or four minutes, you stayed in the bedroom with the dying lady while Mr. Sathasivam went downstairs to close the door?"

"About 2 or 3 minutes."

"Finally, you assisted Mr. Sathasivam to take the body into the garage?"

"Yes."

"Did any idea cross your mind at that time as to why he was taking the body into the garage?"

"He told me, 'Help me to take this to the garage' but I did not know for what reason. No idea crossed my mind as to why he was taking the body there."

"When you came down, you saw the front door locked?"

"Yes."

"You were helping him to take the body through the open verandah at the back?"

"Yes."

"If you yelled at that time all the world might have seen you?"

"Yes. If I yelled anyone would have seen but I did not shout. We went to the garage and placed the body there."

"Then you turned to go back?"

"Yes."

"That is to get away?"

"Yes."

"Now you knew you were free to go?"

"I went to take my shirt and get away. I wanted to get away without informing anyone and I was going in order to save my own life."

"At that stage you were not afraid that Mr. Sathasivam might grab you?"

"I was afraid and that is why I turned and looked back."

"And when you looked back you found that he was quite willing to let you go while he was lifting a mortar?"

"He did not know that I was going away."

"He paid no attention to your going away?"

"I do not know. He saw me going out of the garage into the kitchen but he made no effort to follow me."

"Thus you knew you were free to get away from the most terrible crime that you could ever have set eyes upon?"

"That is so. I went away."

"He said not a word?"

"Not a word."

William, answering further questions of Dr. de Silva, said about 20 minutes must have elapsed after having assisting in strangling and leaving the body in the garage.

"So 20 minutes after all this, Mrs. Sathasivam was still alive?"

"When I left the garage she was alive."

"So when you got out of that house, Mrs. Sathasivam was not yet dead so far as you knew?"

"That is so."

"So that when you got out of that house and if you got assistance, there was still an opportunity, so far as you knew, to save that poor lady's life?"

"I won't say that her life could have been saved."

"Were you afraid that if anybody found you with the jewellery and you were taken to Mrs. Sathasivam, she might still be alive to say that you were the person who took that jewellery?"

"I was not."

"Were you afraid that if you should by any chance be back in that house before she was dead, she would be able to say who squeezed her throat?"

"I did not entertain such a fear."

"Then why did you not tell a single person in that bus stand, 'Heaven's alive. The master has killed the lady and given me this jewellery. Come with me to the bungalow and save that lady's life'?"

"I was frightened, and my idea was to get to my village."

"What was it that you were frightened of?"

"I was frightened of Mr. Sathasivam. I did not know where he would hunt me in Colombo."

"But you could have got to that bungalow with an army of people while he was there with that dead lady. Is that not so?"

"That is so but it did not strike me at that time. I was not so intelligent to do all that at that time."

Justice Gratiaen asked William, "Or was it that your commercial instinct was predominant at that time, to get some money from the murdered woman's articles?"

"No. I was not fond of the money or the articles. The only idea in my mind was to get back to the village as soon as possible," William replied.

Dr. de Silva queried, "Since you were not fond of the articles you did not attempt to throw them away?"

"I did not."

"But in Panadura, you knew exactly how to get rid of your sarong and shirt so that they may not be traced?"

"It did not strike me that I should get rid of my clothes. They were soiled clothes as I was working in the kitchen and I wanted to get some new clothes."

"But then why did you go and leave them in Suppiah's boutique and tell him that you would come back for them later?"

"I did not tell him I would come back for my clothes," said William.

Justice Gratiaen queried, "The soiled clothes that were suitable for a cook were no more suitable for a man who was at this time opulent?"

"As they were soiled I put them away."

Dr. de Silva continuing his cross-examination asked, "Did you not think of going to the Police Station or the betel boutique or to the market place where you went marketing regularly, or to anyone else and saying that Mrs. Sathasivam had been killed?"

"No."

William said when he went home his father asked him why he came from Colombo. He told him that where he was employed the master killed his wife and therefore he came.

"Then what did your father say?" asked Dr. de Silva.

"Father said nothing. He said, 'All right you stay at home'."

"Your father took murder in this stride?" asked Dr. de Silva. William remained silent.

Answering further questions William said he wanted to go to the Police Station but his father did not allow him to go. Other villagers also suggested that he should go to the Police Station but his father did not want him to do so.

William said that he told the villagers that he assisted in the murder but he did not tell that to his father. He said he did not tell his father thinking that he would thrash him. He told his father that he was an eyewitness to the murder after his arrest.

At this stage, Justice Gratiaen directed the Clerk of the Court to issue summons to H.M. Darlis Appu, William's father.

Answering Dr. de Silva's questions further, William said he also did not tell his father that he had money, although he had about 100 rupees in his pocket. He said he spent the whole thing. He did not use a cent of money for household expenses, because this was ill-gotten wealth!

"Therefore, I treated my friends with tea and spent all the money," William said.

Dr. de Silva asked, "Hundred rupees worth of tea?"

"I went for pictures (movies) had tea and enjoyed with my friends".

"You would agree with me that even with the tea price last year, you could not have spent whole of that?" William did not answer.

Answering further questions William said he paid some debts he had and lost about ten to twelve rupees by gambling.

Justice Gratiaen asked William about the different statements he made to Police Officers after his arrest.

"You remember being questioned as to whether you had told Mr. de Saram, or some Police Officer at Matara, that you heard a sound like 'Dadi bidi' upstairs, a noise of something going on there?"

"I did not say that."

"Did you say anything to your father to this effect, that the gentleman in the house had gone somewhere, he returned home later, that the lady went up the stairs with the gentleman, then you heard a wailing sound, and then the gentleman came and pushed you and asked you to go?"

"I did not say that to my father."

"Could your father, unless he invented it, have possibly said anything to that effect to Mr. Koelmeyer, one of the honourable Policemen who is not under criticism in this case?"

"I did not tell him that," said William.

Answering further questions of Dr. de Silva, William admitted that since he went to Mrs. Sathasivam's house to work, she never came down to the kitchen.

"Her only visit to the kitchen was before she died when two men carried her above the floor level to the kitchen, and you were holding the legs?" asked Justice Gratiaen.

William said, "Yes."

Dr. de Silva then asked William how he could explain or suggest any information how the dirt got on to the soles of Mrs. Sathasivam's feet, if her feet never touched the kitchen floor when she was carried through the kitchen.

"I cannot say how they get on to the soles of her feet. Even when she was inside the house she never used any footwear," replied William.

"Do you know that the analyst took samples from the bedroom and found that the content of dirt of that floor did not match with the swab on the soles of Mrs. Sathasivam's feet?" asked Dr. de Silva.

William remained silent.

Justice Gratiaen questioned William about statements he has made to Punchi Singho, a friend of his, and one Piyadasa, a distant cousin of his.

William said on the day he left his village to go to Hungama, he told Punchi Singho that his master killed the lady and he also helped in the killing.

He also told Punchi Singho, "I was given some gold articles. This money is what was realised by the sale of those articles."

Justice Gratiaen asked, "Did you tell Punchi Singho this, as recorded by Inspector Goonetileke after he came to the scene, that one day when you were in the kitchen you heard a loud 'Dadi bidi' noise upstairs and when the gentleman of the house came downstairs, he gave you some jewellery and told you to go away if you wanted to save your life?"

"I did not tell him that," said William.

Continuing his questioning, Justice Gratiaen asked William whether he told Piyadasa, a fellow remand prisoner, also the same story.

"I did not say that."

Justice Gratiaen asked, "According to these stories – this is what you have said – you were always in the kitchen when the murder took place, but according to you the murder took place upstairs and not in the kitchen?"

"I did not make those statements," insisted William.

At this stage Justice Gratiaen ordered the Clerk of the Court to issue summons also to Punchi Singho and Piyadasa to attend Court to give evidence.

Dr. de Silva then asked William to describe everything he did on the morning of the murder in the kitchen in detail.

For example, he asked when and how drumsticks and the ash plantains were peeled and cut and whether condiments or curry stuff were added to those.

William then explained that he cut ash plantains, put a pot of rice to boil, and started scraping a coconut to get coconut milk to add to vegetables to cook.

Showing the knife used by William in the kitchen, Dr. de Silva asked, "This was the knife with which you used to peel the drumsticks?"

"Yes."

William was given a drumstick and the knife and he was asked to peel it and cut it. He took two minutes to peel it and half a minute to cut it, in all about two and a half minutes.

Dr. de Silva then referring to the story that William requested garlic from Mrs. Sathasivam, informed him that according to the accounts book of Mrs. Sathasivam, on the 5th of October, eighty cents worth of garlic had been bought.

"When you wanted garlic that day you found that you had no garlic in your kitchen where the Dover stove is?" asked Dr. de Silva.

"Yes."

"There is garlic in the safe in the room where the gas stove is?"

"There is a little garlic there and in case it is needed there is garlic left upstairs too."

"You now claim that Mrs. Sathasivam also kept garlic upstairs?"

"Yes."

"That is your assertion. Look witness, if you were to be given garlic after Podihamy left, the garlic had to be taken from the gas stove room cupboard?"

"Earlier, when the safe was opened and goods were taken, the garlic was taken upstairs."

Justice Gratiaen asked, "The same day?"

"Not the same day. The garlic is kept upstairs," insisted William.

William admitted that no cupboard key was ever put in to his hands by Mrs. Sathasivam.

Dr. de Silva asked, "I am putting it to you that if you as you say, obtained from Mrs. Sathasivam garlic for your cooking that day, it only had been given by her to you from the cupboard in the kitchen where the gas stove is?"

"I deny that."

One morning during the period of cross-examination of William, Justice Gratiaen addressed the jury and said, "Before we start I wish to say something to you, gentlemen of the jury. I received this morning from anonymous sources a scurrilous letter dealing with certain aspects of this case. I would normally treat the matter with the contempt it deserves, but it occurred to me that the same person or persons may attempt to communicate with you in the same way. If that happens, will you please inform the Court at once and I shall direct the Criminal Investigation Department to try and trace this monster."

Dr. de Silva, continuing his cross-examination, asked William to demonstrate again with the help of a peon how Mr. Sathasivam held Mrs. Sathasivam while carrying her down stairs.

William placed his right arm under the neck of the peon standing on his left and placed his left arm around the body of the peon pinning his right arm.

William said that Mr. Sathasivam went first with her body and he followed.

"One little push by you could have send Mr. Sathasivam rolling downstairs?" asked Dr. de Silva.

William said, "I cannot say."

Justice Gratiaen asked, "When you had reached the bottom of the stairs and when you were passing the door which he had closed, did it occur to you to drop the legs of Mrs. Sathasivam, open the door bolt for your life?"

"It did not occur to me," replied William.

Dr. de Silva questioned William about the injuries he had when he was arrested.

"When Mr. Wickremaratne found you at Hungama, he only noticed the scratch on your cheek?"

"Yes."

"Did you show the scratches on your hand?"

"I did."

William said he explained at both the Hungama Police Station and the Matara Police Station that they were caused when he held Mrs. Sathasivam.

William said he got the injury of the waist when a Police Officer at Modera broke the string, which was around his waist. He said the Police Sergeant before putting him into the Police cell examined him and removed the belt. Then he looked for a knife to cut the waist string he had. As he could not get a knife he snatched the waist string and broke it and doing so his waist got cut.

Dr. de Silva asked William about the banian, the undergarment covering the upper part of the body, he was wearing at the time of the murder.

"It had been taken over. The Crown has taken it over," William said.

"The Crown took that banian?" asked Dr. de Silva.

Then William said it got torn.

"That banian was never obtained by the Police?"

"I have no recollection."

"That was the banian that you wore in that house on the night of the 8th October and at the time when Mrs. Sathasivam was killed?"

"Yes."

"That banian you say was torn?"

"Yes."

Justice Gratiaen asked, "When and how did the banian which you were wearing at the time of the murder ever get torn?"

"Yes. The boxing banian I was wearing at the time of the murder got torn in the village."

"How?"

"I went into the jungle and I was playing about."

Dr. de Silva asked, "You put that shirt on, over your banian in any event to leave this house and I put it to you that was because that banian was torn?"

"It was not torn at that time."

"I put it to you that you thought it necessary to put that shirt over the banian because your banian got torn in your struggle with Mrs. Sathasivam?"

"I did not go to struggle with her. It was Mr. Sathasivam who struggled and killed her."

William said that after leaving the murder scene, he got in to a double decker bus and got down at Wellawatte to inform his eight-year-old cousin that he was going to his village and he was looking for the number of the house his cousin was working.

"So did you go to that bungalow?" asked Dr. de Silva.

"I was looking for the number but I cannot be quite sure as to the situation of that bungalow."

"You were now going to your cousin. Did you go to the house where he was working?"

"I did not go that day."

After walking down the High Street, William said he thought that there was no need to see him and decided to sell the gold chain.

"Why did you change your mind?"

"I thought 'I need not go and see him. I will now sell this chain'. Then I sold the chain, took the money and then went to take a bus."

Dr. de Silva was rather annoyed with this answer.

"Every time I ask you a simple question, you deliver a speech. In that speech I can never find the answer to my question. Please answer my question. My question is this - You then changed your mind about going to see your cousin?"

"Yes."

"Why did you change it?"

"I thought that there was no need."

"So you decided to see and then you decided not to see. Where about in High Street did you decide, 'No. I would not go to see' and turn back?"

"When I went up to that boutique I thought, 'I will sell the chain', and then changed my mind."

William said he did know the owner of the boutique, Edmund, before that day. He said Edmund was getting ready to close the boutique. He went to him and quietly asked him, "I have a chain. Will you buy?"

"Edmund is a perfect stranger to you?"

"Yes."

"You were not afraid to mention that you had this chain with you?"

"I was frightened, yet I asked."

Dr. de Silva reminded him that this chain has come off a lady who was murdered, and not far away from Edmund's boutique there was the Wellawatte Police station.

"Nevertheless you were not afraid?" he asked.

"No," said William.

William said after he sold the chain to Sirisena for 100 rupees at Edmund's boutique, Edmund showed him another boutique on Station Road and said, "We do not know if this is stolen property or not, if something happens do not come here, show that boutique!"

William said either Sirisena or Edmund inquired from him where he got this chain from, but they did not ask whether it was a stolen article.

After selling the chain he went to the 'Ariyasinhala Hotel' to have a cup of tea. Then William said he boarded a bus going to Panadura. When he got down at Panadura, the first thing he did was to have a haircut.

"That was the first stage in changing your appearance?" asked Dr. de Silva.

"Yes."

"Then you went to the shop and bought a new sarong and shirt?"

"Yes."

"You were not ready to carry those two to Matara. You got a man to stitch the sarong, so that it would be ready to wear immediately?"

"Yes."

Justice Gratiaen asked, "What was the colour of the new shirt? The old shirt you said was red?"

"It was a striped shirt, not white in colour."

"And different to the old shirt from the point of view of colour?"

"Yes, it was a different colour."

William said the sarong was also of a different colour from the sarong he was wearing.

"When you put on the new sarong and the new shirt after your new haircut, you would now looking quite a new man. Is that not so?" asked Dr. de Silva.

"Yes. I have not changed, but my clothes were changed," answered William.

"Then you thought it was not wise to carry your old sarong and shirt along with you to Matara?"

"No. There was no need for it and therefore I left them at Panadura."

"Were you not afraid that if you were seen in the old sarong and shirt you would be caught by the Police?" Justice Gratiaen asked.

"No," replied William.

Dr. de Silva asked whether he could remember making a statement to Mr. Koelmeyer regarding the sarong and shirt.

"Did you say this to him, 'I handed my old sarong and shirt that I had made into a parcel to the boy who makes the tea as a present, as I believed if I had the same clothes when I left the bungalow that I might be arrested by the Police'. Did you say that to the first CID officer who was instructed to record your statement?"

"I did not say that," William replied.

During the cross-examination, the Clerk of the Court informed Justice Gratiaen that Professor de Saram wished to make a statement. Dr. Colvin R. de Silva has requested him to be present.

In the absence of the jury, Professor de Saram was called to Court.

He said, "I understand from the counsel for the defence that I am expected to group the blood of the witness who is now giving evidence."

Justice Gratiaen said that an order was made and he allowed it with William's consent.

Professor de Saram said that he had not received the order.

Justice Gratiaen then asked, "Will you take my oral directions?"

"Yes, My Lord," replied Professor de Saram.

Dr. de Silva said, "I understand from the doctor that for the purpose for which I require the grouping, it is necessary not only to group the blood, but also to find out whether the person is a 'secretor' – whatever that means – and for that test it would be desirable to have specimens of the person's semen or saliva, or both, as well as the blood."

'Secretor' is a person who secretes his or her blood group antigens into body fluids such as seminal fluid, saliva, mucus in the digestive tract and respiratory cavities.

A person can be either a secretor or a non-secretor. This is completely independent of whether a person's blood type is A, B, AB or O, and is genetically determined

As a general rule, only about 80% of the population are secretors.

Dr. de Silva wanted Professor de Saram to confirm whether the seminal fluid found in Mrs. Sathasivam's vagina could have been from William.

Justice Gratiaen said William's consent was needed for this and when asked, William consented to give blood, saliva and a sample of semen.

"I think it is only fair William should be told how that operation takes place with the minimum of discomfort, as well as of embarrassment," said Justice Gratiaen.

He ordered the Clerk of the Court to make necessary arrangements with the Officer-in-Charge of the Hulftsdorp prison, to take samples the following morning.

As all four specialist doctors giving evidence in the trial, that is Professors de Saram, Milroy Paul, M.V.P. Peiris and Dr. H.N. Welikala, were present in the Court, Justice Gratiaen asked William to repeat the demonstration how Mr. Sathasivam throttled his wife for their benefit.

William also demonstrated how Mrs. Sathasivam's hands scratched his face and hand during strangling.

He also showed the position of Mr. Sathasivam's hands was, at the moment Mrs. Sathasivam was put on the ground. That is, the thumb on the right side of Mrs. Sathasivam's neck and the fingers on her left.

Questioning William about the stamping of the neck Dr. de Silva then asked, "How did you realize that under another man's foot the voice box under the skin had broken?"

"When Mr. Sathasivam moved his leg and her head turned to a side, I knew that the voice-box was broken."

"If you trampled that throat with your bare foot you could feel that voice box breaking, is it not?"

"But I did not trample her."

"How do you know that the voice box was broken?" Dr. de Silva asked again.

"When the head turned to a side I know that it was broken."

"Why should you think that because the head turned to a side that it is the voice box that broke?"

"When the head turned suddenly to a side I knew that the voice box had broken."

Dr. de Silva asked William what he exactly did in the kitchen on the day of Mrs. Sathasivam's murder.

He handed William a husked coconut and asked, "Now in order to prepare that coconut for scraping, the first thing you have to do is to remove the tuft of fibre at one end of it?"

"Yes."

William was asked to remove it and he said he could do it with a blowpipe found in the kitchen. It was handed over to him. William said that he used it remove the tuft. He rested the coconut on the rail of the witness box and hit the tuft of fibre at the end of the coconut twice with the blowpipe. The tuft broke off.

"Then I split the coconut and sat down to scrape it. In order to scrape the split half I have to clean the nut", William said.

Then he demonstrated how he did it with the split half of coconut found in the kitchen, which was produced in Court. He showed how he held it and scraped it.

"In your fingers at this moment there is a whole lot of fibrous fluff?" Dr. de Silva asked.

"Yes, I had to dust it off my hands by bringing my hands together for the purpose."

"Professor de Saram, you remember, said in Magistrate's Court that he found just over the left jaw of Mrs. Sathasivam, a depression - a depressed injury - in which he found fragments of fine dark powder. He, you will remember, also said that he gave that powder for analysis to the Government Analyst Mr. Chanmugam. And Mr. Chanmugam tells us, you will remember, that these tiny pieces of brown material, on examination were found to be similar to fluff found on coconut fibre?"

William remained silent.

"Mr. Chanmugam found that there was in this depressed injury over the left jaw just the same sort of stuff as you find on the fibres on the back of a husked coconut, just as the one you handled just now. You know that now?"

"I do not know."

"Have you any suggestion as to how that fluff came into that depressed injury just over Mrs. Sathasivam's left jaw?"

"I am unable to give any suggestion."

The fluff, Court production number 101, which was in some transparent paper, was handed over to Justice Gratiaen and then shown to the Acting Solicitor-General and the jury.

Dr. de Silva asked William whether he would agree that such coconut fluff could not come from the bedroom upstairs.

"That is so."

"There was, as I told you on the second day of your cross-examination by me, on the soles of Mrs. Sathasivam's feet, black material such as is found in the house on the floor of the kitchen that you worked in that morning. You know that material too was analysed by the Government Analyst and he found in it tiny particles of siliceous matter, strands of fibre and vegetables debris covered with a black organic matter, which he produced as P102?"

Again William remained silent.

Dr. de Silva asked William about the four stained areas on that saree described by Mr. Chanmugam.

"Mr. Chanmugam tells us the quality of the stains also. 'These stains consist essentially of dark organic matter along with small specks of siliceous particles and are similar to the stains obtained by sweeping the floors of the two kitchens at No.7, St. Alban's Place.' Can you explain how these things came?" asked Dr. de Silva.

"I am unable to explain that," William replied.

Dr. de Silva then asked William whether he could give any explanation as to how Mrs Sathasivam's saree was torn and it contained stains of dark greasy material.

William replied he was unable to explain.

"You have told us that in the entire 11 days of your service at the Sathasivams' the lady never stepped into either of these kitchens?"

"Yes."

"Did you ever see her come into the kitchen wearing this saree?"

"I have not."

"The only time you saw that lady in this saree in the kitchen was when you say you were helping to carry her into the kitchen?"

"Yes."

Justice Gratiaen asked, "At what height were her feet being carried by you when you took her over the kitchen?"

William indicated the height as being about the height above the ground when his hands were hanging by his sides. It was measured and found to be 2 feet 1 inch.

"In all the 11 days that you knew this unfortunate lady, that was the nearest height her feet reached the kitchen floor?" asked Dr. de Silva.

"That is so."

"Can you explain to this Court how stains got on to this saree, of material of the same sort as you find on the two kitchen floors?"

"I am unable to say."

"Do you know that there was on this saree a long tear, where the saree would come just over the breast when it is worn?"

"I do not know."

"It is a seven and a half inch tear, three inches wide and just below at the bottom end of that there are two smaller tears?"

"I do not know."

"Can you tell the Court whether you can suggest any manner in which those tears were caused?"

"I am unable to say."

"That is to say you saw nothing by which you can associate that tear with anybody's hands?"

"I am unable to explain those tears."

"You yourself, according to the position in your evidence, never reached above the two sides of her hips with your hands or feet?"

"That is so."

"I am now going to suggest to you directly from the defence that you, and you alone, were the killer of Mrs. Sathasivam?"

"I deny that."

"I am also going to suggest to you that the killing of Mrs. Sathasivam took place as a result of her coming into the kitchen in which you were that day?"

"I deny that. There was no need for me to kill her."

"And that it was your hands that squeezed her throat unto death that day and nobody else?"

"I deny that and I say it is Mr. Sathasivam who throttled her to death."

"You will agree, won't you, that if this Court is satisfied that she came into the kitchen that day, then your trying to hide that fact shows that you did something to her on that occasion?"

At this stage Justice Gratiaen requested Dr. de Silva to put suggestions to the witness as it would be better than asking him whether he agrees to certain things or not.

"I suggest to you that you are seeking to hide the fact that Mrs. Sathasivam came to the kitchen that day because you attacked her in that kitchen?"

"I deny that. I had no reason to murder that lady. It is the gentleman who killed her and I in obedience to his command assisted him in holding her down."

"You had no reason to obey him?"

"Through fear I obeyed him."

"Is it your position that if a master of yours orders you to kill, that you will kill?"

"There is no necessity for me to kill. In fact he killed and asked me to hold and I held her."

"And when he asked you to hold you were free to leave that room?"

"Though I was free, through fear I did not leave."

"Though you were free, you also went away with the jewellery?"

"He gave them to me. Through fear I took them and went away."

"Though you were free to refuse, you accepted it through fear?"

"Yes."

Referring again to the stocks of condiments kept in the kitchen cupboard, Dr. de Silva asked, "You have admitted that the key of that cupboard was never touched by you?"

"Yes."

"Therefore, I put it to you that the garlic had to be got out of the cupboard by Mrs. Sathasivam coming down to that room?"

"There was no need for her to come downstairs and open the cupboard and take the garlic because there was garlic upstairs too."

Answering further questions William said there was a heap of firewood in the kitchen.

Dr. de Silva showing the piece of firewood found in the garage asked, "Do you know that in the garage there was found, a little away from Mrs. Sathasivam's body, this piece of firewood?"

"When firewood is brought it is put into the garage."

"Therefore when the Police came that day if there was any firewood they should have found it in the garage?"

"Not only in the garage but even outside."

"Do you know that the Police found a heap of firewood in the kitchen?"

"I do not know."

"Do you know that the Police found a heap of firewood under the Dover stove and another heap of firewood by the side of that stove?"

"I do not know."

"Do you know that there is a photograph of this garage?"

"I saw the photograph." (See Figure 9. Page 472)

Dr. de Silva asked whether William knew that the garage shown in photographs did not show the slightest sign of a heap of firewood.

"I do not know that."

"But one solitary piece of firewood literally staring in the face?"

William did not answer.

"I am suggesting to you that when Mrs. Sathasivam was in the kitchen you grabbed her by the throat?"

"There was absolutely no reason for me to do that."

"Answer my question. Is it not a fact that when Mrs. Sathasivam came to the kitchen that day, you grabbed her by the throat?"

"That is not correct."

"Is it not the fact that you took her into the garage from that kitchen?"

"No."

"Is it not a fact that it was because Mrs. Sathasivam came to the kitchen that day that she got the kitchen dirt on the soles of her feet?"

"She did not come to the kitchen."

"Is it not a fact that you stripped her body of the jewellery after you had throttled her?"

"It is not a fact," said William.

Dr. de Silva then referred to the statement William made to the Magistrate after his arrest and asked whether he said, "I put on the shirt and opened the front door."

"I did not say I put on the shirt. I said I took the shirt."

Reading the statement Dr. de Silva said, "Listen to the words: 'I put on the shirt and opened the front door'?"

"Let him write in any way he wants. I said I took the shirt," William said.

Justice Gratiaen asked, "What do you mean by that answer 'Let him write anyway he wants'?"

"He has recorded things that I did not say, putting it out of his own pocket!"

Dr. de Silva then said, "I am going to read to you what somebody else wrote down in Colombo on the 19th, that is Mr. Koelmeyer. I gather that you are trying to explain to us today, that you were so frightened of the murderer that you were anxious to merely get your shirt and not put it on until after you left the house. Isn't that so?"

"Yes."

"Did you say this to Mr. Koelmeyer: 'When I left the garage I went into the room where coconuts are left'?"

"Yes."

"Up to that point of time he has correctly recorded what you said?"

"Yes."

" 'I took my red shirt that was there'?"

"That is also correct."

" 'Wore it'?"

"I did not say that."

"That is where the invention commences, is it not, the truth being that you were too frightened to wear it?"

William remained silent.

Dr. de Silva reading from the statement William made to the Magistrate on the day of his arrest asked, "Then can you give any reason why the Magistrate should invent the same suggestion that you put on that shirt before you left, as Mr. Koelmeyer has done?"

"I do not know why he recorded that. What I told him was that I took the shirt and left the bungalow."

"Where did you put it on in fact?" asked Justice Gratiaen.

"Outside the gate."

"In the middle of St. Alban's Place?"

"Yes."

Continuing the cross-examination Dr. de Silva asked, "According to your previous evidence, you put on that shirt and you also thought it necessary, after getting out of that door, to tell the babies that you were going?"

"Whilst going I told them."

"Why? Here you were running away in fear of your life? Why did you stop to tell the babies?"

"As the babies were there I told them."

"You wanted to leave the impression that you were going, as you might term it, 'ordinarily' from house?"

"Yes."

"What was the necessity?"

"The baby asked 'Where are you going?' and I said, 'I am going away'."

Referring to William's statement recorded by the IGP (See Chapter 4. Page 32) Dr. de Silva said, "Now I am turning to another point. You know when you spoke to the IGP, according to the IGP's record, you had told Mr. Albert de Silva as follows – I am just reminding you about it – 'When Mrs. Sathasivam came into the kitchen while I was scraping coconut, I released the coconut, got up and held her throat with both hands'. In your statement to the IGP, you have said that you said that to Mr. Albert de Silva?"

William remained silent.

"Did you in that way get up releasing the coconut that was in your hands and grab Mrs. Sathasivam's throat?"

"I did not. I told the IGP that it was what I was tutored to say."

"Now I am going to put to you the questions, on your instructions, that Mr. Christie Seneviratne, your counsel, put to the Inspector in the lower court. You have told us today how you were taken into a latrine downstairs?"

"Yes."

"This is the question put by Mr. Seneviratne on your behalf to the Inspector: 'I put it to you that William was taken near the latrine downstairs.' Did you give those instructions to Mr. Seneviratne?"

"I did not tell him that. I do not know what questions he put to the Inspector. I told him that I was taken to the latrine behind the Office."

"Do you suggest that Mr. Seneviratne too had joined the army of opposition against you?"

"I would not say that."

"Mr. Seneviratne, you told 3 minutes ago, carefully questioned you on this matter before questioning the Inspector?"

"He may have made a mistake."

"Or you are not telling the truth, one of the two?"

"I speak the truth; he may have made a mistake."

"Look at the next question. Then Mr. Seneviratne asked, 'I put it to you that while the Police Officers were at lunch, you took William down and offered a bribe of 1,000 rupees and employment if he made a statement exculpating Mr. Sathasivam?' Did you give those instructions to Mr. Seneviratne?"

"I did not give him those instructions."

"So Mr. Seneviratne has invented that also?"

"He may have put those questions. I am not an advocate to instruct him to ask those questions."

"Therefore, the suggestion that Mr. Wickremaratne offered a bribe of 1000 rupees to you is also false?"

"I do not know whether it is false or true!" William said.

Justice Gratiaen asked, "Why don't you know that it is false or true?"

"I cannot remember whether he said so or not. He may have said so."

"You remember Mr. Sathasivam giving you the comparatively trivial sum of 3 rupees, which he took out of an almirah?"

"Yes."

"But when an Inspector of Police offers you a princely sum of 1,000 rupees to implicate yourself on a charge of murder, that matter, you say, may have passed completely from your mind?"

"Yes."

"Do you remember anybody at any time in any connection ever offering you a bribe in connection with this murder or anything else?"

"May have. I cannot remember," William replied to Justice Gratiaen.

Dr. de Silva then questioned William about the time he left the house and his journey to Panadura. This was to elicit from William the probable time William left the scene of murder.

Dr. de Silva asked, "What time would you say you left this house? What is your own guess? I see, automatically your eyes go to the clock the moment you are asked about the time?"

"About 10."

"How long did you spend at Wellawatte?"

"25 to 30 minutes."

"Then you set out to Panadura?"

"Yes."

"I am going to put to you certain facts. In your estimate, how long did you take from Wellawatte to Panadura?"

"About an hour."

"I may tell you, you are remarkably accurate. It takes about 50 minutes. Now, you told us, in the course of your evidence in this court, that you got to Panadura at a time when the next bus for Galle was due to arrive and leave at 2 odd or 3 odd, that was your position?"

"Yes."

"In this court you have said that when you reached Panadura you asked, 'When is the next bus to Galle'?"

"Yes."

"And you were told, you said, that the next bus was at 2 odd or 3 odd? That is what you have said here?"

"Yes."

"Therefore, you arrived there before the two o'clock bus?"

"Yes."

"Would you be surprised to hear that on this day, 9th of October 1951, Galle buses passed through Panadura at half hour intervals?"

"I do not know. I asked a certain woman and I accepted what she told me."

"Not a woman. You went and got down at the bus terminus in Panadura garage?"

"Yes."

"And you enquired there?"

"I asked the woman and that is what the woman told me."

"I will put it to you, on your own showing, if the next bus was at 2 o'clock, you arrived at Panadura sometime after 1.30, let us say about 1.30?"

"It was not even one. When I was asked I gave a rough guess that it was about one o'clock."

"Therefore, I put it to you, that you left Wellawatte, on your own showing, not before 12.30?"

"I do not know that."

"And I am saying, if you spent 25 – 30 minutes at Wellawatte, or you can have more, that you arrived at Edmund's shop somewhere between 11.30 and 12?"

"I deny that."

"Do you know witness that according to Edmund, he was not at Wellawatte at 10.15?"

"I do not know."

"Do you know that according to Edmund, he was away from Wellawatte between 9.50 and 11 o'clock?"

"I do not know."

"Do you know that he says that he returned to Wellawatte from the hospital after 11 o'clock?"

"I do not know."

"You told us in this Court that you met Sirisena on this day?"

"Yes."

"And you told us how you sold that chain to him?"

"Yes."

"Do you know that according to him he left Wellawatte that morning at 8.35?"

"I do not know."

"Do you know that according to him he returned only in the afternoon to Wellawatte?"

"I do not know."

Dr. de Silva then questioned William about lifting of the mortar by Mr. Sathasivam.

William was asked to look at the photograph of the kitchen, which showed the position of the mortar, where Podihamy had left it.

"Do you claim that from the door between the two kitchens you can see the spot where you have placed the mortar?"

"The mortar is not visible."

"You have also said that you never saw Mr. Sathasivam lifting that mortar?"

"Yes. I saw him trying to lift it."

"If you could not see the mortar how do you know that Mr. Sathasivam was trying to lift it?"

"I did not see the mortar as it lay there, but when he was trying to lift it he slanted it and I saw it."

Justice Gratiaen asked William, "Can you see a man or a mortar from where you were standing if that man or the mortar were in the garage?"

"Yes."

"Are you quite sure of that because the whole Court and the jurors went there?"

"I am quite sure," William replied.

Dr. de Silva continuing his questioning asked, "Before you went away did you put that mortar on the lady's body?"

"I did not."

"Did you instruct your counsel that there was any popular superstition in regard to the placing of a mortar on a dead body?"

"I do not know."

"Have you ever heard of such a superstition?" queried Justice Gratiaen.

"I have not," said William.

"Now I am going to ask you witness, did you drag that lady from the kitchen into the garage?" questioned Dr. de Silva.

"No."

"Did Mr. Seneviratne, your counsel in the Magistrate's Court, tell you that Mr. Chanmugam giving evidence in your presence and in Court said that he found signs of a drag mark in front of the door leading towards the garage, that is to say, from the kitchen?"

"No. I was not told. He did not tell me."

"Now, I will tell you if there was such a drag mark leading from the kitchen towards the door leading into the garage, could you give any suggestions as to how it happened?"

"No. I am unable to."

Concluding the painstaking and very focussed cross-examination to show that William, and William alone, strangled Mrs. Sathasivam in the kitchen, Dr. de Silva asked, "Shall I suggest something to you and finish. I suggest to you, that drag mark is a drag mark caused by your pulling Mrs. Sathasivam from the kitchen into the garage, after you had grabbed her in the kitchen?"

"I deny that," insisted William.

After a brief re-examination by Mr. T. S. Fernando, the Acting Solicitor-General, Justice Gratiaen questioned William.

"What time, can you tell us, it was in your estimation when you left the house after the killing?"

"About 10."

"Could it be later?"

"I would say it may be even earlier. Between 9.30 and 10 that I left the house. I cannot say later than 10."

"Now how do you make that estimation?"

"It is a guessed time."

"You see, before you knew that there was this question of 'times' having some importance, you were questioned by Mr. Koelmeyer in the CID office?"

"Yes."

"He asked you specifically?"

"Yes."

"And what did you say then?"

"About 10 or 10.15, is what I said."

"In fact 10 or 10.30, is that not so?"

"I cannot remember."

"That was also your guess?"

"Yes."

"Like your present guess?"

"Yes."

"Except that your present guess fits the case for the prosecution – you realize that?"

"Yes."

"Do you remember being asked about your having had your hair cut and your having changed your sarong and shirt, and counsel asked you whether you went away with a tell-tale banian?"

"Yes."

"What did you understand by the description of 'a tell-tale banian'? What was the tale that the banian was going to tell?"

"I understood it to mean that that was the banian I wore at the time the lady was being murdered."

"Did she clutch at your banian too?"

"No."

"Do you remember, or do you not remember?"

"She did not."

"When did this banian get torn? Can you remember now?"

"I cannot quite remember. It was roughly about 4 or 5 days after I had been in the village."

"How it comes to be torn?"

"We were playing a game called 'Katti-paninawa' (dodging) and we went into the jungle."

"You play this game in the jungle, do you?"

"No, in the paddy field."

"Now, are you quite sure that you saw the children playing on the swing when you left the house for the last time?"

"I am quite sure."

"Did you tell the Police Officers at the Modera Police Station that the children were upstairs at the time you left the house?"

"I did not," replied William.

After Justice Gratiaen's questioning, the jury also asked a few questions about the statement recorded at the Matara Police Station and about feeding the little children left at home.

The next witness for the prosecution was Mr. M. M. Haniffa of 79, Horton Place, Colombo. He said he knew Mr. Sathasivam for about 20 years.

Mr. Haniffa said that he returned to Ceylon by "Himalaya" in which Mr. Sathasivam and his mother also returned. He had shared the same cabin with Mr. Sathasivam.

He said on arrival in Ceylon on the 22nd of September, Mr. Sathasivam asked him whether he could come and stay with him till he found a place to go to, as his wife had filed a divorce case and he could not go home.

However, Mr. Sathasivam actually came to stay with him only on the 24th after spending two nights with Mrs. Sathasivam. Mr. Haniffa said that Mr. Sathasivam stayed with him several nights on and off.

On 8th October, Mr. Sathasivam showed him the summons he had received. After that they left the house together and had drinks in a couple of places.

Mr. Haniffa said at about 2.30 p.m., Mr. Abba Ramachandra, Mr. Sathasivam and he left the Orient Club to go to his place for lunch. On the way, Mr. Sathasivam who was driving Abba's car stopped, and got his two children and Podihamy, who were travelling in a rickshaw from school, to the car. Then they went to St. Alban's Place.

Mr. Haniffa who has met Mrs. Sathasivam once or twice before, went into the house. When Mrs. Sathasivam came downstairs, he took her hand and spoke to her. Mr. Haniffa then asked her whether she could not make up with her husband and withdraw the divorce case. Mrs. Sathasivam did not talk a word about the case.

Mr. Haniffa said after sometime they left the house, went to his place and had lunch. Then Mr. Sathasivam went out in the evening at about 6.00 p.m. in a friend's car. He did not return that night.

On the 9th morning, when Mr. Haniffa was having a drink as usual at the Galle Face Hotel with a friend of his, Mr. Sathasivam came there. Mr. Haniffa's recollection was it was about 10.30 a.m.

Answering a query from Justice Gratiaen he said that the time was about 10.30 a.m., because they left the Hotel at about 11.30 a.m. Mr. Haniffa offered a drink to Mr. Sathasivam but he refused strong things and had an 'Orange Crush'. Then they decided to go to Fort and Mr. Sathasivam got off at the Bank of Ceylon.

They met again little after mid-day and had several rounds of drinks at the Grand Oriental Hotel. Then they went to the Galle Face Hotel and had drinks again!

Mr. Haniffa told Justice Gratiaen that in England he did the same thing, which was called "pub crawling".

After several drinks they went to his house at Horton Place. Mr. Sathasivam then had lunch and went to bed.

Mr. Haniffa said that at about 4.00 p.m., there was a call for Mr. Sathasivam and he woke him up. Mr. Sathasivam had a brief conversation and then told Mr. Haniffa that his wife had been murdered!

"He began to get dressed quickly. Before he finished, there was another call. It was about 10 minutes after the first. It was from Mr. K.C. Nadarajah, an advocate, who asked Mr. Sathasivam to stay till he arrived. Mr. Nadarajah came after sometime and had a discussion with Mr. Sathasivam. They were whispering and I could not follow what they were saying. Then the Police arrived. I saw Mr. Attygalle and Mr. Albert de Silva. Mr. Sathasivam left with Mr. Nadarajah followed by Mr. Attygalle and Mr. Albert de Silva," said Mr. Haniffa.

He said he went to the Fort Police Station that evening to see Mr. Sathasivam, but he could not speak to him.

"I was woken up at about 3.45 a.m. on the 10th by Inspector Thiedeman and he recorded a statement from me. The same day I pointed out Mr. Sathasivam's bag to the Police Officer and he searched the bag and took certain letters from it," said Mr. Haniffa.

Dr. Colvin R. de Silva cross-examining Mr. Haniffa referred to the evidence he gave in the Magistrate's Court earlier, where he has said after the first call, Mr. Sathasivam said that his wife was dead, and that he was going to see what all this was about. He had further said in the Magistrate's Court that Mr. Sathasivam rang up Mr. Nadarajah and spoke to him and then told Mr. Haniffa that his wife had been murdered and Mr. Nadarajah was coming. Mr. Haniffa had further said in the Magistrate's Court that Mr. Nadarajah told him that Mr. Sathasivam's wife had been found murdered and he is coming with Mr. Attygalle and Mr. Albert de Silva.

Dr. de Silva reminded Mr. Haniffa that he had also stated that Mr. Sathasivam expressed great distress when he heard the news of his wife's death.

As there were differences between what Mr. Haniffa said in Court now and what he had told in the Magistrate's Court, Dr. de Silva asked, "Are you in a position to remember anything?"

"I can only say what I can remember."

"So that you are in no position really to speak either of details or of the sequence of events?"

Mr. Haniffa remained silent.

At this stage, Justice Gratiaen stated that it does not seem to be suggested by either side that Mr. Haniffa was trying to mislead the Court but that it was a question of his not being able to remember.

The next witness, Mr. W.L. Bogstra, Director of the company 'Bogstra and De Wildt' giving evidence said that he knew Miss Stevenson since 1934 or 1935 and she was employed in his company for a few months. He confirmed that Mr. Sathasivam had a close friendship with her.

The next group of important witnesses called by the prosecution were to corroborate William's evidence about the time he left No. 7, St. Alban's Place.

Mr. V.S.N. Sanmugam, of 67, High Street, Wellawatte, was a key Crown witness on whose evidence the Crown relied upon to fix the time of Mrs. Sathasivam's murder.

Mr. Sanmugam, examined by Mr. T.S. Fernando, the Acting

Solicitor-General, said he knew Edmund, who had a boutique at 37, High Street, Wellawatte.

He said on the 9th October morning, his servant girl Premawathie, fell ill and he wanted Edmund's help to take her to hospital. Edmund agreed to come with him to hospital.

He telephoned for a 'Quickshaws' cab from a place next to Edmund's boutique. When he came back to Edmund's boutique, Sanmugam said he heard a boy dressed in sarong, banian and shirt inquiring from Edmund for the jeweller to whom a portion of that boutique had been sublet.

At the time, Edmund was closing the boutique to accompany him to hospital.

He heard Edmund asking the boy why he wanted the jeweller. The boy replied that he had some gold jewellery for sale. Edmund with his hand pointing in the direction of Station Road asked the boy to go there.

Sanmugam said that in five minutes a 'Quickshaws' cab came and both of them took the girl to the Out Patients' Department of the General Hospital, Colombo. He said when he set out to the hospital with the girl it must have been about 9.45 a.m.

There the girl was examined by a doctor and admitted to a ward. Sanmugam said that he then returned home and it was about 11 a.m.

Continuing Sanmugam said, next day he read in the 'Ceylon Daily News' about Mrs. Sathasivam's murder. He read the description of the missing boy from the newspapers a few days later. He then read out the description of the boy to Edmund. With a view to discussing the possibility of that boy being the one who had come to Edmund's boutique on 9th October, Edmund wanted to see the description in the Sinhalese papers.

Edmund later read a description of the boy from the 'Dinamina', a Sinhalese national newspaper.

However, there was no reference to any missing jewellery in the papers.

Sanmugam then asked Edmund to help him in tracing the person to whom Edmund had directed the boy.

On 14th October, Sanmugam said he went to Edmund's boutique and Edmund told him that the jeweller whom he had contacted had told him that the boy had sold him a chain. He asked him for the weight and he was told it was 7 ½ sovereigns. He then inferred that it must have been a 'thali' worn by Tamil ladies.

Edmund told him that the jeweller had valued it at 490 rupees but bought it for just 100 rupees.

Sanmugam said that on 16th October, he tried to get Edmund to inform the Police about the boy who came to sell jewellery. But Edmund refused.

Then Sanmugam told the Court that he wrote to Mr. Albert de Silva, Inspector of Police, because the newspapers mentioned his name as the Investigating Officer. The letter he wrote on the 17th was mentioned earlier. (See page 49)

In fact, Mr. Sanmugam wrote a letter to Mr. Albert de Silva again on the 20th. Then he wrote to the Inspector-General of Police on 25th October the following letter.

"I wish to bring it to your notice that I addressed 2 letters dated the 17th and 20th instant to Mr. M.A. De Silva – SP Colombo – (copies of which I hereto annex) but that I have received no acknowledgment of any kind.

I feel that the valuable information I gave in these letters would have in no small measure contributed to the arrest of the missing boy William. It is very discouraging that my action does not appear to have been appreciated or even the ordinary civility of an acknowledgment extended to me. Will you please look into this matter yourself and inform me as to what action you propose to take and whether you will require my services in the future."

While giving evidence, Mr. Sanmugam informed Court that he was feeling weak to continue his evidence. Justice Gratiaen adjourned the proceedings for the day.

When the trial resumed on a Monday after the weekend adjournment, Mr. T.S. Fernando, the Acting Solicitor-General, submitted a medical certificate tendered by Mr. Sanmugam.

The certificate, signed by Dr. G.R. Handy, a consultant physician and a renowned heart specialist of the General Hospital, Colombo, stated that Mr. Sanmugam was suffering from left ventricular failure and had been advised to rest in bed for a few days. 'Left ventricular failure' is the inability of the muscles of the left side of the heart to pump adequate amounts of blood to the organs.

Dr. Handy had further submitted that Mr. Sanmugam would not be able to attend Court for about two weeks and if his evidence was very necessary, it might be recorded in his house.

Justice Gratiaen said that he was wondering whether it would be advisable to record the evidence of the witness in his house. He said he was reluctant to do that unless he could get a reasonable assurance from the doctor that it would do the witness no harm.

"The cross-examination of Mr. Sanmugam is very essential in this case," said Justice Gratiaen. He said he wished to hear the doctor's opinion on the matter.

The Acting Solicitor-General said that he had requested Dr. G. R. Handy to be present in Court and Justice Gratiaen then adjourned Court until the arrival of Dr. Handy.

He arrived in Court a few minutes later. He said that Mr. Sanmugam had been his patient for about three years. He suffered a heart attack at his bungalow on Saturday and his examination revealed he was suffering from left ventricular failure (Heart failure).

Replying to a question by Justice Gratiaen, Dr. Handy said that in the interest of Sanmugam's health, it would be better if there was no cross-examination at all. He agreed that excitement would bring upon another heart attack. However, he could be given some time to rest.

Justice Gratiaen suggested that Dr. Handy might be in attendance during the cross-examination of the witness so that he could tell them when to stop.

Two weeks later, after sitting for one hour at the usual Court premises at Hulftsdorp, Justice Gratiaen adjourned the Court to assemble in the operating theatre of the 'Durdans', a private hospital in Colombo, to hear the evidence of Mr. Sanmugam.

Justice Gratiaen, the court staff, the jury, counsel, the accused Mr. Sathasivam and Dr Handy went to the hospital where Mr. Sanmugam was undergoing treatment for 'Cardiac asthma' or failure of the left ventricle of the heart.

Dr. Handy, who was attending on Mr. Sanmugam, informed Justice Gratiaen, that Mr. Sanmugam had developed a slight heart attack the previous night on being told that he would have to give evidence on that day. "The attack", he said, "Could be brought about if the patient was physically or emotionally excited."

Mr. Sanmugam was in no condition, Dr. Handy said, to attend Court, but if the court was willing to take a risk, his evidence might be recorded at the patient's bedside.

Dr. Colvin R. de Silva, the defence counsel, on being asked what his attitude was, said, "The witness is an untruthful witness and it would be impossible to cross-examine the witness without embarrassing him, though without intention."

Answering questions of the Acting Solicitor-General, Sanmugam said he had spoken to Mr. Sathasivam only once at a platform of the Madras Railway Station. They were in the same bogey together with Mr. S.S. Jayawickrama, another famous All-Ceylon cricketer, when they were returning from Bombay.

Sanmugam denied that Mr. Sathasivam had kicked him on that occasion. Mr. Sanmugam said if Mr. Sathasivam had kicked him, he (Mr. Sathasivam) would not be here!

Replying to Justice Gratiaen, Sanmugam said that if Mr. Sathasivam kicked him, both Mr. Sathasivam and himself would not be there because there would have been a big fight!

Justice Gratiaen adjourned Court for five minutes before the cross-examination began to enable the witness to get a short rest and medical examination by Dr. G.R. Handy, who came in at this stage.

Cross-examined by Dr. Colvin R. de Silva, Mr. Sanmugam denied having been in the same compartment with Mr. Sathasivam. He denied having been under the influence of liquor.

He also denied having met Mrs. Sathasivam on a train in India. He denied that Mr. Sathasivam threw him out of a railway compartment. There was no incident in which he was involved.

Mr. Sanmugam said he did not see William between the day of the murder until the day on which he saw him at the Magistrate's Court on October 24th. He had told Mr. Koelmeyer that he came to

Court as he was anxious to see the boy William.

Mr. Sanmugam answering questions said that if he had received the 1,000-rupee reward offered by the Police for providing information on William, he would have given it to the school for the Deaf and Blind!

Further cross-examined by Dr. de Silva, Mr. Sanmugam said that Premawathie, the patient he admitted to the hospital, was his wife's sister's daughter.

"That is your niece! Then why do you call her your servant? You have referred to her as servant several times in the course of your evidence?" asked Justice Gratiaen.

"She does the household work, My Lord," replied Mr. Sanmugam.

Justice Gratiaen pointed out that in his statement to Mr. Koelmeyer, Mr. Sanmugam had stated that Premawathie was a servant of the tenant. He asked what Mr. Sanmugam meant by that.

Mr. Sanmugam replied that he did not use that phrase. He said it might be an invention of Mr. Koelmeyer!

Dr. Colvin R. de Silva said, "I put it to you that you read the newspaper report at about 5 p.m. on October 17 that a monk had seen the boy, and thereafter sat at the typewriter at 5.30 p.m. to write the letter to the Police?"

"I was not influenced by what I saw in the newspaper," he replied.

He stressed that it was true that he had seen William at High Street on 9th October.

Mr. Sanmugam said that he knew that his information was the first and as such he was entitled to the 1000 rupees reward!

Another key witness for the prosecution was Mr. H.A. Pabilis, the 'Quickshaws' cab driver who took Sanmugam, Edmund and Premawathie to hospital on the 9th morning.

The log sheet of the driver showed the figure 9 indicating the hour, but the numbers indicating the minutes had been erased. That hire was from 32, High Street, Wellawatte, to the General Hospital.

Pabilis said that in the past they were not particular about marking the exact times. Since the murder of Mrs. Sathasivam, exact times of departure and arrival of all their trips were recorded.

Justice Gratiaen quipped, "In preparation for the next murder? I hope neither I nor the jury will be involved in the next case!"

Cross-examined by Dr. Colvin R. de Silva about the time, Pabilis said that his recollection was that the order for the cab was for 9.45 a.m.

He returned to High Street, Wellawatte from the hospital about 11 a.m. He said that he could say definitely that Sanmugam and Edmund were both away from Wellawatte between the hours of 9.45 a.m. and about 11 a.m., because they were with him in the car.

Dr. H.C. Uragoda was the admitting medical officer at the Colombo General Hospital, on 9th October 1951.

Giving evidence he referred to the routine in admitting patients to the Hospital.

He said on 9th October Premawathie was brought to the out patients' department of the hospital by Edmund who described himself as the patient's brother. The time of examination as indicated on the examination card was 10.20 a.m. Dr. Uragoda said that the patient was then admitted to Ward 27B, the ward of Dr. E. M. Wijerama, a consultant physician.

Dr. Wijerama, a distinguished Past President of the Sri Lanka Medical Association, the apex professional medical body in Sri Lanka, later donated his palatial house in Colombo 7 to the Association.

Mr. P. A. Edmund, a trader of High Street, Wellawatte, who accompanied Sanmugam and Premawathie to the hospital, giving evidence said that the 'Quickshaws' cab arrived about five minutes after William left his shop.

If, according to the 'Quickshaws' driver's record the car left his shop at 9.50 a.m., William must have come there about five minutes earlier.

He said that when the Police arrived at his shop he sent a message for Sanmugam through Sanmugam's servant who was at that time passing his shop. Sanmugam came in a rickshaw.

Mr. D.A. Dharmasena, a goldsmith of Wellawatte, giving evidence said that he was employed at Sirisena Jewellers, Station Road, Wellawatte.

He said that at about 10.30 a.m. on 9th October he saw William. He was able to fix the time by looking at the clock in his shop.

Justice Gratiaen then reminded Dharmasena that he had told the Police when they first came to his shop that William had come to his shop between 10 a.m. and 11.00 a.m. A fortnight later he had stated that William came at 10.35 a.m. He now fixed the time at 10.30 a.m. by reference to the clock!

Dharmasena continuing said that he issued receipts to his clients and kept carbon copies of it. Shown a carbon copy of a sale for 100 rupees, witness said that was the transaction with William. The original receipt was given to William.

Justice Gratiaen reminded the witness that on 19th October, he had told the Police that William took the money and went away and thereafter he wrote the receipt.

He knew that the 'thali' was worth 490 rupees. It did not occur to him that it might be stolen property.

He denied that he was trying to shield his brother Sirisena. Dharmasena insisted that it was he who bought the 'thalikody' and not his brother Sirisena.

Confronted with William's evidence that Sirisena came out of the barber's shop into Edmund's boutique and paid him 60 rupees, and then went to Station Road and brought the balance 40 rupees, Dharmasena said that he did not know about it!

He said he issued a receipt to William and he signed it as 'K.M. Martin, 35, Cross Road, Kirillapone'.

The false receipt prepared by Dharmasena was as follows:

"I the undersigned K.M. Martin do hereby certify that, I sold this day to D.C.A. Dharmasena of 54, Station Road, a 'thalikody' weighing 7 sovereigns for a sum of Rs. 490/= lawful currency of Ceylon."

The next witness, Mr. D.A. Sirisena, a 28-year-old man of Imbulgoda, said that on 9th October 1951, his brother Dharmasena bought a 'thalikody' cheap. He said that he had a look at it at about 2 p.m. the same day, before his brother melted it.

Sirisena denied that Edmund, Dharmasena and himself discussed what evidence they would give in that case.

The jewellers at Wellawatte, Dharmasena and Sirisena, maintained that it was Dharmasena who purchased the 'thalikody' at their shop whereas William had stated it was Sirisena who bought it at Edmund's boutique at High Street, Wellawatte.

This was a significant contradiction of key Crown witnesses.

Another witness summoned by the Crown was Arlishamy, a goldsmith, working also as a salesman at a textile shop at Panadura, owned by Mr. M. D. P. Dharmasena, who had a jewellery shop as well.

He said a boy, whom he had identified in the Magistrate's Court earlier as William, came to the shop at about 3.00 p.m. on 9th October to buy a sarong and a shirt. After he bought them he said he had some jewellery to sell. He said William took two gold bangles and a ring from his waist. William wanted 60 rupees for them.

Arlishamy then showed the jewellery to Mr. Dharmasena who offered 30 rupees for the articles, and gave him the money.

Arlishamy said at about 5 p.m. the same day they melted down the gold bangles. He said that they usually melt down the gold jewellery quickly because they required gold. He was shown a block of gold and he identified that it was the melted block of gold. He valued the gold at 200 rupees!

Cross-examined by Dr. Colvin R. de Silva, Arlishamy said Dharmasena later gave him 101 rupees as his share in the transaction!

He said as far as he remembered, William was dressed in a sarong and a banian. He pulled off his banian and wore the new shirt in the shop itself. William wrapped up the banian and took it away with him.

This evidence contradicted what William said in evidence about his banian earlier.

William had said he was in a hurry and wanted to go home before it became dark. Arlishamy said it was about 5.00 p.m. when the transaction was completed.

Replying to a query from Justice Gratiaen, Arlishamy admitted that in the Magistrate's Court he had stated that his suspicions had been aroused and that he had suggested to Dharmasena that the jewellery should be melted down.

Mr. M.D.P. Dharmasena, the next witness, who was the owner of the jewellery shop and a textile shop at Panadura, confirmed that at about 3 or 3.30 p.m. on 9th October, Arlishamy brought two bangles and a ring given to him by a boy. He put them in his drawer and gave Arlishamy 30 rupees. He said that he did not see William that day.

However, Mr. Dharmasena said that on 18th October when the Police brought William to his shop after his arrest, he identified him, contradicting his earlier statement!

Mr. V. Suppiah, the next witness called by the Crown stated that William came to his boutique at Panadura at about 3.30 p.m. or 4 p.m.

William drank a glass of water and gave him a parcel. William told him that the parcel contained a sarong and a shirt and asked him to keep it, saying that he would call for it after going to the junction.

Suppiah said on 18th October Police came to his boutique with William and took the parcel away.

Cross-examined by Dr. Colvin R. de Silva, Suppiah said that in the Magistrate's Court he might have stated that William came to his shop at 4.30 p.m. After giving his evidence he went back and thought about the probable time of William's arrival at Panadura, and he thought the time was about 3.30 p.m. or 4.00 p.m.

Replying to a question of Justice Gratiaen, Suppiah said that he came to Colombo in the car of the previous witness Dharmasena.

Justice Gratiaen remarked, "So by pure coincidence you both have changed the time of William's arrival at Panadura by an hour!"

Inspector M.W.B. Thiedeman, who was the Inspector of Police, Bambalapitiya, at the time of the murder of Mrs. Sathasivam, was summoned again by the Crown to give evidence.

Examined by Mr. T.S. Fernando, the Acting Solicitor-General, Mr. Thiedeman gave a description of the state of the kitchen, the garage and the bedroom at the Sathasivam residence on the day of the tragedy.

Replying to Mr. Fernando, who showed him a series of photographs of the kitchen and garage, Mr. Thiedeman said they were taken from different angles. He said in the kitchen, he found two 'chatties' (clay pots), one containing cut ash plantains and the other containing cut drumsticks.

He said he examined the half coconut he found in the kitchen. There was one strand of coconut in the 'chatty' below the coconut scraper and the half coconut was almost whole, indicating that the scraping had just been begun.

Shown a photograph of Mrs. Sathasivam's bedroom, Mr. Thiedeman said it was taken on the day of the murder.

"There was a white poplin shirt and a napkin there. I did not notice whether the napkin was stained," he said.

"On the table was a bowl with dirty water, indicating that someone had washed the hands after eating string hoppers. On a plate on the table were some string hoppers. They had fine strands quite unlike the ones usually available at boutiques. On the tea table were four fresh eggs," he continued.

Describing what he saw, Mr. Thiedeman said that the bedroom window was open with a half-blind.

"There was no sheet on the bed. There was a 'verti' on the bed, which was crumpled up. The bedroom did not appear to be disarranged. The room appeared to be unswept," he said.

Replying to a query by Justice Gratiaen, Mr. Thiedeman said that on that day he did not give as much significance to the bedroom as he gave to the garage and the kitchen.

He said he spoke to Podihamy and to one of the children as soon as he went to the house.

He then informed the Inspector-General of Police and all the other authorities about the murder.

Mr. Thiedeman said a crowd began to turn up near the residence from about 4 p.m.

Meanwhile the Government Analyst, Police Photographers and other Police Officers arrived.

He said that Mr. Sathasivam and the servant boy William were not in the house at the time.

"I started recording Podihamy's statement from about 5 p.m. in the kitchen. At about 7 p.m., I went upstairs and continued to record Podihamy's statement. I left No. 7, St. Alban's Place at about 11.30 p.m. I had then completed only Podihamy's statement," said Mr.

Thiedeman.

"When I left the house I took with me the mortar, the mirror and other items I found in the garage, and locked them up in the strong room at the Bambalapitiya Police Station. I then left for the Fort Police Station, where I saw Mr. Sathasivam with his mother and Mr. Kandiah," Mr. Thiedeman said.

Continuing his evidence he said then he went to No. 79, Horton Place at about 3.30 a.m. and recorded Mr. Haniffa's statement. He also found a travelling bag, which contained three letters signed by Yvonne. He took those letters into custody.

At this stage the Acting Solicitor-General produced those letters and read them out to Court.

The love letters, written by Yvonne Stevenson to Mr. Sathasivam referred generally to her anxiety to join him in Colombo and urged him to 'get cracking' with the divorce proceedings. The letters also referred to her financial position and to her finding a job in London.

On 10th October, the day after the murder, Mr. Thiedeman said that he visited No. 7, St. Alban's Place again and recorded the statement of Manjula.

When he was there Mr. Chanmugam came and pointed out to him a mark at the edge of the doorway to the garage. He said he however did not see any mark.

"I removed an accounts book kept by Mrs. Sathasivam and a diary. I also found a monitor's exercise book showing an entry of the date of engagement of William and two letters addressed to Mr. Sathasivam by her. She wrote one of them from Aden and the second letter was written from Ceylon," Mr. Thiedeman said. He then produced the two letters together with their copies.

Mr. Thiedeman further said that Mrs. Sathasivam's handbag was in the almirah and he had a look in it. But he did not make a detailed examination.

The following letter addressed to Mrs. A. Sathasivam, dated 8.10.1951, was found in her handbag. It was sent by 'Perera & Sons', a reputed firm of Confectioners, Bakers, Caterers and Dairymen in Colombo, established in 1902.

"Dear Madam,

This account refers to supplies for the last few months. The enormous increase in the cost of ingredients, the maintenance and collection of accounts has made it impossible for us to extend credit for a long time. According to our present practice your credit expires on the 25th instant.

We shall therefore, be grateful if you could send us a remittance before that date to maintain the continuity of your supplies.

Thanking you,

Yours faithfully,

Accountant"

The envelope this letter was sent was not found, perhaps not specifically looked for by the Police.

As this letter was received, read and kept in her handbag by Mrs. Sathasivam, if the time this letter was delivered to her residence was determined, it might have helped to ascertain the time of her death.

For example, if it was delivered at 10.15 a.m., William's story was palpably false, because Mrs. Sathasivam was then alive.

Mr. Thiedeman said that a list was made of Mrs. Sathasivam's jewellery, which was not removed that day. Apart from the jewellery, there were about 125 rupees in cash distributed in different compartments of the almirah.

In the middle shelf there were 12 new sarees. There were 4 others, which were worn about once.

In a cabinet in the dining room there were a number of silver cups. In the almirah there was a pair of binoculars and a set of EPNS ware.

Mr. Thiedeman said on 13th October he took into his charge a slip of paper found inside a pad on the telephone bracket. He gave it to the Examiner of Questioned Documents and it was later returned to his custody.

"After William's arrest, during the demonstration in the CID Office William showed how he held the hips of Mrs. Sathasivam. That was the only demonstration given there. At about 9 p.m. that night I took William to Mr. Rajendram's residence and Mr. Rajendram came in at about 10.45 p.m. He asked the Police Officers to leave his residence and we went on to the road and stayed in the car. At about 4 a.m. the following day William was handed over to fiscal's custody," Mr. Thiedeman said.

He further said that on 27th October, he went into the garage where Mrs. Sathasivam's body was and recovered a pearl dislodged from the ear stud from underneath the rocking horse. It was near the place where the head of Mrs. Sathasivam was.

The police guard to No. 7, St. Alban's Place was finally taken away after Mr. Sathasivam's mother came to live there.

Answering further questions by Mr. Fernando, he said "I contacted Professor Milroy Paul on the instructions of Mr. Koelmeyer, the Superintendent of Police, CID. I also contacted Professor M.V.P. Peiris on his instructions and gave the post-mortem report and the report of the Government Analyst."

Cross-examined by Dr. Colvin R. de Silva, the senior counsel for the defence, Inspector Thiedeman said he drew particular attention of the Registrar of Fingerprints to the mirror, the mortar and the body and expected the fingerprint expert to examine other objects in the garage for prints. He said he did not examine a shoebox, which was near the dead body.

He said he found a sliver of firewood near the main entrance to the garage.

Mr. Thiedeman was then questioned about the slip of paper he found inside a pad on the telephone bracket. The piece of paper with the telephone numbers was not produced in Court earlier. He said he was not responsible for not producing it in Court.

"I inquired about that piece of paper from Mr. Pathmanathan and I also showed it to Jothiswary to see whether she could identify the handwriting. That slip of paper constituted a record of telephone calls made from telephone number 81353. Mrs. Sathasivam was a very methodical woman and it was very likely that she kept a record of the telephone calls. On that there were calls made for nine days up to the day of her death."

"By the time I found that slip of paper, I knew of two telephone calls made that day from that telephone. I made investigations whether there had been any other telephone calls than the two made to 'Quickshaws' cabs. I inquired from Mr. Pathmanathan but not from Mrs. Pathmanathan," he said.

Mr. Thiedeman said, "At about 5.00 p.m. on 14th October, I inquired from Mr. O. P. Mack (Mrs. Sathasivam's lawyer) whether anybody telephoned the firm of Messrs. Mack and Mack on that morning from 81353. I questioned Mr. Mack in consequence of an independent piece of information I received from Sub-Inspector Johnson. After speaking to Mr. Mack, it might have been possible that the additional importance of the document struck me. As a result of the conversation I had with Mr. Mack, I felt that it could prove to be one of the calls made from that telephone on that day."

Questioned further by Dr. de Silva, Mr. Thiedeman agreed that this document was a material one.

Dr. de Silva asked, "Then why did not you produce it?"

"I am not conducting the Crown case," replied Mr. Thiedeman.

Mr. N.M.J. Rajendram, the then Colombo South Magistrate was summoned to give evidence regarding the magisterial inquiry into the Sathasivam murder case he held in 1951.

This evidence included the statement made by Mr. Sathasivam in the magisterial inquiry.

In the absence of the jury, Justice Gratiaen inquired whether there was a precedent for the whole of a statement recorded by a Magistrate being read to corroborate evidence.

Mr. T.S. Fernando, the Acting Solicitor-General said there was no precedent, but it could be done.

"Whatever the interpretation His Lordship gives to the word 'corroboration' they could not ignore Section 157 of the Evidence Ordinance and it is consistent with English law," replied Mr. Fernando.

Justice Gratiaen agreed with that submission and the jury was recalled.

He explained the ruling given in their absence regarding the evidence of Mr. Sathasivam in the Magistrate's Court. He said that the evidence would be admissible in its entirety and he would direct them how to approach that evidence.

The Crown Counsel then read the lengthy record of Mr. Sathasivam's evidence, and his evidence under cross-examination and re-examination, as recorded by the Colombo South Magistrate, Mr. Rajendram.

Mr. Ananda Pereira, Crown Counsel, read out the first portion of the recorded evidence and Mr. Douglas Jansze, Crown Counsel continued the recital with Mr. Rajendram in the witness box.

Mr. Rajendram said that he had taken down in long hand about 3,600 pages of statements of witnesses.

The evidence as recorded, also referred to an incident in the South Indian train in which Mr. and Mrs. Sathasivam and Mr. Sanmugam were travelling. After an argument with Mr. Sathasivam, he kicked Sanmugam out of the train compartment.

Continuing Mr. Ananda Pereira also read the evidence given by Mr. Sathasivam under cross-examination by Mr. Christie Seneviratne, Counsel for William.

Mr. Rajendram, examined by Mr. Ananda Pereira, Crown Counsel, said that on 19th October William was produced at his bungalow around 10.30 p.m. After he spoke to the Police Officers, he found William sleeping in the corner of his verandah!

He then cleared the bungalow of Police Officers and began to record William's statement at about 12 midnight.

Concluding his evidence, Mr. Rajendram said that on 9th April 1952, he committed Mr. Sathasivam and William to stand trial before the Supreme Court.

At this stage, the Foreman of the jury wished to know from Justice Gratiaen whether William's evidence as a witness in the Magistrate's Court should not be made available to the jury. He said they felt it would be better if they knew the whole evidence instead of parts of it.

Justice Gratiaen said that he was afraid it would not be in accordance with his ruling and his understanding of the law.

He said the defence was now seeking to point out that William's statement in the Court was inconsistent with the description he had given to the Magistrate. In view of that allegation, Justice Gratiaen said all the relevant statements made by William in regard to the manner of strangulation would be comprehensively placed before them.

Mr. A.P. Kandasamy, the Assistant Director of the Meteorological Department, was called by the Crown to give evidence. He submitted readings of room temperature on certain days. He said accurate readings were taken three-hourly but he interpolated reading for every half-hour by working out the values as requested by the Crown.

Dr. Colvin R. de Silva, cross-examining Mr. Kandasamy asked, "Will you admit that these half hour values are therefore a simple mathematical operation?"

Mr. Kandasamy agreed. He further said they were reasonable values and explained how the values were arrived at.

Answering a question by Justice Gratiaen, Mr. Kandasamy admitted that Meteorology was not such an exact science as astronomy.

Austin, the laundryman, Mrs. Foenander, and many other lay witnesses, scientists and medical specialists gave evidence for the prosecution.

Justice Gratiaen refused an application made by Mr. T.S. Fernando to call Professor C.J. Eliezer, the Professor of Mathematics of the University of Ceylon as a witness in the trial, as that witness was not called before the Magistrate's Court and as his name did not appear on the indictment.

Before the prosecution case was closed on 4th May 1953, Dr. Colvin R. de Silva applied to the Court to recall William. Mr. Fernando, the Acting Solicitor-General did not object.

Dr. de Silva asked William about what he told Piyadasa, a fellow remand prisoner.

"Is it a fact that you told Piyadasa, subsequent to your giving evidence in this Court, that this accused did not murder his wife but that you murdered her?" queried Dr. de Silva.

"I did not say so. Let him be brought here and questioned," William replied.

"Did you also add the statement to him: I will say I am guilty in my case?"

"I did not say so."

"Did you ever tell your brother Hendrick, I will plead guilty in my case?"

"I said if anybody comes to see me hereafter I will plead guilty."

"That is to say, you said you will state to Court that you had killed Mrs. Sathasivam?"

"I did not say that, but I said I would plead guilty," replied William.

"Guilty to what?" asked Justice Gratiaen.

"I said that I would plead guilty to abetment," answered William.

Dr de Silva asked, "Did Superintendent Crowe ask you whether you told prisoner Piyadasa that you killed Mrs Sathasivam?"

"No."

Dr. de Silva then asked whether he made a suicide attempt at Hulftsdorp jail a few days ago. William denied that and said an inquiry was also held on this, which was a 'frame up' at the instance of some party, who was antagonistic towards him.

William then complained to the Court that after the inquiry into the alleged suicide attempt he had been transferred to the Welikada jail where he had been harassed by Prison Officers more than in Hulftsdorp! He begged Justice Gratiaen to send him back to Hulftsdorp. Justice Gratiaen said that he had no power to issue a direction administratively to Prison authorities.

The defence then called B. Piyadasa, a 21-year-old unconvicted prisoner who was on remand for ten months. He said he had been in Hulftsdorp for six months. Prior to that he was at Welikada Prison. During that period he came to know William and became friends.

He said that there was an inquiry into an alleged attempt on the part of William to commit suicide. He was questioned by Mr. Crowe, the Superintendent of Prisons. At that inquiry he told Mr. Crowe about a conversation in the course of which William told him about the death of Mrs. Sathasivam.

William told him that while he was scraping coconut, Mrs. Sathasivam came to the kitchen and bending down asked him why the strands of the scraped coconut were so thick.

William said that he thought there might be a lot of money and jewellery in the house, so he hit the lady with his elbow and she appeared to be dazed. He then caught her by the neck and squeezed her. She appeared to be dead and then he stamped on her neck. Then he took the bunch of keys, which was tied to the corner of her saree and opened the almirah and took 7 rupees, which was there and went away.

Replying to a question by Justice Gratiaen, Piyadasa admitted having told Mr. Crowe that William told him that it was he who killed the lady and not Mr. Sathasivam, and that he would plead guilty and run away on his way to Court.

Mr. E.R. Crowe, Superintendent of Prisons, Hulftsdorp Jail was summoned next. Examined by Dr. Colvin R. de Silva, he said that he held an inquiry into an allegation of attempted suicide by William and he questioned Piyadasa.

Mr. Crowe said Piyadasa informed him that William told him that it was not Mr. Sathasivam who killed the lady but he (William) himself, and that he would plead guilty and run away on his way to Court. When he put the allegations made by Piyadasa, William denied that he had made such a statement.

The case for the prosecution was closed on the 9th June.

Before making his opening address for the defence, Dr. Colvin R. de Silva applied to court to recall Podihamy to elicit certain evidence. Justice Gratiaen agreed.

Examined by Dr. Colvin R. de Silva Podihamy said that she supervised the work of William when she was at home. She denied that Mrs. Sathasivam supervised the work of William.

She said she gave all that was in the almirah to Mr. Thiedeman. She said she found some sarees missing.

She admitted having stated that the necklace and the earrings to match were presents Mr. Sathasivam gave his wife after his return from England.

CHAPTER 6

EVIDENCE OF THE PROFESSOR OF FORENSIC MEDICINE

Evidence of medical and scientific expert witnesses played a decisive role in the Sathasivam murder trial. Except for Professor Sydney Smith, the Crown called all the other expert witnesses, though it did not accept some opinions expressed by Professor G. S. W. de Saram.

Mr. G. Webster, the Technician of the Department of Forensic Medicine, who went with Professor de Saram to the scene of Mrs. Sathasivam's death took photographs of the body and the scene.

He was summoned to give evidence and he produced 3 photographs he took under the direction of Professor de Saram.

Examined by Mr. T.S. Fernando, Mr. Webster said, "I developed the negatives and I made the films."

The photographs Mr. Webster took at the scene were,

(a) A photograph of the body of Mrs. Sathasivam as she lay on the garage floor

(b) A photograph of Mrs. Sathasivam showing the face, the neck and the upper portion of the saree of the body as she lay on the floor, and

(c) A photograph of the left foot and the ankle of Mrs. Sathasivam.

Mr. Webster was not cross-examined by Dr. Colvin R. De Silva.

Professor G. S. W. de Saram, Professor of Forensic Medicine, Faculty of Medicine, University of Colombo, who performed the post-mortem examination of Mrs. Sathasivam on the 10th of October, commenced his evidence on 8th April 1953

Professor de Saram was an experienced forensic pathologist who was the first Professor of Forensic Medicine of the University of Colombo. Before accepting the post of Professor, he had served as the Chief Judicial Medical Officer, Colombo.

Examined by Mr. T.S. Fernando, Professor G.S.W. de Saram said that Sir Richard Aluvihare, the Inspector General of Police, came to his residence on 9th October afternoon and suggested that he should visit the scene and perform the post-mortem examination.

"Was any suggestion made that the Judicial Medical Officer, Colombo, Dr. P.S. Gunawardene should be associated with you in the post-mortem examination?" queried Mr. Fernando.

"Yes."

"Were you agreeable to that suggestion?"

"No. I said that I would rather not work with Dr. P.S. Gunawardene. Sir Richard agreed to that suggestion," said Professor de Saram.

Answering further questions, Professor de Saram said that he visited the scene of death at 5.55 p.m. and entered the scene through the outer door of the garage.

He said he noticed Mrs. Sathasivam's body lying on its back with the feet towards the inner wall of the garage.

The feet were separated from each other by a distance of sixteen inches, as depicted in the photograph. Her face was turned towards the outer door of the garage and slightly upwards, which was towards the right side of the body.

Professor de Saram said that Mrs. Sathasivam was dressed in a purple, white and red checked voile saree.

In the post-mortem report this is how he described the dress of Mrs. Sathasivam.

"Extending down to just below the knees was an underlying pink petticoat with its upper part as a white bodice fastened with press-studs in front. A portion of the saree draped the left shoulder and was carried round the right side of the chest, and tucked in on the left waist where the saree was secured with a cord. The saree was also secured in front with a safety pin."

He noted that there were two plastic bangles worn over the right wrist and three plastic bangles and one gold bangle over the left. There was a pair of gold brilliant ear-studs on both ears.

He described that the hair was in a single plait lying loosely under the neck and left shoulder.

Professor de Saram said he found 18 external injuries on Mrs. Sathasivam's body.

Copies of the diagrams of the injuries were handed over to Justice Gratiaen, jurors and the counsel of both sides. In the diagrams, he had marked external injuries in green and internal injuries in red.

Professor de Saram described each injury and gave his opinion as to how each one was caused. He explained this during the cross-examination by the defence counsel Dr. Colvin R. de Silva more than in the examination-in-chief, because Dr. de Silva requested more detailed interpretations.

The first three injuries Professor de Saram described were on the lower jaw. They were abrasions.

Abrasions are superficial injuries damaging the epidermis or the outermost layer of the skin.

They can be of three types.

(a) Scratch abrasions: These are caused by moving pointed objects, such as nails, pins, needles etc., over the skin, or the skin moving over such an object.

(b) Imprint abrasions: These are caused when skin comes into contact with blunt objects, with no relative movement between the skin and the object. They are caused by objects such as nails, sole of feet, sole of a shoe, or a bumper of a vehicle in a road traffic accident.

(c) Grazed abrasions: These are caused when a blunt object with a broad surface comes into contact with skin, with relative movement of either or both. They are seen when a person falls on the ground and injures knees or elbows, or when a person is assaulted with a brick or similar rough object.

"By abrasion you mean a scratch mark?" asked Mr. Fernando.

"Yes, it was the rubbing off of the superficial layer of the skin," Professor de Saram explained.

Professor de Saram then demonstrated the exact site of each injury on a peon of the Court.

Injury number 1 was an abrasion, 1¾ inch x ½ inch over left lower jaw extending to left from middle of chin along its lower border. (See Figure 10. Page 472)

This was an imprint or pressure abrasion.

Injury number 2 was situated ½ inch above the middle of injury number 1. It was a linear superficial abrasion, ¼ inch long. It was lying obliquely.

Injury number 3 was situated ½ inch behind and ¼ inch above the rear end of abrasion number 1. It was another abrasion, 2 inches long x ½ inch wide, extending horizontally forwards from the left angle of the lower jaw. This was also a pressure abrasion.

Professor de Saram said that the soft cheek over this abrasion was depressed. Fragments of fine black powder were found along it and on the jaw below it.

Professor de Saram said he scraped it off with his fingernails and gave it to the Government Analyst. "He found this was coconut fluff," said Professor de Saram.

Mr. Fernando asked, "Do you remember that there was a heap of coconut husks in the garage, to the left of the lady, as shown in one photograph?" (See Figure 9.Page 472)

Realising the importance of this question asked by Mr. Fernando, Justice Gratiaen queried whether the presence of the coconut husks in the garage might explain the fine dark powder on the injury.

"I scarcely think so. There was one big bit of fluff that I took from under the jaw and that bit was firmly adherent and I found it difficult to detach it," replied Professor de Saram, indicating the spot he took it from.

Professor de Saram said injuries 1 and 3 could have been caused if a hard, heavy object had been placed against the face.

The next six external injuries (numbers 4 to 9) were on the neck.

Injury number 4 was an abrasion, 1¼ inch long x 1/8 inch wide, consisting of some irregular scratch marks lying obliquely over the right side of the voice box. (See Figure 11. Page 473)

They were more or less a number of interrupted marks.

"These injuries were undoubtedly fingernail marks," said Professor de Saram. His opinion was that these marks were caused by the middle, ring and little fingers of the left hand of the assailant, who was strangling Mrs. Sathasivam from behind, while his index finger was pushing up the chin.

"The top-most mark was probably caused by the middle finger. This could also be an injury caused by Mrs. Sathasivam's own right thumb trying to release the strangler's grip," he said.

Injury number 5 was situated 1 inch to the left of the lower end of injury number 4. It was an abrasion, ½ inch x 1/8 inch wide, consisting of three linear scratch marks, 1/8 inch long and a localised spot, 1/16 inch in diameter.

Answering Justice Gratiaen, he said these were 3 linear scratch marks constituted one abrasion.

He said that the concavity of these marks faced outwards.

Injury number 6 was an abrasion, ¼ inch in diameter, situated 1 inch below the middle of the left lower jaw.

"This was caused by the index finger of the right hand of the assailant," said Professor de Saram.

Injury number 7 was a superficial abrasion, 1/8 inch x 1/16 inch on the left mastoid region (the bony prominence behind the ear). Professor de Saram said this was situated immediately behind Mrs. Sathasivam's ear stud on the left ear.

Professor de Saram said that this injury could have been caused if the ear stud had been pressed back.

The front part of this ear stud was bent and the centre stone was missing. It was found in the garage later, where Mrs. Sathasivam's body was.

Injury number 8 was situated on the left side of the neck, 1 inch from the midline. These were three abrasions, 1/16 inch, 1/16 inch and ¼ inch in diameter, at intervals of ¾ inch and 1½ inches and placed in a line.

He said these were caused by the middle, ring and little fingers of the right hand of the assailant. He thought the hand then shifted closer to the side of the voice box to cause injury number 5.

Professor de Saram said that injuries 4, 5, 6 and 8 were in the region of the throat and could have been nail marks.

Then he described the rest of the external injuries.

Injury number 9 constituted several parallel linear abrasions 2 inches to 1 inch long over the lower part of the front of the neck. Professor de Saram said these injuries were not clearly visible in the photographs.

Injury number 10 was an abrasion, 1 inch x ½ inch, over the middle of the left collar bone.

Injury number 11 was an abrasion, 1 inch x ½ inch, over the front of the left shoulder.

Professor de Saram said the above two injuries were covered by the saree.

The next two injuries were on the left hand.

Injury number 12 was a rectangular abrasion, ¼ inch x 3/8 inch, over inner aspect of the top of left hand, overlying the base of second metacarpal bone. (See Figure 12. Page 473)

Injury number 13 was an abrasion, 1/8 inch in diameter, over the inner aspect of the left wrist.

These two injuries were caused, according to Professor de Saram, when the assailant was removing bangles and trying to remove the remaining gold bangle on Mrs. Sathasivam's wrist.

He said he also had considerable difficulty in removing this bangle at the post-mortem.

Injury number 14 was an abrasion, 1/8 inch long x 1/16 inch wide, over the back of the distal end of the first segment of the right thumb. (See Figure 12. Page 473)

Injury number 15 was also an abrasion, 3/8 inch x ¼ inch, over the outer aspect of right elbow with a corresponding contusion 1/8 inch in diameter. It was ¼ inch deep. Professor de Saram said this was probably caused when Mrs. Sathasivam struck some object when she struggled to save herself.

Explaining what a contusion (bruise) was Professor de Saram stated, "In simple language, a contusion is a rupture or tearing of the deeper tissues. These ruptures are usually associated with bleeding into the part affected. The superficial tissues at surface are not torn. The bleeding is as a result of the rupture of small blood vessels. Bleeding takes place only in a place where there are small vessels."

Injury number 16 was an abrasion, 3/8 inch x ¼ inch over the inner middle top of right big toe. (See Figure 13. Page 474)

This injury was important because of the dark material adherent to feet.

Professor de Saram said "I observed some dark material adherent to the balls of the toes of the right foot as well as the soles, toes, and heel of the left foot. The sole of the left foot was very much darker than the sole of the right foot." (See Figure 1. Page 467)

"All the toes of the left foot were black and it has also extended to the big toe," replied Professor de Saram answering a query from Justice Gratiaen.

Professor de Saram further explained that the dark material adherent to the ball of the foot came off as a crust. "It came off in a crust when I inserted a piece of paper between the skin and the material. The whole thing came off quite easily as a crust. I did this at the scene," he said. He said he gave this, as well as some particles from the right foot, to the Government Analyst, Mr. Chanmugam.

Professor de Saram said that the samples taken from both feet corresponded with the samples Mr. Chanmugam took by way of swabs from the floor of the kitchen.

Injury number 17 was a superficial abrasion ¼ inch in diameter over the top front of the right leg ½ inch below the lower border of the kneecap.

Injuries 12 to 17, according to Professor de Saram, could have been caused by contact with a localised hard surface during the struggle.

"Injuries 16 and 17 might have been caused if Mrs. Sathasivam was kicking about with her right leg during strangling, striking an object in front."

He said there were many objects in the kitchen that could have caused these injuries.

Injury number 18 constituted several abrasions, 1/16 inch to 1/8 inch in diameter, over the back of the chest between the shoulder blades covering an area 2¼ inches in diameter. Underlying this and extending downwards between the shoulder blades from the neck, was a contusion 4 ¼ inches x 3 inches wide.

This injury was unique because this was the only injury found on the back of Mrs. Sathasivam's body.

Professor de Saram thought it was possible that the injury number 18 could have been caused if Mrs. Sathasivam, who was in a sitting position, had been held by the hair and the front of the neck, brought down on the floor with some force with her face upwards.

These were grazed or imprint abrasions.

As readers will find later there was another, perhaps the most likely explanation, given by Sir Sydney Smith, the pathologist called by the defence.

Professor de Saram said apart from the 18 injuries, he also observed, as mentioned earlier, a dark material adherent to the balls of the toes of the right foot, as well as the sole, toes and heel of the left foot.

Shown a photograph of the soles of the feet of Mrs. Sathasivam, Professor de Saram said, "The sole of the left foot was very much darker than the sole of the right foot."

Professor de Saram said he found eleven internal injuries.

Internal injury number 1, corresponding to external injuries 1 and 3, were contusions, 1½ inches diameter and 2 inches diameter. (See Figure 14. Page 474)

Professor de Saram said that this injury was probably produced in the same process as external injuries.

Injury number 2 was a deep contusion, 3 inches x 2 inches x 1 inch, situated over the lower part of the front of the neck.

"It was a fairly big contusion and could have been caused by the pressure of a foot over the neck," Professor de Saram said.

The next two injuries were on the tongue. Professor de Saram said that Mrs. Sathasivam biting her own tongue caused them. It is commonly seen in cases of asphyxia by strangulation. (See Figure 15. Page 475)

Professor de Saram described injury number 3 as three slightly semi-lunar shape lacerations placed in a line on the front third of the left border of the tongue. 3/8 inch below these lacerations and parallel to them were three similar lacerations all forming a horseshoe pattern. Each of them was 1/16 inch deep with surrounding and underlying contusions. Laceration is a split or a tear of a tissue.

Injury number 4 was a contusion, ¼ inch in diameter, over the tip of the tongue, immediately to the right of the midline.

Internal injuries 5 to 8 were on the neck.

Professor de Saram had brought a model of the throat to Court, which was bigger than the normal size of the throat, showing its parts and he described the parts of the throat referring to this model.

He described injury number 5 as two bilateral contusions near the free margin of the epiglottis at its middle. Each measured 1/16 inch in diameter.

This injury was in the region of the voice box.

"The epiglottis," explained Professor de Saram, "Is the lid which extends upwards from the voice box and that lid gets shut when food passes thus preventing the food getting into the larynx." Larynx is the opening of the respiratory passages.

Injury number 6 was a contusion behind the voice box. It was 1 ¼ inch in length and one inch wide, placed vertically. It was ¼ inch deep.

Injury number 7 was a contusion surrounding the vocal chords and the sides of the voice box on each side, situated on the inner aspect. It measured ¾ inch x ½ inch, and 1/16 inch deep with fractures of both upper horns of the thyroid cartilage. The hyoid bone, which was half an inch above the voice box in the neck, was intact. (See Figure 11. Page 473)

Professor de Saram had a normal size model of the neck cartilages showing the fractures in the voice box.

Injury number 8 was a contusion over the front and sides of the voice box and base of the tongue 2 inches x 2 inches x ¼ inch deep. This contusion continued in a downward direction over the front of the windpipe for a further 2 inches x 1½ inches across.

"This was a very extensive injury," said Professor de Saram.

He described the injury number 9 as petechial haemorrhages on the inner surface of the windpipe and bronchi, with congestion.

Petechial or pinpoint haemorrhages are characteristically seen in deaths from asphyxiation, for example, from manual strangulation or strangulation by ligature or hanging.

Injury number 10 was a deep contusion of scalp, extending horizontally backwards from the outer angle of the right eye to 3

½ inches behind the right ear. This involved the lower right temple, the upper half of the external ear and the rear right side of the scalp. Total length of this injury was 6 inches. It was 1 inch wide in front and 2 ¼ inches wide behind. It was ½ inch deep. (See Figure 14. Page 474)

Professor de Saram said he had to cut deep into the scalp to observe this injury and it did not correspond to any external injury he described earlier.

It is the practice of forensic pathologists to make cuts into the soft tissues when dissecting a body to look for deep injuries.

Professor de Saram thought that a blow with a club could have caused this injury.

Professor de Saram said when he went into the garage, he saw a piece of firewood and he thought it could have caused this injury.

He said that the blowpipe found in the kitchen was a very heavy weapon. Only a very light blow with it could have caused this injury. He said it was improbable that the blowpipe caused it.

Internal injury number 11, the only internal injury on the back, was also a deep contusion, 1½ inches in diameter over middle of left shoulder blade. (See Figure 12. Page 473)

This injury was also found after cutting into the deep tissue and there was no corresponding external injury.

Professor de Saram thought that the external injury number 18 and the above injury were compatible with the body being carried and knocking against the lintel of the door or against the plaster that surrounds the door, as the door leading from the kitchen to the garage was only 18 inches at maximum width.

Professor de Saram said that all the injuries were 'ante-mortem', meaning that they were caused before death.

"Mrs. Sathasivam's height was 5 foot and 3¼ inches. She weighed 90 pounds (approximately 41 kilo grams)," Professor de Saram said.

To compare Mrs. Sathasivam's height with that of William's, Professor de Saram was requested to measure the height of William. He was 5 feet 6 inches. Professor de Saram said he measured William's height in October 1951 also.

"He has grown 2 inches since I examined him," said Professor de

Saram.

Continuing further Professor de Saram said Mrs. Sathasivam's eyes were dark brown, cornea was clear and the pupils were semi-dilated.

Professor de Saram explained that in life, the pupils of the eye contract and dilate according to the availability of light, and soon after death, pupils are dilated. (See Figures 16 and 17. Page 475)

"After death, the first thing that happens is that the pupil dilates and then it gradually contracts and dilates again," he said. The contraction is due to rigor of pupillary or iris muscles and dilatation is due to passing off of rigor.

Professor de Saram explaining the pupillary changes remarked that it gave an indication of time of death, which he did not solely rely upon. He emphasized that he did not base his conclusion of time of death on that alone.

Professor de Saram said he found an area of haemorrhage (bleeding), ¼ inch in diameter at the inner angle of right eyeball, with pinpoint haemorrhages over eyelids of both sides.

Professor de Saram said he turned the eyelids up to look for pinpoint haemorrhages. In fact he has noted this at the scene of death. This was the result of the rupture of blood vessels, a feature observed when pressure is applied on the neck.

Mrs. Sathasivam's head hair was black and 30 inches long. Her tongue was normal, except for the injuries described earlier. She had all 32 teeth and there was no peculiarity in them.

Professor de Saram said that he also noted at the scene that 'rigor mortis' was present in the face neck, jaws and extremities. It was 'setting' in the fingers and toes.

'Rigor mortis' is the stiffening of muscles with a shortening of the fibres that occurs after death. Every muscle in the body, including iris muscles of the eye, undergoes rigor. This process is due to the chemical changes that take place in muscles due to lack of oxygen to muscle cells after death. The stiffness usually passes off in 12 to 18 hours when muscle putrefaction sets in.

Professor de Saram said that hypostasis was also present on the body of Mrs. Sathasivam at 5.55 p.m.

"Hypostasis is the discolouration of or staining which occurs after death. The blood being still fluid tracks down to the most dependent parts of the body and produce discolouration," explained Professor de Saram.

After death, blood obeys the law of gravity while it is liquid, and settles into the lowest placed blood vessels in the body causing post-mortem hypostasis or 'lividity'. The heavier red blood cells have a tendency to settle first, imparting a deeper colour to the affected parts.

Mrs. Sathasivam's fingertips were blue indicating 'cyanosis', a characteristic feature of asphyxial deaths.

Professor de Saram has noted that Mrs. Sathasivam's mouth and ears were normal. There were no injuries or natural disease in the anus or sexual organs externally.

Describing the neck injuries, Professor de Saram said that the hyoid bone, which was half an inch above the voice box, was intact. However, the upper horns of the thyroid cartilages were fractured as described earlier.

There were no injuries to the cervical (neck) vertebrae.

After describing the external examination of Mrs. Sathasivam's body in detail, Professor de Saram explained the findings of internal examination.

He said that her scalp was normal and the bones of the skull were thicker than normal. It was about 5/16 inch thick.

The membranes and sinuses of the brain were normal but the brain substance was congested. 'Congestion' is also a feature of asphyxial deaths. Lateral ventricles of the brain had clear fluid. Blood vessels of the brain were normal.

In the chest, Professor de Saram found that the soft parts covering the chest cavity, bones of the chest and the position of chest organs were normal.

In the heart, there were a few small sub-endocardial haemorrhages (bleeding) in the left ventricle. These haemorrhages, found in the inner lining of the cavity of the left heart, is also a feature of asphyxia.

There was slight brown atrophy of the heart. "Atrophy means this. When people are emaciated, poor in health, the heart is deprived of its fatty covering, and then it appears smaller and brownish in colour," explained Professor de Saram.

Rest of the heart, the coronary vessels and the large blood vessels of Mrs. Sathasivam were normal.

Professor de Saram said that the lungs showed sub-pleural pinpoint haemorrhages. There was some sub-pleural emphysema. There were areas of collapse and haemorrhages in the substance of lungs.

Pleura is the outer coating of the lungs. Subpleural pinpoint haemorrhages and haemorrhages in the lungs were also signs of asphyxial deaths. Emphysema according to Professor de Saram was dilatation of the air vesicles or chambers when there is difficulty in breathing, as in asphyxial deaths.

"I found fine white froth with an odour, which I took to be garlic in the wind passages, and in the lung substance. I also found white froth with an odour of garlic on dissection," Professor de Saram said.

The presence of the odour of garlic was a very significant finding, indicating that Mrs. Sathasivam consumed garlic just before her death.

The gullet (oesophagus) was normal. (See Figure 18. Page 476)

In the abdominal cavity, the position of the abdominal organs, the diaphragm and the vertebrae were normal. The liver was congested. The gall bladder contained about half an ounce of dark fluid bile.

The spleen measured 4 ¾ inches x 3 inches x ½ inch and weighed 4 ounces (168 grammes). This was a normal finding.

The stomach was congested and had a few pinpoint haemorrhages. It contained 10 ounces (284 millilitres) of fluid, pieces of string-hopper and coconut with odour of coconut.

Professor de Saram said he put the stomach contents into a measuring cylinder. After an hour he looked at the sediment that had come down to one third of the volume.

"The stomach contents pass first into the small intestines through the duodenum. Between the duodenum and the stomach there is a muscle called pyloric sphincter. That is a muscle which contracts and expands," explained Professor de Saram.

He said that the small intestines (duodenum, jejunum, and ileum) contained semi-digested bits of string-hopper, except for the last three inches at its lower end. Professor de Saram said he cut the small intestines at different levels when they were still in the abdomen so that the contents would not get mixed due to movement. The food was continuous from the stomach.

The large intestines (colon) contained faeces.

Mr. Fernando asked Professor de Saram whether he examined the intestines after they were removed from the body.

"No," replied Professor de Saram.

"In the body itself?"

"Yes."

Professor de Saram explained that the technique he adopted was to check up the distance to which the food has tracked along it, while the intestines were there still in the abdomen. He said once intestines were removed, food could get displaced due to movement. Therefore, he said he cut the intestines open at different levels and examined them when they were still inside the body.

The kidneys were congested and the bladder was empty. The blood vessels of the abdomen were normal.

Professor de Saram stated that there was an old tear at the mouth of the womb and the uterine cavity contained about one drachm (one eighth of an ounce or about three and a half millilitres) of yellowish fluid material. The size of the uterus was 2 ¾ inches x 2 ½ inches x ¾ inch. Both ovaries contained cysts.

The vagina and mouth of womb had thick whitish material adherent to it. "A good deal of that whitish material, I believe, was seminal fluid but there may have been other natural secretions," he said.

Professor de Saram said he gave his opinion that Mrs. Sathasivam's death was due to "Asphyxia from manual strangulation". 'Asphyxia' is a state in which body lacks oxygen because of some mechanical interference with the process of breathing.

He said that he examined Mr. Sathasivam, who was arrested on the day of the murder, at 8.35 p.m. in his laboratory in the Faculty of Medicine, University of Colombo, when he was produced by the Police.

He said he noted that Mr. Sathasivam's fingernails were 1/16th of an inch long.

"I may have measured one or two perhaps, but not every one because they were more or less of the same length," he explained.

"He was not smelling of alcohol and so far as I can say he was rational," he said.

Professor de Saram said he did not measure the height of Mr. Sathasivam.

"When I saw him I took him to be taller than Mrs. Sathasivam."

"We can have him measured now," Justice Gratiaen suggested.

"The consent of Mr. Sathasivam will have to be taken before that is done," remarked Mr. Fernando.

Dr. Colvin R. de Silva said that in the Magistrate's Court when the Crown Counsel desired that Mr. Sathasivam's height be taken, he said that Mr. Sathasivam's consent could be needed but if his consent was taken he would have no objection.

"The retort was then given that the Crown did not need it and Mr. Sathasivam could have it taken if he so desired it. I may state that it has been our position all along and it is our position now that Mr. Sathasivam will be quite willing to permit his height to be taken with his consent," said Dr. Colvin R. de Silva.

Justice Gratiaen remarked rather sarcastically, "I think we can take it that he has not grown since then!"

Professor de Saram then measured the height of Mr. Sathasivam with his shoes on.

He was 5 feet 9 inches in height.

Professor de Saram said that on the 19th of October he examined William and got Mr. Webster to take photographs of the injuries of William. (See Figures 4, 19 and 20. Pages 468 and 477)

He described William's injuries as follows:

1. Over middle of left cheek bone, ¾ inch below the outer angle of the left eye, a triangular white mark with a light scab adherent to lower angle. Its base was 3/32 inch wide and the total length was 3/32 inch. The triangle was lying with the base upwards.

2. An almost vertical white mark, 3/8 inch long x 1/16 inch broad, situated ¼ inch below and 3/32 inch in front of injury number 1.

3. An oblique white mark, ¼ inch long x 1/16 inch wide, situated 3/8 inch below the lower end of injury number 2. It was directed

downwards and forwards to the left angle of the mouth. Over the upper two thirds of this mark was a superficial raw surface 1/16 inch in diameter.

4. A very slight white mark 3/16 inch long and 1/16 inch broad, situated ½ inch behind and ¼ inch below the rear end of injury number 3.

5. A scab area, 3/16 inch long x 1/8 inch wide, situated on the inner border of the left forearm, 2 inches above the inner prominence of the left wrist.

6. A white mark, 3/16 inch long x 1/16 inch wide, over the middle of front of left forearm.

7. A white mark, 3/16 inch long x 1/8 inch wide, lying parallel to and 3/16 inch internal to injury number 6. The upper third of this mark was red and depressed for about 1/16 inch.

8. A horizontal abrasion, 1¼ inches long x 1/16 inch wide over right loin, 3 inches to right of mid rear of body and ¾ inch above the upper edge of the hip bone.

He explained that William had seven injuries (Numbers 1 to 7), which were healing.

"They were consistent with having been received on 9th October," Professor de Saram said.

"Injury number 8 was quite different in point of age. I questioned him and he said that a Police officer pulled him by his waist string and it had cut him. It was quite consistent with that explanation. It was a recent injury," replied Professor de Saram.

He further said that William's finger nails were short and the nails on the left hand appeared cut and those on the right hand appeared bitten.

Mr. T.S. Fernando concluded his examination-in-chief on 9th April morning.

When a forensic pathologist gives evidence in a murder case where he has performed the post-mortem examination, it is customary that the prosecution requests him to produce the post-mortem report and get it marked as a production.

But at the trial, Mr. T. S. Fernando, the Acting Solicitor-General did not mark Professor de Saram's post-mortem report when he gave evidence!

Dr. Colvin R. de Silva began his cross-examination of Professor de Saram with the question, "You were called in this case, if I understood you all right, by special invitation of the Police authorities?"

"Yes," replied Professor de Saram.

"The offence in respect of which the post-mortem examination required to be conducted had been committed within the Colombo Judicial Medical Officer's area?"

"That is so."

"On this occasion when you were invited to conduct this post-mortem examination did a representative of the authorities visit you for that purpose to ask you to do this? I want to know how the invitation was conveyed to you, and by whom, and where?"

"When the message came through that Mrs. Sathasivam had been killed, I was seated in the Criminal Investigation Department (CID) Headquarters in front of Mr. Edwards, Assistant Superintendent of Police (ASP), who is in this Court. I believe Mr. Edwards said, 'Yes, he is here' and I was informed that my services might be required."

"I thereupon telephoned Mr. Webster to have all the apparatus ready. Shortly after that I was informed that it was not coming through just then, and there was some talk of two officers being deputed to carry out the post-mortem examination, so I understood, the Judicial Medical Officer and myself. I then pleaded that whoever it was it did not matter, but to get the Medical Officer there as quickly as possible."

"I said at that time I did not agree to two people and that I would stand down and it was quite all right by me. I thereupon cancelled the order to Mr. Webster, and went home. Then the Inspector-General of Police Sir Richard Aluvihare, accompanied by Mr. Cherubim, the Crown Counsel came to my residence. Perhaps Mr. Koelmeyer and Mr. Edwards also followed and there the Inspector-General of Police asked me to do the post-mortem," said Professor de Saram.

"Your advice was that the medical examination should be as prompt as possible?" asked Dr. de Silva.

"That is so."

"And that it did not matter whether you were asked to do it

or the Judicial Medical Officer, Colombo, so long as it was done promptly?"

"That is so."

"I want to ask you frankly, would you have undertaken to do this post-mortem examination at the invitation of the Police, if you had the slightest suspicion that the Police would at any time seek to challenge the accuracy or care or efficiency of your work?" asked Dr. de Silva.

"No."

"Why the Police authorities themselves chose in this case to get your services specially for a post-mortem examination instead of the usual service of their Judicial Medical Officer was not a matter in which you interfered?"

"No. May I say that there was a directive issued by the late Prime Minister instructing the Police, as I was a trained person with all the facilities for investigation of crime, all important cases should be handed over to me, but that direction I think has not been fully implemented," Professor de Saram said.

He further said that Sir Sydney Smith trained him for 10 to 11 months at the Edinburgh University, Scotland.

"I did work in London in the Scotland Yard Laboratories and I also attended some post-mortem examinations with Dr. Keith Simpson. I also went to Cairo and worked at the Institute there for about six months," he said.

Dr. de Silva then referred to the 'Post-mortem Examination Form' provided by the Department of Health and asked whether the section "Opinion and the reasons on which it is grounded" in this form means doctor's opinion as to the cause of death.

"That is so."

"Every Medical Officer who conducts a post-mortem examination, if he can give, always gives the cause of death as he considers it, on the basis of his post-mortem examination?"

"That is so."

"What was your opinion of the cause of death?"

"I am of the opinion that death was due to asphyxia from manual strangulation. I gave this as my opinion in my post-mortem report and I have given that as my opinion from that day up to this."

"Do you seek in any manner to modify or change this opinion?"

"No," replied Professor de Saram.

Dr de Silva then questioned Professor de Saram regarding the age of William.

"Were you given any idea before your post-mortem examination of what was believed to be the likely age of William?"

"No, I do not remember. Not as far as I can remember."

"Until yesterday, what age were you having for William, as at the date 9th October 1951?"

"About 15 or 16 years."

"That is what you had been made to understand was his age?"

"I believe so."

"Do you know now that the birth certificate of William has been referred to, and that we know his age now?"

"No. I do read the papers at times. I did not gather that information from the papers."

Dr. de Silva told Professor de Saram, "Please accept it from me that William according to his birth certificate, we are informed by the Crown, was born on the 5th of December 1932. Please take that from me for your future considerations. On that footing as on the 9th of October 1951, he would have been a bare six weeks less than completing 19 years of age?"

"Yes."

"Do you know at what age young men are recruited to the Army in our country? Do you know that 18 is the age of recruitment for the Army?"

"I did not know that," replied Professor de Saram.

"Would you say as a medical man in this country, in the village, at 19 a person would be considered a young man?"

"Yes," Professor de Saram replied.

Answering further questions from Dr. de Silva, Professor de Saram said that soon after the post-mortem the Coroner asked him to address his mind to the manner of strangulation and the question of the time of death.

Professor de Saram said that at the inquest, he informed the

Coroner that Mrs. Sathasivam was strangled between 10.00 a.m. and 11.30 a.m.

He said he had discussions with both Crown Counsel who appeared in the Magistrate's Court, Mr. Cherubim and Mr. Thamotheram, about two to three occasions. On one occasion, they were accompanied by the Inspector-General of Police (IGP).

Professor de Saram said he went to the Police Headquarters and had a discussion with the IGP, the two Crown Counsel, Mr. Chanmugam, the Government Analyst, Mr. Koelmeyer of the CID and one or two other Police Officers. Later, he had another consultation with Mr. Crossette-Tambiah, the then Solicitor-General and some Police Officers.

Dr. de Silva further questioned Professor de Saram about other doctors who gave evidence in the Magistrate's Court. He asked whether they contacted him before he gave evidence.

"Professor Milroy Paul spoke to me on 14th October 1951 (that was 5 days after the murder) when I was just coming out after giving evidence at the inquest. He asked about the food in the stomach. I just told him there was food in the stomach."

"On the first day I gave evidence at the Magistrate's Court, Professor Paul spoke to me again. He did so at the Grand Oriental Hotel after the farewell dinner to Professor Collumbine. He wanted to discuss with me something about delayed death after strangulation. I did not discuss with him," Professor de Saram said.

Continuing the cross-examination, Dr. de Silva asked, "You and you alone examined the body of Mrs. Sathasivam from a medical point of view?"

"'That is so."

"A doctor conducting a post-mortem examination observes much more than he notes down in detail?"

"That is so."

"The fact that you have seen the injury makes a difference to your judgement as to whether it was due to a fall or a blow or to friction?"

"That is so."

"When you go for a post-mortem, if the body has not been shifted I believe the doctor is expected to observe the conditions and surroundings in which the body is lying?"

"That is so."

"How many hundreds or thousands of post-mortems must you have done in your career as a doctor?"

"Nearly or over 10,000," replied Professor de Saram.

These questions were asked by Dr Colvin R. de Silva to indicate to the jury the qualifications and expertise of Professor de Saram.

Also it showed the jury that Professor de Saram was in a better position to interpret injuries of Mrs. Sathasivam than other doctors who saw only the photographs.

Professor de Saram, at the request of Dr. de Silva, again demonstrated Mrs. Sathasivam's neck injuries on a peon. He explained in detail how each injury on Mrs. Sathasivam's neck was caused.

During the demonstration he showed how the fingers of the assailant made the marks on the neck of Mrs. Sathasivam. He also placed the ball of his left foot on the left big toe of the victim. (See Figure 21. Page 478)

"In the position in which you placed your left foot over the left big toe of the victim, it pressed on the left big toe of the victim?" Dr. de Silva queried.

"Yes."

"If the person who was bare-footed had kitchen dirt on the soles of the foot, would you expect that kitchen dirt and any portion of it, to transfer itself to the upper portion of the big toe of the victim?"

"Yes."

"On the upper portion of the big toe did you find any dirt?"

"There was," replied Professor de Saram.

Professor de Saram said if the assailant were wearing shoes he would expect injuries on the left big toe of the victim.

He said the two stains found on the saree, according to the Government Analyst, contained matter consistent with their having come from the floor of the kitchen. The saree may have come in the way of the foot of the assailant who was trampling on the left big toe of the victim.

Professor de Saram further said that the presence of dirt on the soles of Mrs. Sathasivam indicated that the strangling took place in the kitchen and not in the bedroom upstairs. Answering further questions from Dr. de Silva, he said he removed the dirt from the soles of the feet of Mrs. Sathasivam and gave it to Mr. Chanmugam, the Government Analyst, to examine.

Referring to the external injury number 7, Professor de Saram said it was caused by the rear portion of the earring of Mrs. Sathasivam.

"The centre pearl of that ear ring was later found in that garage close to where the body had been lying?"

"That is so. Inspector Thiedeman told me."

"It was not found in the bedroom upstairs?"

"I was told so," Professor de Saram replied.

These answers were important to indicate that Mrs. Sathasivam was not strangled in the bedroom upstairs as William alleged.

Questioned about the act of strangling, Professor de Saram was very clear about the position Mrs. Sathasivam was strangled.

"What do you say must have been the position of the lady at the time when the strangling commenced?" asked Justice Gratiaen.

"She was standing. I exclude any possibility of her being on the floor when the strangling commenced," replied Professor de Saram.

"Could she have been at any stage put on the floor and the strangulation continued thereafter?"

"I do not think it is possible. My view is that the strangler got hold of the lady and that in a very short time she became unconscious," Professor de Saram replied.

Professor de Saram said that he saw William's demonstration of how he claims to have held Mrs. Sathasivam while she lay on the bedroom floor, while Mr. Sathasivam was alleged to have been squeezing her throat.

"Given that demonstration, would you have expected bruises on Mrs. Sathasivam's body where William's hands and the knee came into contact?" asked Dr. de Silva.

"I would," said Professor de Saram.

"He not only pressed down on her with his two hands but he also pressed down on her with his right knee. In fact did you notice in his demonstration that it was as if most of his weight came upon Mrs. Sathasivam's body at the three sites where his two hands and right knee were pressing?"

"Yes," replied Professor de Saram.

These answers implied that William's story of how the strangling took place could not be true.

Dr. Colvin R. de Silva then questioned Professor de Saram about the dripping of urine during strangling and the distribution of urine in Mrs. Sathasivam's petticoat.

Professor de Saram said Mrs. Sathasivam's bladder was empty, as she has lost the bladder sphincter control during strangling.

He said that urine may be passed during strangling and if a person was on her feet, urine would flow down the thighs and the front of the petticoat would have got soiled.

Referring to the position of strangling of Mrs. Sathasivam, Dr. de Silva queried, "If the person strangled was lying flat on the floor you would expect that urine on the petticoat in a certain way is it not?"

"Yes."

"How would you describe your expectation?"

"The urine would have been passed at the rear and would have seeped in round the buttocks and thighs."

"If on the other hand, the strangling was done when the person was on her feet, how would you expect the urine to flow?"

"Down the thighs, and the front of the petticoat would have got soiled."

"It would have tended to drip down, is it not?"

"Yes."

Professor de Saram then explained in detail how William's demonstration of strangling by Mr. Sathasivam could not have produced the neck injuries of Mrs. Sathasivam.

Dr. de Silva then questioned Professor de Saram on the injuries found on William when he examined him on the 19th of October, 10 days after the murder.

Professor de Saram said that the four injuries on William's face were caused on one single occasion.

"If the assailant's face was held in the manner William showed, then that assailant's face was well within the reach of the hands of the victim?"

"Yes, the face of the assailant was within reach of either hand of the victim."

"Now you found no injuries on the face of Mr. Sathasivam or on his hands?"

"No."

"You did find injuries on the face of William?"

"Yes."

"If the assailant strangled Mrs. Sathasivam in the manner indicated by William, would you normally have expected more injuries on the hands and on the face of the strangler, than you have found, say on William?"

"Yes, certainly," confirmed Professor de Saram.

"You saw the manner of the strangling which was demonstrated by William here. I am now not speaking of the question of Mrs. Sathasivam being put on the floor, but the grips. What is your opinion of the method of strangling which he demonstrated?"

"That is not compatible with what I found on the body, nor is it compatible, as would be expected, with a man who is trying to strangle a woman who is on the floor," replied Professor de Saram.

Dr. de Silva asked in what way it was incompatible with injuries Professor de Saram found.

"When Mrs. Sathasivam was dragged down on to the floor, the assailant got up and walked round the head to the left side of the victim. There was at that time no indication of a twist of the fingers on the throat, nor was there any evidence to show on the body where those two hands were applied in the way in which William demonstrated it," explained Professor de Saram.

Dr. de Silva reminded Professor de Saram that there were items like the tables, a stone to grind the curry stuffs, coconut scraper and the Dover stove in the kitchen and asked whether Mrs. Sathasivam's injuries on the back of the left and right hands, back of the right elbow, front of the right knee and right foot could have been caused by these.

"You yourself can point to a number of projecting places or things or spots in that kitchen against which her hand and her knees can strike?"

"Yes," replied Professor de Saram.

Professor de Saram, who examined and measured Mr. Sathasivam's nails said, if Mr. Sathasivam has strangled his wife, he would have expected to find deeper injuries and more lacerations in her neck as his nails were long.

"Would there be any marks on his nails - tell-tale marks - ?" asked Justice Gratiaen.

"One would find bits of the skin under the finger nails if they were as long as 1/16th of an inch. But of course, I saw him about 12 hours after it occurred. I did look for such evidence but there was no such evidence under Mr. Sathasivam's finger nails. If he had washed his hands or brushed his nails, that evidence would have disappeared," said Professor de Saram.

He said he gave his opinion that William's injuries on both the forearm and the left cheek were consistent with those having been inflicted upon him on the 9th October 1951, the day of the killing. He said he formed this opinion without knowing what position William would take.

At the request of Dr. de Silva, Professor de Saram demonstrated on a peon how he thought Mrs. Sathasivam was strangled.

Continuing his evidence, Professor de Saram produced the first edition of the book "Forensic Medicine", written by Professor Keith Simpson, which was published in 1947.

He referred to an illustration on page 96, which showed the injuries to the neck, if the victim was throttled by the right hand of an assailant, as demonstrated by William. They were not similar to the injuries on Mrs. Sathasivam's neck.

Professor de Saram was then questioned about the sound William said he heard when Mrs. Sathasivam's voice box was broken.

Justice Gratiaen asked Professor de Saram, "What was broken you say were the horns of the main thyroid cartilage of the voice box?"

"Yes."

Justice Gratiaen asked, "When they broke would the strangler have felt them break?"

"Yes, he would."

"What sort of sensation would he get?"

"He would feel it suddenly 'give'."

"There would be no sound?" asked Dr. de Silva.

"He would feel something happening under the pressure of his fingers. He would feel something happen and I think it is improbable there would be any sound. I have tried out an experiment on a voice box that was hardened by formalin and I had to cut it open, and a person standing a short distance away from me (indicates a few inches) heard it, but I do not think that would be heard in a natural body. The strangler would feel the horns of the thyroid cartilage give way," explained Professor de Saram.

This again contradicted William's story of hearing a sound.

Dr. de Silva then questioned Professor de Saram about the determination of the time of death.

To study the fall of temperature of dead bodies, Professor de Saram said he obtained half hourly temperature charts recorded by the Colombo Observatory on the day of the murder. It showed that the room temperature in Colombo at 8.30 a.m. was 82.5 degrees Fahrenheit and at 11.30 a.m. it was 84 degrees Fahrenheit. The highest temperature recorded was 84.2 degrees Fahrenheit at 2.30 p.m.

"How do you bring the temperature factor into play when you are seeking to assess the time of death of a person?" Dr. de Silva asked.

"First, we take the rectal temperature by inserting a thermometer into the rectum and then you take at the same time, immediately before or after, the temperature of the room. Then you deduct the rectal temperature as registered in the thermometer from 98.4 degrees Fahrenheit. That difference is divided by 0.7 or 0.8 degrees."

Professor de Saram said, "0.8 is the factor by which I estimate the time of death. I divide the temperature drop (difference between the normal temperature, 98.4 degrees Fahrenheit and the rectal temperature), by a specific figure, which is 0.8 or 0.7 degrees, because I have found that for each hour, about 5 to 7 hours after death, on average the usual drop of temperature in this country is 0.7 or 0.8 degrees. The average drop per hour is 0.7 or 0.8 degrees. So, when I divide the difference between the normal temperature, 98.4 degrees Fahrenheit, and the rectal temperature by 0.7 or 0.8 degrees, I get the number of hours that lies between the time of death and the time of examination."

What Professor de Saram said can be further explained by the following formula:

Time since death = $\dfrac{\text{Body temperature} - \text{Rectal temperature}}{\text{Hourly rate of fall}}$

Mrs. Sathasivam's rectal temperature was 93.2 degrees Fahrenheit.

This indicated that the time since death was

$$\dfrac{98.4 - 93.2}{0.7} = 7.4 \text{ hours}$$

Therefore, according to this calculation Mrs. Sathasivam died about seven and a half hours before 6.55 p.m., that was at about 11.15 a.m.

Dr. de Silva asked, "You gave three major factors which you would take into consideration to ascertain the time of death?"

"That is so. They were (1) the temperature of the body (2) rigor mortis and eye changes (3) food in the stomach and intestines."

"Nobody can fix the time of death with mathematical exactitude?"

"No."

"For instance, if you are asked to say whether a person died at 10.30 or 10.20, you would not have been able to say?"

"No."

"But within a certain range you can give what you term as probabilities?"

"Yes."

"And within that range of probability the exact time of death would lie?"

"Yes."

"In giving the time of death for instance as between 10 and 11.30 a.m. all that you are doing is fixing the limits of the two ends of probability?"

"Yes," replied Professor de Saram.

He said, judging by the fall in temperature, he would say that he would fix the time of death as half past eleven. Only on the temperature he would say the limits of probability are between 10.30 and 11.30. He added that temperature method is the most accurate assessment.

"You are saying doctor, in your experiments as checked up subsequently by three cases which you wish to speak of, the temperature drop is 0.8 and 0.7 degrees Fahrenheit per hour in this country?" asked Dr de Silva.

"The average; within 5 and 7 hours after death – that was my original estimate."

"You say you have checked up with three cases?"

"That is so."

"Do they cause you, in any manner, to modify?"

"They do not."

Explaining the experiments further, Professor de Saram said he knew the exact time of death of the prisoners and he took half hourly readings of rectal temperature.

"In carrying out these tests we tried to approximate as far as it is humanly possible with conditions that existed on that day when Mrs. Sathasivam was murdered. We had therefore clothed these bodies in petticoat and saree. The saree which was used for the first two bodies somewhat resembles the saree of Mrs. Sathasivam. The saree that was used for the last body was a new saree. It was of art silk, of similar texture as the other saree. The petticoat that we used for these bodies had the upper part made of taffeta. The petticoat of Mrs. Sathasivam was of cotton," he explained.

"With that preliminary, I should also like to say the other conditions under which we carried out this test. I was informed by the Crown Counsel in the Magistrate's Court, or at my bungalow I believe, that there was a fire burning in the kitchen. Therefore within 5 or 6 feet of these bodies I had a Bunsen burning half way. Everything was approximated as was humanly possible to bring these two cases on parallel lines," remarked Professor de Saram.

A Bunsen burner is a common heat source used for laboratory work.

Answering a question by Justice Gratiaen on the experiments on prisoners, Professor de Saram said, "I have carried out these experiments after I gave evidence in the Magistrate's Court on a suggestion made by Professor Sydney Smith who had been my teacher. Owing to the specific case in hand, I have restricted myself to the rectal temperature I have taken. These are tests and estimates, which I have carried out on bodies where the time of death was precisely known. They were conducted on people who were healthy. They were executed criminals."

Explaining further Professor de Saram said that in all these cases he took half hourly readings.

"In carrying out these tests, we tried to approximate as far as it is humanly possible with conditions that existed on that day when Mrs. Sathasivam was murdered. We had therefore clothed these bodies."

Professor de Saram then produced a chart showing the temperatures of the three executed prisoners' bodies on which he experimented. He also had a graph showing the rectal and room temperatures. He explained in detail how the experiments were carried out.

Table 1 furnishes data about physical build, etc. of the executed prisoners, as these are the modifying factors of the cooling rate. The last column indicates the number of hours that elapsed before the rectal temperature reached 93.2⁰ Fahrenheit, the temperature of Mrs. Sathasivam's body, at 6.55 p.m.

Table 1

Body	Weight	Height	Range of Room Temperature	Number of Hours Since Death
No. 1	112 lb	5'1"	81.0⁰ F - 83.5⁰ F	6 ½
No. 2	152 lb	5'5'	79.0⁰ F - 82.0⁰ F	7 ½
No. 3	130 lb	5'3"	80.0⁰ F - 83.0⁰ F	8 ½

As compared with the above, the corresponding details with reference to Mrs. Sathasivam's estimated time of death are shown in Table 2.

Table 2

Body	Weight	Height	Range of room temperature	Number of hours since death
Mrs. S	90 lb	5'3¼"	81.5⁰ F.	7 ½ - 8 ½

Therefore, Professor de Saram said the estimation of the time of Mrs. Sathasivam's death from all factors as being between 7½ to 9 hours before 6.55 p.m., i.e. between 10 a.m. and 11.30 a.m.

"May I say here and now that I was quite satisfied with my original evidence in Court, but these experiments had been carried out at the instance of Sir Sydney Smith, who suggested that I should carry out these experiments in connection with this case. I should like it to be perfectly understood with justice to Sir Sydney that nothing, except for the factual materials arising from these reports, had been entertained between him and me. Sir Sydney is a person of world repute and whatever insinuation may be made against me, I trust, would not be extended to Sir Sydney," Professor de Saram said.

At this stage the Acting Solicitor-General Mr. Fernando said that he and his juniors have nothing in their minds with regards to the doctor's evidence.

Answering a question by Justice Gratiaen he said that before the Sathasivam case, he had occasion to consider the question of time of death in twenty or thirty cases.

Explaining various factors of the body and environment affecting the rate of cooling, Professor de Saram said that as a general rule asphyxial death was accompanied by a possible rise in temperature in the body of the person who died. That would depend on the extent of struggling in which the subject was engaged before losing consciousness.

Referring to Mrs. Sathasivam, he said any effort at struggling was more or less frustrated by the grip that the assailant had on the lady and she would have become unconscious in a matter of seconds. He said the element of struggling was not borne out by what he found at the post-mortem examination.

Dr. de Silva then questioned the value of rigor mortis or stiffening of the body after death.

He said, "When I tested rigor in toes when I went in, it was still lax. By the time I finished in one hour there was rigor. I would fix the time since death at 12 hours."

"Rigor is a very doubtful sign to be taken by itself. It can only, so far as my estimation goes, very inaccurately give you the estimate of the time of death, because I have seen bodies within two hours in full rigor," Professor de Saram explained.

He said it would take about 8 to 12 hours for a body to develop rigor completely and Mrs. Sathasivam's body was in complete rigor at about 6.00 p.m.

"What is the period you would give that this body had been a dead body from the rigor test alone?"

"I would say between 8 to 10 hours."

"That would take it back to what?"

"8 to 10 hours would be from 6.00 p.m. and that would take it back to between 8.00 and 10.00 a.m.," replied Professor de Saram.

Justice Gratiaen asked Professor de Saram whether in determining the time of death he would modify the estimate he gave on the temperature factor or reject the rigor factor altogether.

"I reject it," replied Professor de Saram.

"In a murder case, would a medical expert, where the question of the time of death was controversial, if he were asked to express an opinion of the time of death based purely on the rigor mortis, would any conscientious medical expert undertake to express any confident view?" Dr de Silva asked.

"No. I would not. He would not in my opinion," replied Professor de Saram.

Next Dr. de Silva questioned about the experiments on passage of food through the intestines Professor de Saram performed on the same executed prisoners.

He asked whether those observations confirmed his opinion about the time Mrs. Sathasivam was killed.

"They confirmed my opinion," Professor de Saram replied.

"Therefore in the light of observations made by you subsequently, you say you stand confirmed in your opinion that death was about three to three and half hours after the last meal?"

"That is so."

Dr. de Silva asked whether that meant whatever the time this meal was taken, it would be at least three hours later Mrs. Sathasivam died.

"That is so," replied Professor de Saram.

"So that this much is certain: If her string-hopper meal was taken subsequent to 8.15, her death you would place as subsequent to 11.15?"

"Yes."

"And may be between 11.15 and 11.45?"

"That is so."

Answering a query from Justice Gratiaen, Professor de Saram said, "In the experiments I held with those condemned prisoners, they ate ordinary hoppers and the conditions of the experiments were such that I could not make very intricate investigation. I could not interfere with prison regulations for the purpose of my experiments by deciding what they should eat."

He said he did check up the time when each of these three people had their last meal.

"Now doctor, you are aware that the crucial question in this case in that aspect of the matter is whether the death was before 10.30 or after 10.30, among other things?" asked Dr. de Silva.

"Yes."

"On this, if the meal was taken subsequent to 8.15 in the morning, there can be no doubt on your opinion in this case that the death was after 11.15?"

"Yes."

"There cannot be even the shadow of a doubt that the death just could not have been at any rate at 9.30 or anything like that, assuming the meal to be subsequent to 8.15?"

"That is so."

Explaining this further Professor de Saram said, "There is just one point I wish to make. That is, that it may be taken up as a ground for argument that I did find at the lower end of the intestines bits of string-hoppers. It may be taken on a hypothetical presumption that because the string-hopper bits were found at the end of that time, that the contents of the intestines had not been absorbed and therefore that there might have been a bit of intestinal hurry."

He said there was uniform distribution of string-hoppers in the intestines, meaning there was continuity of the meal in the food passage.

He further explained that it must not be presumed there was intestinal hurry because there could be lack of digestion of stringhoppers due to lack of pancreatic juice or bile salts. These are secretions coming from the pancreas and gall bladder respectively, that help in the digestive process.

Answering a question about the passage of food in the gastrointestinal tract, Professor de Saram explained that from the stomach, the food passes out into the duodenum through the pyloric sphincter, a group of muscles surrounding the opening of the stomach.

"And the pyloric sphincter itself has to be passed through before you get to the duodenum?"

"That is so."

"What is peristalsis?"

"It is the moving waves of contraction which take place in various segments of the intestines. The stomach forces the food outwards. Peristalsis is the contractions of the muscles which push the food along the intestinal passages. The next section of the small intestine after the duodenum is the jejunum. The next one after that is the ileum. That is the lowest portion of the small intestine. From the ileum you pass on to the caecum. That is the beginning of the large intestine. Between the ileum and the caecum there is a sphincter."

"The order is this – the stomach, the duodenum, the jejunum, the ileum and the caecum. That would be the order of the sections of the intestinal canal through which food would pass after it has entered the stomach," explained Professor de Saram.

Continuing to answer further queries, Professor de Saram said, "There are two aspects of the passage of food once it has reached the stomach. One is the expulsion of the food from the stomach into the small intestine and the other is the passage of the food along the small intestine."

"Do you use either or both of these factors in assessing the time of the death?"

"What I do is to assess the extent to which the 'head' of the meal had travelled along the intestinal tract once it had got out of the stomach. That is the test on which I rely." (See Figure 18. Page 476)

"You do not yourself use the rate of the expulsion of the food from the stomach into the small intestine?"

"Under certain circumstances I would."

"That is you were carrying out experiments on the rate of progress of food through the small intestines?"

"That is so."

"What kind of experiments did you carry out?"

"I found out what food had been eaten before death and I examined the stomach contents and the intestines and estimated backwards."

"Also on condemned prisoners?" asked Justice Gratiaen

"That is so."

"Were they the same three condemned prisoners?"

"Yes."

Referring to the murder case where Mr. John Silva, the driver who was killed after robbing over 400,000 rupees from the Colombo Turf Club a few years ago, Professor de Saram said that six or seven hours after the ingestion of rice, identifiable rice grains were found in the small intestines of the victim in that case.

Regarding the determination of time of death, finally Dr. de Silva asked, "Taking all the various factors you have spoken of into consideration, will you please tell the Court now, combining all considerations together, what you would fix the time of death as?"

"I would fix the time of death as about 11.00 or 11.15 or even 11.30. Not earlier than 10.45. There might be just a chance of 10.30. 10 o'clock would be impossible," Professor de Saram said.

At that stage he handed over to Justice Gratiaen a paper, which had the results of the experiments he carried out.

Dr. de Silva asked Professor de Saram how the deep internal head injury (injury number 10) could have been caused. He said it could have been caused by her head being struck with some object such as the piece of firewood found at the scene. He agreed that her head striking a hard object such as the part of an almirah could have caused it.

Dr. de Silva asked Professor de Saram whether he was given an opportunity to state his opinion on the views of other doctors before he gave evidence. Professor de Saram replied he did not have that opportunity.

"But did you have any conference or meeting with any of those doctors other than those occasions you referred to with Professor Paul?"

"Yes."

"Who are the doctors with whom you have had any kind of official conference?"

"I met Dr. Taylor, Professor Paul and Professor M.V.P. Peiris and another doctor who I believe is called Dr. Jackie Silva. He was, I believe, the Police Surgeon at that time".

"Where was this?"

"At the Galle Face Hotel where Dr. Taylor was staying."

"For what purpose?"

"I understood that Dr. Taylor had expressed a desire to see me and discuss various points. So I went there. I got a message in the morning through Inspector Thiedeman and I checked it up with Mr. Koelmeyer. I confirmed the message and then I contacted Dr. Taylor at the Faculty of Medicine building where he was examining for the FRCS. He came out and he told me that he expressed a desire to see me and that he had written a report."

"We know from Dr. Taylor that he thought that it was proper that he should express his view to you. So did you meet him?"

"I went there and was given the report by Inspector Thiedeman and shortly after that I was ushered in to the room and I met Dr. Taylor there, and the other three doctors also came in. Dr. Peiris I think came in later."

"On that occasion did you express an opinion on Dr. Taylor's view?"

"I expressed a view as to the time of death, but when it came to a discussion as to the manner of the strangulation I had reached the limits of my patience and I told them that if they feel so sure about it they could go and give evidence in Court and that I did not care."

"The conference did not go through to the finish?"

"Not to the finish," Professor de Saram replied.

After Professor de Saram's cross-examination by Dr. Colvin R. de Silva was concluded, Justice Gratiaen asked Mr. T. S. Fernando, "I suppose you will desire to cross-examine this witness?"

"Yes, at a certain stage. I assume I have a right to put certain questions in the ordinary course."

"You have a right to re-examine the witness," Justice Gratiaen said.

Mr. Fernando commenced his re-examination with this question: "In answer to my learned friend Dr. de Silva who put a question in this form, namely 'I want to ask you frankly would you have undertaken to do the post-mortem examination at the invitation of the Police, if you had the slightest suspicion that the Police would at any time seek to challenge the accuracy or care or efficiency of your work,' your answer was 'No'. Are we to take it that that would have been your ordinary approach to post-mortems?"

"No. In this particular case under particular circumstances I had been asked to do it," replied Professor de Saram.

As Mr. Fernando was not satisfied with that answer he repeated the question.

Professor de Saram said, "I have no experience of that before. Under the conditions I would not."

"Do I understand that the way you approach your duties in this kind of matter would be that your opinion should be accepted?" asked Mr. T.S. Fernando.

Justice Gratiaen disallowed that question.

Rephrasing the question Mr. Fernando asked, "Would you have refused to undertake the post-mortem if you had the slightest suspicion that the accuracy of your examination would be challenged?"

"Certainly I would."

"In other words, you would say that before I undertake this examination you must agree to accept the accuracy of my work?"

"The accuracy of the facts, and not my work," Professor de Saram replied.

Dr. Colvin R. de Silva addressing Justice Gratiaen said, "My Lord, I do not wish my question to mean anything other than what it means. Nowhere in that question is a matter of opinion referred to."

Mr. Fernando, undeterred continued his line of questioning.

"Would you stipulate beforehand, that your opinion should

be accepted by the Police if you are to undertake a post-mortem examination?"

"Never."

"You are not annoyed in any way that your opinion is being challenged by the prosecution?"

"No."

"Do you remember Dr. Welikala who gave evidence in this case?"

Dr. Welikala was the radiologist who did some experiments to study the passage of food in the intestines. He gave evidence in the Magistrate's Courts.

"Yes."

"Do you remember Dr. Welikala coming to you with a number of x-ray photographs?"

"Yes."

"He wanted to discuss them with you?"

"Yes."

"Before Dr. Welikala gave evidence?"

"Yes."

"Were you agreeable to discuss the matter?"

"No."

Justice Gratiaen asked, "Why?"

"Because, it was usual for the person who held the post-mortem examination to be informed beforehand of these experiments, so that these experiments may be discussed from all points of view by the person who held the post-mortem examination with the people conducting the experiments," Professor de Saram replied.

"Then your grievance was that you had not been consulted by him before he took the photographs?" questioned Mr. Fernando.

"No. I thought that it was in the order of things that the people who were in charge of this did not want me to partake in this at all. Therefore, when Dr. Welikala came to me I told him 'They don't want me to do it. So you had better give your evidence without consulting me'."

"But the mutual goodwill between you and Dr. Welikala remained unaffected?" queried Justice Gratiaen.

"That is so."

Mr. Fernando asked, "And your mutual goodwill with the other Doctors like Dr. Paul, Dr, Peiris etc. also remained unaffected?"

"Need I answer that question, My Lord?" Professor de Saram asked Justice Gratiaen. He remained silent!

Continuing further questioning, Mr Fernando asked, "In regard to what you said about your visit to Dr. Taylor at the Galle Face Hotel, do I understand you to say that Dr. Taylor wished to see you?"

"So I understood."

"Did you also understand that Dr. Taylor had been consulted by the Police with a view to getting him to give evidence in the case?"

"Yes, he told me that."

"And he had said that before he came into the case he would like to discuss the matter with the doctor who conducted the post-mortem examination?"

"He told me that."

"At the conference, there were Dr. Silva – you need not refer to him at all because he is not a witness in this case – Professor Paul, Professor M.V.P. Peiris, Dr. Taylor and yourself?"

"Yes."

"At the conference, it transpired that all three doctors, Professor Peiris, Professor Paul and Dr. Taylor held a view different to yours with regard to the strangling?"

"I don't know that because Dr. Taylor came up to me one day when I was about to leave for a social and said he wanted to know from which position the strangling was done, and he came at me like that from in front. Then I told him 'If you are so sure about it go and give your evidence in Court. Why do you want to worry me about it?'"

Only during the re-examination, Mr. T.S. Fernando, the Acting Solicitor-General marked the post-mortem report of Mrs. Sathasivam as 'P99'. As mentioned earlier, in murder trials, the post-mortem report is marked by the prosecution during the initial examination-in-chief of the pathologist.

At a post-mortem examination, a pathologist is entitled to take any part of the skin or organ to demonstrate an injury or the cause of death.

"One of the matters mentioned is the preserving of any part that will help in demonstrating the injuries?" asked Mr. Fernando.

"Yes. The reason I did not take the lesion was that I would have mutilated that unfortunate lady's body and I wanted to spare her that," Professor de Saram said. Here the 'lesion' means the part of the skin of the neck showing injuries.

Mr. Fernando questioned Professor de Saram about the position of the mortar on Mrs. Sathasivam's neck, which could have caused abrasions on the face, and referred to an attempted demonstration of that in the presence of two Crown Counsel, in the chambers of the Magistrate's Court.

Professor de Saram said he wanted to know the probable position of the mortar on Mrs. Sathasivam's body, as it was found by the person who first saw it. The Magistrate said that the Crown Counsel informed him that there was no witness who was able to give the accurate position the mortar was found. Professor de Saram then said he could not give evidence on that point.

Justice Gratiaen said, "Is it not fairly clear that what the doctor has told us is, as I understand it, that you first made an application for a demonstration of this mortar in the course of what we might call a private session, between the Magistrate and the witness?"

"Yes."

"And the two Crown Counsel came in and to the best of their ability gave you a demonstration?"

"Yes."

"Subsequently you asked that the demonstration should be repeated in Court and you were then told it cannot be done as it was not possible for any witness to give a precise demonstration?"

"Yes, that is correct," replied Professor de Saram.

As further questioning on the neck injuries of Mrs. Sathasivam by Mr. Fernando continued, Justice Gratiaen asked him, "It is quite apparent that at some stage you will have to ask for permission to cross-examine your witness?"

"Undoubtedly, My Lord."

"I really feel therefore that to avoid judicial interruption, which I want to avoid, I think it will be far more satisfactory if you made this application now?"

"I propose My Lord when we come to the question of the time of death to make the application," Mr. Fernando said.

Justice Gratiaen said, "On questions of fact as I understand it, he was your witness, and while he is in the witness-box it seems to me that you are bound by his statements of fact. If you can contradict that fact by the evidence of another witness, that is another matter. But, if you cannot, and if his facts are incorrect so much the worse for the side that called him. If your questions are to show that what he states as a fact is not reliable, I am afraid you cannot do that without moving to cross-examine your own witness."

Justice Gratiaen said that he could not allow any re-examination for the purpose of allowing the jury to draw the conclusion that evidence of Professor de Saram with regard to facts in examination-in-chief or cross-examination cannot be accepted. "If you make an application to treat him as an adverse witness on that aspect of the matter I will consider it," Justice Gratiaen said.

Mr. Fernando continued with his questioning of Professor de Saram and Dr. de Silva intervened.

He said, "It is my respectful submission that this re-examination does not arise from my cross-examination. The intention of re-examination is to cover something that has arisen in cross-examination, not to provide a basis for some future tribunal. My learned friend got out those injuries and I based my questions on the testimony he obtained from the witness on those injuries. Now my learned friend seeks to clarify them purposely."

Justice Gratiaen then remarked, "Let us be quite frank. It seems to me that you want to cross-examine this witness at some stage. For some reason it is apparent to me you want to postpone that moment. In the meantime, I get the impression that through what appears to be re-examination on certain points, you are seeking to bring in certain answers to questions, which would be relied on for the purpose of weakening the view of the evidence of a person who is your witness. It is for you to decide whether you intend to continue that. Having regard to the fact that we have a long trial it is going to be further delayed by these objections at every stage. It would be of great assistance if you state on what points which emerged in cross-examination you seek to throw doubt."

Mr. Fernando said, "In regard to these injuries, I was careful to get out a description from Professor de Saram. My learned friend got out the possible cause of those injuries, and I want to put to Professor de Saram whether it could be caused by some other cause as well. I am not putting the doctor down as a witness of opinion. If he expresses it, I am entitled to test it."

"That is by getting permission to cross-examine him," said Justice Gratiaen.

This statement of Mr. Fernando indicated that he wanted Professor de Saram to be a witness to the fact, but his opinions would not be accepted.

Mr. Fernando said, "Before I come to that, there are cases where a witness says an injury was caused in a certain way. In re-examination he may say, 'Yes, I also think it is possible to have been caused by some other cause'."

Justice Gratiaen said, "Those are questions put to a person, who being your own witness you accept his answer, but I understand you do not intend to accept them in this case."

"I will leave that also for my observations. I can make an application straightaway to treat the witness as a hostile witness, but there are certain matters which arose in cross-examination and I wish to get those matters out," replied Mr. Fernando.

Justice Gratiaen, perhaps unhappy with that comment finally said, "The present procedure is bound to cause interruptions and it affects our train of thought. This is a serious matter in which everybody wants to get on with the business."

Mr. Fernando then continued with the re-examination.

Answering further questions Professor de Saram said that he was quite sure that one strangler could have finished the job of killing Mrs. Sathasivam. He said he considered the possibility of two people strangling her after he heard William's story.

Professor de Saram explaining the pupillary changes in the eye remarked that perhaps as an indication of time of death, he did not rely upon it. He said he did not base his conclusion of time of death on that alone.

Quoting from Sir Sydney Smith's text book (10th Edition), Mr. Fernando asked, "In judicial hanging, the conditions are extremely different from those in suspension by a cord, for the whole process depends not on asphyxia from pressure on the neck but on fracture or the dislocation of the cervical vertebra (spine) and compression of the spinal cord?"

"Yes," replied Professor de Saram.

Referring to the textbook of Physiology by Samson Wright, Mr. Fernando asked whether Professor de Saram agreed that the rectal temperature was 0.7 or 0.8 degrees Fahrenheit above the normal temperature of the mouth. He agreed.

Mr. Fernando then asked about the discussions Professor de Saram had with Dr. Taylor about the rectal temperature after the death.

At that stage Justice Gratiaen asked whether this is not a good stage where he should move to cross-examine Professor de Saram.

Mr Fernando said that he would, because he had not relied on Professor de Saram and therefore his evidence must be tested by cross-examination!

"Your position is that he was in fact, whatever his opinion may have been, an essential witness on questions of fact, and he has expressed opinions which support the defence to a large extent. The Crown does not accept that part of his opinions on certain aspects of the matter and you want to test it by cross-examination?" asked Justice Gratiaen.

"Yes," said Mr. Fernando.

Justice Gratiaen then told Dr. Colvin R. de Silva, that he personally feels in the interests of justice that opinions on such vital matters as Professor de Saram has spoken of should be tested by cross-examination.

He further said, "My feeling is that although, apart from any question of technicalities, that evidence should be tested by cross-examination, at the same time having regard to the fact that neither the jury nor myself yet know specifically what the case for the Crown is on the medical aspects which are of such importance, I am at present disposed to, subject to argument, allow cross-examination at this stage. And also I think that Professor de Saram should be re-called for cross-examination after all the medical evidence for the Crown has been placed before court."

Continuing Justice Gratiaen said, "Professor de Saram, the learned Solicitor-General has properly and fairly conceded, is not a person who is a witness whose integrity or general competence is challenged at all. But it seems to me from the point of view of the defence that the value of his evidence to the defence would be weakened if there was no opportunity given to the other side to test it by legitimate cross-examination."

"That is my attitude at this stage. I propose, unless you convince me to the contrary, in fairness to everybody including Professor de Saram, to allow the application of the Crown and direct Professor de Saram to be present in Court, so that he can know what is the medical case for the Crown, and thereafter for the Crown to cross-examine him after all the other medical evidence," Justice Gratiaen said.

Dr. Colvin R. de Silva said, "I do not wish to say anything but if I understand Your Lordship right, the procedure Your Lordship proposes is that if any cross-examination is to be permitted of Professor de Saram, that should come after the whole of the other medical case for the Crown has been placed before Court?"

Justice Gratiaen then remarked, "I am myself in a difficulty of not knowing what precisely is the medical case for the Crown! But I have the right in the exercise of my discretion to refuse cross-examination at this stage and I have the right also in the exercise of my discretion to recall a witness for examination, cross-examination or for any other purpose and it seems to me that having regard to the vital issues in the matter here, I would be forced to adopt this procedure. I think that is the fairest way. Would that suit you Mr. Solicitor-General?"

"All that I have said in my opening address so far as I now remember, regarding the medical testimony, is to say that the lady died within one hour of the meal," replied Mr. Fernando.

"I am not criticising at all. It certainly has not been placed before us in any elaborate detail and this was the first time that William gave a particular demonstration. We do not know what the experts on whom the Crown relies are going to say. We are not aware of it. It seems to me, taking that one's duty is to hold the scales on a proper balance between the Crown and the defence, that one must also have a clear idea of the position. You would not have dreamt of calling Professor de Saram if he was not going to support you and the Crown has not been taken by surprise because the Crown led his evidence in the Magistrate's Court," Justice Gratiaen said.

Dr. de Silva said that the Crown also utilized it but has since abandoned it!

"That part of his expert opinion would never have been placed before Court under normal circumstances except by the defence. It was my intention to submit to Your Lordship that the test Your Lordship would apply would be what would be best in the interests of justice. It was my intention to state that I had no objection to this witness being cross-examined on the matters of expert opinion, if a proper application is made," said Dr. de Silva.

Justice Gratiaen then remarked, "Some of the expert evidence given is favourable to the defence though the witness was called by the Crown and certain observations were properly made that the defence would be in a much stronger position to rely on that evidence if it was tested."

Dr de Silva submitted, "I seek to rely on Professor de Saram's evidence but I do not bind myself to it. As far as I am concerned, I act on facts elicited in favour of the defence through witnesses placed by the prosecution. It is my duty, I submit, to elicit it."

"Obviously you are not bound by any witness called by the Crown but you can rely on any opinion which is favourable to you," Justice Gratiaen said.

Dr. de Silva remarked, "Whether the Crown intends to place counter evidence does not interest me. All I wish to submit is that the proper procedure to follow, especially as it is a question where the Crown has the right to cross-examine, which Your Lordship intends to give them the opportunity of, is to, in the light of any cross-examination that is done, give the defence an opportunity to clarify anything we wish to clarify in relation to it."

"I would allow any number of questions to be put by either side in a murder case," said Justice Gratiaen.

After this discussion Justice Gratiaen gave his ruling.

"I refuse permission for Professor de Saram to be cross-examined by the Crown at this stage but that after the evidence of the medical experts on whom the Crown relies has been completed and after points of controversy have been further clarified, I shall, in the exercise of my discretion."

Justice Gratiaen further said that Professor de Saram should be permitted to be present in Court if he so desires, when the medical witnesses of the Crown give evidence.

Then Justice Gratiaen said, "In the meantime there are one or two points which I would like to ask you. What is your recollection of the kind of mark, which you saw on that mortar in that garage?"

"It was a bare foot print. The portion, which was best marked was the front portion and that appeared to be stretched out and not together at least the big toe," replied Professor de Saram.

Justice Gratiaen then referred to the story of William that Mr. Sathasivam stamped his foot while Mrs. Sathasivam was still alive.

"Do internal and external injuries which you did find on Mrs. Sathasivam's neck support the position that a man of the height of Mr. Sathasivam brought down his shod foot on the woman's neck?" asked Justice Gratiaen.

"If he stamped his foot down, more or less to finish her off, I would have expected a broader mark superficially. There would have been an abrasion and if she was still alive I would have expected a certain amount of haemorrhage," replied Professor de Saram.

Answering further questions from Justice Gratiaen, he said that injuries on Mrs. Sathasivam's neck did not support the proposition that Mr. Sathasivam stamped his foot on her neck.

Replying another question from Justice Gratiaen, Professor de Saram said that on 20th October at about 12.30 or 12.45 the Inspector-General of Police came with Mr. Cherubim and Mr. Thamotheram to meet him and had a long discussion with him about the post-mortem and the statement William had made to Mr. Koelmeyer, the Superintendent of Police.

Professor de Saram told them that William's account of the death as appearing in the statement was highly improbable. He also said that the statement William had made to Mr. Wickramarathne at the Matara Police Station, stating that he had personally strangled Mrs. Sathasivam in the kitchen, was more consistent with what he found at the post-mortem examination.

"Having regard to the size and appearance of William in relation to Mrs. Sathasivam, who weighed only 90 pounds, will you express any opinion as to whether William could or could not possess sufficient strength to strangle Mrs. Sathasivam himself?" asked Justice Gratiaen.

"He could have."

"I want you to tell us a little bit more about this asphyxial death by manual strangulation. What actually happens which causes death?"

"There are several features. It is not only the lack of oxygen in the lungs. There are various vessels and nerves in the neck, pressure on which may precipitate asphyxial death. Pressure on the nerves and vessels produce 'certain inhibitions in the heart' causing it to collapse long before asphyxial death," explained Professor de Saram. He also said that death would have occurred within not more than 3-5 minutes.

Although most people can hold their breath for a considerable period without distress, it is remarkable that a sudden compression of the wind pipe can render a person powerless to call for assistance and cause almost immediate insensibility and death.

As Professor de Saram explained death is not a matter of uncomplicated asphyxiation.

In such cases pathologists today prefer to give 'Compression of the neck' as the cause of death.

'Inhibition of the heart' mentioned by Professor de Saram means reflex inhibition of the heart beat causing the heart to stop, through the stimulation of the 'vagus nerve' or its branches, or the 'carotid sinus', a dilated part of the carotid artery (the main artery carrying blood to the brain) in the neck.

'Carotid sinus' has numerous nerve endings, and it also communicates with the cardiovascular centre in the brain stem.

It is concerned with the control of blood pressure and heart rate.

The carotid sinus is at the level of the upper border of the thyroid cartilage, a site commonly involved in strangulation. Even today, the precise mechanism of causing death by this method is a mystery.

Justice Gratiaen informed Professor de Saram, "I just want to ask you one more point. You went to assist in the administration of justice at the special request of the Inspector-General of the Police?"

"That is so."

"You saw this tragic corpse of this frail woman and from the moment you undertook the case up to now have you any desire other than to further the ends of justice?"

"No."

"If any conclusion which you had formed at one stage needs to be modified after further thought, you would not hesitate to modify it?"

"That is so," replied Professor de Saram.

Justice Gratiaen informed the members of the jury that they can ask questions from Professor de Saram when he comes back to give evidence again.

CHAPTER 7.

CONFLICTING MEDICAL EVIDENCE

Just after Professor G.S.W. de Saram's evidence and re-examination by the Acting Solicitor-General Mr. T. S. Fernando, evidence given by Dr. John Frank Taylor during the magisterial inquiry was read in Court, at the request of Mr. Fernando. Dr. Taylor, who was in Ceylon as an Examiner for the Royal College of Surgeons of the United Kingdom in January 1952, passed away after he left Ceylon.

Justice Gratiaen said that evidence of Dr. Taylor, which was recorded by the Magistrate, would be read as Dr. Taylor has since died. "According to our law of evidence his deposition would be admissible and it would be read to you as part of the case for the Crown," Justice Gratiaen told the jury.

Mr. Fernando read the evidence given by Dr. Taylor on 16th, 21st and 22nd January 1952 in the Magistrate's Court.

Professor Milroy Paul was summoned next by the Crown to give evidence. He has given evidence in the Magistrate's Court earlier and he has also observed William's demonstration of stamping the neck of Mrs. Sathasivam.

Professor Paul gave evidence for 8 days of which nearly 4 days were on cross-examination by Dr. Colvin R. de Silva.

Professor Paul said he was the Professor of Surgery of the University of Ceylon, a post he held from 1936, and was also a Visiting Surgeon of the General Hospital, Colombo.

He said he held the degree of Master of Surgery of London and was a Fellow of the Royal College of Surgeons.

Explaining how he was involved in this case, Professor Paul said Inspector Thiedeman came to his residence in either December 1951 or January 1952 and requested him to read through certain documents and give an opinion. Opinion was not requested on any specific issue.

After perusing the following documents he gave an oral opinion to him.

The documents were,
- Postmortem report of Mrs. Sathasivam prepared by Professor de Saram
- Summary of Professor de Saram's evidence in the Magistrate's Court
- Summary of the Government Analyst Mr. Chanmugam's evidence in the Magistrate's Court
- The photographs of the body of Mrs. Sathasivam at the scene
- Professor de Saram's report on the examination of Mr. Sathasivam
- List of William's injuries

Commenting on the photographs of the scene and of the postmortem examination taken by Mr. G. Webster of the Department of Forensic Medicine, University of Colombo, Professor Paul said that Webster was the most expert medical photographer available and if he took the photographs he did not expect any optical illusions to be in the way of those photographs.

Professor Paul said he agreed with Professor de Saram that Mrs. Sathasivam's cause of death was asphyxia from manual strangulation.

Answering questions of the Acting Solicitor-General Mr. Fernando on the method of strangulation of Mrs. Sathasivam, he said he thought that the strangler had used his right hand on the throat and that he was on the right side of the victim and William at a certain stage had come in to assist him and got scratched. He said that the strangler who was on the right side never altered his effective grip.

Professor Paul agreed that Mrs Sathasivam's external injuries on the left jaw (numbers 1, 3 and 9) and the corresponding internal injuries (numbers 1 and 3) were caused by stamping on the neck as demonstrated by William. He said one act of stamping could have caused them.

In the Magistrate's Court, Professor Paul thought that they were caused during the struggle, which occurred on the floor. Then he did not know William's stamping story.

He said that the heel or the front part of the foot might have struck the jaw bone first and then travelled down the neck from the bone to the next prominence. He now thought that his earlier opinion was improbable. He did not think that Professor de Saram's demonstration of the act of strangling could have caused these injuries.

"Flesh contacting flesh could not have caused these injuries," said Professor Paul.

Agreeing with William's demonstration of how Mrs. Sathasivam was strangled, Professor Paul said that there were 7 nail marks on the injury number 4. He said the right thumb of the assailant caused them all and they all faced the middle line.

Answering a question by Justice Gratiaen, Professor Paul however said he could confidently state that the right thumb caused the first and the second nail marks but with the others he was not certain.

Professor Paul, looking at the photograph said that there were seven nail marks in the external injury number 4.

Dr. de Silva at this stage said that he understood that the Crown was proceeding on the footing that they accepted Professor de Saram's view on the factual side. "I do not know whether the position has changed. I wish to know whether it is changed," Dr. de Silva said.

"You cannot stop the Crown questioning another witness," Justice Gratiaen remarked.

Mr. Fernando explaining his position said, "I say that Professor de Saram's post-mortem findings in this report are not being challenged at all, but when he gives an opinion as to the direction of the concavities, that is not a post-mortem finding of his at all."

"That is evidence of fact," said Justice Gratiaen.

Disagreeing with that view, Mr. Fernando said, "That is evidence of his opinion."

Professor Paul, using a magnifying glass to view the injuries in the photograph showing Mrs. Sathasivam's neck, said that he was certain that the concavities of the nail marks were turned towards the mid line. This was exactly opposite to the opinion expressed by Professor de Saram.

At this stage, four magnifying glasses were handed over to the members of the jury to view the neck injuries.

"Professor de Saram said that he could decipher only six nail marks in the injury number 4. You say there are seven?" asked Mr. Fernando.

"I do not know on what basis he counted," replied Professor Paul.

Explaining William's injuries Professor Paul said, "The process of strangulation that was going on would have reduced her to the point at which she would have not been able to exert purposeful resistance. But I think in view of the scratches on William, the marks on William's forearm, there is no doubt at all that she was not unconscious at that stage. She was able to put her hand out to do something but she was not able to do the obvious thing, to tear away the strangler's hands from the throat."

Professor Paul said that he would not exclude Mr. Sathasivam as the strangler because he had finger nails 1/16th of an inch long. Mr. Fernando reading from Dr. Taylor's evidence said that Dr. Taylor also held the same view.

He said injuries on William's face and forearm could have been caused by Mrs. Sathasivam's right hand. Absence of injuries on Mr. Sathasivam was due to Mrs. Sathasivam being stunned by the injury number 10, the contusion on the right temple, which was caused when the head struck the floor, or a projection on the foot of the bed, as shown by William.

However, Professor Paul did not exclude the possibility that this was caused by a blow with the piece of firewood.

"The most probable explanation for the external injury number 18 and the internal injury number 11 on Mrs. Sathasivam's back is that they have been caused in the course of a violent struggle on the floor," said Professor Paul.

Mr. Fernando questioned Professor Paul regarding the injuries on Mrs. Sathasivam's body and opinions expressed by Professor de Saram. He said "As injuries 1, 3, and 9 were ante-mortem, the mortar could not have caused them, because in my view by the time she reached the garage there was no circulation."

Having watched the demonstration and listened to William's account of strangling, Professor Paul said that there was no injury that was not consistent with that description.

Professor Paul said that the ear stud of Mrs. Sathasivam got bent when the head struck the floor as described by William.

Referring to the Government Analyst's evidence that there was semen on the 'verti' found on the bed, Professor Paul agreed that the seminal stains were consistent with Mrs. Sathasivam having had normal marital intercourse some short time before she came by her death.

"With her consent? That is in the absence of any injuries?" asked Justice Gratiaen.

"Yes," answered Professor Paul.

Professor Paul agreed that if Mrs. Sathasivam was strangled on the kitchen floor, as her cloth was not stained at all, she was strangled in the upright position and the most likely position then would be to strangle her from behind. This was also the view of Professor de Saram.

"So you quite confidently exclude any possibility of Mrs. Sathasivam having been strangled on the kitchen floor?" Justice Gratiaen queried.

"Yes," said Professor Paul.

Answering a question from Justice Gratiaen, Professor Paul said that if Mrs. Sathasivam was strangled from behind, she would have tried to wrest his wrist and hands and those would have been injured, not his forearm and face.

"The actual injuries sustained by William in the course of the strangling more or less are of such a kind that they acquit William of being the strangler himself?" Justice Gratiaen asked.

"That is so."

"Even if Mr. Sathasivam now on trial has the most perfect alibi imaginable, you would still entertain doubts as to whether William, having regard to the injuries, was the strangler?"

"Yes."

"In your opinion, the injuries on William are non-purposive injuries?"

"They are purposive up to a point, but in the circumstances of this case if a person was in full possession of her faculties, the minute strangling occurred I would expect her hands to go to the assailant's hand, not to anyone else."

Answering questions of Mr. Fernando on the determination of time of death, Professor Paul said that he also carried out some experiments on dead bodies to ascertain the rate of cooling.

One case was a person who died of typhoid fever. His starting rectal temperature was 107.6 degrees Fahrenheit. His fall of temperature was one degree in the second half hour, 1.2 degrees in the third half hour and one degree in the fourth half hour.

The second case was a person who died of tetanus and his starting temperature was 108 degrees Fahrenheit. His half hourly rate of fall of temperature was one degree in the first three half hour segments.

In another case of cancer, the starting temperature was 99.4 degrees Fahrenheit and she had falls of temperature of one degree in the fifth and sixth half hour segments.

Having measured the rectal temperature of 12 patients in the General Hospital, Colombo (who had no reason to have fever), he said that normal rectal temperature could vary from 98.8 degrees Fahrenheit to 100.4 degrees Fahrenheit.

The temperature under the tongue varied from 98.4 degrees Fahrenheit to 98.6 degrees Fahrenheit.

He said two medical students who were asked to struggle 'for their lives' on a mattress for 2 minutes had their rectal temperature increasing from 99.2 degrees Fahrenheit to 99.7 degrees Fahrenheit. Five minutes after the struggle had stopped, the temperature rose to 100 degrees Fahrenheit in one and 100.2 degrees Fahrenheit in the second. Professor Paul said that the rise in temperature could not be stopped as it is produced by muscular effort and the heat has been already produced. The rise of temperature has nothing to do with the moment of death.

Justice Gratiaen queried, "In other words, you would think it fair to assume that Mrs. Sathasivam having struggled for approximately two minutes before she came by her death, would have had a rectal temperature of 100.1 degrees Fahrenheit?"

"That is so," said Professor Paul.

However, during the cross-examination by Dr. Colvin R. de Silva, Professor Paul agreed that the heat generated in Mrs. Sathasivam's body was not exactly comparable to the heat generated by the 2 medical students because,

(a) The medical students could take deep breaths freely and rapidly as their breathing was not obstructed, and,

(b) They were alive and generating heat by supplying oxygen to the body after the struggle while Mrs. Sathasivam was not.

Therefore, to assume that Mrs. Sathasivam's rectal temperature was 100 or 100.2 degrees Fahrenheit at the time of death was fallacious.

Professor Paul agreed that Mrs. Sathasivam's rectal temperature could be nothing more than 98.8 degrees Fahrenheit before the struggle.

Regarding cooling, he said in his view the rates of cooling were so variable that it would be unsafe to form any definite opinion from the rate of cooling.

Regarding rigor mortis, Professor Paul agreed that it would indicate the time of death between 8.00 a.m. to 10.00 a.m. He said that it was not a safe conclusion.

During the cross-examination, Dr. de Silva reading from Keith Simpson's book "Forensic Medicine", asked whether Professor Paul agreed with the following paragraph.

"Cooling – This is the only reliable index of lapse of time during the first 18 hours after death and its early measurement is often vital to the establishment of exact time of death."

Professor Paul said that he would agree that it is the best of a bad lot, but the word 'exact' in the sentence would be quite inapplicable.

Dr. de Silva also quoted the following sentence from "Taylor's Principles and Practice of Medical Jurisprudence" (1948 edition) and asked whether Professor Paul would agree.

"Of all the changes that occur in the dead body that of cooling of the temperature is one about which we have the most knowledge."

Professor Paul agreed with that and said, "Yes."

"Assuming the initial rectal temperature was 100.1 degrees Fahrenheit, if you estimate the rate of cooling as 0.6 degrees Fahrenheit per hour the time of death would be 7.25 am. If it was 0.7 degrees Fahrenheit per hour, it would be 9.01 and if the rate was 0.8 degrees Fahrenheit it would be 10.19?"

"Where 0.1 degree Fahrenheit makes such a difference in the calculations it would be unsafe to assume that you know the rate of cooling," said Professor Paul. "I think we are making conclusions which are beyond the particular scope of the evidence," he reiterated.

Professor Paul agreed that 0.7 degrees Fahrenheit fall per hour as worked out by Professor de Saram was reasonable. His disagreement was with the starting temperature of 98.4 degrees Fahrenheit.

Regarding the passage of food in the gastrointestinal tract, Professor Paul said that even if she had died one hour after she had string-hoppers, in his experience he would not expect to find any recognizable features of string-hoppers in the small intestine.

"It should be liquid by then. Therefore in 3 hours it is impossible to have recognizable string-hoppers in the intestines," said Professor Paul.

To check this, Professor Paul said he had done several tests on patients.

In the 1950s Professor Paul may not have obtained 'ethical clearance' or 'informed consent' to perform these investigations, for the sole purpose of solving a murder case.

After giving various amounts of string-hoppers, 'sambal' and water to 7 women he aspirated the stomach contents, rather an uncomfortable procedure to patients!

Based on those studies, he said to find 10 ounces (284 millilitres) of fluid in the stomach, Mrs. Sathasivam would have taken 20 ounces of fluid about half an hour before death.

Professor Paul said that death has occurred within one hour of taking the string hoppers and fluid. Whether it was tea, coffee or water, he said that the rate of emptying of the stomach was a more valuable test.

"Do you think that test by itself, if the time of death became a crucial issue, would be sufficiently convincing to your mind for the purpose of deciding whether on that factor alone a man should either be convicted or acquitted?" asked Justice Gratiaen.

"Yes," said Professor Paul.

Dr. Colvin R. de Silva began his cross-examination by asking Professor Paul whether he was interested in the Sathasivam murder case before the Police professionally contacted him.

"Yes," replied Professor Paul.

"I take it, like most people in those days, you also had some views of your own like most people, as to who had most likely committed the murder and so on, previous to your being professionally consulted?"

"No views of that nature. I would not have had enough information to form any view. The views that one would draw are from what was published in the papers."

Somewhat unhappy with that reply, Dr. de Silva said, "You will pardon me for reminding at the very outset, in this case I must tell you one thing. When I put you a question I would like you to please answer that question and then, if you wish to give reasons for that answer, I shall happily give you the opportunity. His Lordship will certainly give you that opportunity. What I want to know is this: My question is not whether you had the facts to arrive at a view. My question is whether you held some tentative view as to who had caused the killing?"

"No definite view."

"I am asking you whether you formed any tentative view?"

"I cannot recall having formed any tentative view," replied Professor Paul.

Professor Paul said when the Police gave him the documents relating to the case they did not ask him for an opinion on any specific issue. He said he gave only an oral opinion to Mr. Thiedeman and not a written one.

He said the first time he met anybody in the Attorney-General's Department was after the trial started.

During the cross-examination, Dr. Colvin R. de Silva asked Professor Paul to give a demonstration of the position of the victim, the strangler and the position from which William could have received those injuries on him as he visualized it, when William was giving evidence in the Magistrate's Court.

"In the demonstration you just gave us the whole length of the legs of the victim were left completely free?" asked Dr. de Silva.

"Yes."

"In the posture you gave to William would you assume that the weight of his body would come on to his forearms?"

He agreed.

Justice Gratiaen asked, "If the strangler strangled Mrs. Sathasivam in that position which you have indicated, was there the slightest necessity for obtaining the assistance of an accessory?"

"No," replied Professor Paul.

"Further, there was no injury on Mrs. Sathasivam's body to indicate an accessory?" asked Dr. de Silva.

"No."

Professor Paul agreed it was theoretically possible that Mrs. Sathasivam was strangled from behind.

Professor Paul said that injuries 7 (behind the ear, on the mastoid region), 10 to 14 (left collar bone and left arm), and 16 and 17 (right toe and leg) could be post-mortem injuries, but he said it was irrelevant to his demonstration of the way of strangling.

Dr. de Silva then reminded Professor Paul that in the Magistrate's Court he had said, "In my view all the injuries Mrs. Sathasivam had were caused in the course of the strangulation." Therefore they must be ante-mortem as Professor de Saram has clearly stated.

He agreed that the external injury number 9 (parallel linear abrasions on the neck) with the underlying contusion of the neck (internal injury number 2) was not a post-mortem injury and could not have caused by stamping on the neck with a shoe after Mrs. Sathasivam was dead.

"Were you frankly satisfied that external injury number 9 was caused while the strangler was strangling the life out of the woman?" asked Justice Gratiaen.

"That is so," replied Professor Paul. He said he was not absolutely certain as to how this injury was caused.

Dr. de Silva asked, "When you find that you have no explanation for an injury in the light of theories that are placed before you, or are constructed by you, does not that become precisely the most important injury in the case?"

"Not if does not upset the theory; if it upsets the theory I would have felt it my bounden duty to mention it to Court," replied Professor Paul.

Dr. de Silva perhaps sarcastically asked, "The statement in this Court in your presence by a young man from Angunabadulla completely shook your faith in your theory?"

Professor Paul admitted it did shake his theory.

Justice Gratiaen also asked "Has he shaken your theory?"

He said, "He has," and added, "There are certain modifications which must be made."

Dr. de Silva found that Professor Paul was now in a difficult position and continued with his cross-examination.

"William contrived to give a demonstration and demolished your theory in the Magistrate's Court and you are now constructing a theory to support William in this Court?"

Professor Paul had to say "Yes."

Justice Gratiaen asked Professor Paul when a doctor swears that from his own observations that abrasions were ante-mortem it amounts to his saying that he saw the necessary marks in connection with those particular abrasions, which would exclude the possibility of them being post-mortem.

"That is not necessarily my criteria. He may have very good reasons for his opinion but that may not be the criteria which I have given in this Court," answered Professor Paul.

Retorted Dr. de Silva, "Will you agree that we can reasonably assume that a Professor of Forensic Medicine in the Ceylon University and an ex-Judicial Medical Officer of Colombo knows what are the standard ways of concluding whether an abrasion is ante-mortem or post-mortem?"

"It is not a standard way. It is not mentioned in Forensic Medicine as such. It is a way which if I observed it would carry absolute conviction to my mind, that is if I saw blood in the streaks," replied

Professor Paul.

Professor Paul however agreed that one person could do the strangulation of Mrs. Sathasivam and a second person was quite unnecessary. In the Magistrate's Court he had said two persons strangled Mrs. Sathasivam because he thought one person was strangling while the other, William, was restraining the free hand of the struggling victim.

"In short, the position you are taking is this. Your position is that you postulate Mr Sathasivam's hand at the throat because William carries injuries on his forearm?"

"Yes."

"It just does not occur to you that a person whose hands were at the throat could have got injuries on the forearm?"

"It was not likely. I would expect injuries on the wrists and hands," said Professor Paul.

Perhaps realising the absurdity of these answers, Justice Gratiaen remarked, "Mr Sathasivam's misfortune, if one can call it a misfortune, is that he has not got the exculpatory scratch marks on the face and arms. If it was Sathasivam who had the scratch marks on the face and arms, and William had none, then the position of the accused would have been reversed?"

"I would not concede that," replied Professor Paul.

"You mean that Mr. Sathasivam is nevertheless guilty?" remarked the Judge.

Perhaps at last, Dr. de Silva got the answer he wanted when he asked Professor Paul, "If the victim recovered from stunning (from the blow to the head) to be capable of semi-purposive reaction, would it or would it not be remarkable that the semi purposive injuries were not on the person nearest to her? If one is capable of semi-purposive reaction would one expect that reaction to be directed at a person nearest?"

Professor Paul perhaps very reluctantly had to answer, "I would."

Professor Paul stated that in all his readings of standard works or any other works, he had not come across any reference with regard to the question of depth of nail marks used for purpose of deciding who the likely assailant is.

Dr. de Silva read the following paragraph from the Keith Simpson's "Forensic Medicine" book.

"Sometimes nail impressions are drawn away and long or short drawn scratches result. The depth and breadth of these may be compared with nails of the suspect and their direction will often show twisting or other evasive movements of the victim."

Professor Paul said that he has also read that passage, but no one has ever excluded one suspect or included another suspect merely on the question of depth.

Dr. de Silva then asked, "Do you claim to be an expert as Dr Keith Simpson?"

"No," answered Professor Paul.

He said that he would have been more convinced if Keith Simpson has gone into Court and said 'I exclude so and so and involve so and so on nail marks'. "Then I would have been inclined to accept him," said Professor Paul.

"If Professor de Saram, who is a reasonably competent doctor to hold a post-mortem as yourself, and who saw that skin of the lady and examined it tells you, as a fellow medical man, that he would expect the lady to have been bruised in that area if somebody held her there bringing his weight to bear, would you dare to challenge it?"

"That would not carry any conviction to me, but I quite concede he may have that honest opinion."

"We must all concede that any doctor in this case is expressing an honest opinion?"

"I do not imply that. Having done the post-mortem he may have arrived at a particular conclusion but the evidence on which he arrived at that conclusion when examining the body at the post-mortem is not in the post-mortem report. You have no evidence at the post-mortem whether a person is easily bruised or not because in manual strangulation where there has been a struggle, how can you say whether a person was easily bruised?" asked Professor Paul.

"Your position is that your fellow Professor of Forensic Medicine in the University of Ceylon is unable to distinguish the quality of the skin, etc. of the body he examined at the post-mortem?"

"Not only he but anybody. No one could. With that information no one could."

"With the information of that post-mortem?"

"Yes."

"What is the information?"

"That there were extensive bruises in certain parts of the body; those abrasions do not indicate to my mind anything."

Dr. de Silva said Professor de Saram has nowhere said so.

"Have you been told that Professor de Saram has said that because there were extensive bruises on some parts of Mrs. Sathasivam's body therefore it was an easily bruisable body?"

"I wish to explain."

"Have you been told that Professor de Saram's evidence is that because there are extensive bruises, heavy bruises on some parts of the body, therefore she had an easily bruisable body?" Dr. de Silva repeated the question.

"I have not been told that."

"Therefore, on what authority do you say that no Professor is entitled to say that?"

"To make it clear, I understood counsel to say that there was evidence from the post-mortem examination that Mrs. Sathasivam had an abnormal tendency to bruise. I see no such evidence in the post-mortem findings. That is not recorded. There is no evidence whatsoever."

"I would like to remind you of one passage given in the light of your evidence in principal examination. Do you remember in your examination by my learned friend the Solicitor-General, you said that the abrasions, though they may be trivial as injuries, can be of the highest importance?" asked Dr. de Silva.

"Can be; yes."

"Whether you said so or not, do you agree that they can be?"

"Yes, they can be."

"Therefore if you find an abrasion which you cannot fit into a theory, will you agree that the abrasion would be of the highest importance?"

"It might be unimportant but it may be of the highest importance too."

"What is your definition of an abrasion?"

"An abrasion is an injury produced by the friction of a rough object."

"In relation to the skin how would you define it?"

"There is one type of abrasion which is quite easy to understand, that is what is produced by a rough object travelling in a line. Then there is another type, which I would not personally classify as an abrasion, but which has been described in this Court as an abrasion that is an imprint; a firm pressure on the skin by an object produces a mark. To my mind that is not an abrasion but I am prepared to call it an abrasion for our purposes."

"What is your third definition of an abrasion?"

"Those are the only two definitions."

Dr. de Silva then read a passage to Professor Paul from Keith Simpson's book on Forensic Medicine, under the heading 'Types of wounds' and sub-heading 'Abrasions'.

"Abrasions are grazes of the skin, would you agree with that?"

"That is what I would expect."

Dr. de Silva continued to read from the passage.

"'And although the fact that they are confined to the cuticle prevents their being grave or serious, there can be no question that they are among the most highly informative and forensically important of all injuries'. Will you agree with that opinion of Keith Simpson?"

"I would not elevate every scratch to a major event. I mean a major event in significance; not in severity."

"There can be no question, says Keith Simpson, that they are among the most highly informative of all injuries. Will you agree with that opinion of Keith Simpson?"

"They might not be. A man might die after scratching his skin. The fact that he scratched his skin might not be informative."

"If you find a scratch there and you find a man dead might it not indicate to you that it is necessary to do something further by way of analysis of the internal organs to see whether it is the scratch of a nail or a hypodermic needle?"

"I will observe it and make notes of it but when I come to Court I would present before Court the relevant details."

"Will you agree that there can be no question that they are among the most highly informative of all injuries?"

"Can be among the most informative. I think that sentence is used with a purpose in that text book, but if you take it by itself you can criticize it."

"Will you agree with this: 'There can be no question that they are among the most forensically important of all injuries'?"

"They are potentially so."

"Therefore, when in constructing a theory of strangulation in relation to injuries on the neck, excluding an abrasion at the base of the neck in constructing your theory can be a very material matter?"

"Yes."

"To fail to inform the Court that you are so omitting an injury in your mind can be to an accused person a lethal matter?"

"I do not agree."

"You remember, I read to you a passage earlier that you had stated that when the strangler got up he had the dead body at his feet. In relation to that I was reading to you the earlier passages. Here is the evidence you gave in the Magistrate's Court on that question whether the lady was dead at the feet of the strangler when the strangler rose from the strangling. I will just read to you the whole thing. You have stated that you disagree with the view that there was any possibility of survival after the strangulation. You remember that?"

"Yes."

"What do you mean by strangulation there?"

"I mean by strangulation the period during which the voice box was compressed."

"Are you assuming in this case one continuous pressure on the voice box or not?"

"I am assuming one continuous pressure."

During the cross-examination Dr. Colvin R. de Silva told Professor Paul, "I suggest to you doctor that you had been prepared in this case to give opinions on non-medical matters?"

"In what respect?"

"I will give you several respects. For instance, you were at one stage prepared to give evidence, were you not, on the dress habits of womenfolk?" Dr. de Silva asked sarcastically.

"If I am asked a direct question – that information was not volunteered by me."

"If you were asked you would volunteer?"

"As anybody else would; as any other member of the public would."

"Who asked you?"

"I cannot remember whether it was the defence or the Crown."

Dr. de Silva quipped, "Never by me. Mr. Cherubim addressed to you a final question, this is what he asked you: 'If the deceased was wearing the petticoat and the saree with the armpits exposed as shown in photographs would you, as a Tamil, and knowing the customs of the Tamils, expect Mrs. Sathasivam to come downstairs in that dress?'"

"I would both expect the deceased to come down in that dress and I would not restrict my opinion only to the Tamils. You gave that answer?"

"Yes."

"Do you think a medical man would give an opinion on the question of how a dead body would lie when it is left finally if two people carried it?"

"That is very relevant to a medical assessment of the case."

"Even if you were not given any data as to how the carrying was done?"

"Yes."

"In other words, you would as a doctor, if you saw a dead body lying about the place, undertake to say how it was carried?"

"It would be very relevant in arriving at the conclusion about the cause of death."

Dr. de Silva perhaps realised that Professor Paul was now in some difficulty.

"In other words, will you undertake from the position in which the dead body was lying if you were told that the dead body had been carried from somewhere else to say how the body was carried?" he asked Professor Paul.

"I could," he answered.

It was Professor Milroy Paul who thought that Dr. Frank Taylor would be a good authority to bring into this case.

Dr. de Silva asked, "At the request of the Police you interceded, as I might term it, to get Dr. Taylor's consent to come into this case?"

"Yes."

"Are you aware of Dr. Taylor's opinion on that question?"

"No."

"He was asked the following question by Mr. Cherubim, Crown Counsel, in the Magistrate's Court after the question about the twelve tears on that saree. 'If Mrs. Sathasivam was strangled in her bed room upstairs by a single assailant and her body taken down to the garage downstairs in what position would you expect the body to be?' Dr. Taylor said 'I do not think there is any answer for that question'. Do you agree?"

"I do not," replied Professor Paul.

"Shown the two photographs of Mrs. Sathasivam's body lying in the garage, Dr. Taylor was asked, 'Do these photos suggest that the body had been laid down'? Dr. Taylor's answer was 'I am not prepared to say'. Do you think that he was quite justified in not being prepared to say if he did not wish to make any conclusion?"

"He was justified in giving that reply."

"You think he could have?"

"I could not answer for him."

"A medical man of his qualifications, you think, ought to have been?"

"I will put it this way. I was prepared to."

"You were prepared to answer what Dr. Taylor was not – 'I do not think there is any answer to that question' – in other words, you were prepared to answer what Dr. Taylor considered unanswerable?" asked Dr. de Silva.

"Yes," Professor Paul replied.

Continuing to compare Dr. Taylor's opinion with Professor Paul's, Dr. de Silva went on, "You were asked: ' If a person strangled the deceased in the kitchen and carried her to the garage and left her what is the position in which you would expect to find the body of the deceased? You will agree that that was precisely what was put to

Dr. Taylor?"

"That is so."

"And the doctor's answer precisely to that question was: 'I do not think there is an answer to that question?'"

"That is so."

Justice Gratiaen asked, "Now your answer would substantially be the same answer whether a single assailant carried the corpse from upstairs or from the kitchen to the garage? The starting point would not make much of a difference?"

"That is so," replied Professor Paul.

Dr. de Silva continuing his searching cross-examination said, "Your answer to the question put to you was: 'A recently dead body is limp and a person is likely to carry the body in the arms with the hips and knees flexed, and the person carrying would leave the body with the hips and knees in that position.'"

Dr. de Silva said that Professor Paul was asked on that point in the Magistrate's Court.

"You were asked, 'By how many assailants do you say Mrs. Sathasivam was strangled?' and you answered 'Two'."

"Yes."

"You have told us that no theory you can think of where two people doing the strangulation, would you be surprised to know?"

"I am not surprised. I said."

"By which you mean one strangler plus the accessory?" asked Justice Gratiaen.

"At that stage of the evidence I considered two people taking part was more likely than one," replied Professor Paul.

"What medical reasons have you?" asked Dr. de Silva.

"One was the injuries on William which were not injuries consistent with his being the strangler; his injuries did not suggest that he was the strangler. Secondly, the position of the body as shown in the photograph."

Dr. de Silva reading further from the evidence remarked that Professor Paul excluded three assailants or one assailant.

"In other words you have said it had to be two assailants, not more, not less?"

"Yes."

"Why it had to be two?"

"Three would be unnecessary; for one thing there was no evidence of three."

"Why not three for medical reasons?"

"I could not conceive of three taking part; that is why I said that."

"Medically?"

"Taking into account the injuries on William and taking the circumstances in which the body was found."

Regarding carrying Mrs. Sathasivam's body to the garage, Professor Paul said according to the photographs and the injuries on the body, two people carried the body to the garage.

"How do you get two, three, four or as a matter of fact half a dozen on photograph?" questioned perplexed Dr. de Silva.

"I could not have conceived of half a dozen persons carrying the body."

"Why can't three carry medically? What is in the way of three carrying it?"

"Could have."

"Medically, what is in the way of 6 people carrying it?"

"Unlikely."

"Why is it medically unlikely?"

"It may be difficult."

"Medically, six people find it difficult to get round a coffin of that size?"

"A coffin is different."

"Why not four, medically?"

"It is unlikely."

"Why?"

"Small woman. I suppose, if there were four, two would be doing nothing and two would be carrying that is the reason I had in my mind."

"What you mean is, doctor, if you were one of the four, you would have been satisfied with one assistant?"

"Yes."

"You do not postulate yourself with your skill and education as a killer?"

"It is quite possible, one could imagine anything," Professor Paul replied.

Further questioning on the number of assailants, Dr. de Silva asked, "You said you postulated two assailants because of (1) the injuries on William and (2) the posture in which the body was left?"

"Yes."

"What has the posture of the body to do with the number of assailants?"

"As I have already mentioned, if it was one assailant that assailant would not have taken the trouble to straighten the body out after it was deposited on the ground."

"Why do you assume he would not?"

"It would be an operation which would take time and quite uncalled for in the circumstances of this case."

"Do you say that the injuries on Mrs. Sathasivam indicate two assailants?"

"No."

"That is definite?"

"Yes."

"It is curious that in the Magistrate's Court you had a different opinion. You said in the Magistrate's Court 'On the injuries on Mrs Sathasivam, I am of opinion that there were two assailants.' Do you remember saying that?"

"I don't remember."

"If you are so recorded would you accept that you probably said so?"

"Probably, but I would like to know what the reasons were."

Dr. Colvin R. de Silva, by this series of questions attempted to discredit the opinion of Professor Paul.

Next, referring to the passage of food, Dr. de Silva read a paragraph from the book "Forensic Medicine" (Eighth edition) by Sir Sydney Smith, which stated, 'The passage of food along the bowel may help in fixing the time since the last meal'.

Professor Paul said, "I have been very puzzled by that passage in that book. I wondered how he came to write it."

"You regard it as a reckless statement in a text book?"

"I would not dream of doing that. When I read that statement, I wondered how he came to write it. I do not imply any recklessness. He was quoting rates of passage of food in the intestines from barium experiments or evidence."

"Do you accept him as an authority on forensic medicine?"

"Yes."

"Would you agree that he is a leading authority on forensic medicine in the Commonwealth of Nations?"

"One of the," said Professor Paul.

"You think that it is the duty that an expert should not give evidence for either side but independently and impartially?"

"Yes."

Concluding the cross-examination Dr. de Silva asked, "The first duty is to give impartial evidence in a Court of law and secondly, to state any difficulties he has in the views he has expressed in this Court?"

"Yes," replied Professor Paul.

It appears that the evidence of Professor Milroy Paul, an honest truthful witness, as all the other medical and scientific witnesses in this case, did not help the prosecution very much.

Professor M.V.P. Peiris was the next witness for the Crown. Examined by Mr. T. S. Fernando, the Acting Solicitor-General, he said, "I am a Fellow of the Royal College of Surgeons England. I was elected a Fellow in 1929. I have been a surgeon attached to the General Hospital, Colombo, from 1930, and a Visiting Surgeon from 1936. I have been an Associate Professor of Surgery, University of Ceylon, since 1952."

"In the course of your work you come into contact daily with injuries on persons?" asked Mr. Fernando.

"Yes."

"And as a result of your experience you claim to be able to speak to the manner in which injuries are caused?"

"Yes."

Professor Peiris said somewhere towards the end of December

1951, Inspector Thiedeman came to see him. He wanted Professor Peiris to express an opinion on the files that were handed over to him in this case."

"Can you tell us what were the documents that were handed over to you?"

"The post-mortem report of Professor de Saram, and the evidence of Professor de Saram and Mr. Chanmugam given in the Magistrate's Court."

He said he was also given three photographs that had been produced in the Magistrate's Court at that stage.

"I believe attached to the post-mortem report was a description of the examination of the accused as well as a description of the injuries found on William?"

"That is so."

"Did you express any opinion to Mr. Thiedeman?"

"Yes. He wanted to know whether I agreed with the conclusions drawn by Professor de Saram and also whether the strangling had taken place upstairs or downstairs, or something like that. I said I was not in agreement with Professor de Saram on the question of the time of death and the deductions made by him on his own findings."

"Did you express any view as to whether the strangling was on the floor or standing?"

"I said that the strangling took place on the floor."

"Did you express any view as to whether the strangler came from behind or attacked from front?"

Professor Peiris said he did not go into details and did not give any opinion in writing.

He said he remembered the meeting he had with Dr Taylor, Professor Paul and Professor de Saram.

"Thereafter, the next thing of consequence so far as you were concerned was that you found yourself in the witness box?" Mr. Fernando asked.

"Well, Mr. Thiedeman came and asked me a second time whether I would give evidence. I said I wanted a few days to consider whether I would agree to come to the witness box. I was trying to get out of it. I was trying to get out of coming and giving evidence again."

"You were a reluctant witness?"

"Yes. But of course I was persuaded to give evidence in the Magistrate's Court. I would much prefer to have all of my time available for surgery."

He said at the time he gave evidence in the Magistrate's Court, he was not aware of William's evidence or the description of the killing of Mrs. Sathasivam.

He agreed that the death was due to asphyxia by manual strangulation. "That I think everybody has accepted and there is no disagreement about that," he said.

Mr. Fernando asked, "Could external injuries 1 and 3 be caused by someone's palm pressing in that region or rubbing in that region?"

"I don't think so. I don't think the soft tissues of the palm could produce those injuries."

"Similarly in regard to external injury number 9, would your answer be the same, that the palm of a person could not cause that injury?"

"There I would be more definite. It is not possible to produce those abrasions with the contusions underneath with the palm."

"Could a shod foot coming with some force in the region of 1, 3 and 9 produce the abrasions?"

"Quite likely."

Mr. Fernando then asked how many nail marks he observed in the injury number 4, described by Professor de Saram in his report as "Irregular scratch mark 1¼ inches long 1/8th of an inch wide."

"Seven."

"Did you have any difficulty in discerning seven nail marks?"

"You can count seven marks there. I have looked at the copy I have got with a magnifying glass. So I know what it is."

Shown the photographs of the neck injuries of Mrs. Sathasivam, he said that the difference is that in one, the lower two marks are drawn with the concavity pointing outwards while in the other the concavities are towards the middle.

"Looking at the photograph it is like one of those puzzles. Concavities are directed inwards and I would say so without hesitation. That is taking all the facts into consideration. In my opinion the concavities of those are directed towards the middle line," Professor Peiris said.

Explaining the injury behind the left ear he said, "During strangling, the ball of the thumb will come in contact with the ear, and if with that you press the ear backwards it is possible to get an abrasion, but taking the other finding that the ear stud was bent, which I have heard somewhere, I don't know whether it is possible to produce a bend in the ear stud and at the same time produce an abrasion with a bare soft hand or the soft tissues of the ball of the thumb."

He said that abrasion number 10 on the collar bone is unlikely to have been caused by the forearm of a person rubbing on that spot.

"The soft tissues of the forearm are not likely to produce abrasions. One should not expect soft tissues to produce abrasions on another soft tissue, even when there is a bone underneath."

"Unless the forearm rubbed against the 'thali' ?"

"Yes."

"Or some rough object came in contact with it?"

"Yes."

Professor Peiris said that injuries on top of the left hand, over the left wrist and on the back of the right thumb were small abrasions caused by a rough surface.

"It will be a terrible thing if doctors had to say accurately how injuries came to be. Would any doctor stake his professional reputation as to how precisely injuries 12, 13, 14 and 15 were caused?" asked Justice Gratiaen.

"Nobody could say that."

"The abrasions of external injury number 18 could have been caused while the victim was on the ground or while the victim was being pressed against a wall in the erect position?" asked Mr. Fernando.

"Yes."

Referring next to the internal injuries of Mrs. Sathasivam, Mr. Fernando queried, "With regard to injury number 10, that was a contusion with no external injury visible?"

"There were no abrasions over it. The likely cause of that injury was a hard object coming into contact with that area."

"You could exclude a piece of firewood like that?" Justice Gratiaen asked showing the piece of firewood found in the garage.

"I think it was unlikely. One would expect even a small portion to be uncovered and be bare, or even with the hair it would cause an abrasion."

Continuing the examination-in-chief, Mr. Fernando asked, "You remember William's demonstration. If the lady was seated on the bed and the strangler got hold of her by the throat and jerked her on to the ground, that portion of the head would strike the floor and that injury would be caused?"

"It is possible."

To explain the method of causation of neck injuries, Professor Peiris demonstrated on a peon of the Court by bringing his shoe down on his left jaw.

Professor Peiris said that the moment the shoe comes down it catches on two prominences the chin and the jaw, and it slips down into the hollow of the neck and one may get a few scratches on the neck.

Mr. Fernando then questioned Professor Peiris about the fracture of the thyroid cartilage of Mrs. Sathasivam's neck.

Justice Gratiaen asked, "Would you expect a strangler while doing that at a point of time when he actually causes the fracture of the cartilage to feel some reaction, that something had happened?"

"I would not expect it."

"Would anything be heard?" asked Mr. Fernando.

"Definitely not. As to feeling one cannot say, but I do not expect it. But as to hearing anything, definitely not," replied Professor Peiris, contradicting William's statement that he heard Mrs. Sathasivam's voice box break when she was strangled by Mr. Sathasivam.

Referring to the length of Mr. Sathasivam's nails and the possibility of having deeper injuries if he was the strangler, as Professor de Saram explained, Professor Peiris said he would not in this case exclude a man merely because his nails were found to be 1/6th of an inch in length.

Professor Peiris agreed that holding a mirror to the nostrils was a well known method adopted to see whether a person was living or not.

Mr. Fernando read to Professor Peiris the following passage from 'Medical Jurisprudence and Toxicology' by Modi (1940 Edition), under the heading 'Tests to determine the stoppage of respiration'.

'The surface of a cold, bright looking-glass, held in front of the open mouth and nostrils becomes dim, due to the condensation of warm moist air exhaled from the lungs, if respiration is still going on, but not otherwise'.

Then he asked, "Do you agree with that?"

"I do," replied Professor Peiris.

Mr. Fernando then questioned Professor Peiris at length on the determination of the time of death.

Mr. Fernando asked whether he would agree with Professor de Saram's statement that according to the rigor mortis of Mrs. Sathasivam's body at 5.55 p.m., her death must have taken place between 8 to 10 hours before that time.

"Yes, I agree with that statement."

"That would take you to between 7.55 a.m. and 9.55 a.m.?"

"Yes. By the rigor test alone you come to within that range. By itself I will not say it is a safe test."

"Have you ever considered post-mortem eye changes to be any guide at all to ascertain the time of death?"

"Post-mortem eye changes are usually not taken into account in considering the time of death. Rigor mortis is bad enough I think and post-mortem eye changes are worse!"

"It is suggested that the rate of fall of temperature in the case of this lady could be taken as either 0.6 degrees per hour or 0.7 degrees per hour. Would you consider those to be reasonable rates of fall for this period?"

"Yes."

Professor Peiris said he did independent experiments with 3 dead bodies to determine the rate of cooling.

"One man had a rectal temperature of 98.4 degrees Fahrenheit at the time of death. He was a very old debilitated man and a miserable looking person, from a medical point of view. He died of debility.

During the first hour the rate of fall in his case was 1 degree, in the second hour it was 0.7 degrees and in the next hour also it was a drop of 0.7 degrees. It shows in the three hours the average rate would be 0.8 degrees. When you consider these experiments of mine, the figure of 0.6 and 0.7 appears to me a reasonable figure, if you consider the cooling of the body for about five hours. That is what has been stated by Professor de Saram and I agree with that. The rate will also vary with the initial temperature. The higher the initial temperature the higher the rate of fall to begin with," explained Professor Peiris.

Mr. Fernando questioned Professor Peiris on the formula to determine the time since death using the rectal temperature and the rate of fall.

Justice Gratiaen asked, "Would you say that it was safe either to hang a man or to acquit him by the mere application of a formula for the purpose of ascertaining the approximate time of death?"

"If the formula gives you a certain rate you can give a margin of error and say that it must be within this reasonable amount of time. If you give reasons and weigh them in your judgment, I think you can apply this formula in a murder case or in any case. It has been always applied in murder cases because it is in murder cases that this crops up."

"You allow a margin of error within safe limits?"

"Yes. This assumes that there is no serious change of temperature at the time of death."

"You think that this is the best method of ascertaining the time of death?"

"It is considered, if not the best, one of the best ways of estimating the time," replied Professor Peiris.

Mr. Fernando continued to question Professor Peiris on the application of the formula.

He suggested that assuming the rectal temperature of Mrs. Sathasivam to be 99.9 degrees Fahrenheit and assuming a rate of fall 0.6 degrees, the time of Mrs. Sathasivam's death works out to 11 $^1/_6$ hours before 6.55 p.m.

That is, $$\frac{99.9 - 93.2}{0.6} = 11 \; ^1/_6 \text{ hours}$$

"That is roughly 7.45 a.m.?"

"I made it out to be 7.42."

"Now assuming a 0.7 degree rate of fall, you work out a sum which comes to 9 $^4/_7$ hours before 6.55 p.m.?"

"Yes."

"How much does that works out to?"

"9.25 a.m."

"So applying these two rates of fall, 0.6 and 0.7, you get 7.42 at one end and 9.25 a.m. at the other end?"

"Yes. Even if you apply a 0.8 rate of fall, it works out to 10.35 a.m."

Justice Gratiaen asked, "Then your conclusion is that it is safe to assume that Mrs. Sathasivam died at some point of time between 7.42 a.m., and 10.35 a.m. at the outside limit. Is that a fair calculation?"

Professor Peiris replied, "From these calculations that is what it indicates."

"So if you take the rate of cooling as a little more than 0.8 degrees?"

"You can take it at 0.9 degrees and it would be 11.30. So that you have a wide range of temperatures and we can be absolutely certain that it must fall within that time. I can take it from 0.6 to 0.9 and say it was somewhere between 7.40 and 11.30 a.m."

Mr. Fernando next questioned Professor Peiris about the passage of food to determine the time of death.

Professor Peiris said that taking all facts into consideration his conclusion was that Mrs. Sathasivam died within an hour of having taken the meal. "An hour being a fairly generous estimate," he said.

"Not possibly more than an hour?" asked Justice Gratiaen.

"Very unlikely."

Cross-examined by Dr. Colvin R. de Silva, Professor Peiris said that he and Professor Paul had discussed the Sathasivam murder case sometimes when they met in the hospital wards.

"Professor Paul has told us that you had conferred on this matter?" Dr. de Silva asked

"That is so. I have spoken to him on the various points in this case."

"You have discussed I take it your mutual difficulties and problems arising from the material placed before you?"

"Yes."

"And I take it you sought to see how far you could accord your views?"

"How far these things could be explained."

"How far you could modify your views and come to a conclusion?"

"It was not our aim to come into agreement, but we were trying to explain the various injuries as best as we could."

"Was it not your aim to arrive at an honest opinion?" asked Justice Gratiaen.

"That is so. But I would like to say that it is not our aim to put forward a joint view whatever it was. Our aim was to give an explanation which each one thought was the correct view. It may be that sometimes I differed from him," replied Professor Peiris.

Answering further questions of Dr. de Silva, Professor Peiris said that on some points, such as whether injuries 7, 10 and 11 were ante-mortem or post-mortem, he did not agree with Professor Paul.

"Then in regard to the nail marks I do not entirely agree with Professor Paul. He was quite confident about the direction of those nail marks. That is, external injury number 4. Professor Paul was quite confident about its direction and how they were caused. I was not prepared to go to that extent."

"That goes for the following questions: (1) direction (2) which fingers caused it (3) what the grip was?"

"Yes, that is so. Those were details on which he and I did not see eye to eye."

Showing the photograph of the injuries of Mrs. Sathasivam, Dr. de Silva asked, "Any other external injury?"

"There is internal injury number 10. From what I read in the papers I think Professor Paul was prepared to say that, that was caused by the edge of the bed but I was not prepared to say that. I noticed these differences not as a result of discussions with him but as a result of what I read in the newspapers."

Referring to the causation of bruises Dr. de Silva asked, "A person may have a body which is more easily bruised?"

"Yes."

"One can speak of a sensitive skin without being committed to the position of saying that there is an easily bruisable person?"

"Yes, quite correct."

"So that the absence of bruises on a strangler's hand nine days after the event need have no relevance on the question of whether he was the strangler?"

"If it is bruises, yes."

"Take this example. Take this very case. Professor de Saram examined Mr. Sathasivam I think at about 7 or 8 o'clock on the night of the very day Mrs. Sathasivam died. Professor de Saram found no bruises or scratches on his hands. As a medical man would you say that those are points entirely in Mr. Sathasivam's favour if you were considering the question whether he was the strangler?"

"Absolutely."

"I wish to put this to you. Professor de Saram examined William, the principal witness in this case, the pardoned principal witness in this case, on 19th October, more than nine days after the event, and found no bruises on his hands. As you have just said that does not necessarily have any bearing on the question whether he was the strangler?"

"Yes."

"If he had bruises could they have disappeared 10 days later?"

"Small bruises would disappear in a short time."

"A person who is being strangled, therefore, may well be able to reach up only to the forearm of the person who is strangling without being able to reach the hands?"

"Yes."

Dr. de Silva then questioned Professor Peiris about the causation of abrasions.

"Anything that is hard and rough is more likely to abrade the skin if it is rubbed against it?"

"Yes."

"If moreover that hard, rough and horny object had some gritty matter then it would make the abrading of the skin surface that it came in contact with more likely?"

"Yes."

"If that hard rough surface with gritty matter on it was brought down hard on the skin?"

"You can get an abrasion."

"And an underlying contusion?" queried Justice Gratiaen.

"It all depends on the force. You can get a contusion as well."

Continuing the cross-examination, Dr. de Silva asked, "Any one of us, without our shoes if we bring our heels down on the soft side of a body, we can very well cause a contusion?"

"Contusion certainly."

"So that we come to this. The sole of a foot which is hard and rough and which may have had gritty matter on it being stamped down hard on this area of the neck and chin may have caused the injuries 1, 3 and 9 you have mentioned?"

"I would say 'yes' to that, but it would be easier with a shod foot. This injury, that is on the neck, it is possible to get that with an unshod foot with sand and grit on it if it is stamped down. That is 1 and 3. Taken all together, I would say it is not impossible to produce it with a naked foot but it will be easier with a shoe."

This opinion was very favourable to the defence.

Querying the story of William about hearing the voice box break, Dr. de Silva asked, "You have told us it is absurd that a person can hear the voice box break?"

"Unless the victim is a very old man where the whole thing is calcified into bone."

"And the strangler's hearing is perfect?" remarked Justice Gratiaen.

"Yes."

"You would rule out any sound being heard probably because there is covering flesh?" asked Dr. de Silva.

"Yes."

"But you could certainly feel that portion of the voice box giving way under the pressure of the foot or hand?"

"You can feel it giving way in that it is compressible, but whether you can take it as a fact which takes place I don't know."

"I am not worried about that. A person squeezing the throat may well feel the throat give way?"

"That is so."

"A person stamping on the bare throat with his bare foot may well feel the throat give way?"

"Yes."

"But a person who has a shoe on cannot feel that way because the shoe leather would intervene?"

"Yes."

Justice Gratiaen asked, "You do not think that anybody who did not actually break the thyroid cartilage but was merely present could possibly know that that particular fracture had occurred?"

"No. You might be able to feel it break. I say might. I grant that it is possible, but nobody else can. Only the fingers that are holding and producing the grip could feel it."

Dr. de Silva questioned Professor Peiris further about the differences of opinion he had with Professor Paul.

Professor Peiris said, "With regard to external injury number 7 my view was that it was a post-mortem injury. His view was that it could be an ante-mortem injury. He believed that convulsions were invariable in the cases of death from asphyxia but I do not agree. I said that it is possible that you may not get obvious convulsions. He was convinced that a bare foot could not produce those injuries on the neck. I said it was barely possible. With regard to the time of death he gave a very wide range. I do not know what he gave but my impression is that it was something between 8 and 11."

Justice Gratiaen remarked, "He expressed no opinion on it. He ultimately expressed a medical opinion based purely on the semi-digested string hoppers found in the small intestines."

Mr. Fernando said Professor Paul took only 0.6 and 0.7 degrees as the possible rate of cooling per hour and he determined the time of death between 9.35 a.m. and 11.15 a.m.

Justice Gratiaen said Professor Paul thought Professor de Saram's rates of cooling were reasonable.

Dr. de Silva then questioned Professor Peiris about the 6 inches long external injury number 10 on the right side of the head of Mrs.

Sathasivam.

"The upper half of the ear has been cut by the blow?"

"Yes. You can see it in the diagram. In the statement too it says that it goes across the upper half of the ear."

At this stage Justice Gratiaen said, "Well, Professor de Saram is in Court and I could ask him if you don't mind it?"

Justice Gratiaen asked, "Professor de Saram, is it correct that the upper half of the ear was damaged?"

"Yes," replied Professor de Saram.

Professor Peiris said this injury was caused when her head struck the foot of the bed or the edge of the bed. As Professor Peiris had not seen the bed, Mr. T. S. Fernando said, "I may say that I have asked Mr. Thiedeman to go and make measurements and be ready to describe it. Mr. Edwards, Assistant Superintendent of Police is asked to telephone and get the bed dismantled and only bring the foot of the bed to Court."

Handing over the piece of firewood Dr. de Silva asked, "Now even for the moment if you assume this piece of firewood, as the weapon with which the blow was struck, if you take especially the flat side of it, it has a relatively smooth surface along the length?"

"Yes."

Professor Peiris therefore agreed with Dr. de Silva's suggestion that there need not be an abrasion on the head as a result of striking with this piece of firewood.

Justice Gratiaen queried, "Can you say now, if you hit defence counsel with this piece of wood that you would be certain to produce an abrasion on his head?"

"I will not say certain, but it is very likely to produce an abrasion with a contusion underneath. It depends on how it will strike."

"It depends on which particular part of the piece of wood came in contact with his head?"

"That is so."

Dr. de Silva continuing the cross-examination asked, "A pretty severe blow with a piece of wood like this could leave this contusion?"

"Yes."

Dr. de Silva then demonstrating the attack on Mrs. Sathasivam asked, "Please think of it this way. She is struck from behind with some weapon of the weight, let us say of this piece of wood, and may be with the flat side of a piece of firewood. With that very act the person is in a position to get hold of the throat of the victim?"

"Yes."

"I am not speaking of the hands, as to which hand was used, but he gets her by the throat, swings her across so as to get her with the back against the wall and the projecting part, thus exercising the pressure harder and increasing the pressure on the throat, rendering her unconscious in that way or bringing her to a stage of helplessness even if she is not completely unconscious, and pulling her into the garage and throwing her down. You can conceive of that, is that not so?"

"Yes, you have to work that out very carefully."

"I suggest to you that there is not a single injury in this case which is not consistent with that rough demonstration I have given?"

"Yes, the injuries could be explained in the way you have said," Professor Peiris agreed.

When Dr. de Silva further questioned about the method of strangling of Mrs. Sathasivam, Justice Gratiaen asked, "Could a one-handed strangling be sufficient without any assistance from the other hand to cause death?"

"It is possible."

"In the demonstration which you gave of a right-handed grip, the right hand by itself was really the effective strangling hand which killed Mrs. Sathasivam."

"That is so."

"The other hand's real contribution would only be as an accessory?"

"Yes."

"Accessory to what?"

"To pressure."

Dr. de Silva asked, "You can conceive of a victim being seized by one hand and pressed against a door-jamb and the strangling being effective as a result?"

"Yes."

"If you were gripping the throat with the left hand and pressing the victim against the door-jamb you could get a completely effective strangling?"

"Yes."

At this stage Inspector Thiedeman was called into the witness box to produce the bed and to speak of matters connected with it.

Justice Gratiaen requested Mr. Fernando, the Acting Solicitor-General to have some photographs taken of the bed to show to the jury.

Professor Peiris also examined the part of the bed that was brought.

Dr. de Silva questioned Professor Peiris about the possibility of the head striking the bed or the piece of firewood causing Mrs. Sathasivam's head injury.

"All the theories are possible?" asked Justice Gratiaen.

"Yes."

"The floor, the wall, the edge of the foot of the bed and the stick?"

"Yes."

Answering questions of Dr. de Silva, Professor Peiris said he had given lot of thought to the injuries on Mrs. Sathasivam's body even after he gave evidence in the Magistrate's Court.

Justice Gratiaen asked, "Having regard to the amount of thought you gave in the Magistrate's Court did you accept the position that external injury number 3 was an ante-mortem injury?"

"Yes."

"You did?"

"Yes."

"Having given further thought you now think that it is impossible that it could be ante- mortem?"

"It is unlikely."

"Impossible?"

"That is so."

"Medically impossible?"

"That is so," replied Professor Peiris.

Dr. de Silva then questioned Professor Peiris about the deposition of fluff on Mrs. Sathasivam's chin, which according to the defence was deposited by the hands of the strangler. Professor Peiris said that if fluff that has settled down on her chin were from fluff that was floating in the garage from the coconut husks, he would not expect it to be ingrained.

Dr. de Silva asked, "If you were told that an additional circumstance was that the fluff at that spot had to be pinched out that would strongly affect your decision on the question whether it could have floated and come to rest?"

"I won't accept it. I won't accept that it had floated."

Dr. de Silva questioned Professor Peiris at length on determining the time since death from cooling and passage of food in the gastrointestinal tract before concluding the cross-examination.

Dr. de Silva quoted from many books during the cross examination which included 'Lyon's Medical Jurisprudence for India' by Waddell and the 'Text book of Practice of Medicine' by Price.

Mr. T. S. Fernando re-examining Professor Peiris also referred to books such as Sir Leonard Hill's 'Human Physiology'.

Once Justice Gratiaen remarked to Mr. Fernando, "You seem to get the most sinister joy reading these most morbid passages!"

During the re-examination Mr. Fernando asked about the experiments Professor Peiris performed on the passage of food.

"One was a woman who weighed 90 pounds (41 kilo grams). At 8 a.m. she was given four string-hoppers and four ounces of tea with a dash of milk. Actually, at 6 a. m. we gave her a cup of tea. Then at 8 a. m. she got this. At 10.30 a. m., she had 8 ounces of tea with a dash of milk. Both were more or less identical. The first woman was 90 pounds in weight and the other 96 pounds (47 kilo grams). The second woman got four string-hoppers and four ounces of fluid, and 8 ounces of tea at 10.30 A tube was inserted and the contents of the stomach were pumped out and we got ½ ounce of fluid with bits of string-hoppers. Then we were not satisfied and we therefore probed further and washed out the stomach and we got more or less clear fluid with tiny little bits of string hoppers. This was 3 hours after the ingestion of the string-hoppers," said Professor Peiris.

"One more point really on this question of the passage of food. Dr. Welikala, the Radiologist, has carried out certain experiments and he told us that in a number of cases which came within his knowledge where he carried out the experiments and took photographs, a woman who had a string-hopper meal mixed with liquid would have the stomach either completely or very nearly empty in two and a half to three hours. Is that in line with your own experience?"

"I do not know exactly what the meal was."

"String hoppers and two cups of tea."

"2 ½ hours would be an outside limit."

At the conclusion of the re-examination Justice Gratiaen told Mr. T.S Fernando, "You have been granted permission to cross-examine Professor de Saram on any question of opinion he has expressed."

CHAPTER 8

CROSS-EXAMINATION OF THE PROFESSOR OF FORENSIC MEDICINE

It is exceptional in a criminal trial that a Forensic Pathologist, who has performed a post-mortem examination at the request of the Crown (State), is considered to be a hostile or adverse witness and is cross-examined by the Crown itself.

As Professor de Saram gave conflicting opinions on several issues relating to Mrs. Sathasivam's death, which were unfavourable to the Crown's case, the Acting Solicitor-General Mr. T. S. Fernando cross-examined Professor de Saram, after the expert medical evidence of Professor Paul and Professor Peiris.

Mr. Fernando began questioning by referring to the time of death of Mrs. Sathasivam.

"You were aware that 10.30 was an important time?" asked Mr. T. S. Fernando.

"Yes."

"You are still aware that 10.30 is an important hour?"

"Yes."

Mr. Fernando then quoted from Professor de Saram's evidence given in the Coroner's Court at the inquest.

"This is what you have said on the 14th of October, in answer to Mr. R.L. Pereira, the Queen's Counsel, who appeared for Mr. Sathasivam then, 'The strangulation must have taken place between 10 a.m. and 11.30 a.m. on the 9th of October 1951?' "

"That is so," replied Professor de Saram.

"You are aware that in this Court you have stated that you now put the time as between 10.45 and 11.15?"

"That is so."

"You have washed away the 10 to 10.45 range? Therefore, from your present estimate in this Court you took a point of time after the crucial time, 10.30?"

"I say that is the most probable time. I said 10.30 a.m. is just possible," replied Professor de Saram.

Continuing the cross-examination, Mr. Fernando asked, "In the Magistrate's Court you estimated the time of death taking certain tests?"

"I had no tests at that time."

"In the Magistrate's Court did you not estimate the time of death with certain tests?"

As no experiments on prisoners were performed at that time, Professor de Saram asked Mr. Fernando, "What do you mean by tests?"

Mr. Fernando said, "Rigor mortis test is one."

"Oh, those tests. I was thinking of the experiments," said Professor de Saram.

Justice Gratiaen then asked Mr. Fernando, "You are not suggesting that this doctor is giving dishonest evidence?"

"No," replied Mr. Fernando.

"I suppose it is purely for the purpose of testing his reliability and accuracy?"

"Yes. Speaking for myself, I do not anticipate even in the future to attack the honesty of this witness," replied Mr. Fernando.

Continuing his cross-examination Mr. Fernando asked, "Then again in the Magistrate's Court you introduced what is called the eye test or pupillary changes test. Don't you agree with me that that is not a test which is taken by any authority?"

"I think it is good for the Attorney-General's Department to understand..."

"We are always willing to learn," remarked Mr. Fernando perhaps sarcastically.

Continuing Professor de Saram explained, "I usually used to work with the Attorney-General's Department. In this case, I have gone out of my way, outside textbooks, to observe certain things in bodies, which are mostly applicable to this Island because this might help post-graduates and under-graduates to estimate time since death. So it is rather difficult, if these questions are going to be decided from text books, for me to do any original work in this country."

"Do you agree that the eye test is not given in any book?"

"No."

"It is your own test?"

"Yes."

"You say you could apply that test in this case?"

"I have applied it," replied Professor de Saram.

Justice Gratiaen asked, "In your present state of investigation of that matter, can you safely apply that in this case?"

"That and rigor mortis are fallacious," Professor de Saram said.

As Mr. Fernando continued to examine Professor de Saram on this, Justice Gratiaen remarked, "This witness has not asked to give any consideration to that test in the Magistrate's Court. You do not rely on the eye test, he does not rely and the defence does not rely on it. Is this part of the cross-examination for the purpose of disproving a test which has not been placed for our consideration?"

"The doctor still relies," said Mr. Fernando.

"No. As I read the evidence in this Court he has made no assessment from an eye test."

Mr. Fernando said, "The doctor gave evidence and he willingly offered to the defence counsel and myself a summary sort of thing of how he estimated the time of death. In that the first thing that struck me was the eye test."

"Up to today neither you nor the defence, nor the witness, has made any submissions to the jury or placed any evidence about the eye test. If you wish to cross-examine on something which has not been placed before us, I have no objection, unless it is for some purpose," Justice Gratiaen said.

"In this case it was left to me not to ask him about the time of death for a particular purpose," remarked Mr. Fernando.

Continuing the cross-examination, Mr. Fernando asked, "Now doctor do you agree that this eye test is really no test at all?"

"May I explain to you? The eye test is really the same process occurring in the eye as occurs in rigor mortis."

Professor de Saram said this because the changes of the size of the pupil after death depend on the contraction and relaxation of the iris muscles. Like all other muscles of the body, iris muscles also undergo 'rigor mortis' changing the size of the pupil.

During the cross-examination of Mr. Fernando, Justice Gratiaen asked Professor de Saram, "In your present opinion, 10 to 10.45 is less probable than 10.45 to 11.15?"

"Yes."

"From a purely medical point of view can you rule out the possibility of 10 to 10.45?"

"No."

"Then 11.15 to 11.30 also you cannot rule out as a possibility?"

"I cannot."

"But you think the highest range of possibility from the medical point of view is 10.45 to 11.00?"

"Yes," replied Professor de Saram.

After the lengthy cross-examination by Mr. Fernando, Justice Gratiaen told Dr. de Silva, "You may question the doctor in regard to matters which are either adverse or favourable to the defence arising out of the permitted cross-examination by the Crown, but not going back to any other matters."

Dr de Silva querying further on the estimation of time of death, asked "Now, doctor, was it any of your concern whether your estimate of the time of death would fit into anybody's case?"

"No."

"I take it, your endeavour was, to the best of your knowledge and understanding in relation to the facts you were able to find, to come to a conclusion as to a probable time of death?"

"That is so."

"I take it as an expert, you have a duty if further knowledge requires your modifying your opinion given 20 months ago, to modify it?"

"Yes."

"If I understood the cross-examination of the learned Solicitor-General all right, it seemed to be an important plan in his case that you have now altered your opinion, had modified shall I say – I prefer to say have developed your opinion – on what was the probable period within the band of time you gave?"

"That is so."

Dr. de Silva, quoting from the recorded evidence in the Magistrate's Court, asked "Now the Crown itself obtained from you the following evidence in the Magistrate's Court – 'To ascertain the time of death the factors I would take into consideration are –
(1) The temperature of the body
(2) Rigor mortis and eye changes, and
(3) Food in the stomach and intestines?' "

"Yes."

"When the Crown led your evidence at that stage it certainly did not suggest, did it, to you in Court that it was, shall we say, something not to be done, to use the eye changes – they never suggested it?"

"No," replied Professor de Saram.

Dr. de Silva by this question showed that the eye changes have been mentioned by Professor de Saram earlier, and was not challenged by the Crown.

Then he concluded his brief cross-examination.

CHAPTER 9

SIR SYDNEY SMITH'S EVIDENCE FOR THE DEFENCE

Both the Crown and the defence realised the significance of Professor G. S. W. de Saram's evidence given in the Magistrate's Court.

For the Crown, it was necessary to challenge Professor de Saram's evidence, which showed the guilt of William and not of Mr. Sathasivam. For the defence, it was essential to strengthen the opinion of Professor de Saram.

Therefore, Mr. Sathasivam's lawyers decided to contact Professor Sydney Smith, Regius Professor of Forensic Medicine, University of Edinburgh.

Professor Sydney Smith had served as the Professor of Forensic Medicine, University of Cairo and Chief Medico-legal Examiner to the British administration in Egypt. He succeeded Harvey Littlejohn as the Regius Professor of Forensic Medicine at Edinburgh University in 1927. The other contender for this prestigious post, John Glaister (Junior) took the post in Cairo and later succeeded his father, John Glaister (Senior) as the Regius Professor in the University of Glasgow in 1931.

Professor Smith was the most reputed forensic pathologist in the United Kingdom in the fifties. He was to visit Ceylon in 1953 as a consultant for the World Health Organization and Mr. Sathasivam's lawyers sent the following letter to Professor Smith.

"Merrill Pereira & Gunasekera   No. 21 Belmont Street,
                                Proctors & Notaries Public,
                                Hulftsdorp, Colombo 12.

13th December 1952

Dear Sir,

Regina v Sathasivam
We are the Proctors for the accused Sathasivam in the above case. Sathasivam stands indicted in the Supreme Court with the murder of his wife. Their former servant, WILLIAM, who stood charged as second accused together with him at the preliminary Inquiry in the Magistrate's Court, has since been pardoned and is now a witness for the Crown.

In the course of the lengthy preliminary inquiry, there arose an important, and even vital, conflict of medical opinion in respect of which we are anxious to obtain your opinion if possible. This 'conflict' was really in the nature of an attack developed by the Crown itself on its own Judicial Medical Officer – Professor G.S.W. de Saram – after he had given his considered medical opinion in evidence. We may say that we would regard as helpful every point, which would help to sustain Professor de Saram's main evidence.

What the points of conflict in the medical evidence actually are, will appear to you from the proceedings in the case, a copy of which accompanies this letter. Since the proceedings are bulky, we have arranged to have the portion of it, which may be relevant for your purposes suitably marked for your convenience.

We refrain from setting out the specific points on which we could be glad of your opinion because we have arranged for bearer to place them before you. We would only like to say that we shall be glad of advice also on any other matters than those bearer will refer to, which may appear important or relevant to you.

Yours faithfully,

Merrill Pereira & Gunasekera"

This letter interested Professor Smith to a great extent as he mentioned in his autobiography, because "Professor de Saram was a former pupil of mine and I have formed a high opinion of his ability and his undoubted probity." Professor Smith agreed to read the evidence brought to him by Mr. K.C. Nadarajah, a junior counsel in the Sathasivam case.

As a strange coincidence, on the same day, 13th December 1952, the Secretary to the Ministry of External Affairs of Ceylon sent a telegram to the High Commissioner for Ceylon in the United Kingdom. It stated that the Attorney-General desires to consult Professor Sydney Smith immediately on arrival in Ceylon about a pending murder case. He wanted to arrange the consultation with Professor Smith via the Home office of the United Kingdom and to inform him immediately. The Attorney-General also wrote to the High Commissioner on 15th January 1953.

A few days later, the Attorney-General's Department was informed that the defence had already contacted Professor Smith.

Therefore, on 17th February 1953, Mr. Vincent T. Thamodaram, a Crown Counsel, wrote to the Inspector General of Police the following letter.

"Please request the High Commissioner to inquire from Professor Sydney Smith whether,

a. He possessed of the relevant facts in the Sathasivam case in which Mr. Nadarajah has contacted him

b. Whether he has issued a report already to Mr. Nadarajah

c. If he has, whether he has any objection to make that report available to Attorney-General of Ceylon, in view of his letter to the High Commissioner on 15th January 1953.

I shall be thankful if the High Commissioner is contacted immediately."

On 26th February 1953, the High Commissioner for Ceylon in the United Kingdom sent a telegram to the Minister of External Affairs.

It stated that Professor Sydney Smith is in possession of relevant facts of the case having read most of the evidence given at the Magisterial inquiry and that he has furnished a report to Messrs.

Merrill Pereira and Gunasekera, the legal firm representing Mr. Mahadeva Sathasivam.

"He has no objection to the report being seen by the Attorney-General but as he has been retained by Messrs. Pereira and Gunasekera, he suggested they or Dr. Colvin R. de Silva, the senior counsel with whom he already had discussions should be contacted. It is for them to decide whether the preliminary report already furnished should be made available to the Attorney-General," the High Commissioner stated.

After studying the documents briefly, on 24th December Professor Sydney Smith wrote a letter to Mr. Sathasivam's lawyers expressing his opinion about the case.

"Dear Sirs,

Regina V. Sathasivam

"I have your note of 13th December relative to the above matter. I have perused the documents and photographs connected therewith which were handed to me by Mr. Nadarajah. I have also had several conferences with him concerning the documents.

"I have come to certain tentative conclusions about the case, but you will readily understand that the documents require a considerable amount of study and I shall have a good deal to do before coming to any final opinion. However, I think it wise to forward for your information some indication of what I think at present. I shall try to give a reasonable opinion on the time of death, the cause of death and the manner of infliction of the injuries, the place where the crime occurred, and certain matters relating to the statements already given in evidence."

Professor Smith said that the case, to a great extent, rests on defining the time of death of the deceased Mrs. Sathasivam, and particularly whether this event occurred before or after 10.30 a.m. on 9th October 1951.

"There is no method known to science which would enable me to decide whether the woman died just before or just after 10.30 a.m.

Even if I were asked to give a decided opinion whether the death occurred at 10 or 11 o'clock, that is to say with the difference of an hour, I should find it impossible to do so. The best one can do is to consider all the available evidence and give an opinion as to the most probable time."

Professor Smith argued that when Podihamy (the domestic aid) left at 8.15 a.m., three adults were left in the house and in discussing the case, therefore, every point which is made concerning the innocence of Mr. Sathasivam must suggest the culpability of William. The issue in this regard has been complicated by the fact that William has made two declarations, in one of which he assumes full responsibility for the death, in the other lays the blame on the accused with himself as an accessory.

"From 10.30 a.m. onwards there is a complete alibi for Mr. Sathasivam and there is some evidence, brought forward by the Crown, which is in favour of his defence, namely:-

1. The evidence of the traffic superintendent of Quickshaws Limited, who deposes that a cab was requested by Mrs. Sathasivam, or at least by a woman with a voice that he associated with her;

2. The evidence of the chauffeur of the taxi which called at the house of the deceased at 10.35 a.m. and who deposed that he saw Mrs. Sathasivam, whom he knew by sight, at the door of the house at that time;

3. The evidence of the son of the legal adviser of Mrs. Sathasivam, who deposes that he had a conversation with her at a time which he places between 10.30 a.m. and 12 noon. He states that he was familiar with the voice of Mrs. Sathasivam and that it appeared to him to be her voice.

The evidence of these three Crown witnesses, if accepted, would place the time of death some time after 10.30 a.m.," wrote Professor Smith.

"It must be remembered, however, that there is also evidence from the jewellers to the effect that William tried to sell the chain of the deceased about 9.45 a.m. This evidence has to be considered against the evidence noted above".

Discussing the determination of time of death, Professor Smith wrote, "Certain other evidence can be derived from the documents placed before me, which may be of some service in helping to fix the time of death. It is established that the deceased was alive at 8.15 a.m. when Podihamy and the children left for school. It would appear that she had a meal of string-hoppers and coconut at some time thereafter, for the parcel of string-hoppers which was to be used for the meal was unopened, when Podihamy left at 8.15. According to Mr. Sathasivam's statement, which is not likely to be accepted without corroboration, Mrs. Sathasivam normally ate late in the morning and on this particular morning, she took her meal when he was dressing (possibly not long before 10 a.m.)."

Professor Smith said that the only other available evidence about the time of death might be derived from:-

1. The state of the food in the alimentary canal
2. The extent of rigor mortis
3. The temperature of the body
4. Certain other conditions, such as the state of staining, the condition of the blood, etc.

Professor Smith discussed each of the above in more detail.

"1. The state of the ingested food: In the stomach there was 10 ounces (about 284 millilitres) of contents consisting of string-hoppers, coconut and fluid. In the small intestine some of this food in a semi-digested state could be traced to a point 3 inches short of the caecum. Food in a fluid state passes through the stomach rapidly, whereas formed elements pass out more slowly. A full mixed meal might be expected to remain in the stomach for 3-4 hours although some of it would start to dribble into the duodenum quite soon after the meal. This particular meal would pass more quickly than a full solid meal and since little of it had passed it would seem that death occurred within about an hour and a half after ingestion."

"If, therefore, the meal were taken at 8.30 a.m. (the earliest possible time) it would be consistent with death about 10 a.m. If it were taken at 9 a.m. it would be consistent with death about 10.30 or if at 9.30 with death about 11 o'clock. Unless we know when the food was eaten, however, it would be extremely dangerous to venture any opinion, for even with that knowledge, the chance of error is considerable, for example food sometimes remains in the stomach for quite abnormal periods and would hesitate to attach much weight to this evidence standing by itself."

Next, he dealt with rigor mortis or stiffening of the body.

"2. Rigor Mortis: Rigor as a rule commences in the head and neck about two to three hours after death, gradually passes down the trunk and limbs, finishing with the fingers and toes. Complete rigor should be found accelerated by heat and retarded by cold, and is accelerated by fatigue or exertion before death. The atmospheric temperature when the body was examined at 6.55 p.m. was 81.5 degrees Fahrenheit, which would tend to accelerate the onset of rigor as would any struggle which occurred just before death. The body of Mrs. Sathasivam in this case showed rigor in all the muscles of the body except the fingers and toes at 5.55 p.m. If we take it that such a degree of rigor would in these conditions be found in about 6-8 hours, we might assume death to have taken place at about 10-12 a.m. with a strong probability that it was nearer 12 than 10, and I think we might tentatively put it round about 11 a. m."

Professor Smith next dealt with the most accurate method of determining the time of death, cooling of the body.

"3. Temperature of the body: The temperature of the body in health varies a little on either side of 98.4 degrees Fahrenheit, which is usually considered the normal. After death, heat is lost to the surrounding objects at a rate depending largely on the difference in temperature between the body and its surroundings, thus if the difference is extensive, the fall in temperature is rapid for the first few hours then becomes slower until it reaches a point within a few degrees of the air temperature, when the heat transfer is retarded.

This is quite natural, for the internal heat of the body has to make its way to the surface by conduction through the tissues. When the air temperature approximates the body temperature, the fall is very slow. In this case, where the difference between the body and its surroundings was only 16.9 degrees Fahrenheit, the general rate of loss would be much slower than in cooler weather."

Professor Smith said that the rate of cooling depends not only on the difference in temperature between the body and the surroundings, but also on many other factors. He listed them as follows:

*On the weight of the body and the relative extent of surface from which heat is lost; thus in a small or light person, heat is lost more rapidly than in one of average build.

*On the amount of fat in the subcutaneous tissues, a good layer of fat tending to retard cooling.

*On the clothing – the amount and its nature; cooling being retarded according to the amount and nature of the covering, and,

*On the exposure to air currents or moisture, any movement of the air tending to accelerate heat loss.

Referring to Mrs. Sathasivam, Professor Smith said that she weighed only 90 pounds, was poorly nourished, clad only in a petticoat and saree and part of her body was in contact with the concrete floor of the garage.

"Each of these conditions would tend to accelerate the rate of cooling. On the other hand the fact that the garage was completely closed would no doubt lead to a higher temperature in the garage in the earlier hours which would in turn delay cooling."

"The temperature of the garage at 6.55 p.m. was 81.5 degrees Fahrenheit, that is to say assuming the body to have a temperature of 98.4 degrees Fahrenheit at the time of death, the possible loss of temperature before equilibrium would occur would be 16.9 degrees. The temperature of the body at that hour, however, was 93.2 degrees Fahrenheit. That is to say that it had lost only 5.2 degrees Fahrenheit, which represents a loss of roughly a third of the possible heat that it could lose notwithstanding the fact that the balance of circumstances were favourable for an accelerated rate of cooling. If we take the rate of cooling to be 0.7 degrees Fahrenheit per hour, in the first few hours, we arrive at the conclusion that death occurred about 7 ½ hours before the examination – that is to say about 11.30 a.m."

"If the temperature of the body had been raised by the struggle, allowance would have to be made for this unknown factor and we must also make allowances for the fact that we are dealing with a very small woman under circumstances which predispose to more rapid cooling."

"Considering all these circumstances, including the possibility of a slight rise in temperature before death and the various conditions disposed to accelerate the rate of cooling, I think we are not far wrong to place the time of death to be round about 11 a.m."

Expressing caution, Professor Smith said, "The whole of these deductions are open to error and it would be foolish to assume the rigid accuracy of the time factor in any biological phenomena, but taking the whole of the information to be derived from the post-mortem examination, I would be inclined to 10.30 a.m. than before that hour."

In his letter Professor Smith then referred to the cause of death and manner of infliction of the injuries.

"From the post-mortem report it is clearly established that Mrs. Sathasivam met her death by manual strangulation in which considerable violence was used. The disposition of the injuries about the throat and jaw (injury numbers 4, 5, 6 and 8) as defined in the post-mortem report and shown in the photographs, suggest that she was attacked from behind or towards her left side, the fingers of the left hand of the assailant being pressed into the tissues about the right side of the throat and the thumb on the left side of the jaw."

"I base this assumption to a great extent on the observation of what appears to be nail marks on the skin of the neck on the right side with the concavity directed to the left. There are however marks which are probably nail marks on the left side of the throat which may have been due to the fingers of the right hand grasping the throat at the same time – I should like to see a clearer photograph or sketch before giving a precise opinion about the way in which these were inflicted. Consideration should be given to the greatly contused marks which would result if the victim were throttled while on the ground with the assailant using both hands."

Referring to the head injury his opinion was, "The deep contusion of the scalp on the right side (10 inches from the outer angle of the eye to 3 ½ inches behind the right ear, six inches long, one inch wide and ½ inch deep), appears to have been caused by a blow from a club or stick, it is unlikely to have been caused by a fall unless the head struck the edge of a table or similar object."

"The bruise between the shoulder blades, 4¼ inches x 3 inches (injury number 18) similarly appears to have been the result of a severe blow or probably by forcing the back against a projecting edge such as the door-jamb. The deep contusion (internal injury number 11) of the left shoulder blade may be related to it."

Professor Smith wrote that the other injuries do not call for comment except to note that injury number 3 on the left lower jaw contained material like fluff from coconut fibres as mentioned in the Government Analyst's Report.

"This may be significant in deciding the locus of the attack," he mentioned.

"The only other injury which appears at present to warrant mention is the slight abrasion on the mastoid process behind the left ear due to damage from the left ear stud, which was bent and the central pearl missing."

"This damaged ear stud and the injury under it behind the left ear tends to confirm that the attack was made from the left or from behind using the left arm, for if attacked from the front with the right hand used to grasp the throat and the left hand to hold the hair behind, as described in the evidence of William, it is difficult to see how the ear stud could have been bent or pressed into the tissues behind," Professor Smith wrote.

He further explained that from an examination of the injuries, "I find no reason to assume that more than one person was concerned in the murder."

Then he discussed the place where the crime occurred.

"The body was found in the garage with clothing somewhat racked up, lying on its back with legs somewhat apart. The bladder was empty."

"The saree was soiled with material which on analysis was similar to material from the floor of the kitchen. It was also torn in several places."

"The petticoat was stained with seminal matter and urine."

"The feet were soiled on the lower surface with material similar to material from the kitchen."

"The pearl missing from the left ear stud was found on the garage floor near where the body was lying."

"A billet of wood was found adjacent to the body but there is no information whether any hairs were found on it."

"There were no urine stains described in the bedroom. There was no sign of disorder in the bedroom. Seminal stains were found on the clothes in the bedroom."

"The statement of the boy William was to the effect that the murder was committed in the bedroom by Mr. Sathasivam with the help of William and that the body was then carried down by them and placed in the garage."

Professor Smith indicated if this were so, there seems no reason for finding a considerable amount of dust from the kitchen floor attached to the feet of Mrs. Sathasivam.

"This dust could not have got there by dragging the body through the kitchen in any reasonable way. The assumption must be that Mrs. Sathasivam was in the kitchen before the murder took place and would agree with the other statement of William that the attack took place there. The pearl, which was loosened in the attack on the woman, probably fell out at once and it is difficult to believe that the pearl remained adherent to ear or clothes during the jolting which would occur in carrying the body from the bedroom, downstairs through the kitchen to the garage, and then fall out when the body was laid down."

"It is possible of course, but the assumption is in favour of the pearl falling when the assault took place or shortly afterwards. This would favour an assault in the kitchen as suggested by William's confession."

"The horizontal bruise on the right side of the head which I think was caused by a blow from behind if the assailant was right-handed, might well have been a blow from such a billet of wood as was found near the body. A careful examination of this may reveal the presence of hair which would confirm the suggestion, but the absence of which need not negative it."

"The body was not in the bedroom when death took place for the bladder was probably emptied about the time of death. The absence of signs of a struggle in the bedroom might have a certain significance but if the woman were suddenly and violently attacked it is unlikely that she would put up much of a struggle."

He mentioned that the above deductions suggested that the murder occurred in the kitchen or garage.

Explaining the manner of the attack he indicated, "It would be expected in such circumstances as I have outlined in the method of attack, that the left arm or hand of the assailant would be scratched by the fingers of Mrs. Sathasivam and it appears from the reports that Mr. Sathasivam bears no scratch marks either on his face, hands or arms."

Concluding the letter he said, "The above report is, as I have said, quite tentative for I have not yet perused the documents sufficiently closely nor have I paid any attention to the opinions expressed by various experts. I am not convinced that there was not an attempted or completed rape though this must of course be difficult to prove, knowing that Mr. Sathasivam had sexual connection with her on the morning of the crime. This does not preclude rape by another and it may be possible to group the seminal matter on the petticoat and sheet respectively to ascertain whether they both fall into the blood group of the accused."

Professor Sydney Smith articulated opinions expressed in this letter when he gave evidence in Court, which certainly favoured Mr. Sathasivam and confirmed the opinions of his pupil Professor de Saram.

Professor Sydney Smith wrote to Professor de Saram the following letter soon after he wrote the above to Mr. Sathasivam's lawyers.

"My dear de Saram,

I have your note of the 17th and am very glad to hear that you are keeping well.

I do not think I shall be able to visit Ceylon as Consultant for the World Health Organization until September or about that time as I shall have to complete my time here in July.

I have, however, been in touch recently with the legal advisers in the Sathasivam case. I became very interested in it and told the Advocate that from my reading of the case, my conclusions were very much the same as yours. They want me to come out and give evidence when the case comes on and I may be able to do it.

There is one thing that I would like you to do, quite between ourselves, and that is to make a number of observations about at half hour intervals at most from (a) per rectum, (b) from the liver, the thermometer being pushed into the liver by means of the incision from the abdominal wall and (c) the muscles of the thighs. I would like the temperature of both taken in a strictly comparable way, one of the legs being covered with artificial silk or similar covering, the other bare, the temperature of the air to be taken at the same time as each observation. If you could possibly let me have these within the next week or two I should be obliged.

I will look into the matter you raise about the phenothiazine in due course.

I hope that you and your family are enjoying the Christmas and New Year holidays and that you will be able to let me have the information that I want as soon as possible," he concluded.

On 30th December, Professor Smith wrote to Dr. A. I. Kayssi, Director of the Medico-Legal Institute, Baghdad, Iraq, and Professor Mohamed E. Emara of the Medico Legal Department, Kasr-el-Aini, Cairo, Egypt, two similar letters which said, "I am writing particularly to ask you to do something for me. Would it be possible for you to take the record of the temperature fall of twenty bodies or so, recording the temperature half-hourly at least for 10 or 12 hours, and thereafter just at any time that suits. I would like the temperatures taken (1) per rectum, (2) with the thermometer pushed into the liver from a small incision made in the abdominal wall, and (3) in each leg in the muscles of the thigh, one of the legs being bare the other covered with a layer of cotton or artificial silk. With the records, I would like to have the range of air temperature at the same time and if you can give me an idea of the weight of the body and the circumference of the limb I should be greatly delighted."

Dr. Kayssi, who was also the President of the Medical Professions Association of Iraq, replying one month later informed the difficulty in performing the experiments giving reasons.

"The reasons are:

1. We receive corpses at the Institute from the Police after a lapse, as a rule of at least five to ten hours.

2. Corpses from the hospital are claimed by the relatives immediately after death or the performance of the autopsy, and relatives are generally unwilling to leave the corpse for any length of time.

Despite this, I shall try to let you have results as soon as possible though since the receipt of your letter no suitable corpses have been admitted to the Institute."

Once the Magisterial inquiry of the case was concluded, Dr. Colvin R. de Silva and Mr. K.C. Nadarajah brought the evidence led in the Magistrate's Court to Professor Sydney Smith at the University of Edinburgh.

Professor Sydney Smith mentions in his autobiography about this visit and the reconstruction of the crime.

"When I had read all the evidence, examined the photographs, and discussed the matter with counsel for the defence, I carried out a reconstruction of the crime in the way I thought it had occurred. I did this in my laboratory in Edinburgh, the scene of many other such reconstructions. I had the benefit of the assistance of the two defence counsel - although they were of surprisingly little help when I asked them to show me how a saree was arranged!"

"I wanted to know whether the tears in the victim's saree coincided with the position of the wounds on her back. The saree is wrapped round the body in a particular way and fastened at the side. Neither of the lawyers knew how it was done, although both were married men. In the end we had to seek the help of a young lady from Ceylon who was working in the department above my laboratory."

"Everything seemed to fit perfectly, and with the help of the two defence counsel the crime was reconstructed with considerable realism. My typist, who played the part of the murdered woman, looked quite terrified when Dr. de Silva pushed her up against the door and pretended to throttle her!"

Professor Smith refers in his autobiography about William's pardon. "He was given a conditional pardon on turning Queen's Evidence, which seems to me rather odd. It was no business of mine, but I thought that it would have been much simpler if both men had been tried for the murder. As it was, every point made in favour of Sathasivam was inevitably evidence against William, who was not on trial."

"If William had committed the crime himself it seemed unlikely that it was for the jewellery and three rupees. The dead woman's saree was torn in several places, and a large stain of seminal matter was found on her petticoat. I thought it likely that the murder was an unintentional sequel to an indecent assault."

On 9th January 1953, Professor de Saram informed Professor Smith the results of his preliminary studies on fall of temperature of two executed prisoners.

Five days later, replying to Professor de Saram, Professor Smith wrote, "I have received your note of the 9th this morning and was very interested in the readings of the two cases and will be glad to have more. These I will regard as strictly confidential and I don't need to say that it is quite essential that any observation that you are making should also be in the strictest confidence between our two selves."

"It would be injudicious to make any comment on the cases until we have more but the figures of these two present several anomalies which, if they are found in subsequent cases, will require very careful consideration indeed."

"I am not quite clear how the readings were taken. The red figures you gave me were with the "Chemical Thermometer". Is this the ordinary mercury bulb thermometer that we normally use for taking readings, or is it some special type? How precisely are you taking the liver temperature? Are you inserting the thermometer through a small incision from the external skin or is it placed against or in the liver after opening the body, and is the thermometer used a mercury thermometer or a thermocouple? Further, in connection with the thighs – were these taken with the thermometer embedded deeply in the thigh muscles and buried to the same extent in each case? If you were able to do it, it would be interesting to find whether the temperature varied between the inner and outer sides of the thigh. It is just possible that the radiation may be less on the inside of the thigh because it will receive some radiation from the opposite thigh. I am also not quite clear whether the Cambridge skin thermometer was the one used for taking the rectal temperatures."

"Thank you very much indeed for your co-operation in this matter. I am getting parallel experiments carried out in two or three different places, the results of which I will let you know in due course."

On 28th February, Professor de Saram communicated with Professor Smith again and wrote, "I have now received the petticoat in the case for the grouping of seminal stains. I have found sperms in fair numbers in an area marked in red by the analyst and the grouping is AB. This stain is principally on the inner aspect of the fabric. There are also other and larger stains showing fluorescence marked in black and which I presume, are those reported by him as urine stains. These areas are more evident on the outer aspect of the fabric. These areas will be examined also for semen, and if positive grouped. I have also noted that the fabric of the petticoat is somewhat different to that of the material I have employed in the cases I have reported to you; if anything, the latter would, in my opinion have rather tended to delay cooling."

"Would also wish to let you know that although my communication with you has been in strict confidence, the transport of the bodies of the prisoners to my laboratory has been observed by persons on the University premises; but though these persons have in no way been connected with the case, it is just possible that a question may be put to me in the witness box as to what I was doing with the bodies; especially as I have been debarred from carrying out routine autopsies and the Judicial Medical Officer occupies the same building as I. I could always evade answering such a question, but I should wish you to advise me, please. I have been summoned to attend Court on the 20th March."

"If you are coming out, I think it best that I should not meet you until you have given your evidence. I intend getting away from Colombo as soon after my evidence has been taken as possible. I should be deeply disappointed, however, should you return to U.K. without my meeting you. I shall be very obliged if you will drop me a note to the above address when you wish to see me."

On 5th March 1953, Professor Sydney Smith replying to this

letter wrote, "It is extremely interesting to note that you have been able to group the seminal stain on the petticoat. You must now find the blood group of Mr. Sathasivam and that of William. It should be easy enough to get the blood group of Mr. Sathasivam, but to get the group of William will probably be opposed. If, however, it is possible to have the group of the accused and should it not fall into Group AB, then the evidence will be crucial. On the other hand if it does fall into AB it will leave the matter very much as it is, for it is generally assumed that the seminal stains are the result of the coitus, which we know occurred on the morning before the crime."

Continuing he said, "I also note that you have some worry about the question that may be asked you in connection with the transport of dead bodies to your laboratory. I don't think you should have the slightest hesitation about your attitude in this matter. If I were you, I should state quite definitely that they were obtained for the purpose of taking continuous record of the temperature, that you have these records which are available for the Court, and that if the question is asked do not hesitate to say that you have also communicated them to me. I will be quite ready to produce the graphs showing the rate of loss of heat and I think you will agree that the heat loss so charted falls into line with what you and I would expect. I should not, if I were you, try to evade any question at all for we are both out for the same thing and that is to get as near the truth as we possibly can."

"I am told that the case will occupy a long period and that I am not likely to be called until the middle of May. It seems rather extraordinary in view of the fact that you are starting on 20th March, but no doubt there are a great many witnesses."

"I think that we should not meet or discuss the case in any way until after the evidence is given, because there must be no hint of collusion. Up to the present, as you will have observed, beyond quoting factual material no communication about interpretation has passed between us. We must, however, make quite sure that, after I have given evidence, we must meet for I should be very disappointed indeed if I returned from Ceylon without having seen and talked things over with you. I will keep your address by me and let you know when I expect to be there," concluded Professor Smith.

However, William was not a 'secretor' of his blood group antigens in semen. Therefore, even though William's blood and semen samples were analysed by Professor de Saram, no conclusion could me made on whether William had sexual intercourse with Mrs. Sathasivam.

After the trial commenced, Professor Sydney Smith was requested to arrive in Ceylon to give evidence. The most suitable dates for Professor Smith, who had a very busy schedule, was late May 1953.

Dr. Colvin R de Silva, who considered it essential that Sir Sydney should give evidence, decided to inform him about the evidence so far led in the case, and wrote a letter from his residence 'Nihathamane', Pendennis Avenue, Colombo 3, on 9th May 1953.

"My Dear Sir Sydney,

I have to thank you for the letter you wrote to me just before leaving for Canada. I am sorry the evidence dispatched to you did not reach you in time. Now that you will have to see it all on your return, you may find the sheer volume of it forbidding. The worst of it is that even as I write, the Crown medical evidence is only just reaching its end. I am afraid its perusal will therefore be very tedious.

You were correctly informed that William made out that the lady was still alive in the garage when he finally left the house. I was not unmindful of its possible implications in relation to the issue of the time of death. But we have met it in three ways. Firstly, we got the doctors into contradiction with him on the possibility of her being alive at that stage. Secondly, it matches up with the suggestion that William stamped on her neck in the garage. Thirdly, we shall use it to show that it fits in with our position that she was finally killed in the garage.

The most important new point that has been made in the medical evidence relates to the contents of the alimentary canal. The Crown has shifted its position on the point again by suggesting an entirely new approach to this question at the trial.

You will remember that Professor de Saram went on the rate of passage of food in the small intestine. The Crown then counterpoised the test of the rate of gastric evacuation as being more reliable and also claimed that Dr. Welikala's experiments and Dr. Paul's experiments brought the period down to within one hour.

By the time they came to this Court, the Crown seems to have realized that this did not go far enough and so they for the first time suggested at the trial Court the new test of the rate of digestion of food.

The position of Doctors Paul and Peiris is as follows on this point. They claim that the presence of undigested string-hoppers in the stomach and semi-digested string-hoppers in the ileum from one and the same meal is impossible save on the hypothesis of intestinal hurry or rush. This, they say, brings the period since taking the meal down to 15 minutes to 1 hour.

I have no doubt that this new after-thought of the Crown doctors is fallacious and I have met the position in broadly four ways.

Firstly, we have suggested that this is a very unreliable test anyhow. Secondly, we have pointed out that the presence of semi-digested food in the ileum may be due to reduced digestibility and not to intestinal hurry. Thirdly, we have stressed that starch is digested mainly in the small intestine and only to a very unimportant extent in the stomach by the saliva brought down along with the food, and that therefore, starchy food can be for a long time in the stomach without being digested. Finally, and above all, we brought them to the position that the period of 15 minutes to 1 hour is as from the time of last taking any fluid, and that therefore any assessment of the time factor must depend on first proving that the solids and liquids were taken together. They concede that otherwise the period has to be longer.

On this question of whether the solids and liquids were taken together, I believe and I am advised that the position is entirely in our favour. The string-hoppers were not only in the stomach but also along the whole length of the 22 feet of small intestine. This suggests a goodly period since the solids were taken. Then the volume of liquid in the stomach is pretty large – too large to have been taken at the same time as the solids because then it would be necessary to assume both an enormous meal and a remarkably large quantity of fluid. Accordingly, the assumption of a fluid being ingested after a considerable lapse of time from the string-hopper meal itself would seem to be both probable and natural.

I have set out the above matter fully because I shall need to discuss it with you in detail and concretely on your arrival as a special matter, over and above the tests previously discussed with you.

I think you would also like to know that your correspondence with the Crown has been put in at the trial. Through this method we have established in advance your neutrality as a witness and thereby facilitated your being called out of turn to suit the difficulties of arranging for your presence here.

The main purpose of this letter is to inform you of these arrangements, though I have left them for the end.

We have had to wedge you in rather tightly between your return from Canada and your necessary return from here to Great Britain for the Coronation. I had also noted that you had not been quite fit and therefore thought you might like a few days rest before you come out. I do hope you are fully recovered and are fit and well. Anyhow, I have arranged that you will also have time for rest on arrival here.

Our real difficulty has been to fit in the planes and we were also worried about Comet arrangements. However, the Proctors have been informed by telephone that seats have been reserved as follows:-

1. Edinburgh to London — - 19th May
2. London – Colombo by Comet — - leaving 20th May
   — - arriving 21st May.
3. Colombo – London by Argonaut — - leaving 30th May
   — - arriving 31st May
4. London – Edinburgh — - 1st June

I am sorry that the return journey is by Argonaut. There is no Comet that could take you in time on the arrangements for taking your evidence. This is quite apart from the fact that the Comets to London have been booked full months in advance because of the coronation.

Our present plan is to give you a day's rest on arrival and then to complete necessary consultations over the weekend so that we can lead your evidence on Monday, 25th May. We are arranging to have your evidence specially taken so that your departure on the 30th is completely assured.

I am sorry I cannot meet you myself on arrival as I shall be in

Court, but Mr. K. C. Nadarajah will be at the airport to receive you. We have arranged for the Galle Face Hotel as being the best in Colombo, and also for Mr. Nadarajah's car to be at your disposal. If there is anything that you wish attended to or arranged for you, we shall be only too glad to have the opportunity.

Further medical evidence up to 5th May was posted to you on the 6th of May, and the medical evidence thereafter up to and including yesterday (8th May) is being posted to you today. As the parcel goes as 2nd class mail, it will make for quick delivery if contact is maintained at your end with the Edinburgh Post Office. The cross examination of Professor de Saram is due to be continued on Monday 11th May. This will be held here against your arrival.

It will be the period of the Buddhist Wesak celebrations when you are here and you will therefore have the opportunity of seeing a characteristic national festival of ours," concluded Dr. de Silva.

As planned, Professor Sydney Smith arrived in Sri Lanka on 21st May and he was met at the Ratmalana Airport by Mr. K. C. Nadarajah and Miss Manouri de Silva (Now Mrs. Muttetuwagama), the daughter of Dr. Colvin R. de Silva. (See Figure 22. Page 478)

"Sir Sydney Smith, Regius Professor of Forensic Medicine and the Dean, Faculty of Medicine, Edinburgh University, arrived in Ceylon yesterday by the B.O.A.C. Comet after a 6000 mile flight to give evidence in the Sathasivam murder trial," reported the Ceylon Daily News.

As soon as he arrived in Colombo, even before going to his hotel, Professor Smith wanted to see the house where Mrs. Sathasivam was murdered, as he had arrived at certain conclusions about the place of her strangling. He wanted to see in particular the kitchen, the garage and the passage between them.

When he did see the passage leading from the kitchen to the garage he found a projection there, a staple, which fitted into the picture that he had formed of how the back injury on Mrs. Sathasivam could have been caused.

This is how Professor Smith mentioned in his autobiography what he did when he arrived in Ceylon.

"At Colombo the defence, led by Dr. de Silva, met me at the airport and wanted to take me to my hotel. I asked them if the kitchen in the house had been examined for a projecting hook or staple, and they said this had not been done. I asked if we could go there then, and they said it was easy enough to reach from the airport, so off we went. The house had long since changed hands, and the new owners were living there, but they allowed us to look round the kitchen. I was rather pleased to find, just 3 feet 6 inches from the ground, on the wall between the kitchen and garage, a staple which had been used for hooking the door back. It was exactly the sort of thing I had expected to have caused the bruise on Mrs. Sathasivam's back."

"The little detour from the airport aroused some comment at the trial. I was asked, among other things, if I had gone to the scene of the crime before having breakfast or a bath. The judge was impressed because none of the medical experts appearing for the Crown - except Professor de Saram, of course - had ever bothered to go to the house. His Honour said he had had to have the bed brought to the Court to get them to examine it."

"While I had been at the house I had been able to see the upstairs bedroom where William said the crime had been committed, the staircase, the kitchen, and the garage, so that I had a fairly clear picture of the case."

"But the thing that created the greatest impression was the fact that I had deduced the existence of the wall staple while reconstructing the case in Edinburgh, and then come to Ceylon and gone straight to the house and found it just where I expected it to be."

On the 21st of May itself, Dr. Colvin R. de Silva, made an application to call Sir Sydney to give evidence on 27th, as he would have to leave by plane on May 30th.

Mr. T.S. Fernando, the Acting Solicitor-General said that although he could not formally agree to a witness being called out of turn, before the case for the prosecution was closed, the Crown welcomed Sir Sydney's evidence and therefore he had no objection.

Sir Sydney Smith commenced his evidence in Court on 27th May and the Court House and the veranda outside were packed to hear his evidence.

Examined by Dr. Colvin R. de Silva, Sir Sydney said he has had experience in Forensic Medicine for about 40 years.

He said he had been consulted first by Mr. K. C. Nadarajah and later by Dr. de Silva. The whole brief containing the evidence led in the Magistrate's Court and the medical evidence had been placed before him.

Regarding strangling, he said it was not necessary that there should have been more than one person to have committed the murder.

Dr. de Silva, reading Professor de Saram's report on the injuries found on William, asked whether those injuries could have been caused if William was the strangler. He replied that the injuries on William's hands and cheeks were consistent with injuries a strangler would receive.

Sir Sydney agreed that the death was undoubtedly due to manual strangulation.

Commenting on the method of strangling, he said there was nothing to conclude that Mrs. Sathasivam was strangled from the front. He said there were no conclusive clues that she was strangled in the standing position either. "It could be either way," he said.

Sir Sydney demonstrated with the aid of a court peon how the strangler could have come by the injuries on his left arm and his left cheek. He pointed out in the demonstration how the right arm of the victim could scratch the left cheek of the strangler and inflict the injury on the left arm of the strangler.

Regarding the act of strangulation, Sir Sydney was of the opinion that when Mrs. Sathasivam was strangled she did not put up a violent fight. She probably made one or two scratches on the assailant before she lost consciousness. Death must have occurred between half a minute to two minutes. Sir Sydney said that he put it down to the lower limit than the higher one.

In his opinion, he said, strangling had been done between the kitchen and the garage.

When Dr. de Silva questioned about the dirt found in the soles of the feet of Mrs. Sathasivam, Sir Sydney said he was aware that the left sole of her foot was dirtier than the right. He was also aware that on the balls of her left feet the dirt flaked off easily.

"That showed that Mrs. Sathasivam had walked into the kitchen and had not walked out of it," Sir Sydney said.

Replying to a query from Justice Gratiaen, Sir Sydney said if Mrs. Sathasivam's body was carried with her feet two feet above the ground as William said, he could not explain how the dark material could have adhered to her feet.

Referring to the only head injury Mrs. Sathasivam had, he said that a blow could have been caused by a firewood similar to the one that was produced in Courts. When she was struck on the head with a piece of firewood she would have been pushed back against the door-jamb. In that process, Sir Sydney said that he would have expected to have seen the two injuries found on the back of head and the shoulders of Mrs. Sathasivam.

Commenting on the presence of a pearl ear-stud found in the proximity of Mrs. Sathasivam's body, he said that the stone got dislodged at the place where the stamping was done.

He said its presence was a pointer to the place where the strangulation occurred. He said stamping of foot caused the injuries 1, 3, 7 and 9, and the ball of the big toe dislodged the pearl. He said that all the injuries were caused by one single act of stamping and they were consistent with stamping with a bare foot.

Shown a 'thalikody', Sir Sydney said that if it came in the way of the assault, it could have caused injuries 1, 2, 3 and 9.

Sir Sydney said he had considered the possibility of a sexual assault on Mrs. Sathasivam. In fact it had occurred to him and he had asked that investigations be made in that direction even at a later stage.

Replying to a query from Justice Gratiaen, Sir Sydney said that there was sufficient evidence in the manner and posture in which the body was found to suggest that there had been a possibility of a sexual assault.

Sir Sydney said that pressing the lady against a door-jamb could have caused the injury on the back of the shoulder.

Sir Sydney, commenting on the conflicting opinions about the injuries on Mrs. Sathasivam's neck, said that the doctor who saw the actual injuries would be in a better position to determine it than one who saw them in a photograph later.

Dr. de Silva showed Sir Sydney the piece of firewood and asked whether it could have caused the head injury of Mrs. Sathasivam. He answered that it appeared too light. Then he asked permission of Court to try out its toughness and struck it twice against a pillar. The firewood did not break. Sir Sydney then said it appeared to be tougher than he thought, and that the injury could have been caused by a piece of firewood like that.

He stated that the iron blowpipe found in the kitchen was very heavy and that would have caused a much deeper injury.

Sir Sydney then demonstrated in Court how he thought the victim had been strangled and carried to the garage. He said that while the victim was being carried, her toes would have been dragged along the ground.

He accepted that the injuries on the dead body were ante-mortem, that is, caused before death.

He further said that the injury over the mastoid bone might have been associated with injuries 9 and 3 and the stamping could have bent the shaft of the ear-stud and dislodged the pearl. Although a shod foot or a bare foot could have caused the injuries, he said a shoe could not have got into an angle underneath the chin or the jaw.

Referring to the ear-stud found in the garage, he was of the opinion that the stone in the ear-stud got dislodged at the place where the stamping was done. He was very clear on that point.

Answering Dr. de Silva's questions on the time of death, Sir Sydney said that in assessing the time of the death he would take temperature and the setting in of rigor. He said he would take the food in the alimentary canal last. It would be dangerous to assume on facts, which they did not know.

Sir Sydney said from the fall of temperature, his estimate of the time of death of Mrs. Sathasivam was between 11 a.m. and 12.00 noon. Considering the general conditions under which rigor mortis occurred, he was of the opinion that death had occurred at 11 a.m. he said.

Considering the passage of food in the gastro-intestinal tract, his opinion was that she might have died two and a half hours after her meal, or even later.

Cross-examined by Mr. T.S. Fernando, the Acting Solicitor-

General, Sir Sydney said that he asked Professor de Saram to carry out certain experiments.

Mr. Fernando asked whether placing the mortar would dislodge a pearl from the ear-stud, which had already loosened. Sir Sydney disagreed with this suggestion after witnessing a demonstration with the mortar placed on the head of a peon.

He said that the moment he saw the original photograph with Mrs. Sathasivam's legs apart, it occurred to him that the possibility of rape should be investigated.

When Mr. Fernando was cross-examining Sir Sydney further, Justice Gratiaen inquired from Dr. de Silva what the position of defence was on that matter and whether the defence was making a charge that William has raped Mrs. Sathasivam.

Dr. de Silva said that the defence had only dealt with the question of rape after the Crown had, on its own, raised the question of excluding rape. Thereupon the defence, he said, joined issue with the Crown, in order to establish that the preponderance of probable material available was in favour of rape.

"Rape was not necessary for the defence, but we wish to drive home the point that although there was no conclusive evidence, rape might well have been committed," explained Dr. de Silva.

Sir Sydney, further cross-examined, said the injury on Mrs. Sathasivam's head could have been caused by a blow with an object from behind or it could have been caused by the head striking a sharp edge of the wall.

Sir Sydney said that his impression was that having received the blow on the head, she had staggered back and hit herself on the door-jamb.

"At this stage she must have lost consciousness and her body would have sagged forward. The assailant then would have dragged her into the garage," Sir Sydney said.

Sir Sydney admitted that if during the struggle in the bedroom upstairs, the head was brought down to the ground and struck the ledge of the bed, it would cause an injury similar to the head injury found on the lady.

On further cross-examination by Mr. Fernando, Sir Sydney

emphasized that he was inclined to believe that it was a bare foot that caused injuries 2, 3 and 9 and not a shod foot because the injury under the chin could not have been caused by a shoe.

"A rubber-soled shoe would tend to slip up. If however, it was a leather shoe with nails it might hold better," Sir Sydney said.

Mr. Fernando said there was no evidence that it was a rubber-soled shoe.

At this stage, Dr. de Silva intervened to say that the Crown had put questions to all its witnesses on the assumption that it was a crepe rubber-soled shoe. He objected to the Crown now changing its position.

"The Crown had put into the box its own pardoned witness who was an alleged eye witness of the incident and did not choose to question him on the kind of shoe that was used. It could not now introduce a leather shoe to fit in with its fanciful theories," he said. He submitted that even Inspector Thiedeman had referred to crepe rubber-soled shoes Mr. Sathasivam was wearing.

Mr. Fernando said that Inspector Thiedeman had spoken of shoes which Mr. Sathasivam was wearing at 9.00 p.m. that day. There was no evidence that accused was wearing the same shoes at the time of the murder.

Replying to query from Justice Gratiaen, Sir Sydney said that he could not comment on stamping by a shoe if he did not know the nature of the sole of the shoe used.

Further cross-examined by Mr. Fernando, Sir Sydney said that judging from the photograph of the neck, there were 6 or 7 nail marks on the neck of Mrs. Sathasivam and the marks showed that they were made by the left hand.

He was of the opinion that Mrs. Sathasivam herself could have made some of the nail marks during the struggle.

Questioned on the determination of time since death, Sir Sydney said he did not know how the stomach contents could indicate that Mrs. Sathasivam had died within an hour of taking the meal.

In his autobiography, Sir Sydney mentions this cross-examination.

"When I was cross-examined I was asked how long it took for

food to pass from the mouth to the lower end of the small intestine. I replied that though it was simple enough to give an average time, that average could not apply to a particular case. It was much the same as asking how long it took a horse to run a mile. It depended, I said, on the breed of the horse, its condition at the time, upon the trainer and upon the jockey; whereupon his Lordship, who had some interest in horse-racing, leant over to me and said, 'And the owner, Sir Sydney, and the owner!' This was received with much amusement by the local audience, known as they did the vagaries of horseracing in Ceylon."

Mr. Fernando asked Sir Sydney whether it was possible that the assailant might have applied the dirt on Mrs. Sathasivam's feet to mislead the investigators.

"Yes," he replied.

He mentions in his autobiography that Justice Gratiaen elaborated the absurdity of this suggestion in his extremely fair summing up.

At the request of Mr. Fernando, Sir Sydney demonstrated how the assailant would have struck Mrs. Sathasivam's head with a piece of firewood.

He agreed that the head striking the ledge of the bed might have caused this injury.

Answering questions on cooling of the body, he said in this case it would not be safe to assume that the temperature of Mrs. Sathasivam had increased shortly before her death as a result of muscular activity. It might or might not have risen. He had postulated that the rectal temperature at the time of death was 98.4 degrees Fahrenheit.

Referring to the experiments Professor de Saram has performed, he said he expected Mrs. Sathasivam to have lost heat more rapidly than in the case of the executed prisoners as she was thin and sparely built, and because of her light clothing.

Sir Sydney explained that his instructions to Professor de Saram were to carry out the experiments as far as possible under similar conditions.

Sir Sydney was cross-examined at length on convulsions (fits) and whether they always accompanied asphyxial deaths, such as strangulations. Mr. Fernando read several passages from many standard medical textbooks on the subject.

Referring to the passage of food in the intestines, Sir Sydney said he was of opinion that she might have died 2 ½ hours after her meal or later.

He further stated that in his opinion strangling was not done on the floor.

Mr. Fernando then referred to the famous Sydney Fox murder case where Sir Sydney Smith gave evidence for the defence, disagreeing with the opinion of Sir Bernard Spilsbury.

Sir Spilsbury was considered 'the father of forensic pathology' and 'the most brilliant scientific detective of all time'.

Sir Sydney said that there was a difference of opinion between him and Sir Bernard Spilsbury where Sydney Fox was charged in 1930 with killing his mother. The question arose whether Mrs. Fox died of heart failure or strangulation.

Sir Sydney Smith's evidence was concluded on the third day and he left for London on the same day.

He mentions in his autobiography about the response to his evidence.

"At the beginning of the trial local opinion in Colombo was strongly against Sathasivam, and I personally received a number of letters cursing me for interfering with the course of justice, which apparently meant the hanging of the accused. One writer said that he was praying the Almighty to strike down the aeroplane in which I was travelling back to Britain. This seemed a bit unfair to the other forty or so passengers on the plane, but by Divine Providence they and I were spared!"

CHAPTER 10

EVIDENCE OF THE RADIOLOGIST

Another expert witness the Crown relied on to support their theory that Mrs. Sathasivam died before 10.30 a.m., was the Radiologist, Dr. A.H.N. Welikala.

Examined by Mr. Douglas Jansze, the Crown Counsel, he said that he was the Assistant Radiologist of the General Hospital, Colombo.

"I am due to assume duties as Radiologist early next month when Dr. H.O. Goonewardene retires. I hold a Diploma in Radiology from the London University and a Diploma in Radiotherapy from the Royal College of Physicians and Surgeons. I am also a Visiting Lecturer in Radiology at the University of Ceylon and I have been an Examiner in Radiology in 1948 and 1949 for the Society of Radiographers in London," said Dr. Welikala.

He said that he was requested by the Police to perform certain experiments in connection with the Sathasivam murder case. He was also instructed by the Director of Medical and Sanitary Services to carry out these experiments.

Dr. Welikala said that the Police sent him three ladies to perform the experiments on passage of food in the stomach and intestines. At his request, Inspector Thiedeman also sent a fourth lady for the experiments.

"You informed Inspector Thiedeman that the subjects who were to be produced before you should not have had any meal that morning?"

"Yes."

"They were asked to have a plain cup of tea at about 6 a.m.?"

"Yes, with a little sugar; nothing else."

"The purpose of your experiments was to show how the stomach empties itself when a particular type of meal is given?"

"Yes."

Dr. Welikala said he gave one lady a suspension of barium sulphate to drink and took a series of x-ray photographs. Barium was given to trace the passage of the meal in the stomach and the intestines. It had no effect on digestion of food. It was really a 'tracer'.

Shown the series of 15 x-rays he took, Dr. Welikala explained that the time taken by barium sulphate to pass through the stomach and intestines.

Dr. Welikala said that to the other three ladies he gave two and a half string-hoppers, one dessert spoonful of coconut 'sambal' and two cups of tea, sprinkled with one ounce (about 28 millilitres) of barium sulphate.

To one lady he said he also gave nine ounces (about 250 millilitres) of tea.

Dr. Welikala explained that the objective of the experiments were to try to work out the approximate rate of gastric emptying. That is the rate at which the stomach emptied itself into the intestines.

During the cross-examination by Dr. Colvin R. de Silva, Dr. Welikala said that his experiments showed that stomach took two and a half to three hours to empty itself completely.

"I would also say, given the same conditions, the head of the meal would take from 2 hours 20 minutes to more than 3 hours to reach the caecum. I cannot say very much more from these experiments," Dr. Welikala said.

Dr. de Silva asked, "Given the fact that a meal containing string-hoppers which had reached to within three inches of the caecum was found in Mrs. Sathasivam's small intestines, would you in relation to your experiments point to the following inference? That the meal had been in the stomach and the alimentary canal for some period, which approximates to the 2 hours 20 minutes and 3 hours, the period you gave for the head of the meal to reach the caecum?"

"Yes," replied Dr. Welikala.

This answer certainly favoured the defence.

Dr. de Silva questioning Dr. Welikala further asked, "That would suggest to you a single string-hopper meal because of the presence of it in both places in continuity?"

"Yes."

"So with the string-hoppers present in that way on your three experiments with the three ladies, it would point to a meal having been present somewhere between two to three hours?"

"Yes."

Dr. de Silva then asked another crucial question from Dr. Welikala.

"In the condition we have found in Mrs. Sathasivam's stomach, based on your experiments, it would point to a meal taken between two to three hours earlier?"

"Yes."

Dr. de Silva asked Dr. Welikala, from the experiments on the three ladies, what were the general conclusions he would safely arrive at, assuming that each person had the liquid meal and the solid meal at the same time, as Mrs. Sathasivam did on the day of her death.

Dr. Welikala said that his opinions would be,

(A) That the stomach starts emptying almost immediately after taking the meal,

(B) That half the stomach would be empty within one hour of taking the meal, and,

(C) That the stomach would be completely empty in three hours.

During the re-examination, the Acting Solicitor-General Mr. T.S. Fernando asked about emptying of the stomach in each case.

"In your experiments, in the case of the first lady, at the end of one hour, what was the nature of the meal in the stomach?

"Over half the stomach was empty."

"In the case of second lady, at the end of one hour?"

"More than half the meal was within the stomach."

"In the case of the third lady, at the end of one hour?"

"About half the meal was in the stomach," answered Dr. Welikala.

Dr Welikala's evidence did not help the case for the prosecution. Dr. de Silva cleverly used his evidence for the benefit of the defence.

CHAPTER 11

EVIDENCE OF THE FORENSIC SCIENTISTS

The Department of the Government Analyst in Ceylon provided all the scientific services to the Police in investigation of crime. Even after half a century the situation is the same. The Department, though short-staffed, ill-equipped and devoid of modern technology today, has specialists in all branches of forensic science – toxicology, serology, ballistics etc.

When there is a murder or a suspicious death, this Department is informed by the Police and depending on the availability of personnel, one or more relevant scientists visit the scene.

Mr. W. R. Chanmugam, the Government Analyst, was the Head of this institution at the time of the murder of Mrs. Sathasivam and he was requested by the Police to visit the scene.

At the trial, Mr. Chanmugam was summoned to give evidence and Crown Counsel Mr. Ananda Pereira first examined him.

He said he has been trained at Scotland Yard and the Metropolitan Police Laboratories in London. He was a Fellow of the Royal Institute of Chemistry and Toxicology and has served the Department of the Government Analyst for eleven years.

He said he received a message from the Police on the 9th of October 1951, and he went to No. 7, St. Alban's Place, arriving there shortly after 4 p.m.

At the time of his arrival, Inspector Thiedeman was there. Professor de Saram and the finger print expert Mr. T. Thalaisingham had not yet arrived.

Mr. Chanmugam said he was taken to the garage where the body of Mrs. Sathasivam was lying. He examined the scene but did not take any specimens until Professor de Saram arrived.

"There were two kitchens in this house - the Dover stove kitchen and the gas stove kitchen. In the Dover stove kitchen, I noticed half a coconut lying beside a coconut scraper, with a few strands of coconut still on the coconut scraper. I also saw a chattee (a clay pot used for cooking food) under the scraper in which there were strands of scraped coconut. I saw a grinding stone with some yellow or orange coconut on it," described Mr. Chanmugam.

"This suggested that a 'sambal' or something like that had been ground on the stone. I saw two chattees (clay pots) on a table there, one containing cut pieces of ash plantain and the other cut pieces of drumsticks, without any curry stuff added. On the ground near this table, I saw portions of the skin of an ash plantain which had been cut."

Mr. Pereira queried whether looking at the kitchen at that time, he was able to form any impression as to whether it was in a normal condition or in a state of disarrangement.

"There was no state of disarrangement. There was one table with articles on it. Nothing had fallen off," replied Mr. Chanmugam.

He said that on the floor of the kitchen he noticed what appeared to be a drag mark near the door leading to the garage.

The drag mark was about a foot and half in length trailing towards the door. It was 1½ inches to 2½ inches broad. It was a wavy line and had stopped short of the doorway, up to about 1½ feet from the door.

Mr. Chanmugam said that he wanted to take a photograph of this, but Inspector Thiedeman told him that it would be irrelevant, as so many people had passed through. Therefore, he did not make any note of it.

Inside the kitchen by the side of the Dover stove, Mr. Chanmugam said he noticed a heap of split firewood. Close to that heap, there was a small heap of kitchen floor sweepings.

"There was no vegetable substance in it. It was merely floor sweepings, dust, ash and things like that. There was a built-in cupboard, which contained some items of curry stuff. He could not remember whether it was closed or not. Adjoining the Dover stove kitchen there was another kitchen, which had a gas cooker in it, and on the gas cooker he found a metal saucepan with rice, which was slightly warm. There was no fire. It was warmth retained from some earlier point of time," he said.

When he opened the saucepan he found that the rice was very nearly boiled. He said he would call it under-boiled but was edible.

In the dining room, there was a dining table and near that there was a shelf containing some uncooked vegetables.

Near the foot of that shelf he found a few strands of peeled off outer fibre of drumsticks. They were long strands about 3 or 4 inches in length.

Mr. Chanmugam said then he went into the children's room and Mrs. Sathasivam's room upstairs.

"When I went into the room I was informed that it was occupied by the deceased Mrs. Sathasivam. There, I observed a bed with a sheet on it, which appeared to be crumpled up. That was a 'verti' cloth (a piece of white cloth) with a blue border. I also saw a striped pyjama sarong, which had been thrown on the bed. Looking at the bed, I got the impression that it was in a state of disarrangement. It had not been made up after it had been slept in. I saw a ceiling fan in the room, which was on at the time I went there. I noticed an almirah in the room. One of the doors of that almirah was ajar. On the flight of steps coming from the top, on the third step, I found a splinter of firewood about 4 inches long and about the thickness of little finger, about a quarter of an inch in diameter. The Police were requested to take charge of some of these productions at that stage," Mr. Chanmugam said.

He said he noticed that the bathroom floor was wet.

Explaining the observations he made at the garage where Mrs. Sathasivam's body was, Mr. Chanmugam said, "By the side of the head of Mrs. Sathasivam I saw some articles - a rocking horse and a rather rickety clothes horse and a wooden mortar. When I saw the mortar it was inverted. There was a footstool halfway between the garage door and the body. On that footstool I saw a hand mirror. The mirror was lying with the mirror side downwards halfway between the body and the door, which had the trelliswork. I saw a stick of firewood, that was lying on the floor just by the side of the body."

Mr. Chanmugam said he took charge of the body at 7.30 p.m., after Professor de Saram examined the body and handed to him certain things which he had got from the body.

In Court, Mr. Chanmugam identified the three little bits of fluff taken from Mrs. Sathasivam's body and given to him by Professor de Saram.

He said he saw Professor de Saram removing this fluff from the left side of Mrs. Sathasivam's chin.

"I took it to the laboratory for examination. One of the bits was used up in the process of examination because I applied some chemicals to test it. On examination, these particles were identified as light spongy material similar to fluff found in coconut fibre. By fluff I mean the outer substance," explained Mr. Chanmugam.

"Can you give us any idea of the tests?" asked Mr. Pereira.

"I tested that first for 'lignin'. That is the woody material that is found in a spongy type of wood. I cut sections of this and cut sections from a different type of lignin from other types of wood and found them dissimilar to the soft spongy material from other woods. They were similar to the spongy material found in coconuts. This kind of material would be expected to be found on the floor where coconuts are kept or handled or where husks are kept."

Mr. Chanmugam explained, as any good scientist would do, that although it was similar to coconut fluff, it might not be coconut fluff at all. He said it might be palmyrah fluff, but later he told Court that palmyrah was not commonly found in Colombo!

"When you say it is fluff from coconut, it is from the fibre part of the coconut. It is not from the other parts of the coconut tree?" queried Mr. Pereira.

"No."

"It is not from the outer hard skin of the husk itself. It is from the substance of the husk?"

"Yes," Mr. Chanmugam replied.

Explaining how Professor de Saram removed the dark material from the sole of the left foot of Mrs. Sathasivam, he said, "Professor de Saram borrowed a penknife from somebody and scraped it off. I cannot tell you what amount of force he used to take it off. I was more concerned in collecting the material as he scraped it off and not let it fall on the ground."

He said superficial particles came off easily whereas deep ones had to be scraped off with a knife.

"On examination, the deep material consisted of tiny particles of sandy matter, strands of fibre and vegetable debris covered by black organic matter."

"The superficial material contained a few grains of sand, fluff and coconut fibre. Most of the fluff was stained dark and similar to the deep material but a few particles of fluff were light brown. There were also a few strands of short pointed hair probably from a dog."

Mr. Chanmugam said that Professor de Saram handed him some dark material, which he removed from the sole of the right foot of Mrs. Sathasivam, which was also scraped with a knife. It was similar to the deep material of the left foot but of a lighter colour.

"I saw the two feet of Mrs. Sathasivam. The left foot contained more of this matter and was darker," explained Mr. Chanmugam.

He also took charge of certain things from the garage on his own.

One was a specimen of fluff from the floor of the garage near the feet of Mrs. Sathasivam. It contained rat dung, some pieces of shell and nails and other vegetable debris.

He took another specimen of fluff from the corner of the garage within two feet of the face of Mrs. Sathasivam, to her left.

"Analysis showed that it was a mixture of fluff and fibre from coconut, light brown in colour and uncontaminated by any organic matter. On the left of the body there was a heap of coconut husks. It was 3 feet from the body of Mrs. Sathasivam. It was somewhat similar to what Professor de Saram took from the chin of Mrs. Sathasivam, except that its composition was fluff and fibre, but the specimen from the chin consisted only of fluff."

"On the following day," Mr. Chanmugam said, "I again went to No. 7, St. Alban's Place and obtained specimens of dry swabs from various parts of the house. They were swabs of cotton wool without moistening them. I rubbed them on the floors in various places in the house."

On analysis, he said he found that the dark substance adhering to the sole of each foot of Mrs. Sathasivam was similar to the two swabs taken from the two kitchens, but different to those found in Mrs. Sathasivam's bedroom.

These findings quite clearly were favourable to the defence, confirming that Mrs. Sathasivam walked in to the kitchen.

Answering a query from the Justice Gratiaen, Mr. Chanmugam reiterated that the material found in the bedroom was certainly different to the darker material on the soles of the feet.

"Substance on the soles of her feet could have come from the Dover stove kitchen as well as from the gas stove kitchen," he said.

On the 1st of November, he received from Professor de Saram the saree and the petticoat Mrs. Sathasivam was wearing when she was killed.

The total length of the saree was 6 yards and its width was 46 inches. It had a grey portion stitched along one edge, which was used to tuck the saree in around the waist.

Answering a query of the Crown Counsel, Mr. Chanmugam said that he found certain tears in the saree, twelve in all.

"The first tear is a large 'T' shaped tear 7 ½ inches x 3 inches with jagged edges, 12 inches below the top and 2 yards from the free end. I have marked it in pencil. There are safety pin marks at the top edge," explained Mr. Chanmugam.

Himself a Tamil, he said he was familiar with the manner in which Tamil ladies wore their sarees. "The cloth is made up into folds and pinned up and that is how there are pin marks," said Mr. Chanmugam.

Mr. Chanmugam then explained in detail the nature and extent of all the other 11 tears.

He said he noticed several dark stains on the saree.

"These stains consist essentially of dark organic matter. I took it by extracting that with ether (a chemical) and there was a small bit of sand, which again had cobble shells - very small particles. They were similar to the material found on the floors of the two kitchens. One large stain lent itself best for comparison. The others were just examined by me under a powerful lens. The matter was extracted from the large stain. Under the lens, they all gave a similar appearance but only one stain was large enough to permit a comparative analysis," explained Mr. Chanmugam.

He further said that it was an old art silk saree, which tears fairly easily indicating it had been in use for sometime.

On the 23rd of January 1952, Mrs. Sathasivam's petticoat was again sent to him from the Magistrate's Court to examine for seminal stains. Five days later, the saree was also sent for examination for seminal stains.

He said he found seminal stains on the petticoat but not on the saree.

"I also examined the petticoat and the saree and I found urine stains on both", said Mr. Chanmugam.

"On the petticoat, it was a very extensive area and it was at the back. In front also you have two patches, but not so extensive as behind," he said.

At that stage the petticoat was draped on a peon of the court who was 5 feet 1 1/2 inches in height and Mr. Chanmugam indicated the positions of the urine stains and the seminal stains. The seminal stains were right at the back. Witness indicated the positions of the urine stains at the back and in front. He said that there were two patches, which were towards the bottom of the petticoat. He also found urine stains on the saree.

Mr. Chanmugam said that it was not possible to say exactly how Mrs. Sathasivam wore her saree. He demonstrated on a peon how she may have worn the saree and said that a lot depended on where exactly she decided to tuck in the loose end of the saree.

"It is impossible to get any precise location of where the stains were at the time the saree was worn by Mrs. Sathasivam," he said.

He was then questioned about the 'verti' cloth found in Mrs. Sathasivam's bedroom. He found that it was also stained with semen.

Justice Gratiaen asked, "Is that a typical sleeping garment which a

Tamil gentleman would wear?"

"I believe so. I adopt it myself as it is of softer tissues. Many Tamil gentlemen use that kind of 'verti' for sleeping in. In this case, I saw the position of the 'verti' myself and it was in a position indicating that it had been used as a sheet to sleep on."

Mr. Chanmugam said he examined William's sarong after his arrest on the 27th October for seminal stains and found nothing on it.

Mr. Chanmugam further said that he found a squarish rectangular piece of cloth in Mrs. Sathasivam's bedroom lying on a chair. "I examined it for seminal stains and the result was positive. It was a kind of garment which was consistent with a person using it to wipe himself after having intercourse," he said.

It is clear that Mr. Chanmugam's evidence, though led by the prosecution, certainly helped the defence.

During the cross-examination Dr. Colvin R. de Silva stressed the issues that were in his favour, especially the dirt on the soles of the feet.

"You were given three specimens of material taken from the soles of the feet of Mrs. Sathasivam as she was lying there dead in the garage?" Dr. de Silva asked.

"That is correct."

"Two of the specimens were from the left foot?"

"Yes".

"All three consisted of dark material such as you would find on the bare feet of a person who had walked about in a place where you could get such dirt on the feet?"

"That is so."

"So the purpose of your taking swabs from the floors of the various parts of the house was to investigate whether it was possible to come, through scientific analysis, to a conclusion as to the floor of which part of the house this matter on the soles of the feet came from?"

"It would have contributed towards that. Professor de Saram and I have worked in collaboration. We have done a lot of work together," answered Mr. Chanmugam.

The excellent teamwork practised by forensic experts even in 1951, though sadly lacking today in Sri Lanka, was evident from an answer of Mr. Chanmugam to a question by Justice Gratiaen.

He said, "Professor de Saram, the Finger Print people and I go to a scene as a team and each one takes what may come under his purview or hand over what has been taken by one person to the other. In this case, I did not want to touch the body until Professor de Saram came."

Referring again to the material on the soles of the feet, Dr. de Silva asked, "So you were addressing yourself in your scientific analysis to the question where in this house could this material on the soles of the lady's feet came from?"

"Yes."

"Then you found there was a possibility of making a differentiation between the swab of the gas stove kitchen floor and the swab of the Dover Stove kitchen floor?"

"Yes."

"When you made that differentiation you found that the differentiation led to a closer identity between the material on the soles of the feet and the material in the Dover Stove kitchen?"

"That is so."

"From that, as a scientific man, I take it that ordinarily you would draw the inference that the material on the soles of the feet came from the floor of the kitchen?"

"Not exclusively from the Dover Stove kitchen. A contributory portion could have come from the gas stove kitchen floor also."

"In other words, if she had walked through the gas stove kitchen to the Dover Stove kitchen, what you found on the soles of the feet would be consistent with that process?"

"Yes," replied Mr. Chanmugam.

Justice Gratiaen asked, "Would you then eliminate it entirely as having come from the floor of the gas stove kitchen?"

"You can," replied Mr. Chanmugam.

Dr de Silva reiterated his position by asking Mr Chanmugam, "Then clearly on your scientific evidence she walked on the Dover Stove kitchen floor?"

"Yes," he replied, perhaps to the immense satisfaction of Dr. de

Silva.

"Then if a person came into the kitchen and there was fluff on that kitchen floor, it could come on to the feet?"

"I suppose if there was fluff on the floor anybody could have picked it up."

"It is also consistent with her having had her feet on the floor in the garage?"

"That is so."

"I will ask you to consider what your view of the matter is, as a scientific man. Imagine the lady walking or standing on the kitchen floor. The contents of the scrapings taken from right against the soles of the two feet of the lady are consistent with her having thus stood or walked on that kitchen floor?"

"Yes."

To clarify this further, Justice Gratiaen asked, "The black substance, which was in the closest proximity to the foot, is consistent with that?"

"Yes," Mr. Chanmugam replied.

Continuing the cross-examination Dr. de Silva asked, "Then consider her one way or another being dragged towards the garage. The one drag mark you found is consistent with some portion of one of her feet dragging along that floor when she was being dragged to the garage?"

"Yes, if the drag mark was made by Mrs. Sathasivam."

Justice Gratiaen then asked, "To put it in a more general way, is the drag mark you saw consistent with it having been made by the foot of a person who was being dragged across the kitchen?"

"Yes," replied Mr. Chanmugam.

He agreed that if Mrs. Sathasivam was dragged into the garage from the kitchen, the stuff that would have adhered to the sole of the left foot last was consistent with stuff from the floor of the garage.

The final question of Dr. de Silva on this issue was, "From the reconstruction of the scientific possibilities one can visualize two feet walking in the kitchen, one of those feet dragging along and a foot at least heavily on the floor of the garage?"

Mr. Chanmugam said, "Yes."

Dr. de Silva then questioned at length about the tears and the stains in the saree.

Mr. Chanmugam agreed that the stains consisted of greasy material consistent with what was seen on the kitchen floor.

Mr. Chanmugam was then asked about the mortar at the scene. He said he could remember seeing a clear light brown mark on that mortar. It seemed to him to have the size and order of the outline of a footprint in light brown mud.

Justice Gratiaen asked, "Were you there when there was a suggestion of it being photographed?"

Mr. Chanmugam said that as Mr. Thiedeman was there he felt that it was under his purview.

Answering Dr. de Silva's questions on the urine stains on the petticoat, Mr. Chanmugam said that the urine patch at the back of the petticoat has reached right down to within 3 inches of the bottom hem of the petticoat.

Dr. de Silva described the patch as having a shape like a very distorted map of South America!

"There is a long portion of this patch which is several inches wide reaching downwards?"

"Yes."

"How wide is the portion of that large patch near the bottom end of the hem?"

"3¾ inches wide, and at about a foot above, it is 5 ¾ inches wide," said Mr. Chanmugam.

Then Mr. Chanmugam was asked to draw the shape of the patch at the back of the petticoat. He said the total length of this patch was 30 inches from top to bottom.

Mr. Chanmugam then described the other patches in the front of the petticoat.

"The upper patch is smaller than the lower patch. The upper patch is more or less a circular patch. The bottom end of it is about 11 inches above the hem. The bottom of the smaller patch goes down to 12 inches of the hem. The smaller patch is 4 inches in length vertically and 3½ inches in width horizontally. The base of that larger patch extends right to the hem of the front of the petticoat."

"It is as if had there been more cloth below the hem, the patch would have extended beyond?"

"Would have continued."

"Those two spots in front, are they suggestive of the urine dripping downwards when the person is standing?"

"It is difficult to say whether that is the result of the urine that has come directly in contact with it when she was standing. It is consistent with one of two ways, either the urine dripped down the thigh and then came in contact with the petticoat, or that it had sort of dripped on to the petticoat."

To clarify this further, Justice Gratiaen asked, "If somebody was lying down and urine dripped down, you would expect the flow to take a different direction altogether?"

Mr. Chanmugam agreed.

This answer clearly helped the defence theory that Mrs. Sathasivam was strangled while she was standing.

Dr. de Silva's cross-examination was followed by a brief re-examination by Mr. Ananda Pereira. It was more a damage limitation exercise by the Crown.

After the re-examination Justice Gratiaen asked further questions about the drag mark.

"With regard to the drag mark which you have now marked on the sketch, have you any doubt about it?"

"No doubt."

"Describe that drag mark," Justice Gratiaen requested.

"It was about 1½ feet in length and was slightly wavy as I have shown on the sketch and it was about 2 to 2½ inches in width. It looked to me as if a foot got dragged along or as if somebody had slipped his footing and gone; it was not a complete outline. It was a sort of a drag mark."

"Would it be fair to conclude that it was not the kind of mark which you would expect to find as having been left there by people who were merely walking about the kitchen in the course of their normal work?"

"No."

"Nothing like that at all?"

"No," replied Mr. Chanmugam.

The Registrar of Fingerprints, Mr. T. Thalaisingham was another scientist who visited the scene of the murder.

He was summoned to give evidence by the prosecution and was examined by Mr. Ananda Pereira, Crown Counsel.

He said that he found a hand mirror on a wooden bench. He picked up the mirror and examined it for fingerprints. He said there were no decipherable prints on it owing to the uneven surface of its handle.

Mr. Thalaisingham also examined the wooden mortar found at the scene of the murder for fingerprints, but they were not there. He said he encircled the area where there was a mark on the mortar with a piece of chalk.

Shown a photograph of the mark of the mortar by the Crown Counsel, Mr. Thalaisingham said it did not resemble a foot. "It was some foreign matter which looked like drying mud. It was light brown in colour," he said.

For the prosecution, it was essential to identify the handwriting of the letters produced during the trial.

The Examiner of Questioned Documents and Hand-writing Expert, Mr. T. Nagendra was summoned to give evidence for this purpose.

He was examined by Mr. Douglas Jansze, Crown Counsel. He was shown some letters signed by Miss. Yvonne Stevenson as "Yvonne" and addressed to Mr. Sathasivam.

Mr. Nagendra said those letters, dated 27th September 1951 and 29th September 1951, began 'My Dearest Pet lamb' and 'My Dearest' and 'Darling'.

He confirmed that the handwriting of all these letters were the same.

CHAPTER 12

EVIDENCE OF SIR RICHARD ALUVIHARE, THE INSPECTOR-GENERAL OF POLICE

It is extremely rare nowadays for an Inspector-General of Police (IGP) to get directly involved in an investigation of a murder case. However, when Sir Richard Aluvihare, the IGP heard about Mrs. Sathasivam's tragic death, he got himself directly involved in the case by visiting the scene, deciding who should do the post-mortem examination and questioning of William. Therefore, he became an important witness in the trial.

Strangely, the IGP was summoned by the Defence at the Magisterial Inquiry. But in the Supreme Court trial, the IGP was called by the Crown to give evidence.

Describing the administrative structure of the Police, he said in October 1951, there were three Superintendents for Colombo. They were Superintendent of Police, Colombo (Mr. C.C. Dissanayake), Superintendent of Police, Crimes (Mr. M. Albert de Silva), and Superintendent of Police, Criminal Investigations Department (CID) (Mr. Koelmeyer). Mr. Aluvihare said that the Superintendent of Police, CID was Superintendent for the whole Island.

Mr. Koelmeyer worked directly under the IGP and the CID worked directly under him.

"When information of a crime is given to the Police, it would be the Crimes Branch that would take it up. The general investigation of crimes in Colombo Division is in charge of the Crimes Branch, Colombo. They would have available to them the assistance of any other branch. In this case, the proper branch to have taken up the investigation of the murder of Mrs. Sathasivam would have been the Crimes Branch of Colombo of which Mr. Albert de Silva was the Superintendent and Mr. Attygalla, the Assistant Superintendent," explained Mr. Aluvihare.

He said that he received information of the murder of Mrs. Sathasivam between 4 and 4.30 on the afternoon of the 9th of October and he decided to visit the scene.

"Of course it is not very usual for you to visit scenes of murder yourself?" asked the Acting Solicitor-General Mr. T.S. Fernando.

"I use my discretion. I do not visit scenes in every case of murder," the IGP replied.

He said he arrived at No. 7, St. Alban's Place at about 5 o'clock. Then he contacted Professor de Saram at his bungalow and suggested to him that he should do the post-mortem in conjunction with Dr. P.S. Gunawardena, the Judicial Medical Officer, Colombo.

"Professor de Saram was not agreeable to doing it with some other doctor and said that he would rather do it alone or not at all. I then decided that Professor de Saram should do it by himself," said the IGP.

He informed Court that on the morning of 18th October he received information from the Police Central Information Room at Fort that the servant boy William had been arrested at Matara.

Answering Mr. Fernando, he said late that night Mr. Albert de Silva contacted him over the telephone from Panadura.

"Did you make any suggestion to Albert de Silva as to where the servant boy should be brought to when he comes to Colombo?"

"I suggested Bambalapitiya Police Station because that was the investigating Police Station and that would be the normal Police Station he should be brought to. Then I had a conversation with Albert de Silva about the place and decided that William should be taken to Modera Police Station."

"Between Bambalapitiya Police Station and Modera Police Station there are a number of Police Stations?" asked Mr. Fernando.

Dr. Colvin R. de Silva then made an objection, commenting "I would submit that any disagreement between Police Officers as to where William should be taken has no relevance certainly at this stage of the case."

Justice Gratiaen intervening asked, "I am afraid this is the same matter which I raised in the course of your opening Mr. Solicitor-General. We are not investigating the conduct of any Police Officer with regard to this change of decision as to where William should be taken. How is it relevant to the guilt or innocence of Mr. Sathasivam?"

"Bambalapitiya would ordinarily be the Police Station where William should have been taken to and there is evidence to show that he did make a certain statement at Modera," said Mr. Fernando.

Dr. de Silva said that William denied in this court that he ever made a statement at Modera.

"Whether William made a statement or not or whether any Police Officer disbelieved him or not, as far as the guilt or innocence of Mr. Sathasivam is concerned, he cannot be held to be responsible for any errors on their part unless you allege a conspiracy," Justice Gratiaen told Mr. Fernando.

Commenting further, Mr. Fernando said, "The credibility of William is an issue in this case and a number of questions have been put to him to test his credibility. My submission is, if that statement is material in this case, then the circumstances in which that statement came to be made is also material."

"Are you suggesting now that it is a matter for the jury to take into account that there was something sinister about the decision not to take William to Bambalapitiya Police Station and that it is of that kind of sinister character, which is relevant to the guilt of Mr. Sathasivam?"

"No, My Lord. What I wish to submit is that if the credibility of William is relevant then the circumstances under which he came to make his statement are relevant, and the venue of his statement is also relevant."

Dr. de Silva then said, "One cannot put questions about a statement of William, whom they have pardoned in this case, introducing into this case the differences in the various branches of the Police as relevant to the case. I have no respect for their failure. I shall at the proper time ask the benefit of that failure to accrue to me."

Mr. Fernando replying said that his submission was that he was entitled to ask why a material witness in this case was taken to a particular Police Station and not to another place. "My learned friend questioned William for two days in regard to various things he had said at Modera," he replied.

Justice Gratiaen said, "He denied having made a complete statement. I can understand your leading evidence in rebuttal in order to contradict a witness, but to meet in advance a possible contradiction that may arise is not in the order of things."

Mr. Fernando then informed Justice Gratiaen, "There is no other opportunity for me to lead this evidence."

Dr. de Silva said, "I very respectfully submit that this case has to go on the evidence in this Court. My learned friend is attempting to introduce into this case some alleged disagreement between Sir Richard Aluvihare and his subordinates. It is for my learned friend to show that that is relevant to this case."

Justice Gratiaen commented, "It seems to be perfectly clear up to this point that William flatly denied a single contradiction, which so far has only been suggested as having been made. William says in effect that wherever he went he told the same story."

"Part of the statement which William made to Mr. Koelmeyer was actually read by my learned friend and the circumstances in which that statement came into existence I submit would be relevant," said Mr. Fernando.

"At this stage all that is relevant is that Sir Richard Aluvihare, who is perfectly entitled to do that as Head of a Department responsible for running the Police Force, decided to take away an investigation from one Branch of the force and hand it over to another," Justice Gratiaen commented.

"I would submit that the circumstances in which he came to make that decision would be relevant. Does your Lordship rule that I cannot put any question in regard to William being taken over to

Modera?" asked Mr. Fernando.

Justice Gratiaen replied, "The fact that he was taken, certainly, that is common ground."

After this interesting discussion, the IGP said that he was not aware that a statement of William had been recorded and he went there with the idea of meeting William and finding out what had happened.

"I did not know at that stage that a statement had been recorded," said the IGP.

He said that Mr. Albert de Silva, Mr. Adihetty and Mr. Wickremaratne were present at Modera and he telephoned Mr. Koelmeyer and asked him also to come. William's statement was read out to him by Inspector Wickremaratne and the IGP listened to that statement.

The IGP said he asked Mr. Albert de Silva about the statements William made and then he decided that William's statement should be recorded afresh by the CID. He read that statement the same afternoon and he got the boy William and put certain questions to William. Then he asked Mr. Koelmeyer to produce the boy before the Magistrate and get his statement recorded.

"Then Sir Richard, I believe you took the decision finally to take the case over from the Crimes Branch and hand it over to the CID?" asked Mr. Fernando.

The IGP said he gave the order the next day.

Dr. Colvin R. de Silva cross-examined the IGP about William's statement he recorded.

"I am asking you this so categorically because William has said almost in so many words that you had fabricated this document?" said Dr de Silva.

Before the IGP answered the question, Justice Gratiaen remarked, "In the Magistrate's Court you were called as a witness for the defence?"

"Yes."

Justice Gratiaen told Dr. Colvin R. de Silva, "Up to date you have been relying on the prosecution witnesses and now this witness the prosecution is relying on?"

Mr. Fernando remarked, "He called this witness in the Magistrate's Court and here he is objecting to my getting out from him what I want."

"When I call a witness I should imagine, subject to Court, that I am in control of the defence," Dr. de Silva said.

Mr. Fernando retorted, "And I am looking after the prosecution."

"And I am controlling both of you. Now let us go on with the case," requested Justice Gratiaen.

Dr. de Silva then questioned the IGP at length about William's statement.

"He made it pretty clear to you that he was admitting having made a particular statement implicating himself solely to Mr. Albert de Silva, but asserting that he made that statement because he had been tutored to do so by an Inspector of Police?" asked Dr. de Silva.

"That is what I understood."

Dr. de Silva then read William's statement, sentence by sentence to the IGP. (See Page 32)

The IGP confirmed that William stated that the Inspector asked him to say that Mr. Sathasivam came to the kitchen after the lady was killed, gave him eight 10 rupee notes and asked him to leave the place. Then William made that statement to Mr. Albert de Silva at the Police Office, Matara.

Dr. de Silva said that William denied making such a statement to the IGP.

The IGP said William further stated, "The Inspector told me that if I made the statement that I already referred to, that he would employ me in his bungalow as a servant."

Further questioned by Dr. de Silva on what William said, the IGP read from the statement.

"He now states that the Inspector told him that he would give 1000 Rupees if he made the statement that the Inspector desired him to make."

"William did make that statement to you?" Dr. de Silva asked.

"Yes," the IGP replied.

After reading William's statement the IGP said, "The signature at the bottom is mine and I identify it and I added my title and date to it."

Dr. Colvin R. de Silva then questioned the IGP about another vital piece of missing evidence.

"At No. 7, St. Alban's Place, a slip of paper was found, what I believe, had noted a number of telephone calls?"

"No, not as far as I remember. I do not remember that."

Dr. de Silva said that he would just read him a passage from Mr. Thiedeman's evidence, which may help to recall the point he was asking the IGP about and read the following section from Mr. Thiedeman's evidence.

"On 13.10.51 when I revisited the scene I found a writing pad on the wooden shelf where the telephone is kept. Inside that pad I found a slip of paper, which contained what appeared to be a record of telephone calls. I took this slip of paper into my custody, but not the pad. The pad was an ordinary writing pad used for writing letters. This pad was the size of an exercise book. I have no recollection of having seen the pad on the 9th. The shelf on which the telephone stands is about 12 inches by 12 inches. When I saw the pad on the 13th, the pad was on the shelf. I saw a row of numbers on the slip of paper. Actually, there was not on this paper the telephone numbers which had been called, but there were rows of figures in sequence and tabular form. So far as my recollection goes the figures against '9' (that is the date 9th October) were 1, 1, 4."

Dr. de Silva asked the IGP, "Were you informed of a record like that?"

The IGP replied, "No."

Concluding his cross-examination, Dr. de Silva asked the IGP regarding contacting Professor Sydney Smith. The IGP said that at the request of the Attorney-General's Department, the CID contacted the Ministry of External Affairs. The Ministry then contacted the High Commissioner in the United Kingdom.

The IGP said that Sir Velupillai Coomaraswamy, the Deputy High Commissioner in the United Kingdom, wrote to Sir Sydney Smith to get advice for the Attorney-General's Department.

CHAPTER 13

THE CASE FOR THE DEFENCE

Since the time of Mr. Sathasivam's arrest on the afternoon of the day of his wife's murder, he maintained that he left No. 7, St. Alban's Place at 10.30 a.m., and at the time his wife was alive and healthy.

After the arrest, Mr. Sathasivam was produced at 8.55 p.m. on the same day before Professor G.S.W. de Saram to be examined. He found that Mr. Sathasivam had no external injuries. His finger nails were projecting about 1/16th of an inch.

Mr. Sathasivam did not smell of alcohol and Professor de Saram recorded that Mr. Sathasivam was 'rational'.

At the magisterial inquiry, Mr. Sathasivam, who was then the first accused, made a voluntary statement on the 31st of March 1952.

He said, "I was the husband of the deceased. I married in 1941. After my marriage, my wife and I lived in my father's house in Campbell Place for about a month. After that my wife and I lived at my wife's house at Horton Place. My wife and I got on quite well."

"My first child was born in St. Mary's Nursing Home and from there my wife went back to her father's house. My second child was born in 1945. That child is Yajnarupa. I cannot remember quite well but it was somewhere between the birth of these two children that my wife and I had some disagreement. After the disagreement my wife and I got on very well."

"My third child Manjula was born in 1947 and my youngest child Rajendrani was born in 1948. I was and I am very fond of my children. I was fond of my wife. I still mourn over her death," he said.

Continuing his statement Mr Sathasivam said that his father-in-law, Mr. Rajendra, died in 1946.

"I am not sure of the date. But I know that he died before the birth of my last child. After my father-in-law died my wife and I lived at Horton Place. My father died in 1950. My wife and I came to live at No. 7, St. Alban's Place I think in 1949."

"I am a sportsman. Cricket is my special game. I captained the All Ceylon team. I am a member of the Tamil Union Club and was the captain of its cricket team. I have travelled a fair amount as a cricketer. Towards the end of 1950, my wife returned to Ceylon from England before I did. She left England before I did as she fell ill and she could not stand the severe winter. I was myself ill with pneumonia at this time. It was very difficult at this time to get a sea passage. My wife returned to Ceylon by sea. On my wife's way back to Ceylon she wrote to me a letter. I remember receiving this letter. It was dated 2nd February and was sent from Aden as the post mark showed."

He said his wife wrote of a certain matter, which she had apparently come to hear of on board the ship.

"I replied to that letter from England. In reply to my letter to her, my wife wrote to me another letter on 13th February. She wrote from 'Sukhasthan', her father's residence. The house No. 7, St Alban's Place is called 'Jayamangalam'. I received this letter before I left England. I left England on 1st March 1951. When I returned from England I had just recovered from an attack of pneumonia and I was asked to be careful."

"When I returned to Ceylon my wife was living with her mother at Horton Place. On the day of my return to Ceylon, my wife and I came to live with the children at No. 7, St. Alban's Place."

Continuing, Mr. Sathasivam said he left Ceylon again and returned on 22nd September. He said, he went to the house No. 79, Horton Place, the house of Mr. Haniffa.

"Even after that I did not stay away from my wife's house. I used to go to No. 7, St. Alban's Place. Between 2.10.51 and 9.10.51, I spent the nights at my wife's house on more than one occasion. On the night of the 8th of October I slept at No. 7, St. Alban's Place. I came home about 1.30 a.m. on 9th."

"That night, I slept in my bedroom, where my wife sleeps. My wife and I had one bed and both slept on this bed that night. I woke up in the morning of the 9th of October, about five minutes to 9 o'clock."

"When I got out of bed I opened the door of the bedroom. There is a clock on the landing, and as I opened the door I automatically looked at the clock as I usually do, and that is how I remember the time I got up."

"I went to the bathroom and I brushed my teeth and did a wash and came back to my bedroom. This would have taken me about five minutes. I found a cup of coffee got ready by my wife as she always does. I drank my coffee, lit a cigarette, took up the morning newspapers and got back to bed."

"I remained in bed for a minute or two. I then got up to answer a call of nature and taking the newspaper I went to the lavatory. I was in the lavatory for about 10 minutes. I came back into bedroom with my newspaper and got into the bed and continued to read the paper until I had finished. This would have taken me about ten minutes. I cannot say exactly."

"My wife and the two younger children were in the bedroom. These two children do not go to school. I remember that I had some chocolates I had brought the night before and I gave them to the children. We were teasing and playing with them. This may have gone on for about 5 to 10 minutes."

Mr. Sathasivam said that he then had sexual intercourse with his wife.

"After that I had a bath as I was going out. After my bath I came back to the bedroom. While I was rubbing myself down I remember my wife telling me, 'Summons has also been served and I do not know what I could tell Mr. Mack if I conceived!'"

"I remember my telling her jokingly, 'If you conceive we will get hold of Proctor Mack to be the godfather!'"

Continuing his statement, Mr. Sathasivam said he ate two half boiled eggs which his wife gave him and had some string-hoppers and coffee.

"I did not see my wife eat, up to that stage, but I cannot say whether she ate before waking hours. Up to the time I ate the eggs I did not see her eat anything."

"My wife is a Hindu. Sometimes my wife and I eat together and if I go out early I eat before her. She always eats late. At the time I ate, my children may have been there. While I was dressing, my wife sat down on the bed and she ate string-hoppers. At this stage the children were in the room. They were seated on the ground and my wife had given them string-hoppers on their plates, which are unbreakable plates. My wife had finished her tea."

"My children are lively and mischievous. They play all over the house. When I am in the bedroom I have to leave my wristlet on the top of my almirah to prevent the children getting at it."

"While I was putting on my pair of shoes, I told my wife to telephone for a 'Quickshaws' cab from the telephone in the bedroom upstairs. I saw my wife ring for a 'Quickshaws' cab. I finished my dressing and came downstairs with my wife and children."

"I was downstairs for a couple of minutes. I remember I went to the Frigidaire and had a glass of iced water, as I was very thirsty. The reason was I had had a lot of drinks the night before and I was thirsty. I had a glass of iced water and then the 'Quickshaws' cab arrived."

"I forgot to state something. Before I left the house I telephoned Mr. Haniffa's bungalow and I was informed by someone there that he had gone with Mr. Newton Perera. The 'Quickshaws' cab arrived. I got into the 'Quickshaws' cab and went away," said Mr. Sathasivam.

Mr. N. M. J. Rajendram, the Magistrate then queried, "When you went away was your wife alive and well?"

Mr. Sathasivam said, "Very much alive and well. I saw her."

"It is alleged by the Crown in this case that you killed your wife?" the Magistrate asked Mr. Sathasivam.

"I deny this," replied Mr. Sathasivam.

Mr. Sathasivam said from St. Alban's Place, he went in the car towards Fort.

"I stopped at the Galle Face Hotel. I met Mr. Haniffa and Mr. Newton Perera there."

"I had a glass of orange juice. I had smoked a cigarette and my throat was worse because of the drinks the night before. Then I went to various places. I ultimately came back to the Galle Face Hotel and from there Haniffa, Newton Perera and I went to Haniffa's bungalow. We reached Haniffa's house about 3.15 p.m. I had some lunch. Haniffa did not have his lunch. Haniffa's condition was not very good. He was drunk. Newton Perera was in the same condition as Haniffa, if anything slightly worse!"

"After lunch I got into bed and slept. While I was sleeping I was awakened by Mr. Haniffa to answer a telephone call from my mother."

"My mother lived at that time in an annexe in Serpentine Road, about 50 yards away from the Tamil Union Club. I went to the telephone. I cannot remember the exact words of the conversation, but I could give the substance. My mother asked me why I did not come there, meaning to her house in the morning. This she asked me as I go to see her every morning or by lunch time. This is my usual practice. I told my mother that I had gone to Fort and had got held up and I would come to see her on my way to the Club."

"I also told her that I had a letter from the estate addressed to her and some papers which I would bring along. She asked me where I had got the letter from. I told her that I had stayed at home last night and I had got the letter. She then asked me, 'How is baby?' referring to my wife. I told her she was all right and then rang off."

"After that conversation I went back to bed. I fell asleep again. I was awakened again by Mr. Haniffa, as there was a telephone call. He told me that Mr. Nadarajah was calling."

"A few minutes later, Police Officers Mr. Albert de Silva and Mr. John Attygalle came to Mr. Haniffa's residence in Mr. Nadarajah's car," Mr. Sathasivam said.

This is how Mr. Albert de Silva described in his evidence in the Magistrate's Court, the arrest of Mr. Sathasivam that day.

"As Mr. Nadarajah approached the house, I saw Mr. Sathasivam get out of the house and coming towards Mr. Nadarajah. Both Mr. Nadarajah and Mr. Sathasivam walked towards us and we met them halfway. Mr. Attygalle told Mr. Sathasivam that I have to place him under arrest for the murder of his wife. Then Mr. Sathasivam said,

'My God, I am innocent. How can it be? My wife was alive when I left the house.' Mr. Sathasivam was taken to the Fort Police Station. He wanted to go home and see the dead body. I told him it would be unadvisable to do so as there was a vast crowd, which may turn hostile. Then Mr. Sathasivam just wanted to see the children and I said that cannot be allowed."

Mr. Sathasivam's defence was therefore, when he left No. 7, St. Alban's Place at 10.30 a.m., his wife was alive.

After the prosecution case was closed, before summoning witnesses for the defence, Dr. Colvin R. de Silva, the defence counsel, made an opening address to the jury.

He stated that it was his intention in terms of the Criminal Procedure Code to place before Court exercising the right vested in the defence, a certain sequence of events in the case of the prosecution.

Criticizing the actions of some Police Officers, Dr. de Silva said, "The Police had perpetrated this greatest injustice by arresting Mr. Sathasivam for the murder of his wife."

"It is also Mr. Sathasivam's position that when the Police arrested him they had certain evidence which pointed the finger of guilt away from him."

Contrasting the events following the murder, Dr. de Silva said, "Mr. Sathasivam was found in the city of Colombo in a place where those who knew the circumstances could find him. But William had fled from that house and changed his appearance by changing the clothes he wore."

"Therefore, the task of the Police should have been not to pursue the unfortunate husband, but the servant who had decamped with the jewellery and the 'thalikody' worn by Mrs. Sathasivam."

"If the Police had not listened to back stair gossip and coloured stories, they should have taken Mr. Sathasivam to help them in their investigation instead of placing him under arrest on a charge of which he was completely innocent," said Dr. de Silva.

"Mr. Sathasivam who was taken into Police custody was not reticent but gave all the information he had to help the police in their investigations. He answered all the questions put to him by his interrogators and also freely submitted himself to be examined by a doctor whom the police had specially chosen for the purpose," Dr. de Silva added.

He reminded the jury that Mr. Sathasivam had subjected himself to an interrogation by the investigating Police Officer for over an hour.

"That conduct of Mr. Sathasivam was most unlike of any guilty person accused of a murder of the nature of which he was accused," remarked Dr. de Silva.

Further criticizing some aspects of the Police investigation, Dr. de Silva said, "Nowhere in the lands where the British system prevailed had there been an investigation carried out in such a spirit, as was evidenced in the investigation of this case. It was a sad commentary on the protectors of the Queen's Justice that there should have cropped up between the two wings of the police a difference of opinion as to the line of investigation they should have pursued. The mode of investigation had not changed after the change over from the open wing to the secret wing. And they had not checked up evidence that had come before them which was material but had contented themselves with investigating irrelevancies."

Dr. Colvin R. de Silva, continuing his opening address to the jury, said that the police had a certain set of circumstances before them.

"William had absconded and jewellery had been stolen. Soon after the arrest of Mr. Sathasivam, the 'Quickshaws' driver in whose car he had left No. 7, St. Alban's Place, was questioned. That 'Quickshaws' driver had categorically testified that when Mr. Sathasivam left St. Alban's Place, Mrs. Sathasivam was at the door."

Dr. de Silva said that the Police had later discovered a corpse in the Mahaveli river and tried to prove that, that was the corpse of William who was then missing.

"The Police had tried to establish that Mr. Sathasivam was not just a murderer but was also a double murderer!" he said.

"The Police took Ragel, the driver who was dismissed by Mr. Pathmanathan on a complaint by Mrs. Sathasivam, to see the corpse and he identified it as that of William."

"But in that instance the Police relied on the evidence of Professor de Saram, who on seeing the body said it could not be that of a boy of 19. The Police thereupon continued the search for William, but it was not a search for a possible murderer, but a search for a possible witness to a murder," Dr. de Silva said.

"At this time," continued Dr. de Silva, "There was an action for divorce pending in the District Court against Mr. Sathasivam. That action was not for adultery but for malicious desertion. There was an agreement between Mr. and Mrs. Sathasivam by which Mrs. Sathasivam had allowed him freedom to marry Yvonne Stevenson on condition she was left alone," said Dr. de Silva.

"We have the evidence of Mr. Allen Mendis of the 'Quickshaws' Company, who would testify that it was Mrs. Sathasivam who telephoned for the 'Quickshaws', which took Mr. Sathasivam away from his house on 9th October. The 'Quickshaws' driver, M.L.A. Perera would testify that at 10.30 a.m., as he took Mr. Sathasivam out Mrs. Sathasivam was alive in the house."

"There is also the evidence, the most important of all of Mr. O.P. Mack, Proctor, who would testify that he had told Inspector Thiedeman that Mrs. Sathasivam telephoned his firm between 10.25 and 12 noon on 9th October and that he himself answered the telephone giving her the information about the serving of summons in the District Court case."

Dr. de Silva then referred to the incidents that led to the arrest of William and the events that followed at various Police Stations and at the Office of the Inspector-General of Police.

"Between the arrest of William and his questioning by the Inspector-General of Police, William had led the Police to various places where the jewellery stripped from the corpse had been found. It was quite clear that William was an absconder who had run away with the jewellery," said Dr. de Silva.

"William also had injuries on him and one dared argue that they were inconsistent with that of the murderer. William had even confessed to the Inspector-General of Police that he had killed Mrs. Sathasivam but the strange topsy-turvy investigations found a new device. It was later made out that William had made that confession under Police pressure and Police influence."

Dr. de Silva continuing said that later the Police found themselves in conflict with their own medical officer, Professor de Saram, who had been called in to conduct the post-mortem examination.

"Professor de Saram was the man who saw the marks on the body of Mrs. Sathasivam. He was the man who examined the hands of Mr. Sathasivam immediately after the murder and declared that those hands could not have strangled her to death."

"For the first time a new theory had been introduced. That was that the absence of injuries proved that a person was the murderer! If the jury accepted that position any one of them might be charged by the Police with having entered by the back door of No. 7, St. Alban's Place and murdered Mrs. Sathasivam," he said.

Dr. de Silva continuing said that subsequently the servant who confessed to the Inspector-General of Police that he was the murderer was pardoned and made the chief witness on whose evidence the Crown depended for its charge of murder against Mr. Sathasivam.

"William had conquered the doubts of the Attorney-General and had conquered the heart of the Crown," he said.

"The time factor given in the Crown case fitted in entirely with the time of death, 11 a.m., as given by Sir Sydney Smith, who stood vindicated in the evidence given in the case."

"A look at the place made all the difference in the understanding of a case and it was a sad fact the two local experts did not care to visit the scene of the murder before they arrived at their conclusions. But Sir Sydney had come 7,000 miles across the world and the first thing he did was to visit and study the scene and the possible cause of injury between the depressions of the shoulder blades, and Sir Sydney concluded that Mrs. Sathasivam had been pushed up against a doorjamb in the kitchen."

Dr. de Silva further said that the mortar did not lie in the way it was tried to be made out by the Crown. It was William who himself had placed that mortar on the body of Mrs. Sathasivam whom he had rifled.

Dr. de Silva, dealing with the evidence of William on the stamping with a shod foot and the breaking of the voice box, said, "It was either William's own barefoot covered with fluff or William's hand with coconut fluff on it which caused the fracture of the voice box. I suggest that it was both the hands and the bare foot of William that caused that injury."

Dr. de Silva said that William who was the conqueror of legal hearts was not the conqueror of people's stomachs.

"That was why Podihamy said that she supervised the cooking and in her absence Mrs. Sathasivam did the supervision. I do not see why a careful housewife should refrain from walking into the kitchen which is her true domain and supervise the cooking done by the inexperienced cook William," he said.

"It was only under stress that the Crown tried to explain that the injury on Mrs. Sathasivam's head was caused by knocking on the edge of the bed."

Dr. de Silva queried why William was not asked where the head struck.

Dr. de Silva continuing his address said that William had disposed of the torn banian most probably because it was stained with blood from the injuries on his cheek or from the injuries found on Mrs. Sathasivam. He said the fact that Mr. Sanmugam had seen only the shirt and the poplin sarong, which William wore but had failed to see the injuries on the cheeks of William showed that Mr. Sanmugam was not speaking the truth.

Concluding his opening address Dr. de Silva said that the Police investigation was not satisfactory in some respects. "It appeared that some police officers investigated thoroughly any piece of evidence against Mr. Sathasivam but ignored those that were favourable to him."

During the trial Dr. de Silva called witnesses to prove this. He commenced the defence case on the 9th of June 1953.

Mr. O.P. Mack was the first witness called by the defence. He was a partner of P.D.A. Mack and Sons, the legal firm handling Mrs. Sathasivam's divorce action.

Sometime between 10.30 a.m. and 12 noon on 9th October, he said he received a call from a lady who wanted to know whether summons had been served in the divorce case. Mr. Mack thought it was Mrs. Sathasivam although the lady did not say who she was.

Mr. Mack said that on the evening of 9th October (the day of the murder), he went to the Havelock Golf Club of which he was a member. He heard some members talking of Mr. Sathasivam and somebody said he had battered his wife to death!

He was surprised and told them that Mrs. Sathasivam had spoken to him over the telephone that day. It was between about 10.25 a.m. and 12 noon. He was able to fix the time because his father had left for the Courts at that time.

He said Mrs. Sathasivam called for his father and in his absence he asked whether he could take down a message. She wished to know whether summons had been served on Mr. Sathasivam and he told her that it had been served the previous day.

Continuing his evidence Mr. Mack said, "Inspector Thiedeman spoke to me on 14th October at my house in 8th Lane. He asked me a few questions about the divorce case but did not record a statement."

Cross-examined by Mr. T.S. Fernando, Mr. Mack said he was now not quite certain that it was Mrs. Sathasivam who telephoned him. At that time he was certain, but later doubts had arisen in his mind, because if Mrs. Sathasivam had died earlier, she could not have spoken to him. He had never seen Mrs. Sathasivam but he had spoken to her over the telephone four or five times.

He said that in the Magistrate's Court he might have said two or three times. In any case, even at that time he could not have been certain about the number of times he had spoken to her.

Further cross-examined by Mr. Fernando he said that a Police Sergeant recorded his statement on 1st November. He said he would not deny that he had told the members of the Havelock Golf Club that either Mrs. Sathasivam or her mother, Mrs. Rajendra, had telephoned. "It was however quite unlikely I said that," Mr. Mack said.

"When Mrs. Sathasivam telephoned, I did not ask who was speaking. I thought I recognized her voice. I might have told the Police that a lady telephoned and that I assumed it was Mrs. Sathasivam," he said.

"But on 9th October I had no doubt that it was Mrs. Sathasivam who spoke. I recognized her voice so well that I did not bother to ask who telephoned. Later, when I heard all sorts of stories that she had been dead at 9 a.m. that day, I began to doubt whether it was Mrs. Sathasivam who had spoken to me," Mr. Mack said.

Mr. Fernando asked, "But why did doubt arise in your mind when you heard those stories?"

"Because dead people don't talk!" he replied.

Continuing, Mr. Mack said now he had doubts whether it was Mrs. Sathasivam who actually telephoned him.

Justice Gratiaen asked, "Are you now certain that it was not Mrs. Sathasivam?"

"No, My Lord," he replied.

This issue could have been easily clarified if a statement from Mrs. Sathasivam's mother was recorded or she was summoned to give evidence.

Unfortunately, this was not done.

Mr. Allen Mendis, 42-year-old Traffic Manager, Quickshaws Ltd., Bambalapitiya, was another witness called by the defence.

'Quickshaws Ltd.' was established in 1950 and it was considered an efficient and popular taxi service in Colombo, with 47 cabs and employing 90 drivers. All bookings made through telephone calls to the company were registered in a book.

Mr. Mendis said most of the business was transacted over the telephone and they were familiar with customers who called regularly. He was familiar with No. 7, St. Alban's Place and the call used to come always from a lady. She had originally introduced herself as Mrs. Sathasivam.

He himself had taken down several orders from Mrs. Sathasivam. He remembered that there used to be regular calls about 8 a.m. and about 10.30 a.m. The morning calls used to be to take the children to school.

"On 9th October I was on duty and the usual call came in at 10.30 a.m. from Mrs. Sathasivam. It was a lady's voice. I have associated this voice with the lady who has spoken to me as Mrs. Sathasivam previously. In consequence of my previous conversation before 9th October, I had come to be able to identify the voice of that person who had spoken to me as Mrs. Sathasivam. It was the same voice that spoke to me on 9th at 10.30 a.m. when the booking was made," said Mr. Mendis.

"When the person who spoke to me on the telephone told me the number of the house, I said on telephone 'Mrs. Sathasivam?' The voice answered 'Yes'. I said I would send a 'Quickshaws' cab and then she said, 'Thank you.' I then put down the entry as 'Sathasivam' and not 'Mrs. Sathasivam'," he said.

Mr. Mendis was almost certain that it was Mrs. Sathasivam's voice.

Referring to the entry on page 265 in a document of Quickshaws Ltd., Mr. Mendis said that there was an entry at 10.30 a.m. on 9th October 1951.

The entry read '10.30 a.m. Sathasivam. St. Alban's Place'.

At this stage Dr. de Silva referred the witness to several entries on the booking register on dates prior to 9th October, which indicated that there had been regular calls from No. 7, St. Alban's Place, for 'Quickshaws'. There were regular calls at about 8 a.m. All those calls came from Mrs. Sathasivam. There were also regular calls at about 10.30 a.m. There were also many calls at other times of the day.

Mr. Mendis said that Mr. Thiedeman came to the office and wanted to see the bookings for the month of October. Then Mr. Thiedeman asked him who had taken the order at 8 a.m. and he told him that it was taken down by Mr. V. E. H. (Vere) de Mel, the owner of Quickshaws Ltd. The order at 10.30 a.m. was taken down by him, and he told Mr. Thiedeman that Mrs. Sathasivam had given that order.

Mr. Mendis denied having told Mr. Thiedeman that he could not remember who telephoned.

Mr. Thiedeman asked him why he put down 'Sathasivam', and to that he answered that he could not exactly remember.

As his mind was particularly directed to that entry he could remember that call was made by Mrs. Sathasivam at 10.30 a,m. on 9th October.

Mr. Mendis, cross-examined by Mr. T.S. Fernando said that as far he remembered, always the caller from No. 7, St. Alban's Place was Mrs. Sathasivam. He said she had a particular way of speaking when booking cars. She always said 'Can you send me one?' and then gave the address.

Mr. Mendis said, "On 9th October I had no doubt whatsoever that it was Mrs. Sathasivam who telephoned, and I had no doubt about it the next day when Inspector Thiedeman questioned me."

Re-examined by Dr. Colvin R. de Silva, counsel for the defence, Mr. Mendis said that the Police had taken the log sheet of 9th October belonging to driver M.L.A. Perera, who drove Mr. Sathasivam from St. Alban's Place to Galle Face Hotel.

Mr. Mendis said that in their business they had to develop the faculty of recognizing the voices of their customers. Recognition of voices generally pleased customers, who felt they were being given personal attention. They had developed that faculty to a great degree in their business.

He said customers had different peculiarities when placing orders and those peculiarities helped them to identify the customers. On 9th October Mrs. Sathasivam telephoned for a car in the usual manner, using that particular formula. Mr. Mendis said it was Mrs. Sathasivam who had telephoned or it was a perfect imitation.

Replying to Justice Gratiaen, Mr. Mendis said Mrs. Sathasivam had been regularly telephoning for cars for about three or four months before 9th October and he had no doubt that Mrs. Sathasivam telephoned at 10.30 a.m. on 9th October.

Mr. Mendis said that a person telephoning as Mrs. Sathasivam has spoken over the telephone many times before 9th October, especially to take the children to school. As a result, he addressed her as Mrs. Sathasivam over the telephone.

Mr. M. L. Aron Perera, 50-year-old 'Quickshaws' cab driver, giving evidence next stated that at about 10.30 a.m. on 9th October, he had his car at Gomes Petrol Shed, Wellawatta.

"From there I was instructed from Headquarters. The instructions were 'Mrs. Sathasivam needs a car.' I arrived at No. 7, St. Alban's Place before 10.30 a.m. I stopped the car just outside the verandah, in front of the front door step, opened the rear door and waited. I waited for about 2 to 3 minutes and I saw Mr. Sathasivam come down the stairs. The stairway could be seen from the place where I was standing."

Mr. Perera said that Mr. Sathasivam got into the car and sat down in the rear seat and lit up a cigarette.

"Then I closed the rear door and came round the cab and sat in the driver's seat. I asked him where he wished to be driven. He told me to drive him to Galle Face."

At that time he saw Mrs. Sathasivam standing leaning against the door of the house. As far as he could remember, she was still standing there when he drove off. He had seen both Mr. and Mrs. Sathasivam earlier.

As requested by Mr. Sathasivam he drove him to the Galle Face Hotel. He said he dropped Mr. Sathasivam there and returned to the closest taxi stand.

Mr. Perera said that he knew Mrs. Sathasivam before 9th October 1951. He had been employed by Dr. Lucien Gunasekera, son of Sir Frank Gunasekera. He said he had seen Mrs. Sathasivam when he used to visit her residence with Dr. Gunasekera, who attended to her father.

"I had seen her about two or three years before 9th October. I knew her sufficiently to recognise her at sight," he said.

He had also seen her at No. 7, St. Alban's Place, and had also taken her in a 'Quickshaws' cab.

Replying to further questions, Mr. Perera said this was the first time he appeared in a Court of law. When the Policeman came to fetch him, he was surprised and asked what offence he had committed.

Mr. Perera said he was taken to No. 7, St. Alban's Place. When he approached the house, he found a large number of people around it. Even at that time he did not know anything about the murder. At the house he was questioned about the murder and he told the Police that it was a '*raja aparade*' (great injustice) on Mrs. Sathasivam because she was alive at the door when he left with Mr. Sathasivam. He said he did not give thought to who could have killed her.

Mr. Perera said on 9th October he was questioned by an Inspector. One of the questions expressly put to him was whether he saw Mrs. Sathasivam at the time Mr. Sathasivam got into the cab at 10.30 a.m.

"I told the police that I saw her," said Mr. Perera.

"You stated to the Police that you saw Mrs. Sathasivam standing at the door?" asked Dr. de Silva.

"Yes. It is true that I saw Mrs. Sathasivam at the door," Mr. Perera replied. "When I saw Mrs. Sathasivam she appeared quite normal and she was looking on. I remember the Police asking me what she was wearing. I gave the description of her saree."

Cross-examined by Mr. T. S. Fernando, Mr. Perera said he could not say who gave him the instructions to go to the Sathasivam residence. The instructions were, 'Mrs. Sathasivam needs a taxi'. Only when he got into the car he knew the hire was for Mr. Sathasivam.

Mr. Perera said that he knew Mr. Sathasivam earlier. During the drive to the hotel he was speaking to him.

He said he saw Mrs. Sathasivam after Mr. Sathasivam got into the car. He glanced at her for a second. She was wearing a white-faded old saree. It had small flower designs on it. He also remembered she was wearing a blouse.

In the Magistrate's Courts, when he was re-examined by the Crown Counsel, he said that he saw Mrs. Sathasivam dressed in a saree.

"I think she was dressed in a white jacket and an old white saree with dots and small flowers," he had said.

"Do you know that when Mrs. Sathasivam was found dead she was wearing a saree which consisted of an all over pattern of white and purple rectangles, 0.5 inches x 0.7 inches and interposed with red and white, red and yellow, and red and blue flowers?" asked the Crown Counsel.

Mr. Perera replied, "I do not know."

Next witness summoned by the defence was Mr. P. Ramanathan, a merchant residing at 68, High Street, Wellawatte, who said that he was a good friend of Mr. Sathasivam. When Mr. Sathasivam did not have a car, he used to travel in Mr. Ramanathan's car.

He said he met Mr. Sathasivam at the Tamil Union Club on the day he returned from England. Mr. Sathasivam was there with his wife.

Mr. Ramanathan said that on the evening of 9th October, one Mr. Sivasangaran telephoned him at his residence. About five or ten minutes later he telephoned him again. As a consequence of what the caller told him he telephoned No. 7, St. Alban's Place and asked for Mr. Sathasivam. He then called for Mrs. Sathasivam and was told she too was also out. It was about 5.30 p.m.

He then tried to get at Mr. Sathasivam at the Tamil Union Club, and later at Mr. Haniffa's residence. Mr. Ramanathan said he found Mr. Sathasivam at Mr. Haniffa's residence. Mr. Sathasivam asked the witness from where he was speaking and wanted a lift to the club. The witness told him that he heard some shocking news and that he would tell him when he met him at the club.

He did not tell Mr. Sathasivam anything over the telephone, because he did not believe that Mrs. Sathasivam had died. In fact he inquired from Mr. Sathasivam how his wife was getting on and whether she was ill. He replied, "She was hale and hearty."

Mr. Ramanathan said Mr. Sathasivam rang him a little later, and told him that Mr. Nadarajah was in his bungalow at No. 7, St. Alban's Place. Mr. Sathasivam asked him what he had heard. He told him that he had heard that Mrs. Sathasivam was dead. Mr. Sathasivam exclaimed, "Dead! Dead!" and replaced the receiver.

Mr. Ramanathan said that he rang Mr. Haniffa's residence again and was told that the Police had arrived and taken Mr. Sathasivam away because he had murdered his wife. Mr. Ramanathan said he was shocked to hear that.

Mr. K.C. Nadarajah, the Advocate who visited Edinburgh to meet Professor Sydney Smith, giving evidence next said he knew Mr. Sathasivam for nearly 11 years. He was also a member of the Tamil Union Club and they both had been members of the General Committee of the Club. He had never visited Mr. Sathasivam at home. They usually met at the Club. He did not know that he lived at St. Alban's Place.

On 9th October after he returned from Matugama Magistrate's Court and when he was getting ready to go out for a swim with his family, the telephone rang. Mr. John Attygalle, the ASP told him that Mrs. Sathasivam was dead and wanted him to call over.

He told him, "Don't talk nonsense." He said he had known Mr. Attygalle for about ten years.

Mr. Nadarajah said then he went to No. 7, St. Alban's Place and he saw some Police Officers and Mr. Pathmanathan. Mr. Attygalle wanted him to try and find Mr. Sathasivam. He got in touch with Mr. L.M. Fernando, who was a good friend of Mr. Sathasivam.

At that time Mr. Nadarajah's wife and daughter, who were in the car outside, came into the verandah and were seated there. Just then the telephone rang, and his wife shouted to him "Satha", and almost dropped the receiver!

Mr. Sathasivam asked him, "What the devil are you doing in my house?"

He replied, "Never mind all that, where are you speaking from?"

Mr. Sathasivam replied, "I am at No. 79, Horton Place at Mr. Haniffa's house." He told him to wait there till he came over.

Mr. Nadarajah said later he together with Mr. Albert de Silva and Mr. John Attygalle, went to Mr. Haniffa's residence and met Mr. Sathasivam. Mr. Sathasivam wanted to go to No. 7, St. Alban's Place and see the body of his wife.

Mr. Nadarajah said that he prevented him going there, because the temper among the people gathered at the house was very hostile. Mr. Sathasivam was insisting on seeing the body, but he told him that he would be able to see it the next day when he would be called to identify the body.

Meanwhile, Mr. Attygalle told Mr. Sathasivam that he was arresting him for murdering his wife. Mr. Sathasivam was later taken to the Fort Police Station.

Mr. C. J. Oorloff, a proctor, summoned by the defence giving evidence said that Mr Allen Mendis, a close friend of his, told him on 10th October (the day after the murder) that Mrs. Sathasivam had phoned him for a cab the previous day. However, he did not mention any particular time.

The defence then called B. Piyadasa, a 21-year-old unconvicted prisoner who was on remand for ten months. He said he had been in Hulftsdorp prison for six months. Prior to that he was at Welikada Prison. During that period he came to know William and became friends.

He said that there was an inquiry into an alleged attempt on the part of William to commit suicide. He was questioned by Mr. Crowe, the Superintendent of Prisons. At that inquiry he told Mr. Crowe about a conversation in the course of which William told him about the death of Mrs. Sathasivam.

William told him that while he was scraping coconut Mrs. Sathasivam came to the kitchen and bending down asked him why the strands of the scraped coconut were so thick.

William had said that he thought there might be a lot of money and jewellery in the house, so he hit the lady with his elbow and she appeared to be dazed. He then caught her by the neck and squeezed it. She appeared to be dead and then he stamped on her neck. Then he took the bunch of keys, which was tied to the corner of her saree and opened the almirah and took 7 rupees, which was there and went away.

Replying to a question by Justice Gratiaen, Piyadasa admitted having told Mr. Crowe that William told him that it was he who killed the lady and not Mr. Sathasivam, and that he would plead guilty and run away on his way to Court.

Mr. E.R. Crowe, Superintendent of Prisons, at Hulftsdorp jail was summoned next. Examined by Dr. Colvin R. de Silva, he said that he held an inquiry into an allegation of attempted suicide by William and he questioned Piyadasa.

Mr. Crowe said Piyadasa informed him that William had told him that it was not Mr. Sathasivam who killed the lady but he (William) himself, and that he would plead guilty and run away on his way to Court. When he put the allegations made by Piyadasa to William, he denied that he had made such a statement.

Dr. de Silva next summoned Mr. F.J.M. de Saram, the Assistant Superintendent of Police (ASP), Nuwara Eliya, who was the last witness to give evidence for the defence.

Mr. de Saram said he was the ASP Matara in October 1951.

He said on 18th October, William was brought to his Office after his arrest by Inspector Wickremaratne. Inspector Goonesinghe, who was the Inspector-in-Charge of the Matara Police Station did the questioning while Mr. Adihetty and he listened.

Mr. de Saram said that William told them that on 9th October he attended to the household duties and was scraping coconut in the kitchen. Then Mr. Sathasivam came and pulled him by the ear and found fault with him for not washing the lavatory upstairs. Mr. Sathasivam then paid him 5 rupees and dismissed him. He took his clothes and went away.

Later, Mr. de Saram said William began to tell another story. That was that he was in the kitchen when he heard a noise upstairs.

At that stage Mr. Albert de Silva and Mr. John Attygalle arrived from Colombo and the interrogation was interrupted.

Mr. de Saram said that William was taken by car to Colombo and he was taken out of the Police Station to the car with a towel over his head to prevent people seeing him.

"That night I telephoned Sir Richard Aluvihare and told him that William had made a number of statements. First he had incriminated Mr. Sathasivam. Later he incriminated only himself," said Mr. de Saram.

With this evidence, Dr Colvin R. de Silva closed the case for the defence.

At this stage, Mr. T. S. Fernando called 3 witnesses including Mr. M.W.B. Thiedeman and lead evidence in rebuttal.

Examined by Mr. Fernando, Inspector Thiedeman said that on 14th October he went to Mr. O.P. Mack's residence to question him about a telephone call from Mrs. Sathasivam.

He said he also went to the 'Quickshaws' office and met Mr. Allen Mendis and checked on the telephone calls received on 9th October.

Cross-examined by Dr. Colvin R de Silva, Mr. Thiedeman said that he made a note of these conversations in his book after he returned to the station. He did not write it as Mr. Mack said it, because he was in a hurry to get back to the station.

"At the 'Quickshaws' office too, I did not take down the statement of Mr. Mendis as he made it, as I was too tired. Besides, the office was too busy, and Mr. Mendis also was busy," said Mr. Thiedeman.

Dr. de Silva submitted that this procedure appeared to have been adopted whenever there were any bits of evidence in favour of Mr. Sathasivam. He asked whether Mr. Thiedeman was too weary to wield a pen.

Dr. de Silva asked, "Did you appreciate the importance of that statement?"

"Yes," replied Mr. Thiedeman.

Mr. K.A.D. Nanayakkara of the CID, who recorded the statement of Mr. O.P. Mack, was another witness summoned by Mr. T.S. Fernando.

Mr. Nanayakkara, examined by Mr. Fernando said he remembered recording the statement of Mr. Mack. He said Mr. Mack told him that a female spoke and inquired about the divorce case summons being served, and that he assumed that it was Mrs. Sathasivam.

The last witness called by Mr. Fernando was Mr. D. Weerasooriya, who was the Inspector of Police, Wellawatte, in October 1951.

He said that he went to No. 7, St. Alban's Place, about 7.00 p.m. on instructions from Mr. John Attygalle. He then went to the 'Quickshaws' office and brought Mr. M.L.A. Perera, the driver, to the scene of crime. He said Mr. Perera told him that he got an order to go to No. 7, St. Alban's Place, to meet Mr. Sathasivam.

Cross-examined by Dr. Colvin R. de Silva, Mr. Weerasooriya said he also told him that he saw Mrs. Sathasivam when Mr. Sathasivam went away with him in the car.

Hewa Marambage Darlis, father of William, was summoned to give evidence by Justice Gratiaen as mentioned earlier.

Questioned by Justice Gratiaen he said that he did not know where William was when he had left his home, nor did he ask him where he had been when he returned home.

Darlis denied that he told Mr. Koelmeyer that when William returned home he asked him why he came back. He also denied that he told Mr. Koelmeyer that William told him that the master came home late one day, went upstairs with the lady, then there was a cry heard from upstairs, and the master then came downstairs and pushed him out.

Cross-examined by Dr. Colvin R. de Silva, he said that when he was questioned he uttered whatever came to his mouth first!

"A gentleman who was there at the time of the questioning threatened to break my ribs. So through fear I said whatever came to my mouth," he said.

Questioned whether it was Mr. Koelmeyer or Mr. Edwards (both of whom were in the Court) who threatened him, the witness said it was a different person. He said it was a fair stout gentleman.

Further cross-examined, Darlis said that he did not remember now what he told Mr. Koelmeyer.

Dr. de Silva asked, "Will you deny that you told Mr. Koelmeyer that your son came home on the 13th or 14th?"

"I cannot say that. I said whatever came to my mouth!"

"Does that reflect your attitude today in this Court? Are you now saying whatever comes to your mouth?" asked Justice Gratiaen.

"Yes, My Lord!" he replied.

Further cross-examined, Darlis said he was an illiterate man. He did not tell Mr. Koelmeyer that William told him there was a cry upstairs. Mr. Koelmeyer had recorded what he did not say. He denied that he told Mr. Koelmeyer that William had told him that he had changed his sarong and wore a new sarong and came home. He denied further statements made by him to Mr. Koelmeyer, and repeated that he uttered whatever came to his mouth!

As mentioned earlier, Mr. N. M. J. Rajendram's record of the Magistrate's Court evidence was read fully during the trial.

One witness who gave evidence at the Magistrate's Court was Inspector of Police, Mr. M. Albert de Silva.

Answering questions of Dr. Colvin R. de Silva he said, soon after his arrest William had told him that Mrs. Sathasivam came to the kitchen while he was scraping coconut. Then he released the coconut and got up, held her throat with both hands from behind, took her to the garage and killed her.

"Did William in fact make such a statement?"

"Yes," replied Mr. Albert de Silva.

"Later William said that Mr. Sathasivam came down and asked him to get up and open his hand and he got up and held out his open palm. He placed eight 10 rupee notes in his palm. Mr. Sathasivam asked him to run to the village. He put the money in his vest and picked up his shirt," Mr. de Silva said.

"I was hanging about the place for a while then I heard the noise from upstairs. I looked towards that direction. I saw Mr. Sathasivam dragging Mrs. Sathasivam down the steps of the stairs holding the hair with one hand and railing with the other. I ran away from the house," William told Mr. de Silva.

Mr. de Silva said, "Then I told William I cannot understand this and to give me a little explanation. Then William reverted to his original position."

William then said, "I was scraping coconut when Mr. Sathasivam came down the stair case and called me upstairs and took me to the corridor and told me, 'You must join me to kill the lady'. William said that he told, 'I am afraid.' Then Mr. Sathasivam told me, 'If you don't join me I will kill you.' Through fear I consented."

Continuing, Mr. Albert de Silva told the Magistrate's Court, "William then said that Mrs. Sathasivam was seated on the bed and Mr. Sathasivam then went up, held her by her hair and put her down and throttled her and asked him to hold her by the legs. Mrs. Sathasivam struggled and in the course of the struggle her hand came into contact with his face and left the marks. She appeared to be dead. Mr. Sathasivam then trampled her with the shoe and both of them took the body and left it in the garage. Then Mr. Sathasivam gave him 3 rupees and asked him to go away. He left the place, got into a bus and reached Panadura at about 3 p.m."

Mr. Albert de Silva said then he started questioning William on this story.

Cross-examined by Mr. Seneviratne, the counsel of William, the second accused in the Magistrate's Court, before he was pardoned, Mr. Albert de Silva said, "At no time in this inquiry I wanted to assert the function of this Court to decide the innocence of either of these accused. My sole concern was to find the truth and place them before the Courts. To do this I was not allowed. The unnecessary interference by the Inspector-General of Police hindered me from doing this."

Mr. Albert de Silva, cross-examined next by Mr. Cherubim, the Crown Counsel said, "Before Professor de Saram came to the scene I saw a mortar in the garage. I did not notice any impression on the mortar before Professor de Saram did, as I did not examine it. The same evening Mr. Thalaisingham, Registrar of Fingerprints was at the scene. He is an expert on finger and footprints. I cannot remember Mr. Thalaisingham putting a circle in chalk on the mortar. I cannot remember him examining the mortar as I was not in one place. When Professor de Saram drew our attention to the mortar and suggested that it be photographed, I remember Mr. John Attygalle asking Mr. Thiedeman to take necessary action."

Re-examined by Dr. Colvin R. de Silva, Mr. Albert de Silva said, "I have been cross-examined for three days in this case. I have been cross-examined into every incident I have spoken to in my evidence-in-chief. I stated in cross-examination that William made three different statements to me at Matara. I informed the Inspector-General of Police at the first opportunity I contacted him after I left Matara that William had made more than one statement to me."

It is pertinent to mention that Mr. Albert de Silva had a distinguished career in the Police.

This is how the Ceylon Police Gazette on 30th June 1948 documented Mr. Albert de Silva receiving the award of "King's Police Medal for Distinguished Service".

"Makalandage Albert de Silva joined the Police Service in August 1913, and was promoted to the rank of Assistant Superintendent of Police in 1938. He is now Superintendent of Police, Colombo (Crimes).

He has the highest reputation for honesty and integrity and is known affectionately in the Force as 'Honest Albert'.

Before he came to Colombo he was in charge of Sabaragamuwa Province where he earned the respect of all concerned for integrity, honesty and zeal."

There is no doubt that the jury must have carefully considered Mr. Albert de Silva's evidence in Magistrate's Court before reaching their verdict.

CHAPTER 14

COUNSEL'S ADDRESS
TO THE JURY

After the defence closed their case and evidence of Mr. Thiedeman and others in rebuttal was concluded, Dr. Colvin R. de Silva, the defence counsel, began his address to the jury. It lasted for 3 days.

He said that for over fifty working days the jury had been engaged in the joint endeavour to see whether a fellow citizen in the dock was guilty or not guilty of the charge of murder.

He reminded them that on 31st March 1952, in the Colombo South Magistrate's Court, Mr. Sathasivam left the dock and entered the witness box.

"When he chose to do that, he took the first lawful opportunity to declare to the world that he was innocent," said Dr. de Silva.

He pointed out that in the cross-examination in the Magistrate's Court, Mr. Sathasivam was told that Mr. Sanmugam and Edmund had said that they had seen William negotiating the sale of the jewellery at High Street at 9.45 a.m., to which Mr. Sathasivam had replied that it was impossible because he had left home at about 10.30 a.m. and his wife was alive then.

"That was the fundamental issue. Our case is that Mrs. Sathasivam died after 10.30 a.m. while according to the Crown case it was before 9.30 a.m.," Dr. de Silva said.

"For William, who according to his own story had participated in the attack, to be at High Street, Wellawatte, at 9.45 a.m. the Crown would have to allow at least 15 minutes. That would push back the time to 9.30 a.m., without taking into account the time occupied in going to Wellawatte from Bambalapitiya by bus. If they took into consideration William's own story then for William to be at High Street at 9.45 a.m. the attack would have had to take place earlier than 8.15 a.m. when Podihamy, the 'ayah', (domestic aid) was in the bungalow," he said.

Dr. de Silva then referred to the allegation made against Mr. John Attygalle by the Crown and said that it was an allegation that should never have been made.

"Mr. Attygalle was not a gatecrasher in the case. He was investigating the case under the supervision of Mr. Albert de Silva. There were also other Police Officers associated with him. But the Acting Solicitor-General had put it to M.L.A. Perera, the 'Quickshaws' driver that Mr. Attygalle had given him a description of the saree in which Mrs. Sathasivam was found dead."

"Inspector Weerasooriya had also told them that at no time did Mr. Attygalle give driver Perera a description of the saree. The driver himself had denied it from the witness box, but still the highest law officer of the Crown next to the Attorney-General, had thought fit to make that allegation," he said.

Dr. de Silva also said that the defence relied on the whole group of the prosecution evidence and at the close of the prosecution case the defence could have stopped as no case was made out against Mr. Sathasivam.

"But in a case like this, the defence is not concerned only with the mere verdict of 'Not guilty' but the defence wanted to show that Mr. Sathasivam was positively innocent of the charge made against him and was free to go on into the world without any clouds of doubt hanging over him," said Dr. de Silva.

"If the defence was concerned only with the verdict of 'Not guilty', then they could have stopped where the Crown stopped, but they proceeded further to show that Mr. Sathasivam was not merely not guilty but was positively innocent of the charge made against him," emphasised Dr. de Silva.

"For one and a half years Mr. Sathasivam had been facing the ordeal of an unjust charge hanging over him, although there was not even the vestige of a foundation for a case for the prosecution. The law demanded that the jury look at a case as it was laid down before them."

"The defence evidence fell into five groups. The first three of which taken individually, could by itself be decisive if accepted by the jury," said Dr. de Silva

"It was evidence in this case, not allegations that the jury should consider."

"It was evidence when Mr. Sathasivam said that he left his house at 10.30 a.m. and cooperated with the Police by giving them his movements that day, which had proved to be correct."

"The second group of witnesses consisted of Mr. O.P. Mack, Mr. Allen Mendis and Mr. M.L.A. Perera. The third, Sir Sydney Smith and the fourth, Mr. Pathmanathan. The remand prisoner Piyadasa and Mr. Crowe, the Superintendent of the Remand Prison, formed the fifth group. We would also rely on whole groups of witnesses brought by the Crown."

"In respect of the five groups, the jury need not be decisive on Mr. Nadarajah, Mr. Ramanathan, Piyadasa and Mr. Crowe, but all the five groups taken together were decisive," he said.

Dr. de Silva explained that if they took the evidence of Mr. Sathasivam and accepted it, that was alone decisive, so was the evidence of Mr. Mack, the evidence of Mr. Mendis, M.L.A. Perera and Sir Sydney Smith. If this evidence was accepted they would have to acquit Mr. Sathasivam. If they rejected the evidence of all the witnesses but accepted the evidence of one witness, then on the doctrine of reasonable doubt they had to acquit Mr. Sathasivam, said Dr. de Silva.

"A tremendous proportion of this case, both at the Magistrate's Court stage and at this trial, has been devoted to medical evidence and never in the history of the Island has there been staged, within the arena of the Court, so titanic a battle of medical evidence," said Dr. de Silva

He compared that effort to the mountain that laboured and brought forth a mouse!

He said that the doctors who had been brought to contradict the defence case had supported Sir Sydney Smith.

"The two surgeons who believed they were against the defence as far as the medical evidence was concerned entirely supported the defence," he said.

Dr. de Silva submitted to the jury that if they took the evidence of the three groups of witnesses who spoke to the time of death, or of anyone of those three groups, they would have to acquit Mr. Sathasivam. He pointed out that Mr. Allen Mendis and Mr. Mack had stated that Mrs. Sathasivam was alive at 10.30 a.m.

The same applied to the evidence of the 'Quickshaws' driver M.L.A. Perera.

Referring to the evidence of Sir Sydney Smith, Dr. de Silva explained that it was expert evidence. Sir Sydney's opinion was that all factors taken into consideration, Mrs. Sathasivam had died not earlier than 10.30 a.m., probably round about 11 o'clock, with the weight of his opinion towards 12 o'clock. If that opinion was accepted, then too the case was over and the verdict should be 'Not guilty'.

He explained that the bedrock principle of our law was that the accused was presumed to be positively innocent unless and until he was proved positively to be guilty.

"In a civil matter, even if a wrong verdict was given no irreparable harm could occur, because the wrong could be righted. But in a murder trial if there was a verdict, which resulted in an accused person being deprived of his life, it could never be remedied. That is why I say the law is not merely merciful but is just and wise," he said.

Dr. de Silva then referred to the 'doctrine of reasonable doubt' and said that the application of the evidence of Mr. Allen Mendis, Mr. Mack, the 'Quickshaws' driver Perera and Sir Sydney Smith must necessarily result in a verdict of 'Not guilty', even if the jury was not positively convinced by that evidence.

Explaining this point further, he said that even if they should entertain any doubt about the veracity of the evidence of anyone of those witnesses, they could return no other verdict other than a verdict of 'Not guilty', until they could positively reject their evidence.

"The Crown," Dr. de Silva said, "Could ask for a verdict of guilty only by asking the jury to consider William as a truthful witness. If there should be the slightest doubt that William was not a truthful witness, then too the verdict could be none other than that Mr. Sathasivam was innocent."

He also reminded the jury that William was a pardoned accused, who on his own admission was an accomplice to the crime. He explained that, according to the law, if they were to believe an accomplice they should make sure that he had been corroborated on material factors before they could consider him a truthful witness.

He next referred to the evidence of Messrs. Mendis, Mack and M.L.A. Perera and asked the jury to consider first, whether collectively and separately there was any reason to suspect them.

"Mr. Mack was a proctor for Mrs. Sathasivam and Mr. Mendis was the Traffic Manager of Quickshaws Ltd. There was no doubt about their integrity. Perera was a driver and he hailed from a different walk of life. But there was no question about his integrity either. All these three men, in different situations had testified to Mrs. Sathasivam being alive at about 10.30 a.m.," said Dr. de Silva.

Dr. de Silva then referred to the paper found by Inspector Thiedeman on 13th October, four days after the murder, inside the telephone pad at No. 7, St. Alban's Place. The telephone number of the telephone upstairs, 81353, was written on top of this.

Dr. de Silva said that there was no doubt whatsoever that the figures were in the handwriting of Mrs. Sathasivam. It contained on the left hand side, reading downwards, the dates 1 to 9 and against each date the calls made each day, and then the total. Against the figure 9 there were the figures 1, 1 and 4, which represented that there were two separate calls and then a group of 4 calls. Altogether, there had been three separate entries.

He pointed out that Mr. Thiedeman had said that the first two entries, numbers '1' and '1', were in the handwriting of Mrs. Sathasivam but there was some doubt about the third entry, number '4'. He had also stated that the first entry was at 8.15 a.m. for the 'Quickshaws' cab to take the children to school, and the second entry was the call made at 10.30 a.m. for a 'Quickshaws' cab for Mr. Sathasivam

Dr. de Silva said that if those two calls were made at 8.15 a.m. and

10.30 a.m. respectively, and if those calls were in the handwriting of Mrs. Sathasivam, it was then unbreakable and fundamental evidence. It was the final corroboration and proof of the truth of the evidence of Mr. Allen Mendis that Mrs. Sathasivam was alive at 10.30 a.m., on the evidence of that piece of paper alone.

He pointed out that the Crown now suggested that the lady who telephoned Mr. Mack at about 10.30 a.m. or thereafter was not Mrs. Sathasivam but Mrs. Rajendra, the mother of Mrs. Sathasivam.

Dr. de Silva said that the Crown had not put Mrs. Rajendra into the witness box because it was clear that she was not prepared to tell a lie. If Mrs. Rajendra had actually telephoned Mr. Mack after 10.30 a.m., the simplest thing would have been for Mrs. Rajendra to get into the witness box and say, 'I phoned Mr. Mack about 10.30 a.m.'

Dr. de Silva submitted that it was actually Mrs. Sathasivam who telephoned Mr. Mack's office after Mr. Sathasivam had left No. 7, St. Alban's Place. She had obviously telephoned to speak to Mr. Mack senior, but when she found that he was away, she asked his son who had answered her question whether summons had been served. Mr. Mack had said 'Yes', and had entered that fact in his diary.

Dr. de Silva next referred to the evidence of Mr. Mendis and said that it was clear that he and the others at Quickshaws Ltd. specialized in recognizing the voices of their regular customers. That fact had been sufficiently established by the example he had given. He had stated in evidence that on one occasion when Inspector Thiedeman had telephoned him he recognized his voice and said, 'Good morning Mr. Thiedeman' before Mr. Thiedeman had introduced himself. That fact was not denied by Mr. Thiedeman when the Crown led evidence in rebuttal later.

Dr. de Silva next referred to the evidence of Inspector Thiedeman and said that a fact that had been very noticeable was that he had followed a uniform procedure in regard to evidence that was favourable to Mr. Sathasivam. He had gone to the 'Quickshaws' office at 3.30 p.m. fatigued beyond repair, questioned Mr. Mendis and examined his books.

"He did not take down anything Mr. Mendis told him because he was in too much of a hurry to get back to the Police Station. Thereafter, he got out of the 'Quickshaws' office sat in his car and made a note of what Mr. Mendis had told him. The hurry had disappeared. It was at a much later stage that Mr. Koelmeyer recorded a statement of Mr. Mendis. Mr. Mendis was a Crown witness in the Magistrate's Court and his name was placed as a witness on the back of the indictment, but it was I who had to call Mr. Mendis as a witness in that Court," Dr. de Silva said.

Dr. de Silva emphasised that from most respectable and reputable sources he had proven that the evidence of Mr. Mendis that Mrs. Sathasivam telephoned him was true, and that when Mr. Sathasivam left his house that day, his wife was alive and was standing at the door of her house, watching the departure of Mr. Sathasivam.

Mr. M.L.A. Perera had known Mrs. Sathasivam well and recognized her as he left No. 7, St. Alban's Place, with Mr. Sathasivam in his car.

"What was material was not what Mr. Mendis wrote in his note book, 'Sathasivam' or 'Mrs. Sathasivam' but that Mr. Perera went to No 7, St. Alban's Place and saw Mrs. Sathasivam. When Mr. M.L.A. Perera came to know of the death of Mrs. Sathasivam he exclaimed that it was a 'grave crime', because he had seen her that morning. His was the evidence that the defence had to rely on and they could not ignore that evidence as untrue, for he was a disinterested and truthful witness," Dr. de Silva said.

"William on his own showing could not have arrived at Wellawatte at 9.30 a.m. and reach Panadura in the afternoon at 3.30 p.m. even by giving time for the haircut which William stated he took. He must have left Wellawatte after 12.30 p.m. The pot of rice, which was warm at 4.00 p.m. was kept on the fire late that morning. But if it was put on the fire at 8.30 a.m. it would have been stone cold by 4.00 p.m.," he emphasised.

Dr. de Silva said that if the jury believed William's own time testimony, it would have taken much more time in doing the things, which he stated he did that morning.

Continuing Dr. de Silva said, "William said he went to the Bambalapitiya bus stand and waited about 20 minutes during which time three Galle buses passed him. Then in desperation he got into a

Mt. Lavinia bus and went to Wellawatte. According to his evidence, the time factor could not be made to fit into the Crown case and make William be seen at High Street, Wellawatte, at 9.30 a.m. On the contrary, William's movements fitted into the defence case like a glove when William stated that he got to Panadura in time for the 2 o'clock Galle bus."

Dr. de Silva pointed out that from every point of view there was concrete evidence that Mrs. Sathasivam died after 10.30 a.m. that day.

Continuing Dr. de Silva said William was an intelligent fellow quick on the uptake. "He had," Dr. de Silva suggested, "Been shaped, reshaped and completely rounded off by the various Police Officers who questioned him at successive stages. He had been questioned by the Police Officers as a probable eye witness and had been confronted with known inaccuracies."

"He had been thus questioned and confronted with so many known inaccuracies that he being quick in the uptake had been able to fit the tale he now told the Police into the facts known to the Police. He had opportunities to shape his own evidence and adapt it as he wanted," remarked Dr. de Silva.

Referring to the confession made by William, Dr. de Silva said that in his 21 years of experience at the Bar he had never come across a confession like that!

"Here was a witness," Dr. de Silva argued, "Who was virtually saying that the Police Officers had taken that same grip that Mr. Sathasivam had used on Mrs. Sathasivam before he (William) had demonstrated it."

Dr. de Silva then referred to the evidence of remand prisoner Piyadasa to whom William had stated that it was not Mr. Sathasivam who killed his wife but he (William). When William was asked whether he said so he denied it, but stated that when he was in the Court he had met his brother with whom he got angry, lost his temper and said 'I will plead guilty'.

Dr. de Silva asked the jury, "What was the meaning of all that?"

Continuing his address to the jury Dr. de Silva said, "William was defiant like a trapped animal when he was giving evidence in this Court. Crown did not even dare to re-examine William to clear the difficulties raised by the cross-examination. They thought that discretion was the better part of valour!"

"William had also denied having made to Sir Richard Aluvihare a confession of the killing of Mrs. Sathasivam."

"If ever a man was officially encouraged to lie in their Court, that man was William and he was pardoned! Never in the history of judicial administration and in our Courts was a man brought to accuse a fellow citizen like that pardoned witness William, who changed his statements from minute to minute," said Dr. de Silva.

Dr. de Silva addressing the jury then discussed the medical evidence in detail and supported the evidence of Professor de Saram, who was the Crown Pathologist.

Referring to Professor de Saram's evidence Dr. de Silva said, "He was an unfortunate man who found himself in the position of being nobody's witness. He was called by the Crown, but his evidence was availed of by the defence. In fact there was nobody to re-examine him!"

Dr de Silva paid a tribute to Professor de Saram who he said had been for many years the Judicial Medical Officer of Colombo and whose integrity and honesty had never been questioned by either side of the Bar until the hearing of that case.

Dr. de Silva reminded the jury that the Crown had in the Turf Club case where Mr. John Silva was murdered, accepted and relied completely on Professor de Saram precisely on the question of the time of death of Mr. John Silva.

Referring to Sir Sydney Smith's evidence, Dr. de Silva said Sir Sydney stood confirmed and not contradicted by the Government doctors on the temperature question when he fixed Mrs. Sathasivam's time of death at 11 a. m.

"Sir Sydney had applied the scientific method known in logic, general science and arithmetic as the method of successive approximation. Sir Sydney had also taken into consideration the three medical tests. They were the rate of cooling of the body, rigor mortis and the condition of the alimentary canal. All standard medical books agreed that the rate of cooling of the body was far and away the most reliable of those three tests," Dr de Silva submitted.

Reiterating to the jury the medical opinions of time of death of Mrs. Sathasivam, Dr. de Silva said, "Both Professor de Saram and Sir Sydney Smith agreed that Mrs. Sathasivam must have died at 11 a.m., or after 11 a.m., and that her body had been cooling till 7 p.m. when the body temperature had dropped to 93.2 degrees Fahrenheit. Professor Peiris had categorically stated in that Court that he could not reasonably exclude 11 a.m. as the time of death. All the medical evidence in the case legally testified to the fact that Mrs. Sathasivam died after Mr. Sathasivam had left the house at 10.30 a.m. If the jury accepted that, Mr. Sathasivam is innocent."

Referring to the credibility of the evidence of William, Dr. de Silva stressed that all the evidence pointed to the guilt of William.

"Mr. Mahadeva Sathasivam asks for justice, not merely a verdict of 'Not guilty' which is inevitable, but that he is innocent, and you seven gentlemen of jury will have to give that decision of yours with an abiding conviction," pleaded Dr. Colvin R. de Silva concluding his 3-day address to the jury.

This request of Dr. Colvin R. de Silva was so unusual, Justice Gratiaen commented on it in his summing up.

Mr. T. S. Fernando, the Acting Solicitor-General, then began his address to the jury paying a tribute to Dr. Colvin R. de Silva, the defence counsel, for the address he had made.

Mr. Fernando said that it was their hope that every man charged with murder or any other lesser charge would always have as able a defence.

He then pointed out that when he studied the brief, about one thing he was certain and he knew there would be no doubt about it. That was that Mrs. Sathasivam had died of asphyxia from manual strangulation.

He next appealed to the jury to go only by the evidence led in that Court. He said it was possible to be influenced by what they read in the newspapers or heard people talking about.

Analysing the evidence in the case, Mr Fernando said that there was the evidence of William and the evidence that tended to corroborate William's evidence.

Explaining this further he said, "There was the medical evidence by which I proved that Mrs. Sathasivam had died substantially before 10.30 a.m. it would corroborate William's evidence. There was the evidence of Mr. Sanmugam that he saw William at the High Street shop at 9.45 a.m. That was also corroborative evidence."

He next referred to William's conditional pardon and said that the jury was not called upon to consider why or how he came to be pardoned. They were not concerned with that. That was a matter, which had been vested with the Attorney-General. The duty for the jury was to see whether William was substantially speaking the truth, he said.

"We all admit that William was not innocent. He was an accomplice. But the jury should decide whether he was speaking the truth when he said he saw Mr. Sathasivam strangle Mrs. Sathasivam in the room upstairs," Mr. Fernando stressed.

Dealing with the family relations of Mr. Sathasivam, Mr. Fernando said that after the birth of the first child Jothiswari in 1942, a divorce case was filed, but the relatives intervened and they were reconciled and Mr. and Mrs. Sathasivam had three more girls.

"Then came Miss Yvonne Stevenson to whom Mr. Sathasivam was attached as was proved by their goings about in Colombo," he said.

"Then we find Mr. Sathasivam and his wife going to the United Kingdom and Mrs. Sathasivam returning to the Island alone. At Aden, she had written to Mr. Sathasivam stating that she was writing in desperation before he fell between two stools."

"Mr. Sathasivam came back in March 1951 and went back in May. Mrs. Sathasivam filed her divorce action and the cause for the action was malicious desertion," Mr. Fernando said.

Continuing his address, Mr. Fernando quoted from a letter of Miss Stevenson to show the attachment between Mr. Sathasivam and Miss Stevenson.

"In her letter she states, 'Give me the right to be with you and I will come . . . ' 'Get cracking on the divorce . . . ' 'If you lose the divorce you will not get me.' In her next letter she stated that she had got the first nice job she had but she would 'chuck' that up and come to him. That showed how much Miss Stevenson loved Mr. Sathasivam," Mr.

Fernando said.

Then in Mr. Sathasivam's own evidence he stated that till the last he was trying to get his wife to withdraw the divorce case.

Mr. Fernando pointed out that if the divorce action filed by Mrs. Sathasivam went through, Mr. Sathasivam would have had to pay alimony to his wife and also bear the expenses of the children. In addition, he would have had to support Miss Stevenson and if after some years he got tired of her also, as he had got tired of his wife, then he would be in further difficulty.

Mr. Fernando then showed the jury the small-sized shirt William wore on the day of the murder and told the jury that this was the boy whom they were asked to believe was the person who had such a firm grip as to break the thyroid cartilage.

"You were told not to look at the shirt but at the hands, yet you must look at the shirt that the boy wore," Mr. Fernando said.

Stating that he wished straightaway to dispose of the bogey of rape, Mr. Fernando said he regretted that suggestion should have ever been made.

"At least let not the deceased lady be tainted with rape, even in her death," Mr. Fernando pleaded.

"If they took the rape theory out of their minds and took the suggestion of robbery, then they would see that that morning William began to do the most disagreeable tasks in the house such as cut drumsticks and scrape coconut. If he was contemplating robbery the easiest thing William could have done was to have battered Mrs. Sathasivam's head with the blowpipe instead of having recourse to the difficult method of killing by strangulation."

"Either the experiment carried out on the executed prisoners was wrong or they must grant that various bodies behaved in different ways in cooling. It would be entirely fallacious to apply the rate of cooling as found in the executed prisoners unless those bodies cooled in the same conditions as those in which the body of Mrs. Sathasivam was found. If the surrounding air was warm in one place and cool in another, it would take a longer time to cool."

Mr. Fernando then recalled the demonstration of the murder given by Sir Sydney Smith.

"If according to that demonstration, a blow was given to Mrs. Sathasivam on her head, it would naturally have dazed her, and she would have sagged. It would then have been natural for the strangler to strike her another blow and finish her off or to allow her to drop on the ground and then give her a second blow."

"Instead of that, for some strange purpose, the strangler, according to Sir Sydney's demonstration propped up the sagging body and proceeded to strangle her. He said it would be very unnatural for a person to prop up a sagging body and strangle the neck to his heart's content instead of simply striking a second blow on the head of the already dazed person," Mr. Fernando said

Referring to the nail marks on the external injury on the neck, he said that it was important to remember that there was a nail mark 1½ inches in length. It was mentioned in Professor de Saram's post-mortem report.

He said that that nail mark could only have been caused by the right thumb, and that supported the story of William in regard to the manner of strangulation.

He next referred to the dislodged part from the earring, the bent shaft, and the injuries on Mrs. Sathasivam's neck. "They were consistent with the trampling of the neck and face by a shod foot, and the placing of a heavy mortar on the face," he said.

Mr. Fernando next referred at length to the medical evidence with regard to the time of death. He said that the case for the Crown was that the death of Mrs. Sathasivam had occurred well before 10.30 a.m. He reminded the jury in detail the medical evidence of Professor de Saram, which attempted to bring the time of death to about 11.15 a.m. He also dealt at length on Professor Paul's evidence based on the alimentary canal test, and said that he had stated that death would have occurred by 9.30 a.m.

"Having regard to the overall rule regarding the cooling test, the higher the temperatures of surrounding air the greater was the rate of fall. The tests on the executed prisoners had shown that the bodies have behaved entirely against the rule. Therefore, I do not think that it would be correct to say that those experiments were conducted in comparable conditions as the body that cooled in the garage at No. 7,

St. Alban's Place, on 9th October 1951."

Referring further to the time of death, Mr. Fernando said that the evidence of Professor M.V.P. Peiris was in accord with the evidence of William and therefore the death occurred before Mr. Sathasivam left the house.

Referring to the medical evidence of Professors Paul and Peiris, he said that the defence had tried to make out that there were many differences of opinion between them.

He pointed out that if there was some disagreement between them it was not on medical matters but on non-medical matters.

"The defence had suggested, that he had been unfair in his cross-examination of Sir Sydney Smith. He explained that he would have been failing in his duty if he did not elicit certain information, which he considered relevant to this case from Sir Sydney Smith."

"Sir Sydney had stated in the course of his evidence that they had to accept Professor de Saram's report, because he was the doctor who had held the post-mortem examination on the body. I am therefore entitled to ask Sir Sydney Smith whether he had done so in the Sydney Fox case. In that case Sir Sydney had not accepted the evidence of Sir Bernard Spilsbury that there was a bruise on the larynx of Mrs. Fox, who had been strangled by her son and the jury had brought in a verdict of guilty of manual strangulation while Sir Sydney then held, and still holds bona fide, that Mrs. Fox had died of natural causes. I request the jury to remember that fact," Mr Fernando said.

He said Sir Sidney Smith's evidence could not be accepted in regard to the time of death as his assumptions were false.

Mr. Fernando next referred to the attitude of Mr. Sathasivam on the day of the tragedy. He had no doubt, established a perfect alibi about his movements leaving the home by 'Quickshaws' at 10.30 a.m. He referred to Mr. Sathasivam's evidence in the Magistrate's Court and said that Mr. Sathasivam had referred to telephone conversation with his mother in the afternoon of 9th October. His mother had concluded her conversation by asking "How is baby?" meaning Mrs. Sathasivam.

Mr. Fernando said that according to the evidence of Mr. Pathmanathan and Mr. K. Sathasivam, by that time Mrs. Sathasivam, the mother of the Mr. Sathasivam had been informed about the death. He could not understand why, on the other hand, Mr. Sathasivam's mother, who on 8th October, the previous day, had gone to No. 7, St. Albans's Place, and padlocked the telephone, should ask how his wife was getting on. He asked whether they could possibly believe that story.

Referring to William, Mr. Fernando submitted it was strange that he decided to kill Mrs. Sathasivam on the very day after summons was served on Mr. Sathasivam.

"Why did William choose that amazing day? And why did he employ that unusual method of strangulation? William was a Southerner, who would have known other methods of killing, he would have known that a person could be more easily killed by clubbing, knifing, stabbing etc."

"There was in that kitchen that heavy blow pipe with which he could have killed her. You are asked to believe that he chose the unusual method of striking her a blow dazing her, propping her up, and then strangling her," Mr. Fernando remarked.

"If robbery was the motive for William to kill Mrs. Sathasivam, I could not understand why he left behind a number of valuable things. He had sold the 'thali' for only 100 rupees. It showed that he did not realise the value of that article," Mr Fernando continued.

He said that Mr. Sathasivam held William by hand and took him upstairs and it was quite possible that the coconut fluff on William's hand could get on to Mr. Sathasivam's hand and after that get transplanted on the injuries caused by Mr. Sathasivam. Regarding the role of William he said Mr. Sathasivam used William to point the finger of guilt away from him and William was therefore a vital necessity to commit the murder and not an unnecessary luxury.

Commenting on the first statement of William, Mr. Fernando said that Inspector Wickremaratna asked him to make a false statement.

Mr. Fernando referred to many instances in the evidence given by the three defence witnesses, Mr. Mack, Mrs. Sathasivam's Attorney, Mr. Perera, the 'Quickshaws' cab driver and Mr. Mendis, the 'Quickshaws' Manager, where they showed they were not in a position to give detailed facts.

Mr. Fernando said that the Crown had been connected with Professor de Saram for so long that their criticism of his evidence was done more in sorrow than in indignation.

He remarked that it was sad that it should have fallen to his lot to lead evidence against Mr. Sathasivam, whose prowess in the cricket field he had the privilege to see.

"But justice is no respecter of persons," Mr. Fernando said concluding his address to the jury.

CHAPTER 15

JUDGE'S SUMMING UP AND THE VERDICT

The Supreme Court trial of the Sathasivam murder case lasted 57 days.

Justice Gratiaen commenced his address to the jury on the 24th of June 1953, reminding the members of the jury that it was exactly three months and four days ago that they were empanelled to try the prisoner in their charge.

He stated that he was quite certain that all of them were well aware of the responsibilities of the oath they took on that occasion. He reminded them that leaving out the inevitable Public Holidays, they have been sitting for 57 days to listen to the evidence and to listen to the most helpful submissions of the learned Counsel for the Prosecution and the Defence.

Justice Gratiaen's address to the jury in this case is of the highest quality and his excellent analysis of evidence is of educational value to members of both the medical and legal professions. Therefore, I have included here most of his address to the jury, with very little editing.

Justice Gratiaen told the jurors, "Gentlemen, the responsibilities of jury service fall far more heavily on some than on others, according to the doctrines of chance which is an essential feature of the system. I am very conscious of the great inconvenience which the performance of this public duty must have caused, not only to yourselves, but also to your employers."

"When this case is over, I think that each of you may justly claim that he has performed his duty sufficiently and well to justify a claim for exemption for the rest of your lives from jury service, and let me tell you now that if any of you desire to claim that privilege it is only necessary that you should address the Registrar of my Court, and the exemption will be granted."

Justice Gratiaen then paid a glowing tribute to the two counsel, Mr. T. S. Fernando, the Acting Solicitor-General and Dr. Colvin R. de Silva, the senior defence counsel.

"We have received great assistance, gentlemen, both from the learned Solicitor-General and from Dr. Colvin R. de Silva. Their most able addresses at the concluding stages of the trial have made my own task considerably lighter, and let me tell you now that if I do not refer in the course of my charge to every single argument which was addressed by one advocate or the other, it does not necessarily mean that I am inviting you to ignore them."

"Learned Solicitor-General told you that he and Dr. de Silva were born in the same village in the same Year of Grace. It is pretty evident to all of us that the Fairy Godmother who controlled the destinies of that particular village in that particular year must have smiled more than graciously on these two little infants, because as you have seen for yourselves, she bestowed on each of them the enviable gift of eloquence which had lightened some of the dark moments of a trial which must from time to time have appeared to you quite interminable!"

Justice Gratiaen eloquently summarised the inherent safeguards in trials by jury to uphold the principle that a man is innocent until proved otherwise.

"Trial by jury for the administration of justice has provided many safeguards out of respect for the principle of the presumption of innocence of which I have told you. If all or any of these earlier safeguards have, for one reason or another, been neglected or abused, then it only means that the task of the jury has been made more difficult."

"The first safeguard is that there should be a thoroughly competent and impartial inquiry of the crime by the Police themselves. The Police in this country in order to assist themselves in their work of investigation have very important statutory rights, which are denied even to the Police in England. They have the right to compel answers to questions. It is their duty to start their work of investigation without preconceived notions, and without ignoring what might turn out to be a most important clue and without leaving anything to chance."

"They should have the assistance also of experienced pathologists, analytical chemists, handwriting experts and such persons and work in the closest collaboration with them. They have a special duty to the suspect because he has no machinery available to him to go about collecting evidence as of right in order to prove his innocence. He, if it be a charge of murder, will be on remand, as this man has for twenty months."

"If the clues which are found are not followed and pursued to the end they might cause great hardship. They might even cause a grave injustice, but be that as it may, the difficulties of a case are greatly increased if the work of the Police at the very commencement has not been thoroughly well done. You can't prevent a Police Officer entertaining suspicion one way or the other. It may be that there was one group of Police Officers who were convinced that it was William who had committed the murder, and the other group may have had a strong conviction the other way."

"All I can say is that the ideal policeman, belonging to either category, who has any suspicion in his mind, any preconceived theories that he entertains, would necessarily call for even greater caution in the manner and method of investigation."

"After the Police investigation was complete and they decide to charge a particular man there follows or should follow an impartial magisterial inquiry. The task of the Magistrate is not to decide whether a man is guilty or not, but to decide whether the evidence placed before him is of sufficient weight and sufficient substance to place the suspect on trial before a jury."

"Magistrates here have some wider powers at the moment, some embarrassing powers, very much wider than they possess in England. A Magistrate under our present Criminal Procedure Code is not merely a judge called upon to decide whether there is a prima facie case or not against the accused, but he himself has the powers of controlling the investigation, and therefore, the law requires that any relevant evidence should be available to him which points one way or the other, and also that any documentary evidence which might assist, should not be withheld from him. No important clue should be kept away from him."

"Then, gentlemen, follows from the Magistrate's Court, an impartial scrutiny by the Attorney-General's Department. They scrutinise the evidence and decide whether there is enough evidence to place the accused on trial before you, and they have wide powers to order the re-opening of the investigation by the Magistrate and placing further evidence before him."

Justice Gratiaen reminded the jury that William and Sathasivam were jointly committed for trial for the murder of Mrs. Sathasivam in the Magistrate's Court.

"The Attorney-General in the exercise of his undoubted discretion, which in a free democracy it is our duty to respect, decided to offer a conditional pardon to one accused and try the other, and in the exercise of the right to call for further evidence, he caused William, the pardoned man, to give evidence against Sathasivam in the Magistrate's Court, and it is that evidence on which, principally, the Prosecution in this trial bases its case against Sathasivam."

"Throughout also, gentlemen, the Police had the assistance of lawyers, in the early stages I think they were called Legal Advisers, who were able to sift impartially the evidence in a quasi judicial manner. Do not forget that the lawyers appearing for the Prosecution in a criminal case here, or elsewhere, as the Solicitor-General quite correctly pointed out, are meant to be ministers of justice to assist the Courts in the administration of justice. That is their proper function."

"Please realise that we are not here to pass judgement on the Police or the Magistrates or the Attorney-General or anyone else. We are here at this stage to judge a particular man on the particular evidence, which has been placed before you. Every time a man is on trial the administration is also on trial."

"If you feel after you have heard my submissions for your consideration that some clues should never have been ignored, your task is still the same, rather your task is far more difficult because in regard to most important clues in a murder case, if you do not pursue them at the proper time you destroy your bridges before you cross to the other side, and it is too late afterwards to repair the possible damage and possible injustice caused by that act."

Justice Gratiaen continuing his summing up enumerated the functions and duties of the jury and the judge.

"Now, finally what are your functions and what are mine? I am here, gentlemen, to control the trial, to see to the best of my ability that the essentials of justice are not disregarded. It is my duty also to rule out all irrelevant evidence and even to shut out evidence, which might only have some very remote relevance, but which if placed before you for a limited period might certainly have a far more prejudicial general effect than is justified in a criminal trial."

"It is my duty to see to it that other material facts, which were even not part of the case for either side, but which have come to my notice through an examination of the police record which I have access to, do come before you."

"For instance, there was some document which I referred to and which I am very glad that the learned Solicitor-General in due course did produce for your consideration, such as that telephone chit. I also consider it my duty to place before you proved contradictions between what witnesses said here and what unknown to the accused they had said somewhere also to a Police Officer. Then it is my duty too to give you my directions on the law, and finally on those directions – there are a very few of them – you must assure that as a person trained in the law as I am giving you proper directions."

"In fact, you are bound to accept them as the law, and if I am wrong well there are other tribunals to put me right. Then it is finally my duty to try and clarify the issues which you must consider, marshal the facts in order to assist you to arrive at a just verdict, but please remember this, you are the sole judges of fact. I am here only to assist you as best as I can to come to a right judgement, and the right judgment must be one, which perfectly satisfy your conscience."

"Even if I were to tell you what my own opinion is on the whole case, or any particular issue which forms part of the case, please realize that you are perfectly entitled after considering what I say, or what I may appear to say between the lines, to disregard it. In fact it is your duty, unless my apparent view or expressed view commends itself to you. You are the judge, and on this part, the most crucial part of the case, I am only an assistant judge. I will try to help you, but it is your responsibility and not mine."

Justice Gratiaen then explained the jury a very useful formula when bringing in a verdict.

"In many of the cases over which I have presided, I often suggest a formula to jurors as to the state of mind which would justify them in bringing a verdict against a man. Having examined all the evidence with anxious care, having faced up to the difficulties instead of evading them, if you can say 'We are sure that he is guilty, and we are sure, that we shall always be sure, that he is guilty', then it is your duty to convict. It is a duty which society imposes on you. If you are not sure, or if you are honestly not sure that you will always be sure, the man must go free."

Justice Gratiaen informed the members of the jury, how they should approach the concept of the burden of proof.

"I suggest to you the manner in which you should approach the problem arising in regard to the burden of proof in a criminal case, as one or other of the learned counsel who addressed you earlier said that in civil cases, Courts are necessarily and properly satisfied, if they come to a conclusion one way or the other, merely on a balance of probability."

"As far as a criminal case is concerned, having regard to the respect which society pays to the life and liberty of individuals, a balance of probability is not sufficient to justify a conviction. It must be something higher than that. I agree at the same time that you cannot get a decision, which is always demonstrably true, as you would expect, say, in the case of a proposition in mathematics. But it must be the highest degree of certainty which human beings conscientiously approaching their task can reach, in judging other human beings."

"Gentlemen, this case has taken a very long time, apart from the difficulties which were involved by the consideration of so many conflicting issues, some of which resolved themselves after many days almost overnight, but you see, most of the time was necessary to be spent because this is rather an unusual case."

"The case has been presented to you on the footing by both sides, that only one of two men could possibly have committed this murder, Sathasivam or William, and in the result the Crown has undertaken to establish two essential facts."

"Firstly, they have undertaken to prove beyond reasonable doubt that it was Mr. Sathasivam and no one else, who strangled this unhappy lady to death. In the course of that attack, they have necessarily been involved in a sort of rear-guard action, because to establish the first proposition it became vitally essential to their case that they should also establish the second proposition, namely, they had to claim by the evidence to establish beyond reasonable doubt that it was not William who was the strangler."

"If William had been himself in the dock on a charge of murder, then the issue before you would have been whether William's guilt had been established beyond reasonable doubt. But as it is, Mr. Sathasivam and Mr. Sathasivam alone who is in your charge on this grave issue. The additional subsidiary issue is, has the innocence of William been established beyond reasonable doubt?"

By these statements, Justice Gratiaen clearly indicated to the jury that they have to take into consideration the evidence presented or highlighted by the defence to suggest that William and William alone was the strangler.

"I hope you will appreciate that vital distinction. The charge against Mr. Sathasivam, with which alone you are concerned, is that before 9.30 on the morning of the 9th of October 1951, he strangled his wife to death. In some cases, gentlemen, it is necessary for the Presiding Judge to give a fairly elaborate ruling as to the necessary ingredients of the offence of murder. In this case there is no such necessity. I will tell you why."

"A man is guilty of murder if he voluntarily causes the death of another human being with the intention of causing death. The case for the Crown is that the accused committed before 9.30 on the morning in question, a premeditated and carefully planned murder in regard to which his intention had been previously communicated to somebody else."

"The Crown says that the motive for this crime was to enable Mr. Sathasivam to be rid of an inconvenient wife, in order that he might thereby regularize a guilty association with another woman. In order to achieve that object, he had planned to avoid the embarrassment of paying a sum of 300 rupees as alimony to his wife, who had already instituted proceedings against him for divorce, on the ground of malicious desertion."

"The Crown has also alleged that there was a special motive of a particularly sordid act, namely, that he hoped by killing his wife to benefit himself by inheritance at least to a half share of her estate as her legal heir."

"Whether there is any evidence that he had grounds for such a hope I really do not know. Whether it is suggested that he hoped to benefit in this way with the knowledge that he was her heir to an extent of a half share under a will which has not been proved, or as an intestate heir under the somewhat complicated law applicable to the inhabitants of the Jaffna province, to which as far as I am aware there is no proof that Mr. Sathasivam belonged – all those are matters in doubt. However, that is the plan alleged."

Justice Gratiaen then listed the ingredients of the case for the Crown.

He said that the Crown accused Mr. Sathasivam of following acts.

(a) Having done this defenceless woman to death by manual strangulation, having, to use the words of the learned Solicitor-General, first lulled her into a sense of false security by enjoying the privileges of their nuptial bed with her.

(b) Having strangled her, he finished off the job by stamping on this unhappy woman's neck or throat with his shod foot, at a time when she lay helpless and breathing her last at his feet.

(c) He then as planned arranged this murder so skilfully as to throw inevitable suspicions on a servant boy.

(d) With a diabolically cynical regard for Hindu custom, which governed his wife and himself he did remove the 'thalikody' which he had placed around her neck on their wedding day, until that neck was the neck of a corpse.

(e) When that planned state of affairs had been realized he then proceeded to strip the corpse of the 'thalikody' and other articles of jewellery, and rifled her bag.

(f) Handed over some little money and those fairly valuable articles to the humble accessory, who had helped him in this murder, as a reward for the assistance he had given him by holding her legs after a few minutes of strangling, and then the additional assistance of ceremoniously carrying the corpse past an open window overlooking the neighbours' houses. If one looked further overlooking a police station, where they dumped this woman together in a garage.

(g) He then went upstairs again and took a looking glass in order that he will be quite certain that the woman had breathed her last.

(h) After the accessory had gone to sell these ill-gotten gains and spoils, Mr. Sathasivam callously remained behind in a house with one corpse and two little children aged 4 and 2.

(i) He proceeded to make the case against the departed William doubly certain by daubing the corpse's feet with kitchen dirt because William's legitimate activities were confined to the kitchen.

(j) He stayed behind for one whole hour, at least one whole hour with the sure and certain knowledge, and apparently with the knowledge which proved to be justified, the knowledge that William would not bring back neighbours, bring back even the police to the very scene of the crime where the murderer would have been caught in the act of daubing the feet of some one he had murdered."

"Well, gentlemen, if after giving your most anxious consideration to all the evidence you have heard, you are convinced that this is an acceptable story, need I trouble you with legal discussions as to whether he was guilty of murder; a murder committed with murder in his heart. Because, if you are convinced of that gentlemen, you are then convinced that it was a murder committed without any mitigating circumstances whatsoever; neither mitigating circumstances which the law recognizes nor would there be mitigating circumstances which in my confident belief, no person vested with the additional prerogative of mercy would dream of exercising."

Justice Gratiaen then considered the 'motive' for the murder. He analysed the evidence presented to show the presence or absence of motive of Mr. Sathasivam and William.

"Now gentlemen, we have heard a great deal on the question of the motive for crimes such as murder. We are on rather dangerous ground there, let me warn you. If a man accused of murder can point out to you, that demonstrably there is no possible understandable reason for his having committed a diabolical crime, that will be a very strong point in his favour, so strong that you would insist on compelling evidence to satisfy your consciences that a man has committed an apparently motiveless crime."

"But if, on the other hand, the prosecution alleges as part of its case that a particular accused person was actuated by a particular motive, then gentlemen the existence of that motive must itself be established beyond reasonable doubt. If it is not established to your complete satisfaction then you must discard it and consider the question of guilt or innocence on the rest of the case."

Justice Gratiaen said, "The authors of learned legal text books have told us – I will quote the words – 'To penetrate the mind of man is out of human power, because circumstances which appear on their face value to present powerful motives may never have occurred as such in actual fact' ."

"Gentlemen, shortly I will place before you for your consideration the motive which the Crown has undertaken to establish as part of its case. But I will with great respect submit to you as judges of fact, that having regard to the grave issues which we are considering, it would be very much safer to say this: If the rest of the evidence convinces you that Sathasivam is guilty, then you may well be satisfied that there must have been some powerful motive which activated his somewhat tangled and complicated mind at that time."

"But if on the other hand, you are not convinced by the rest of the evidence that Sathasivam murdered his wife, then, as the books say, to eke out a weak case by any attempt of proof of motive is an extremely unsatisfactory and hazardous process."

"Gentlemen, there can be no doubt, can there, that at this particular time Sathasivam's mind in regard to his most intimate, private and domestic affairs was neither commendable nor satisfactory.

There were two women in love with him; one of them was his own wife. The wife had reached the stage, apparently before his return from England, when she felt that there was no further hope of their attempting to re-establish a perfectly happy home. There was the other woman in England, who herself wanted the same divorce. One gets the impression that Sathasivam himself had reached the stage when he really did not know what he wanted with regard to his future life, with one woman, or with the other, or with both!"

"You remember the gist of Mrs. Sathasivam's disillusioned letter from a ship, which was passing through Aden earlier that year. You will remember another letter, which she wrote to him when she was in Ceylon and he was in England. The gist of her complaint seems, that although she loved him, although in between accusations she would pause to describe how one of the daughters had grown more beautiful than ever, how playful the new puppy she had brought had become, yet she was harping back on these memories of his association with another woman."

"Her attitude seemed to be this, that her husband, whose protestations, true or false, that there was no adultery in the affair, seemed to want the best of both possible worlds. If you summarize her complaint one got the impression that she was saying to herself that his attitude was not so much 'how happy could I be with either' but 'how happy could I be with both!' "

"In fact, that was precisely what was suggested to him in his cross-examination in the Magistrate's Court and which he admitted gentlemen, in the stress of cross-examination. The question put to him was about his affairs with these two women: "You wanted the company of Yvonne and you also wanted to remain the husband of your wife" and the wretched man said 'Yes'."

Justice Gratiaen said that when two women wanted to divorce him, he sends a cablegram to one saying, 'Come out, the divorce is going through'.

"Then he goes back to his wife and asks her to withdraw the case and all the time they are living together as man and wife. In certain moments probably there might have been recriminations and counter-recriminations."

"At other moments what do they do? Go together to patch up the domestic quarrels of Mrs. Sathasivam's sister with her husband. They have celebrations over the reconciliation, which they have brought about and as Mrs. Sathasivam's brother-in-law Mr. Pathmanathan said, 'I was very grateful to them. I would have done anything for them, but there was nothing I could do for them. They seemed perfectly happy'."

"Now gentlemen, if he really wanted to marry Yvonne Stevenson, if he sincerely wanted that, there was the divorce action which would give him what he wanted. If he did not want the divorce action, then nothing on earth, except perjury could have permitted Mrs. Sathasivam to win her case, because if she was obviously a truthful woman, and in divorce actions the law requires that where a case is defended or undefended, it is the duty of the plaintiff's counsel to place the truth, the whole truth and nothing but the truth in regard to domestic relations before the Court."

"If she spoke the truth and admitted that on the 22nd of September when the husband arrived, pending the action had been refused admission to her house, that the husband went to her sister Mrs. Pathmanathan's bungalow, and he rang up his wife and said 'I want to see the children, and I want to see you', what happened? The wife and the children went to Mrs. Pathmanathan's house and they all went back together as one family."

Justice Gratiaen reminded the jury that same evening they braved a suspicious world by visiting the Tamil Union Club together.

"On the 24th they go to an estate outside Colombo to bring about reconciliation between Mr. and Mrs. Pathmanathan. On the 26th they take Mrs. Pathmanathan to the same estate, and two reconciled couples, as far as one's eyes could see it, returned together after a celebration."

"Then there is the question of alimony. He wanted to get rid of the obligation to pay alimony. Well then, he had two courses open to him. One was to see that the divorce action was completely sabotaged, to use the Solicitor-General's own words, by bringing about a reconciliation and a complete condonation by not one act of intercourse, but many acts of intercourse! Suppose he did not do that, then the question of alimony would have to be decided."

"Gentlemen, he was unemployed. He had no income except for an allowance, which he obtained from his mother. His wife had an income, and everybody who has ever appeared in the divorce courts is fully aware that alimony is assessed by the Judge after consideration of the joint incomes of both the erring and the innocent spouse."

"However, as I have said, a man in that unhappy complicated and confused state of mind, if he did murder the woman, surely you would have no difficulty in saying to yourselves, there must have been some reason for it. That is the state of mind which satisfies a conscientious jury, very properly, because they say to themselves, the case is proved by the really reliable evidence and not disproved by any demonstrable absence of motive."

"Then we come to the motive for the other suspected strangler – William. Well there, gentlemen, I think that any juror who was trying, not Sathasivam but William, would, if he were satisfied by the evidence against William have very little difficulty at all on the motive for the murder by him."

"Indeed, the Crown has asked you to accept as part of the case for Sathasivam that William's motive to take part, as an accessory in Sathasivam's cause was the filthy motive of financial gain. He says he was attracted, the Solicitor-General says he must have been attracted, by the offer of jewellery worth 300 or 400 rupees. Well, if a man of any collar size whatsoever, of any size of shirt, is prepared to assist in a murder for 300 or 400 rupees worth of jewellery, would it be very difficult to find a motive for an actual unassisted killing, provided of course, that that killing was proved?"

"I would like first to touch upon it, and then ask you finally to forget what the Solicitor-General very properly described as the bogey of rape. Sir Sydney Smith has told you that when he was sent all the relevant papers and photographs to Edinburgh, he as a person trained to assist professionally in the investigation of grave crime, merely took the view that the possibility of a sex motive was a matter for careful and competent investigation."

"He did not look at the photograph and say, 'Well we need not bother about the rest of it. There was a sex motive for this crime'. He has said, as any cautious man would say with that idea in mind, this is a matter, which should be examined."

"Justice Gratiaen reminded the jury that Sir Sydney Smith had suggested to the defence that although many months had passed since the 9th of October 1951, they should make a belated attempt to go into that question and that they should get blood tests of William and the seminal stains tested.

"Well, gentlemen, by a coincidence the blood stains of William proved negative - he is one of these mysterious people who is a non-secretor - and therefore the results were completely negative, and from that point one could go no further. Sir Sydney Smith says that if he was pursuing the matter himself at the proper time, he would have given considerable thought to the suspicions created in his mind by what seemed, prima facie, to be an unusually large quantity of seminal stains in the vagina, in the little napkin by the bed and in the petticoat, and he said, as far as he was concerned, he would have applied further tests to examine the further quantity in the vagina and uterus."

"Well, that was not done, and Sir Sydney Smith himself as a responsible expert giving evidence for Sathasivam, but as he claims, and I think the Solicitor-General accepts that claim in a neutral capacity, summarized the theory of stains in this way - that having regard to the limited investigation which has proceeded up to the present point of time - it would be quite unfair, if William was in the dock, to introduce the theory that sex might have been one of the motives for the crime."

"Well, gentlemen, the defence, I think, could perhaps have said, 'Does it not still leave an uneasy feeling in your minds - not for the purpose of condemning William - but for the purpose of assessing Sathasivam's guilt? But the defence, as I understand Dr. de Silva's last submission, does not claim a finding."

"So, with due respect, I would endorse, for your consideration, what the learned Solicitor-General has said, 'Let us leave out that aspect of the matter out of respect for the lady'. Whoever sought to prove that motive had left us in a state of only saying that it has not been proven at all either way."

Justice Gratiaen at this stage made further general observations as to how a jury should approach its task in any criminal case.

"You must have before your minds, throughout your deliberations when you retire to consider your verdict, the hallowed principle that any man accused of a crime must be presumed to be innocent until that presumption has been displaced, not by suggestions, not by unsubstantiated insinuations, but by evidence which brings you to a compelling and an abiding certainty in your minds that the man is guilty."

"It must be that degree of certainty which is the highest which can be achieved by human beings judging another human being. Nobody can ask for a higher degree of certainty in that, but it would be quite unjust to be satisfied with any lesser degree of certainty."

"This is a principle, introduced into our country well over a hundred years ago, under the label of British Justice. It has taken very deep root in our soil, so deep that, since Ceylon gained the right to control her own destinies, we still adopt that principle as part of our heritage. What does the application of this principle mean in this particular case, gentlemen?"

"It means that no jury can brand a man as a murderer out of deference to the insinuations of lawyers or even out of respect for the hunch of any Police Officer."

Justice Gratiaen said that that meant however distinguished the person is, juries demand and claim that they should be presented with evidence, which compels them that the hunch is justified.

"If there be such a case, it is the quality of the evidence and not the hunch which has any relevance to your decision. So, it would be with the hunches of other people that a man is necessarily innocent. It cuts both ways."

"The principle also reminds us, gentlemen, that the stigma which attaches to a self-accomplice, a person who has admitted that, even as an accessory, he has committed an offence punishable by death, is not removed merely because an Attorney-General, however respected, however illustrious he may be in the law, has conferred on him a conditional pardon."

"I am sure that the Attorney-General would entirely endorse

my statement. Indeed, when I come, in due course, to give you, as simply as I can, my directions as to how jurors should approach the evidence of an accomplice, I shall direct you that the fact that a man is a conditionally pardoned witness by reason of the very conditions attaching to his pardon and by reason of the obvious interpretation of those conditions by the accomplice himself, call only for greater caution from a jury."

"There are a few more other pitfalls which a jury, I am sure, would easily avoid. We have not reached that stage of penetration of the mind on others to be able to say that so and so is a murderer because he has the look of a murderer."

"Still more monstrous would it be to say that so and so is obviously the murderer because somebody else does not look like a murderer. You know, you really cannot judge Sathasivam in this case by the size of William's shirt at least, that is my respectful submission to you who are the judges of facts; nor can you judge Sathasivam by the suggestion that William cannot be a murderer because it was Mrs. Sathasivam herself, so we are told, who employed William for she was not an excellent judge of character."

"Gentlemen, this is a very serious case, and that is not the way to approach this case," continued Justice Gratiaen.

"There are two men with whom you are principally concerned in this case – Mrs. Sathasivam married one, and employed the other. I have no doubt that she was quite convinced in her mind that neither of them would ever dream of murdering her!"

"Now we know that she was wrong. We know that she was wrong, at least, in respect of one. William says that she was wrong in respect of both – indeed gentlemen, William tells us that Mrs. Sathasivam grossly misjudged William himself. She would not have employed him if she thought that he was capable of assisting in strangling her for a reward of 300 or 400 rupees!"

"You see, that size of a shirt may possibly have had some relevancy, if it could convince you that no person wearing a shirt like that could possibly possess the strength to strangle. Is there any evidence of that? As I asked Sir Sidney Smith myself, 'Before you answer a question of that nature would you prefer to look at a man's shirt or at his hands?'

As I see the case on this minor aspect, Sathasivam obviously possesses the strength to strangle his wife if he was so minded."

"We have Assistant Superintendent of Police, de Saram's description of the boy William, we will call him a boy, when he was arrested on the 18th October, he said he had a fair pair of shoulders. William, himself, says he had experience as a person who rowed a '*padda*' boat in the village rivers and streams."

"So that, gentlemen, is it humanly possible for judge of fact to decide the case as between the respective potentialities for strangling of a cricketer on the one hand and a rowing man on the other? I suggest that one should leave it at that," said Justice Gratiaen.

Then he reminded the jury the important dates in the case.

"In February 1940, the marriage between Mr. and Mrs. Sathasivam was registered. Exactly a year later, the marriage was solemnised according to Hindu rites – the 'thalikody' was placed round her neck. During the ten and a half years of that marriage, it is quite evident that there had been many ups and downs, more downs perhaps than ups, and I do not think Mr. Sathasivam himself would dispute the fact that the downs were largely of his own making!"

"He seems to have unfortunately, perhaps because he was a spoilt child, a particularly idle fellow, had very few short and rare periods of employment. If the evidence of events which preceded this tragedy be any guide, he seems to have joined a band of people belonging to the 'idle rich', whose philosophy was well described by a sage who said that 'work is the curse of the drinking class'. But that does not mean that he is a murderer."

"Well then this marriage brought four young daughters to the world who at the time of the tragedy were 9, 7, 4, and 2. The mother seems to have been deeply devoted to her children and a good mother in every respect."

"The father himself, as far as one can judge by the evidence, was also very fond of these children, but, of course, as happens in so many homes, particularly in regard to children of that age, it is the mother who actually pays more attention to their requirements. In fact, in one of her letters Mrs. Sathasivam does acknowledge the fondness of this man for his daughters, because when she was complaining of his attitude to her in a moment of pique she said, 'You tolerate me because I am the mother of your children. I do not want that kind of tolerance'."

Justice Gratiaen reminded the jury that in October 1944, "There seems to have been a somewhat serious dispute and on that occasion it was the husband who brought an action against his wife for divorce. That was settled fairly early by relations."

"By the year 1950 he seems to have formed an association with this lady Miss Stevenson and rumours seem in due course to have reached Mrs. Sathasivam herself. You have the evidence of Mr. Bogstra of discussions in which a married man was somewhat hysterically searching for Yvonne who had gone apparently to India. According to Mr. Bogstra, Mr. Sathasivam had even then announced his intention to marry this Yvonne Stevenson. How permanent those intentions were it is for you to judge."

Justice Gratiaen then referred to the visit of Sathasivams to England.

"On the 1st of November 1950 Mr. and Mrs. Sathasivam went to England together. In February 1951, she returned alone. You will remember there were one or two unhappy letters in which, having heard of these rumours, she complains of his neglect of his home life and his obligation at home and that he preferred to go about dancing and keeping the company of other women, although she seems to have accepted the assurance that he had not been unfaithful to her, in the more sinister sense of the term."

"In March 1951, Mr. Sathasivam himself came back to Ceylon, but for a very short time, because in May 1951 he went to England again. Yvonne was there and the correspondence which was found in Mr. Sathasivam's suitcase in Haniffa's house makes it pretty clear that she at least was deeply devoted to him and was prepared to make some sacrifices to come to him, but not, as the Solicitor-General points out, unless there was some certainty of a permanent attachment."

"Now I might just mention in passing about these letters of Yvonne Stevenson, that there at least the person who, according to the Crown, was a master planner of a murder which he was trying to foist on somebody else, did make a little slip, because those letters were left behind and are certainly a strong part of the case on which the Crown relies."

"Now the next important date seems to be the announcement by Mr. Sathasivam that he was returning to Ceylon in the 'Himalaya' in September 1951. Mrs. Sathasivam promptly filed a divorce action on the 7th of September 1951 in which she alleged that Sathasivam had deserted her on the 19th of March 1951 when he had gone back to England."

"According to our Roman Dutch law, desertion has to be proved to be of so permanent a kind that there was no hope of any reconciliation between the husband and wife or of their coming together again. Well, on the 22nd of September Sathasivam returned with his mother in the 'Himalaya'. I have already reminded you gentlemen of the circumstance that the wife had apparently sent a message that she did not want him to come and stay with her."

"Well, we do know from what Podihamy told Inspector Thiedeman, that Mr. Sathasivam brought Mrs. Sathasivam some gifts of jewellery when he arrived, and according to what Podihamy said, that was part of the jewellery which was found to be missing after the murder. She said it was jewellery which he brought her when he returned on the 22nd of September 1951."

"Now gentlemen, while the divorce action was pending, one thing has been established beyond reasonable doubt, and that is this: that from the 22nd of September, 1951, until the 2nd of October, 1951, notwithstanding the alleged desertion of March 1951, these two people lived together openly as man and wife at No. 7, St. Alban's Place with their children. Whatever secret communications might have been passing between him and the Stevenson woman during that period, there can be no doubt that as far as he was concerned he and his wife were living together as man and wife, sharing the same bedroom, sharing the same bed, living together in the fullest sense of the term."

"Knowing for myself as a member of the legal profession the respected senior partner of the firm of lawyers which was acting for Mrs. Sathasivam, I think it is safe to assume that Mr. P. D. A. Mack senior could not possibly have known this."

"Certainly, if he had heard of it, he should have dropped the case like a hot brick, because if ever there was a collusive action - if such an action was to be continued, it would have been that it would be making a mockery of the divorce Courts of this Island. That a man and his wife should go together to the Tamil Union Club, meet their friends on the day of his arrival, that they should go and mix with the other members of his family and her family on the basis that they were a married couple and that either of them should go before the Courts and say 'He left me on the 19th March 1951 and never returned thereafter' would have been something which no Court could have tolerated."

"It has been suggested by the Crown, suggested, not proved, that even this living together as man and wife was part of a deliberate plan for some purpose. He was not living with her in the ordinary sense of a domestic couple, but that he had deliberately compelled her to have intercourse with him as his wife, and that she submitted to that act through some sense of fear."

"Gentlemen, if she was afraid during the period 22nd of September to the 2nd October, she had many people to whom she could have expressed that fear. It could not have been some question of a general and vague fear which she might have expressed before he came; it would be the question of the fears of a woman after she had willingly at her sister's house agreed to receive him back to their home."

"She could have complained to her proctors that he was forcing his way into the house, forcing his attentions on her. She could have complained to her mother, she could have complained to her eldest sister Mrs. Pathmanathan, she could have complained to Mr. Pathmanathan, but one must assume that there was no such complaint."

"Is it not equally possible gentlemen that this woman, who without question loved her husband, was earnestly hoping that by the threat of the divorce action, that unless he mended his ways the home would be broken, was not fighting for her home?" asked Justice Gratiaen.

"That is a counter-suggestion; is that not equally possible? Try and visualize for yourselves the method of approach, which Mr. and Mrs. Sathasivam adopted, two days after they came together again, the arguments, which they must have used to try and persuade Mr. and Mrs. Pathmanathan to come together again."

"Is it quite fanciful to visualize either Mr. or Mrs. Sathasivam saying, 'Good heavens! What are you people quarrelling about? Look at us. With all the troubles we have had, here are we now reconciled'. We again could imagine Mrs. Sathasivam with all her love for this man, nevertheless taking the view that she was dealing with a somewhat mercurial personality who still wished not to be happy with either woman, but to be happy with both."

Justice Gratiaen then referred to the other important event that took place.

"On the 29th of September, a young man, nearly 19 years old, had come with a very humble wardrobe consisting of the banian and the shirt which you have seen for yourselves."

"He arrived from the village in search of employment. Mrs. Sathasivam had borrowed until then a servant from her sister, and she employed William. We shall have to consider William's character in some greater detail at some later stage, but does it not seem to you gentlemen a terrible thing that in the city of Colombo, so many people take risks by employing in a casual way, these unknown domestic servants who are not even registered?"

"I am not talking now at all or suggesting the possibility of William an unregistered domestic servant was the murderer. I am not suggesting that at all. Take him at his own face value."

"These women, not very well off, like Mrs. Sathasivam, whose husbands have helped to squander their dowry money, it seems to me, just by way of passing reference, that there should be more protection in regard to casual employment of people of that kind," remarked Justice Gratiaen.

"Well then gentlemen we come to the period the 2nd of October 1951 to the 8th of October 1951. Mrs. Sathasivam, whatever may have been her secret and unexpressed feelings as to the chances of redeeming this broken home, certainly expressed and manifested a firm determination to get summons served."

"She therefore realized herself that it would be quite out of the question for her to ring up her proctor and say, 'The man who deserted me is living with me. Will you please get a special Fiscal's server to come here and have him served here in the house, which he deserted according to me six months ago'. So something had to be done about it and she threatened that if he did not leave the house, she would."

"She said 'I will go to the Y. W. C. A. until the summons is served'. Then he tells us he said, 'Very well, I will go to Haniffa's'. He said that on oath and submitted himself to cross-examination before the Magistrate on the point that he was in a huff, and gentlemen, frankly shall I say this is not a Court of morals?"

"Here is a man, doing his best to persuade his wife to give up a divorce action, and in his huff he sends misleading cablegram to Miss Stevenson saying 'Come to Ceylon, the divorce action is under way!' She had written earlier saying 'Get cracking with the divorce' and it was 'cracking'. So he went to Haniffa's, but according to Podihamy, William and Sathasivam himself, in spite of the nominal change of residence, he came back on at least three occasions between the 2nd and the 8th of October."

"What kind of menage was this, gentlemen, I really cannot say. What were his intentions? What were her intentions? During that period did she complain to her proctor saying 'This wretched man is still returning to the house though I am determined to go on with the action'? Well, it is difficult gentlemen to fathom the minds which were working at that time, but we do know this, by arrangement, at an agreed place, viz. Haniffa's house, the Fiscal's server who had been told to go to Haniffa's house on the morning of the 8th of October, did arrive and serve summons on Mr. Sathasivam at 7 o'clock, an hour at which apparently he was not accustomed to be awake at all!"

"Of course the service of the summons did not interfere with his normal customary habits, be they commendable or not. He and Haniffa and the others went round the same old round, had their late lunch, or on their way to the late lunch they accidentally passed the two elder Sathasivam children returning from school to their house."

"So Mr. Sathasivam stopped the car which he was driving, it belonged to somebody else, picked up the children and Podihamy, and went. Then came Haniffa's blundering attempt, in a state of some intoxication to bring about a reconciliation, which Sathasivam with his rather more magnetic personality, failed to achieve. Well, he got short shrift from Mrs. Sathasivam and they left."

"On the night of the 8th of October, Sathasivam returned again to the house and knocked at the door. The wife came down, she admitted him and William heard them going up talking on this occasion, in English."

"Now, was there anything sinister gentlemen about the time at which he chose to arrive and to obtain admission? On that we can only go on Podihamy's assessment of Mr. Sathasivam's habits, that even when there was no divorce, he used to come at one in the morning."

"You see, he seems to have been the neglectful member of this household. From what one can gather, I suggest it would be a little unsafe, if not quite unsafe, to draw any sinister inference from the fact that he chose to go home at one o'clock in the morning. Every day, they kept his dinner for him, but he does not come till after the door is closed and his friends had retired for the night."

Having analysed the activities of Mr. and Mrs. Sathasivam up to the day of the murder, Justice Gratiaen gave a vivid account of what happened on that day.

"Now we come to the tragic day itself. The household was roused in the usual way. There were the two children getting ready for school, and we know from Podihamy the time when – what every one would have regarded as perfectly natural – certain incidents occurred."

"The children had their morning cup of milk at 7 o'clock. In the morning, Mrs. Sathasivam, as usual, had a cup of coffee with milk, and she gets busy; she sends William for string hoppers, and on this occasion she sends for 6 eggs as well; she sends for the morning newspaper, and Podihamy feeds the two elder girls."

"At 8.15, which is a fixed time, Mrs. Sathasivam who had, according to her custom on a school day, not yet had her morning meal, telephoned for a 'Quickshaws' cab, which arrived, and off they went to school – Podihamy and the two elder girls. Podihamy cannot tell us when the two younger children are fed, and when Mrs. Sathasivam later on has her meal. What she does when her husband is also there is itself a matter left in some obscurity, but we know by now certain definite facts from Podihamy."

"When the three of them left in a 'Quickshaws' cab at 8.15, Mrs. Sathasivam was seated in the small children's room reading her newspaper, copy of the 'Ceylon Daily News', and reading her letters. The children were about and had not yet been fed. There was a parcel of string hoppers still tied up in the newspaper in the children's room."

"Podihamy said Mr. Sathasivam was asleep on the bed. There is only Podihamy's evidence on that point – there can be no doubt because there is a little human episode, which we were told about. These children, little ones, were playing upstairs making the usual noise, which children usually make, and Mrs. Sathasivam in so many words says, 'Don't make a noise. Daddy is asleep'. Podihamy told them, 'Quiet baby, Daddy is asleep'. Those were, I should imagine, the last words which Podihamy heard from the lady whom she had looked after when she was a small child."

"Then, gentlemen, I want you to regard what happens next by assuming that No. 7, St. Alban's Place was a darkened stage. The curtain is down after the first act at 8.15."

"The second act covers the period 8.15 to 9.30. It was enacted on a completely darkened stage. Then the curtain drops again and the third act covers the period of time 9.30 to 10.30, and then the curtain goes down again. Acts 2 and 3 were played on that tragic stage in complete darkness as far as you and I are concerned."

"The prosecution has undertaken to place before you evidence which is of so compelling a quality as to convince you that it reflects on to that stage such a body of illumination that you can see for yourselves what happened during Act 2, and then later during Act 3, as clearly as if you were there yourselves."

"They say that you must be driven by the evidence to the abiding conviction that during Act 2, between 8.15 and 9.30, Sathasivam woke up, possibly made his final attempt unsuccessfully to secure the withdrawal of the divorce case, and that he then conceived finally that the time has arrived for the execution of the diabolical plan, which perhaps has been hatched in his mind quite sometime, and that he went into the kitchen to secure the services of an accessory who was admittedly quite unnecessary for the purpose of effectively killing the woman, but who was vitally necessary to be the stooge on whom the finger of guilt points."

"In all William's stories, one thing is clear, and that is, that a few minutes, or perhaps more accurately, a few seconds before Mrs. Sathasivam died, William was seated on a coconut scraper in the kitchen scraping his coconut, getting the meal ready, and it is said that you could see clearly now, through the assistance of this credible witness, the husband saying, 'Please come and help me William' and you remember the conversation."

"William replied, 'I really cannot help you to murder your wife' but the master said, 'You must help me to murder my wife because, you see, there is a divorce action which I shall otherwise lose. I will give you a lot of gold jewellery, worth 300 to 400 rupees. Don't be afraid. Come up with me,' and he took him upstairs; and you know the story William says when he was there."

"There is a little point of disagreement between the Crown and William. William says that no threat was uttered, but that he was petrified, too frightened to rid himself through the open door and to go out from this hideous scene, which he said he had enacted. William said that they went upstairs and he was released so that he could have made good his escape, but he was too frightened!"

"He watched for a few tense moments the woman being held by the right hand and pulled by the hair by the left from the bed which Sir Sidney Smith says would have been an ideal place on which to strangle anyone."

"Then he put her down, and when he had her down there, Professor Paul said, if he wanted to strangle a woman on the ground Sathasivam happened to have a perfect and natural grip for a right handed person, he got up and went round the head and came to the other side and adopted, what Professor Paul, the Crown expert, says was a most unnatural position from which to strangle the woman."

"William watched the strangling effectively executed from that unnatural position. But the woman moved her hands about and moved her legs about and so at the request of the strangler he held the woman by the hip, until what Professor Paul thought must have happened, the strangler stood up with his victim dead at his feet, but she was not dead."

"She was still breathing her last. If she had eyes to see we hope she did not see what she would have seen, the shod foot of her husband come down as William demonstrated. It was so effective that the man who did not feel the voice box, said, 'And then the voice-box broke'. The voice-box broke and the time had come for William to receive his reward, and the 'thali' and other jewels were taken away from this corpse of a woman, ninety pounds in weight."

"Then Sathasivam said, 'You must have some cash as well, and he opened the almirah, took out the bag, gave him three rupees and said to him, 'You must have some small change as well'. William knew so much that he knew there was small change. He knew it, not because he opened the bag and looked for himself, but because the contents and value of those coins were also communicated to him by the strangler."

"He said, 'You have had your reward, watch here, I will go down and close the front door', and there William watched, in that room with the corpse. Of course, he had the jewels himself which the corpse had been wearing just before, and Sathasivam came and said, 'We will carry this woman together down to the garage', and then the corpse was dumped down there."

"By that time really William had seen and done enough for three or four hundred rupees worth and he went and got his shirt, because he was wearing a banian, which William says when last seen was torn, but nobody has ever seen it since that day. He transferred the jewels to a more convenient place, put the money in his pocket and left the house. But one remarkable thing happened, he says. He was standing at the doorway between the two kitchens."

Justice Gratiaen then referred to a photograph taken at the scene. "I asked Thiedeman where this photograph was taken and he said it was somewhere from the direction of the doorway between the gas stove kitchen and the Dover stove kitchen. It gives you a very clear picture and a fairly good impression of what a man standing at that doorway would see if he looked in the direction of the garage."

"He would have seen a chair, a table with some objects on it, but even with the most penetrating eyes he could not possibly have seen the corpse because the corpse was not there. And with even more penetrating eyes than that he could not possibly see the mortar where he tells you the mortar was always standing, because the mortar he says, was against the wall in which direction the feet of the corpse were pointing. He showed us where the mortar was when he helped to carry the corpse in. It was against the wall near the plank."

"Gentlemen, just glance at this photograph, and tell me whether it is humanly possible for a terrified boy looking from the doorway between the two kitchens in the direction of the garage to see a man taking up the mortar or trying to pick it up? He says he saw the man stooping to pick it up. If he could not see the mortar could a boy in that frame of mind know what the man was picking up? It is a matter I suggest for your earnest consideration as judges of fact. I will tell you why, and I will deal with that perhaps more fully when we come to the evidence of accomplices who were present at the commission of a crime."

"William was there at the murder. He tells you that he had bolted before any mortar was placed across the neck of the woman. How did that detail come to his knowledge unless he was present in the garage and saw it placed across the neck, which he says did not happen? If he did it himself, he would have known that there was a mortar across the neck and then, of course, if he was guilty all he did do was to say somebody else did it."

"Those are little details accomplices know about and the temptation in the way of accomplices who know all the details are just that. He knows what happened, he saw how it happened and there is the temptation, if he be guilty, which is another question for you, to say, 'Well, what I really did I will say somebody else did'. But here is something he did not see, and according to his own demonstration here he could not have seen."

"How then was it he came to know that the mortar which he and Sathasivam had passed as it lay by the side of the corpse, how could he know possibly the connection it would have to the corpse in the garage?" asked Justice Gratiaen.

"I looked at that picture because the learned Solicitor-General did suggest I think yesterday that from where William says he was standing he could see into the garage. That is perfectly right. You can see into the garage, but how in heaven's name can you see the hidden object which he assumes the strangler was stooping to pick up?"

It is clear that Justice Gratiaen was developing an argument, which questioned the credibility of William's story.

"Well before 9.30 William has left the house, said goodbye to the children, and at one end of the stage we are invited to follow him to the bus stand at Bambalapitiya. He misses two or three buses. He gets off at High Street, Wellawatte. He goes in search of a cousin but he changes his mind just opposite 37/1, High Street. Well then 9.30 has gone."

"We must come back to the other end of the stage during Act 2," continued Justice Gratiaen.

"There we are invited to observe through the process of logical reasoning Mr. Sathasivam making his preparations for one whole hour to plant this diabolical crime, which he had committed, on his unfortunate accessory – the daubing of the feet; the use of a hand mirror without his fingerprints on it because Mr. Thalaisingham says it is not a very good medium."

"So there again he is fortunate in his plan. Then he goes upstairs and no doubt he washes his hands, removes any evidence, which might have been there for Professor de Saram to observe later in the night. The mortar has been placed on the victim for what purpose none of us know. All we know is that William's counsel – I don't think it will be safe to saddle William with that theory, or knowledge of that theory - William's counsel suggested that there is some well known superstition about placing mortars across the necks of the dead. None of us have ever heard of that."

Justice Gratiaen then referred to the telephone call to Mr. Mack, the proctor of Mrs. Sathasivam.

"I think one suggestion was that Sathasivam might have been the person who feigned the voice of a woman asking about the divorce case. Then we must assume if that story be true, that in that little telephone chit which was discovered by Thiedeman three days later beside a pad near the telephone, that at least one or more, possibly two of those final numbers giving a number of telephone calls made from that telephone on the day of the murder, were written by Mr. Sathasivam."

"Then we come to the end of Act 3 on the darkened stage, because what happened after 10.30 there is no mystery about at all, because on a perfectly lighted stage the 'Quickshaws' cab arrives and Sathasivam goes to the Galle Face Hotel and carries on what was apparently at the time his daily round of idleness with the idle rich," commented Justice Gratiaen.

He reminded the jury a suggestion made by William's counsel in the cross-examination of Mr. Sathasivam in the Magistrate's Court as an additional proof of the consciousness of guilt. That was Mr. Sathasivam, a man who never drank anything but Whisky and soda from 10.30, was in such an uneasy frame of mind that he first had an orange squash before he proceeded to the more stimulating drinks.

"There they are drinking at the Galle Face Hotel, stopping at the Bank of Ceylon, drinking at the Grand Oriental Hotel and so on until they get to Haniffa's house."

"Meanwhile let us go back to No. 7, St. Alban's Place. Sathasivam has done his work, not only of murder, but planting the murder on someone else, leaving behind a corpse and two small children. It is horrible to think, is it not that if this story is true, that the father of these two children left them stranded in that lonely house of death? One trembles if one has enough imagination to think that perhaps while they were playing about in the kitchen they were spectators to the daubing of the feet. It is all monstrous, is it not?" asked Justice Gratiaen, indicating that this theory of the prosecution was very unlikely.

"Well, Podihamy and the children returned at 3 o'clock. The laundryman has arrived and he has seen for himself. The laundryman has taken his clothes bundle away just as any other laundryman would do. Mrs. Foenander comes and uses the telephone and sees this horrible sight for herself. How fortunate for the planner, was it not, that she did not want to use the telephone between 9.30 and 10.30 that morning?"

"Podihamy first goes upstairs, quite ignorant of what had taken place, finds some evidence that the almirah had been left open, anyhow she gets the coins to pay the rickshaw, coins which were available of course by the generosity of William, because they had been offered to him, then she comes down and from that moment everybody in the house knows that there had been a terrible murder!" said Justice Gratiaen.

"At 3.15 precisely, we get another fixed point of time. Mrs. Foenander telephoned the Bambalapitiya Police and summoned them to the scene. The relatives were also summoned."

"Mr. Sathasivam was asleep after lunch in Haniffa's house. We have evidence that Assistant Superintendent of Police, Mr. Attygalle telephoned Nadarajah, the advocate, if you believe him, indicating that Mr. Attygalle was on the look-out for the suspect."

"Gentlemen, one thing is clearly understandable about this whole case of suspicion. Could you blame the relatives of Mrs. Sathasivam, when they went there and saw what had happened? Can you blame them for suspecting Mr. Sathasivam, the absent husband?"

"Even his own relatives, such as K. Sathasivam were apparently not aware, as his drinking companions were aware, that his telephone address was now Haniffa's house. One can imagine, could one not, the communicating of that suspicion to the Police Officers who arrived. If they shared the suspicion one could not blame them. One can visualize the communication of those suspicions to the professional experts like Professor de Saram, Mr. Chanmugam and others when they were summoned to the scene."

In his address to the jury, Justice Gratiaen referred to the conduct of the Police and various allegations and counter-allegations made.

"There has been some suggestion with which I shall have to deal at a later stage, that at least one section of the Police have behaved in a most suspicious manner in their investigations."

Justice Gratiaen said, "We are not here to judge the Police. As I said before, we are not a Royal Commission appointed to investigate the techniques of Police investigations. We are not here to praise or to condemn the decision of Sir Richard Aluvihare on the 19th of October 1951 to transfer the investigation from the Crime Department to the Criminal Investigation Department. We are only concerned with the evidence which both groups of investigators with their accumulated skill has presented to the prosecution, and offered as proof of Mr. Sathasivam's guilt."

"But I attempted to make it clear that if there was any allegation by one side or the other that any evidence placed before you is suspect, because of the improper intervention of any Police Officer in this Island, that of course, however unpleasant the task may be, is a matter for your consideration, because if the witness concerned, be he for one side or the other, is open to suspicion.

"In some cases, the allegations have been made but the allegations have not been proved. I will give you just one instance in passing."

"A 'Quickshaws' driver named Perera was brought to No. 7, St. Alban's Place, by an Inspector who is not suspect and he was brought there on the instructions specially given by Mr. Attygalle. It was suggested in cross-examination that something, which the 'Quickshaws' driver had said, was not a matter within his own knowledge but what he had been prompted dishonestly and improperly to say by Mr. Attygalle."

"I have said that, that allegation has not been proved. It is for you to say whether or not it has not been convincingly disproved by the Inspector who recorded the 'Quickshaws' driver's statement, for he says that from the moment the 'Quickshaws' driver was taken to No. 7, St. Alban's Place, until the moment he left, he and the 'Quickshaws' driver were together."

"A few questions were put to the driver by Mr. Attygalle in the presence of the Inspector and there was no prompting, or time for prompting, or opportunity for prompting."

Later on in the summing up, Justice Gratiaen paid another compliment to the Acting Solicitor-General, Mr. T. S. Fernando.

"The Solicitor-General has presented his case substantially so very fairly and he is a person for whom I have very great regard and shall always have. We lawyers in our profession appear to be rather less sensitive than members of other learned professions appear to be. We in the course of our duty give knocks and receive knocks and we remain friends afterwards. The minor external abrasions are quickly healed and there are never any internal bruises of any depth at all. But when it is ones duty to say what one thinks is right, one says it."

"All I will say is that I would very much have wished it that that particular allegation when it was disproved against that particular Police Officer had been withdrawn. Counsel make allegations on instructions and sometimes we regret to find that the instructions, which we believe, are not correct and who gave these instructions on this occasion it is not for me to say."

"As I say, I wish it had been withdrawn gentlemen, for one reason among many others. You see when this case is finally over, when the pink shirts and the flowered sarees are tucked away, when the verdict has been pronounced, when the Solicitor-General in the exercise of his important duties in presenting cases before able juries and Dr. de Silva in his turn is bringing under his spell, the administration of justice must go on and the Police are a vital link in the system."

"It is sad that in a case where the suggestion of conspiracy between the Police and the accused has been publicly announced is not part of the case for the prosecution, that we should have allegations made against Police Officers still in public service, still investigating other crimes, that their names should be besmirched, without proof."

"We know that Advocate Mr. Nadarajah was frustrated in his earlier arrangements to take his daughter swimming in the Galle Face Swimming Pool, that he came to No. 7, St. Alban's Place. If you believe him, he had been trying to contact Mr. Sathasivam at the request of the Police, and eventually Sathasivam had rung up the house and this telephone call was received."

"Mr. Sathasivam was claiming that he wanted to come there and Nadarajah says that because of the temper of the relatives and the temper of the crowd, he thought that was not at all desirable. You will remember that Pathmathan, a brother-in-law himself, says that even the mother of Mr. Sathasivam was cold shouldered when she came rushing to the scene and her step-brother said, 'We better get away. We are not wanted here.'"

"Two senior officers then in charge of the case asked them to leave and they went with Nadarajah and Mr. Sathasivam was arrested, I think I am right in saying, between 5 and 5.30 in the evening – and if I am wrong perhaps someone will correct me. Well, gentlemen, so ends the 9th of October."

Justice Gratiaen then commented about delay in the Court cases.

"Mr. Sathasivam has been in custody since that time. One of the scandals of the present time is the horrible delay in bringing men to justice for serious crime. It is unfair and monstrous to the accused person; it is unfair to witnesses who are called upon to strain their memory by giving details of what happened 18 months ago."

"If this man is innocent, the delay is indefensible. If he be found guilty by you, nevertheless this delay surely constitutes an unnecessarily cruel form of refined torture, but those are matters gentlemen which the Attorney-General's Department and the Judge, I regret to say, are powerless to remedy."

"The other possible suspect, William, had also gone away. He had departed to his village, and from his village to another village and admittedly, as he told Koelmeyer, I think, he was in hiding. The investigation is proceeding. More clues are discovered, some of them perhaps at a leisurely pace."

"You will remember that the key of that bed room was taken away, quite properly, by Mr. Thiedeman on the day of the murder itself. Nobody could enter and nobody could tamper with what was there until he had got the permission of the Police."

Justice Gratiaen then referred to the telephone chit found in the bedroom, 4 days after Mrs. Sathasivam's death.

"Nobody disputes the words 'Telephone number so and so' and 'Telephone calls' or whatever the words at the top of that piece of paper, were in Mrs. Sathasivam's hand-writing. Nobody disputes her characteristic regard for the minor financial details of her affairs, that against each day, horizontally she would check up, so to speak, the number of the calls, either singly or collectively and they would be totalled at the end of the list. Nobody disputes that the first one, at any rate, on the 9th was hers."

"Gentlemen, either the whole of that document is genuine or the last two figures of that document against the crucial date represent the work of a forger. If they were forged they must have been forged before Mr. Sathasivam left the house for the last time. If it was a genuine document, it is true that Mrs. Sathasivam had telephoned for her husband's 'Quickshaws' from that house, it is true that it was she who telephoned Proctor Mack, then, gentlemen, that is the end of the case against Sathasivam."

"If on the other hand, there is good ground for suspecting that he had the cunning to enter those figures himself and if that matter was investigated, that would surely be a strong point against him. Well, what happened to that document?" asked Justice Gratiaen.

"We know that Thiedeman made notes on the day of the discovery, as he himself admits, saying to himself, 'This is a very important clue. The first one against the date of death is clearly the telephone call for the 'Quickshaws' at 8.15 made by Mrs. Sathasivam. The second one might well be, and the other four calls may possibly be, to her relatives', and he says, 'I will ask Mr. Pathmanathan about this'."

"On the 13th instant Thiedeman had that document. On the 14th he has proceeded a little further in his investigations because he makes another note in which he says 'I have been to the 'Quickshaws' office, checked, cross-checked and done everything else and I have found the following facts'. The word is 'facts'. It does not mean that those are facts which the Crown must accept".

Justice Gratiaen said, "But those were the opinions honestly entertained that day by the Inspector of Police who, according to law, whatever departmental arrangements which an Inspector-General of Police may make, was the person charged with the statutory obligations of holding the investigation, with the statutory right of interrogating witnesses, with the statutory obligation of bringing people whom he suspects before a Magistrate to be charged, and finally with statutory obligations, when reporting the matter to the Magistrate, to send to the Magistrate all the documents and productions which may be relevant. He then went to Proctor Mack still pursuing this clue."

"Later, you will have to consider whether the witness Mack is a liar or a mistaken witness, or whether he is a witness whose impression as to the identity of the person who telephoned him between 10.25 and 12 noon on the 9th was a correct impression."

"But Mack tells us that Mr. Thiedeman told him about this telephone chit and that he told him, among other things, that he had checked up some of the calls and that he had checked up, at least, one call to the Pathmanathan house by Mrs. Sathasivam, explaining one of the four calls, and that he had checked another call from somebody whose name Mack cannot recollect."

"Thiedeman gave evidence in rebuttal, and Thiedeman says that, to the best of his recollection, no such conversation took place. He says it is not unlikely that he may have mentioned about the telephone chit, but he has no recollection whatsoever of having told Mack anything about what Pathmanathan told him."

"In fact, says Thiedeman, that although the whole of the crime file contains not a single reference to a further questioning of any member of that household as to whether Mrs. Sathasivam had telephoned them after 10.30 that day, he now remembers, one and a half years or more after the event, that Pathmanathan told him that on that day, 9th of October 1951, Pathmanathans' telephone could not possibly have been used because a tree had fallen across the line."

"Gentlemen, if that is true, you must bear it in mind because it could only then be a complete invention on the part of Mack, apart from his recollection of his own telephone call, when he said that Thiedeman did tell that one call to the Pathmanathan household had been checked."

"I wish to pursue a point which had not occurred to me, which the learned Solicitor-General, quite properly made, because he thought it was a matter for your consideration as judges, regarding Mr. Sathasivam's conduct when he heard of the murder of his wife for the first time."

"It was suggested that there was good ground to fill in a few gaps in his evidence from something in Haniffa's evidence, which would justify a jury, in a murder case, in inferring that Mr. Sathasivam's mother had been the first person to telephone her son and inform him of his wife's death somewhere between 3 and 4 in the afternoon."

"Because, if that was so gentlemen, even though Haniffa says that as soon as Mr. Sathasivam heard that his wife had died he seemed distressed and he rushed off to change, saying that he was going home, the fact remains that for at least one to one and a half hours he did not go home. We will leave it at that."

"But I did make it a point to look at the evidence on that particular issue and I will give it to you in that connection. What I did find – which I am sure the Solicitor-General, Dr. de Silva and all of us have forgotten – was this."

"At 3.15 was the first telephone call, informing the outside world that there was a corpse in the garage – that was Mrs. Foenander's call to the Police. The next call was from the daughter, the eldest daughter of the Sathasivams, to her grandmother, Mrs. Rajendra, and to her aunt, Mrs. Pathmanathan. The witness Pathmanathan, the brother-in-law of Mrs. Sathasivam, told us – it just shows how we forget – that his wife telephoned him in his office and said, 'Baby is dead! Come at once. We must go to the house.'"

"So, gentlemen, there were two telephone calls received in the Pathmanathan house on the afternoon of the day of this murder but says Thiedeman he was told when he asked about a telephone call after 10.30 from No. 7, St. Alban's Place to the Pathmanathan house that a tree had fallen across the line. He said, 'I now recollect Pathmanathan telling me that a tree had fallen across the line'."

"Gentlemen, if that is responsible evidence of Thiedeman, then Pathmanathan was lying. If it is an invention of Thiedeman, his evidence is unworthy of a Police Officer."

"Particularly unworthy for any reason, gentlemen. If Mack is speaking the truth, leaving out his own call, there are about two other telephone calls which form part of the final four calls, and was that not a highly important document for an Inspector of Police in the discharge of the duty entrusted to him by the law to place before the Magistrate?"

"But what happened? In fairness to Thiedeman he says, 'My Lord, I am only the nominal complainant. If it was left to me that document would have been sent to the Magistrate'. But instead what happened to that document?"

"Gentlemen, that document we now know, was handed to the Examiner of Questioned Documents, very properly, to see if there was any reason for suspecting its authenticity. He was asked to look for erasures and he said there were no erasures. That document, according to Thiedeman, was then placed or deposited in the CID strong box."

"Would it not be a terrible thing if the truth, which we can never necessarily know for certain because nobody bothered to inquire, is that those two figures are in this unhappy lady's handwriting?"

"Some suggestion has been made that there is an absence of dots and dashes against those two figures. As I see it, there is an absence of dots and dashes against some other admitted figures as well. But we do know this, that when through the courtesy of the Attorney-General who acted most commendably in bringing that document to light, the Examiner of Questioned Document was asked whether he saw any significance in the dots and dashes, he said that was far too insignificant to have the slightest importance."

"Supposing the matter had been investigated and it had been found that the figures were forgeries, then also would it not be a terrible thing that you should not have the advantage of that proof in a murder case?"

"Clues are meant to be followed. Documents like that should not be tucked away in CID strong boxes when juries, presiding judges and counsel are trying murder cases. That decision in a sense stands condemned by Thiedeman himself, because he said he would have thought it his duty to place that before the Magistrate for what it was worth. It may well be, I do not know, that after complete investigation, after recording of the statements of every possible relative of Mrs. Sathasivam to whom she could possibly have telephoned, that the clue might have been properly rejected. But you don't reject a clue at the start."

"Gentlemen, it is not a very happy feature of this case that the Defence has complained that at certain stages it had become the attitude of the Police to say, 'The man is guilty. Anything that any witness may say in his favour is so obviously false that it is not worth investigating'. It is not for me to endorse that observation. I am not a judge of fact, but I do say this in all earnestness, if documents and clues are tucked away and with-held and not investigated can you blame the Defence Counsel if he makes that charge?" asked Justice Gratiaen.

"You get a lot of things which leave an unhappy feeling in the minds of people who are conscientiously trying to do their duty in the administration of justice. One of the greatest difficulties, which always confront us, is when something which may or may not have provided a convincing finale one way or the other is left undetermined because it is inconvenient or because the investigator is careless."

"Because the investigator is in a hurry, as Thiedeman was on one day, or sleepy as he was on the next. When you get certain witnesses you get ample zeal in the investigation of the witness."

"Take Proctor Mack, a professional young man, whose evidence at the best if believed by you, is evidence of an opinion as to the matter on which he had an honest view at the best. Three times it was found necessary to interrogate him. Twice it was recorded. On the third occasion, there was apparent a certain contradiction on the face of the document. Well that was good Police work."

"They tested him and they probed his evidence. He was left in a state of doubt. But then you get other witnesses. At long last, Mr. Sanmugam's statement was recorded by the Police. Does he stand on such a demonstrably higher plane of credibility than Proctor Mack that one interrogation is quite enough? It may be," said Justice Gratiaen.

The exact time William sold the gold 'thali' at a boutique at Wellawatta was crucial to determine the time when Mrs. Sathasivam was strangled. Justice Gratiaen critically analysed the evidence of Sirisena who bought the 'thali' from William.

"We will get another witness who came before you, the man called Sirisena, who everybody admits is the most despicable receiver of stolen property. One statement of his was recorded, in which he purported to give on the vital question of time, details with regard to all his movements. It is common ground now that William sold the 'thali' in Edmund's boutique at 37/1, High Street, Wellawatte."

"The question is at what time did the transaction take place? In the Magistrate's Court Edmund, Sirisena and Dharmasena it is now admitted lied. They all said that the transaction took place in Sirisena's boutique and not in Edmund's boutique. That evidence was led on that basis in this murder enquiry."

"Now, gentlemen, Sirisena relies on an alibi for himself, and as the Crown says, he had got a convenient younger brother who was willing to take the blame. But now we know that it was Sirisena who bought it, and we also know that Dharmasena the little boy was willing to be the stooge. He had no interest in the transaction at all, except to take a message. When did the sale take place?" asked Justice Gratiaen.

"Sirisena says that he has a document which he says supports him on the point he said. He says he left at 8.45 in order to go to Dickman's Road with some things that were ready for a customer, but that he decided after leaving to go to Pettah and then return to Dickman's Road where he got the 50 rupees and then returned to Wellawatte. It is now everybody's case that it was Sirisena who was the purchaser."

"Would it not have helped you and me in assessing the credibility, shall we say of the vital witness Sanmugam, if we were comforted with the knowledge that Police Officers who are quite willing to go three times to a Proctor's office to record his statement, had taken the trouble to check up on Sirisena's movements, so that we could know for certain when it was that Sirisena was available to buy anything that day?" asked Justice Gratiaen.

He then brought to the notice of the jury, some important clues the Police have failed to investigate.

"We have another difficulty, gentlemen, another uninvestigated clue, which I respectfully suggest must necessarily create a difficulty in the mind of any conscientious juror, although it is not for me to say whether that difficulty is or is not insuperable."

"Mrs. Sathasivam's private handbag was upstairs. In that handbag was a letter from a reputable firm of Bakers, 'Perera & Sons', threatening to cut off her supplies of bread unless she paid the bill which was outstanding, before the 12th of that month."

"One thing is certain. This careful woman probably put the envelope in which that letter arrived into her waste paper basket, which nobody looked at, but the letter itself she put in her handbag in order that it might receive her attention, so that she could pay the bill and see that her children did not go hungry."

"When did she get that letter? It is dated the 8th October. What is the sum total of the evidence which the prosecution places before you for the purpose of deciding, gentlemen, whether she opened that letter and put it away in her bag for later attention?"

"Did she get it before 9.30, which if clearly established is not inconsistent with Sathasivam's guilt, although it does not prove it, or did she get it after 9.30, in which case the whole of the prosecution story seems to me, and I trust to you, to be completely destroyed, unless of course one's imagination could go still further and say well, really, what is the use of investigating that matter. Is not a man who is capable of daubing the feet of his wife's corpse not equally capable of receiving a letter from a postman, putting it in her bag so that he could rely on it as an alibi?"

"Whether you would have been attracted by that suggestion or convinced of his innocence, was it not fair to us that, that matter should have been investigated. What was the extent of that investigation, gentlemen?" asked Justice Gratiaen.

"In a murder case, when at that time there was no anticipation of William being pardoned, was it not fair to Sathasivam and was it not also fair to William himself who was a co-accused on a charge which involved, if he was guilty, the extreme penalty?"

"On that occasion in connection with that document Thiedeman went to the office of 'Perera & Sons', Colpetty, and he asked some questions. What the answers to the questions are we do not know. He then said, 'I am now recording the statement of so and so of this establishment'. The next sentence runs 'I am now leaving to the CID Office on the instructions of so and so'. He had to go on an urgent summons to the Police Office."

"Nobody bothered after that to find out whether 'Perera & Sons' letter was posted, and if so, posted when, or whether it was sent by a delivery peon, and if so delivered when, and if it was by a delivery peon whose initials were on that book, if there was such a book, as having received the document. On what date was it received? If it was sent by post what time is the first delivery of any letters to the residents of St. Alban's Place, Bambalapitiya. Gentlemen, is it not a terrible thing if the truth is that that letter was received by Mrs. Sathasivam from a postman after 9.30?"

"You see what you have got to do now gentlemen. You must say, 'We do not know what a proper police investigation would have revealed, but we are so convinced that the evidence of William the accessory, the self-confessed accomplice, is true, and we are so attracted by the compelling quality of Sanmugam's evidence, that we can say to ourselves we are perfectly sure, that if they had bothered to find out the truth, the truth must have been that she received the letter and put it away in her bag long before she submitted to the hands of a strangler.' Those, gentlemen, are disturbing features, are they not? Do they or do they not increase the difficulties of jurors in the performance of their task?" Justice Gratiaen asked.

"If that prisoner in the dock who is now in your charge is guilty, would it not be a terrible thing for the administration of justice if you say to yourselves, 'We are inclined to think he is guilty. If we had only known the time when 'Perera & Sons' letter reached No. 7, St. Alban's Place, we would have been sure, and because we are not sure, such evidence as the Police have bothered to collect is not of quite that compelling quality which jurors demand.' Is it not also a terrible thing that if the investigation of that clue did establish that the letter was received after 9.30, then surely the most sinister writer of anonymous letters might well have been satisfied that there was no case to make out against the man?"

"Gentlemen, Professor Paul told us graphically, truly, that half a minute in a man's life in certain circumstances might be an eternity. How exactly in terms of eternity one would assess twenty months of either an innocent or a guilty man awaiting his trial I do not know. I would also like some mathematical proposition about the relationship between eternity and one whole hour in the mind of a murderer, with his wife's corpse - two little children - daubing the corpse's feet."

"Now gentlemen, I have quite frankly told you as a person whose duty it is to assist you in your task that to my mind there are many enormous difficulties many of which are of the creation of the Police themselves."

"I am not telling you therefore that you must acquit. That is for you to decide. But by the time I have concluded my charge to you, I shall certainly tell you what I, as your respectful adviser, would say are difficulties which individually and collectively must be examined with the most anxious care, and you must ultimately find, before you convict, that those difficulties are not insuperable."

"That is how I suggest you should approach your task. It may be that you may say, well, in spite of those difficulties, we are sure that there could not have been a solution favourable to Mr. Sathasivam, if the clues which were not fully investigated had been investigated."

Justice Gratiaen emphasized to the jury what the Crown has to prove beyond reasonable doubt.

"The Crown has to prove to you beyond reasonable doubt, first of all, that William can confidently be eliminated from the strangler's end. It is a far more a formidable task than would have presented itself to a lawyer appearing for William, if he were charged for murder, but it is that formidable task which the Crown has undertaken."

He said that the jury must also be satisfied beyond reasonable doubt that the murder, not merely might, but must have been committed before 9.30.

"You must be convinced that the murder must, not merely might, have been committed in the bedroom upstairs. Therefore you must be in a position to say that you can confidently eliminate the kitchen as the scene of the crime."

"You must be satisfied beyond reasonable doubt that William's version, whether on the merits of his own evidence or of the circumstantial evidence, convincingly establishes a strangling upstairs on the ground," continued Justice Gratiaen.

"You see gentlemen - I think I am not saying anything which is controversial when I say this - can you say to yourselves, 'We do not like William's evidence, he is not the kind of witness that we would accept under any circumstances, he has lied, his story is improbable and there are all the other difficulties'. But can you say, 'Really we think that the truth is that Mrs. Sathasivam was strangled to her death in the kitchen and that it was a strangling against the kitchen wall which explains more rationally the stains on her feet and the urine stains which dripped down her petticoat, but still, although that means that William's whole version is false, still we have a sneaking feeling or still we are convinced that the person who strangled that poor woman, against the wall leading from the kitchen into the garage was Sathasivam and not William?'"

"I mean, to put it in a slightly fantastic way, can you say, we are convinced that the murder took place as the Defence suggests, but really William absolves himself, therefore we eliminate William in that way and find Sathasivam guilty?"

Justice Gratiaen told the jury that the case for the Crown was the case they had to judge.

"The case for the Crown is that in the eyes of their principal witness - in answer to me, quite specifically on the point - I asked him: 'Did Mr. Sathasivam kill the lady in the kitchen?' He said 'No'. So that we cannot speculate, we cannot go outside the case and look for other theories, because however agreeable an exercise that may be we are dealing with a particular case that a particular man killed a particular woman in a specific and particular way. That is the case which you must either accept or reject in its entirety."

"The defence version was," continued Justice Gratiaen, "Nothing like this occurred at all. Mrs. Sathasivam was alive at 10.30."

He then analysed the evidence Mr. Sathasivam gave in the Magistrate's Court.

"I was asleep as Podihamy says at 8.15. I was asleep much longer than that. I then woke up and I lit my cigarette and then I went into the lavatory and I came out and I read the 'Daily News'".

Justice Gratiaen said that the 'Daily News', which was last seen in the children's bedroom, was found lying on the floor of the bedroom where Mr. Sathasivam says he read the Daily News.

"He then says, 'My wife and I had intercourse with one another' and that is demonstrably proved by the evidence on the bed and the evidence of that little towel found by the bed. He then says 'I got ready to go out. I had my meal of string-hoppers and the 'sambol', and I had two eggs'. Is that right? Well, it is proved in the handwriting of Mrs. Sathasivam herself that six eggs were bought, and it is proved by Thiedeman that when he went there after the death had been committed, there were four eggs there."

"These are little items of corroboration on matters of detail that does not carry the case any further, but they are not disproved anyway. He says 'I then went and had a bath', and when the Government Analyst arrived in the afternoon or the evening and went upstairs taking swabs, he found that the bathroom upstairs had a wet floor. He then says 'I started dressing, and while I was putting on my shoes, my wife, who had been having her meal there, at my request, telephoned for a 'Quickshaws' cab. A 'Quickshaws' cab came and then she saw me off. She was perfectly hale and hearty'."

"If you are convinced that Sathasivam's story is substantially true, obviously you acquit him," Justice Gratiaen told the jury.

"If you are convinced that his story is false, that William's story is true, obviously, you must convict. But, if the evidence of Mr. Sathasivam and the evidence of Sir Sydney Smith, who tells you that in his considered professional opinion the woman could not on all the medical evidence have been dead before 10.30 and therefore obviously before 9, if the evidence of the 'Quickshaws' driver who claimed to have seen this lady at 10.30, if it is true, obviously it considerably strengthens the case for the defence and it is the end of the case for the prosecution," said Justice Gratiaen.

"But if the evidence is even of such a quality that it raises honest substantial doubts in the minds of seven conscientious men called upon to judge a fellow man, then those honest doubts, gentlemen, resolve them in his favour."

"He is not required to prove his innocence. What he is required to do is to place evidence before you, either through the lips of prosecution witnesses or through the defence, which is sufficient for you to be able to say, 'We honestly are not sure, we honestly are not convinced.'"

Justice Gratiaen then drew the attention of the jury to the importance of scientific evidence.

"I want, gentlemen, now to ask you to consider certain aspects of the case which are presented by what one would describe as the real evidence - that is, real evidence as opposed to the oral testimony of witnesses and evidence of that nature. Real evidence is necessarily, and nearly always necessarily, spoken to by witnesses, and they often are of such a character that they assist judges of fact to draw certain helpful, or even valuable, and perhaps, in some cases, vital conclusions."

"You will remember that even before Professor de Saram arrived, Mr. Chanmugam, the Government Analyst, was summoned to No.

7, St. Alban's Place, on the afternoon of the murder. He, a trained investigator, who was expected particularly and required particularly to look for clues on which his particular expert knowledge might prove valuable, himself had a look at the corpse."

"Naturally, he did not interfere with the body or touch it in any way, and he noticed for himself what Professor de Saram himself regarded later as a very important clue - namely, the dark stains on the feet of this lady, and presumably he formed a tentative conclusion as to this being a clue as to where the lady might have been standing at some stage, either in the course of the strangulation or shortly before it."

"He thereupon decided, in anticipation, to take for analysis, swabs from the garage, the kitchen, the upstairs bedroom, the children's room, the Dover stove kitchen, the gas stove kitchen and so on."

"Professor de Saram has given you a description of the nature of those stains. He says there was dark material adhering to the balls of the right toes and the sole of the left toe and also above the ball of the big toe and the first toe. There were also similar stains but not quite so dark or thick - I do not know which he meant by it - on the right sole and right foot. You have got those photographs before you. You have - I am not going through in such details with you - got the corpse full length on the floor. You see for yourselves the marks on the left foot. We have been told that it is common ground that there was similar discolouration on the sole of the right foot."

Justice Gratiaen stated that the analysis of the swabs taken by Mr. Chanmugam conclusively established that the material found on the soles of the feet and above the left foot came from the dirt on the kitchen floor.

"There is no question about that and there is no controversy on that issue whatsoever," emphasized Justice Gratiaen.

"William says that the strangulation took place upstairs in the bedroom. The floor of that room has been described to you as a fairly clean, polished floor with Mansion polish. Mr. Chanmugam, who is a prosecution witness - please remember - says that it was the best swept floor in the whole of that house but nevertheless it contained very fine sand."

"Now, the analysis which was carried out by Mr. Chanmugam establishes, again beyond any point of controversy, that the texture of the material found on the soles of the corpse's feet were entirely different to the material which you would expect to find if a person walked upstairs and got his feet stained."

"Now, Professor de Saram says that having examined the feet, you can see for yourselves, and the marks on the ball of the right toe, heel and the sole of the foot, and similarly the mark on the heel of the left foot and sole of the left foot, that is exactly what he would expect to find, if a person walked on that particular dirty kitchen floor, what he would get on his or her feet if he or she was walking there or stood there bare-footed," explained Justice Gratiaen.

"Mr. Chanmugam has himself told us that the impression he got was that it looked to him as if Mrs. Sathasivam had walked in the kitchen. He said, 'I saw this before Professor de Saram arrived and I regarded it as a clue'. Now these two gentlemen are trained observers, and I think the defence is entitled to claim, just as Dr. de Silva did in fact claim, that the best people and the most competent people to offer an opinion as to even the bare possibility of the alternative suggested by the Crown, were these two gentlemen."

"Are you convinced, gentlemen, that this is a wholly non-technical matter?" asked Justice Gratiaen.

"Is it so perfectly clear that any juror without looking at the marks, where the marks were, without looking at the feet can say, 'We are as competent as anybody else to express an opinion upon that point?' Can it be confidently stated that it is a non-technical issue, that Professor de Saram and Mr. Chanmugam could themselves have given us the benefit of their observations as to where exactly on a particular foot the stains were expected to come, if Mrs. Sathasivam were standing or walking on a dirty floor?"

He said that the Crown relied wholly on the fact that when Professor de Saram for the purpose of analysis decided to pick a sample of that material from the left foot, the outer part of that material flaked off.

"The rest was not flaking off and could not be flaked off. After that particular material came off on that sheet of paper as Professor de Saram explained, there was still dark material left on both feet.

How did that come there? What is the explanation for that?" queried Justice Gratiaen.

"All I can say, gentlemen, is this. That you must decide whether it is completely a non-technical matter, and if so whether you as men of the world and men of common sense are perfectly competent without the assistance and opinion of Professor de Saram and Mr. Chanmugam to decide one way or the other, and if so, whether you are convinced that the impressions sworn to by both those gentlemen, may well be wrong and in fact, having regard to the burden of proof that lies on the prosecution that they must be wrong."

"If it is a non-technical matter we will leave Professor de Saram out of it because he is really nobody's witness, but let us take Mr. Chanmugam. Even if it was a non-technical matter, is he himself not a man of the world who should have been given an opportunity of saying what he, a witness called by the Crown, had to say about that matter? If it is a technical matter and if it might be a technical matter, are we not treading on rather dangerous ground in hazarding as laymen in a technical matter an issue of that nature?"

Justice Gratiaen reminded the jury what Mr. Chanmugam, a prosecution witness said, 'I got the impression that she had been walking in the kitchen that day'.

Though he was not asked one question to test the reliability of his opinion, Justice Gratiaen said that if the case was closed without calling Sir Sydney Smith into the witness box as a defence witness, the suggestion could not have been put to anybody at all.

"While Sir Sydney Smith having read the description what he observed in the evidence of Professor de Saram and Mr. Chanmugam, and having seen the photographs which have been produced, told you on oath that in his opinion, it was the most important factor in the whole case. On this issue, whether there was strangulation of a standing victim in the kitchen or there was beyond doubt the strangulation of the victim lying on the bedroom floor upstairs he put it rather graphically. He says, in my opinion on that evidence the victim walked into the kitchen and never walked out again!"

"There was some question about the marks and stains above the left foot, and Professor de Saram stated that in his opinion the explanation for the dark stains on that foot - on the sole - was that a bare footed strangler might well have at some time placed his weight on the women's left foot. His opinion was that that would explain not only the dark material on the left foot but also the fact that it was thick."

"Then there was another question. It was suggested that it was a remarkable and sinister feature about these stains that if a woman walked barefooted on a dirty floor, that one would naturally expect a similar extent of stains on both feet. It is for you to consider whether that would not be more reasonable, a more reasonable argument in the case of an evenly polished stained floor and less reasonable in the case of a kitchen floor, which is certainly not intentionally dirty evenly throughout the whole area."

Referring to evidence of Professor Paul and Professor Peiris who gave evidence on many points, Justice Gratiaen said that in their examination-in-chief, no question was put to them with regard to that matter.

"Paul says that he did offer a certain opinion in the Magistrate's Court about it, but he was not asked that opinion here by anybody and we don't know what his opinion is, whether it would have been the same or not. Professor Peiris was also not asked."

"Now Professor Peiris did however make a certain concession in the course of his evidence upon this point."

Then Justice Gratiaen told the jury what Mr. Chanmugam said on that point.

"You will remember that the evidence is that there was some fluff also adhering to the sole of the foot. On that point he was questioned."

Question: "Then if a person came into the kitchen and there was fluff on that kitchen floor it would come on to the feet?"

Answer: "I suppose if there was fluff on the floor anybody could have picked it up."

Question: "It is also consistent with her having had her feet on the floor in the garage?"

Answer: "That is so."

Question: "I will ask you to consider what your view of the matter is as a scientific man. Imagine the lady walking or standing on the kitchen floor. The contents of the scrapings taken from right against the soles of the two feet of the lady are consistent with her having thus stood or walked on that kitchen floor?"

Justice Gratiaen said then he interpolated a question to clarify the matter.

Question: "The black substance which was in the closest proximity to the foot is consistent with that?"

Answer: "Yes."

Justice Gratiaen then referred to what Professor Peiris said.

Question: "If on top of that you found that the lady who had been killed and whom that particular suspect states never entered the kitchen that day or any day when he was there, has got kitchen dirt on the soles of her feet, you would regard that as still further strengthening the matter which you think was necessary for him to explain?"

Answer: "Quite right."

Question: "If further you held the view, that the person who was being strangled had to be brought up against a hard object, let us say the wall for instance, and you found the sole of one foot having material such as would be found in a kitchen floor and having it more thickly coated than the sole of the other foot, that also would be consistent with a picture of a person struggling and being pushed against the wall?"

Answer: "Yes."

Continuing his address to the jury, Justice Gratiaen said, "Now, was it not fair to Professor Peiris, that when he made that categorical admission that he should have been asked what view he honestly entertained about the alternative suggestion, which was placed before you at such a late stage of the trial? Well, those are matters gentlemen which emerge from that item of real evidence."

Justice Gratiaen made further critical remarks about the conduct of the Police at the scene of Mrs. Sathasivam's death.

"If the lady had those marks on her feet as a result of walking in the kitchen what about William? Should not William have had marks like that as well? I should imagine the answer is obviously 'Yes'. Did one single policeman look anywhere to see if any encrustations of kitchen dirt had come off somewhere after William walked out of the kitchen? Because whether the lady's feet were daubed after her death or whether they got stained while she as a living woman walked into the kitchen, William's feet must have been stained. Is it suggested, therefore, that he could not possibly have left any stains elsewhere?" asked Justice Gratiaen.

"Instead of looking about this place, as far as I can understand the unhappy Inspector Thiedeman was concentrating mainly on the kitchen that afternoon. He tells us he attempted to ring off the kitchen and he kept the bedroom under close supervision though he did not go into details very much, but what happened?"

"We are told that members of the family, whom one might almost be inclined to forgive if they walked across the kitchen, but the head of the Police Department himself with legal advisers specially attached to his department, walked across the kitchen. They were all there, brass hats, legal advisers and everything else and when Mr. Thiedeman was asked why did you allow that, he said 'I did my best but if Senior Officers come across who am I, an Inspector of Police to interfere?'"

Justice Gratiaen said there was one rather important point as to where the strangling took place.

"William says that never did Mrs. Sathasivam on that day walk downstairs and certainly never into the kitchen. On that kitchen table was found some pieces of garlic being prepared to make a curry. William admits that he went upstairs and asked for some garlic that morning. He says that the lady gave him the garlic, which she kept upstairs. Nobody saw any other garlic upstairs."

Justice Gratiaen said, "It seems a strange place does it not, to keep your garlic, when Podihamy tells us that to her knowledge, the garlic was kept in the kitchen safe in the Gas Cooker kitchen!"

"There is another point in that issue as to whether she never came downstairs at all that day. You will remember gentlemen, that after William's arrest, his father Darlis was sent for and he was interrogated by Superintendent Koelmeyer, who had by that time taken over the investigation."

"Well, Darlis tells us, that in answer to questions he said whatever conveniently came to his mind! He had been frightened by a nonexistent policeman that he would be beaten up unless he spoke the truth and when he was threatened that his ribs would be broken if he did anything but speak the truth, he felt that the best thing to do under the circumstances was to invent things."

"Now what did he say to Koelmeyer and how did he come to gain any knowledge of the facts which he spoke to? Darlis lives miles away from St. Alban's Place, Bambalapitiya, in a village south of Matara. Whether it was an upstair house or a downstair house he did not know unless someone who had recently come to meet him gave him the necessary information. And what did he say? Gentlemen, it is important on this, and even more so on another important and vital aspect of this case."

Justice Gratiaen reminded the jury what Mr. Sathasivam in his sworn evidence in the Magistrate's Court said.

"My wife saw me off at the doorway when I got into the 'Quickshaws' at 10.30 and I never came back."

Continuing Justice Gratiaen said, "It is an issue as to whether the wife saw him off. But it is certain that he did leave and it is certain that he never came back. Why does Darlis, from a source, which is not very difficult to speculate about, say to Superintendent Koelmeyer, 'My son came back and he told me that the master left the house'. That is true. That is common ground. And he says 'And then the master came back'. That is not true admittedly. Then what happened when the master came back? 'The lady and the master went upstairs and I heard a wailing noise upstairs'. That he heard a wailing noise upstairs is not true."

"But there is the admission that when the master came back, that is after the master had admittedly left the house, the lady was downstairs, either to go upstairs or into the kitchen."

"Please ask yourselves, whether with all the elaborate details which William gave us day after day under the stress of cross-examination, which you must remember in his favour, two things were clear; one is that before she died he was at the kitchen coconut-scraper. Equally common to all the stories is, Mrs. Sathasivam never stepped into the kitchen. Gentlemen, so much so that William gave us such a graphic description of Mrs. Sathasivam being carried into the garage across the kitchen, but even there he was particularly careful to hold the two feet above the ground," said Justice Gratiaen.

"Is that all true, or was there some secret thought in his mind that whatever happened, it would be a most damaging thing to admit that dead or alive, that Mrs. Sathasivam's feet touched the kitchen floor that day?"

"Of course, we shall come in detail to all the different versions which he gave. But while he was giving one version after another, this so called accessory, never knew that a Government Analyst and a Government Pathologist were walking about in the garage looking for telltale evidence, which might point to the circumstance that this woman had been standing at some stage of that morning in the kitchen. That is one of the items of real evidence, which you must bear in mind on this very important issue, as to where the strangling took place."

Justice Gratiaen was again very critical of the Police for not taking a photograph of the one and a half feet long wavy drag mark trailing towards the door of the garage, observed by Mr. Chanmugam.

"Now gentlemen, he tells us in elaborate detail what happened when he claims to have seen that drag mark that afternoon. He says, he wanted to take a photograph of it and a Police Inspector said that it was irrelevant because the brass hats and others and the members of the family had been walking through the kitchen already. But he tells us this, that it was not the kind of mark that he would expect to find if someone was merely walking across the kitchen."

"He said it was consistent with the foot of a person being dragged across the kitchen. He said, 'It looked as if the foot got dragged along or as if someone slipped'. Somebody said - I do not think it is at all fair to insinuate even that somebody was acting improperly – 'I do not think it will help'. Well gentlemen, people like Mr. Chanmugam are trained observers, who are summoned to a scene of a crime, concentrate particularly on aspects in respect of which they are specialists."

Reminding the jury that Mr. Chanmugam was trained at Scotland Yard and the Metropolitan Police Laboratory, London, Justice Gratiaen said, "He has given evidence in our criminal Courts for many years, and I think you can take it that the Prosecution and the Defence and all judges before whom this gentleman has appeared have always found him to be a man of unquestionable integrity, and of remarkable skill and ability, who has contributed more than his fair share to the detection of crime in the cause of justice."

"He was a man who on this particular occasion admittedly did go into the kitchen, admittedly took swabs from the kitchen floor. He was a man, and the only man as far as I can recall from the evidence, who saw and described the kitchen sweepings in the corner of the kitchen, from which the Crown suggests the dauber took what he needed from the corner of the kitchen."

"He has given us, if you recollect his evidence, in the minutest detail, what he saw on the kitchen table and he has even told us about the length of the vegetables that had been chopped up and about the coconut scraper and the quantity scraped! Gentlemen, he swears to that. He is a Crown witness. It was not suggested to him anywhere in the evidence, as far as I can see, that he was either lying - which I am sure no one would suggest - or that he was making a genuine mistake."

"Thiedeman's version was never put to him. But at a later date, Thiedeman tells us that he was certainly not the Inspector of Police to whom any drag mark was shown on the 9th. But that he does remember, that on the 10th, that was the day when he was sleepy and understandably so, because the whole of the previous night he had been working in this case, and that part of his evidence whatever view you take, I believe it to be perfectly true, but he says on that day Mr. Chanmugam asked him in the presence of Mr. Attygalle and Mr. Adihetty, pointing to something, 'Can you see a mark?' Not where the drag mark was drawn on the sketch for your assistance by Mr. Chanmugam, but somewhere else, another mark or alleged mark, and he says they all looked with their trained policemen's eyes, and what did they find - just the bare floor - nothing resembling a drag mark. They all shrugged their shoulders and presumably said 'Poor Mr. Chanmugam must also be tired as we are'."

"Well, was Mr. Chanmugam speaking the truth? It does not necessarily mean that what Mr. Thiedeman was saying was untrue, because it is not unlikely perhaps that is was shown to another Police Officer there."

"There - but remember this - a Police Officer on the one hand and this respected Government Analyst on the other."

"Treat them as people of equal veracity, standing on the same high plane of credibility and ask yourselves whether you prefer to believe the eyes of a man who says he saw something or whether you prefer to believe the eyes of a man who said he did not see something. Well if you are not satisfied that there was a drag mark, that bit of real evidence takes us nowhere," said Justice Gratiaen.

"We might have been able to judge exactly who was speaking the truth and how vitally relevant that wavy mark in that particular place was, if somebody had not prevented Mr. Chanmugam from taking the photograph that day. But it was never taken, so it is a question of just believing him or not."

"Now, gentlemen, what is the significance of the drag mark? The significance of the drag mark is a matter, which you must carefully consider when you examine Sir Sydney Smith's theory, based purely on the medical evidence, as to how the strangling took place and where it took place"

"You will remember that his theory was that at a certain stage, Mrs. Sathasivam was being strangled against a particular projection, which he found near the door leading out of the kitchen towards the garage. Then she fell unconscious and sagged back, picked up by the strangler still alive, still 'vital', to use that medical term, which I hope we shall all forget when this case is over, and that she was dragged out by one person as Sir Sydney Smith demonstrated - this old gentleman of 70 - with a peon, and he took him out through the door and he says, I have read the evidence about this drag mark and to use his own words, he said, 'It is exactly what I would have expected to find if my theory of the murder in the kitchen is true.'"

"You will remember, he explained that while Mrs. Sathasivam was being dragged like that, her toes must have been trailing along the floor and he was asked whether he would not expect to find some abrasions, at least, upon the toes which had been dragged in that fashion."

"His answer was, 'Well, you know I thought of that myself' and apparently Sir Sydney Smith's nurse has been subjected in her own way to all kinds of experiments, but he says it was not the same kind of floor, it was a cement floor. And he says, - he considered it professionally - he would not expect to find it, and taking the difference in the floors into account, he did not get abrasions on the nurse's toes."

"He was then further cross-examined about this drag mark as to whether there was such a drag mark at all, and in his rather picturesque way he smiled at the Solicitor-General and said, 'Well, that drag mark is your evidence, you know.'"

"That is the evidence of Mr. Chanmugam, the Government Analyst. Sir Sydney seemed almost to shrug his shoulders and say, 'I come all this way to give evidence and I am surely entitled to expect that evidence of fact, led by responsible officers of the Government was true evidence.'"

Justice Gratiaen said that Sir Sydney Smith did not have the advantage of knowing that Mr. Thiedeman was to give evidence later.

"Now, that is a second piece of 'real evidence', which you must not fail to bear in mind. What conclusions you would draw from that is a matter for yourselves because it is useful gentlemen, in this difficult case, with so much hard swearing one way and the other, to look at the real evidence, and see while we are starting from reality, whether you can get somewhere."

Continuing Justice Gratiaen said, "You see gentlemen, people trying a murder case where murder is alleged to have been committed in a particular way – such as, a particular person strangling a victim on a particular floor upstairs – like others faced with that task or not, merely would know as people solving for their entertainment jigsaw puzzles, and even if there were those of you, who do entertain yourself with a jigsaw puzzle, that you do not start with the solution and work backwards!"

"Certainly, in a murder case like this, you must not start with a picture of Sathasivam at the starting point upstairs and working backwards from that to fit everything else like a jigsaw puzzle."

"Let us get the witnesses who may be lying and who may not, and who has no necessity to lie in a case like this, when there are two suspects, only one of them could possibly have been suspected of this particular crime. Let us start away from the throat. Let us start from the feet and work upwards - I do not think it is an experience which anybody can conjure - and then let us see if, at the end of all our investigation, you can see as clearly as at the start, that Mr. Sathasivam and nobody else has strangled her neck."

Justice Gratiaen then requested the jury to look for a third piece of 'real evidence', which he said he only heard about rather late in the case.

"In fact, we would never have heard about it till after the case for the Prosecution was over, except that Sir Sydney Smith, owing to other engagements, had to give his evidence before the close of the case for the Crown."

"Now, all of us went to that house. There was a guide in Inspector Thiedeman who has conducted most efficiently and most helpfully. I seem to remember, when we had spent quite some time there, in a moment of unusual zeal, I suggested that you seven gentlemen might go back into the kitchen and have another look."

Justice Gratiaen asked the jury, "Did you look for a door-jamb or did you find a particular staple? I certainly did not."

"Even Professor de Saram, apart from the question of his opinions, with his meticulous attention for details in post-mortem matters and one who has specialised in examining all possible places where the crime may have been committed, never told us about it. Inspector Thiedeman never told us about that," commented Justice Gratiaen.

"Poor Professor Paul and poor Professor Peiris could not help us on that point because up-to-date these two brilliant surgeons, who have confidently excluded, as the scene of the crime, a particular kitchen, and confidently preferred, as the scene of the crime, the floor upstairs, candidly confessed, at the very early stage of the evidence of each, when I asked, 'Have you looked at this kitchen? Have you gone to No. 7, St. Alban's Place, and have you seen the bedroom floor?' 'No. Nobody asked us. I never went there'".

"Gentlemen, I would myself have been very much happier in my own mind if even one of those two doctors, who had never driven from our local Harley Street to Bambalapitiya, after hearing what Sir Sydney Smith had bothered to look for and found, had gone to that place, had a look at that staple, then came back to this Court asking to be recalled in the interest of justice, and said, 'We have now bothered to go to the scene of the crime, we have seen that particular projection in the wall,' and either said to us, 'Honestly we still stick to the same opinion', or 'Honestly we have changed our minds'."

Justice Gratiaen continued to praise Sir Sydney Smith, which was an indirect criticism of the evidence of Professors of Surgery, Paul and Peiris.

"I will make a confession for myself, gentlemen. Well, Sir Sydney Smith was in the witness box there. On the very first day that he appeared before us giving evidence, Professor Peiris, naturally interested in the evidence of another professional man, came and sat where one of these ladies is seated, and as that new fact was brought to our notice, I caught the eye of Professor Peiris and really I would very much have liked to have said, 'Would you mind now going to No. 7, St. Alban's Place, and please come back and say whether or not you have altered your views?' Now, it was not for me to control the movements of Professor Peiris, and the case proceeded."

"So, we shall never know whether or not these two distinguished surgeons would or would not have clung to that particular theory as tenaciously as they did, as most honest men were entitled to. Now, what was their evidence, gentlemen?"

"You will remember that Sir Sydney Smith, who is 70 years of age, and who came by a Comet plane, had to ask all of us to talk louder because he was still suffering from the disturbance in his ears."

"He said, 'Before I went to my hotel, I had worked out some theories and I was worried about one thing and I asked to be taken to that house. I looked into all those rooms and on the wall of the kitchen just by the door-jamb through which one approaches the door leading to the garage where the corpse was found, I discovered 3 feet from the ground on the door-jamb, a rounded staple, and that projection was capable of producing an injury on the back and a bruise on the back of Mrs. Sathasivam , if she was pushed against it in the course of the strangulation'."

"He said, "Now that fits in with my theory of strangulation in the kitchen. I searched for evidence as to whether or not there was just such a projection and it confirmed the theory to my satisfaction. It is very important'."

"Whether Sir Sydney Smith, as a witness in this case suffers the same fate or not, which it is suggested he suffered twenty three years ago, when Sir Bernard Spilsbury, another giant, gave evidence expressing a contrary view to his in England, I do think that he has taught a lot of us, who do our business in the Courts, and a lot of us who are and will be giving, professionally, medical evidence on vital matters, to look about when you go to the scene of a crime, so that you will always be able to state, if the issue be ever like this again, 'I think it was on the kitchen floor, which I saw, and I think the strangulation was effected against a particular projection, which I saw', and not merely, 'I am convinced in fact that it was not a strangulation on a floor in the bedroom, which I did not see.' How can any professional man risk giving evidence of the scene of the crime without bothering to visit it?" asked Justice Gratiaen.

"The other explanation is, and I have no doubt it is true, and we have great respect for those gentlemen, they were merely asked to give purely theoretical evidence, those were the words of Professor Paul, on a medical issue. In other words they were told, even if something is half technical and half non-technical keep out of the kitchen dirt and speak to the medical issues on a theoretical plane, where as we, in this case, and all other cases, are not concerned with theoretical strangulation. We are concerned with human vital issues."

"Why in the name of Heaven those two people, for whose integrity one must have so much respect, why when a hint was given, why was it not taken?"

"I said, 'Did not the Police take you there?' They said, 'No'. You see it was rather important because of the three doctors on whose evidence the Crown relies."

"Firstly, the unfortunate Dr. Taylor who died before he could see the house, and Professor Peiris who would not or was not allowed to see it and Professor Paul. All of them say this: 'They did not exclude the possibility of strangulation against any hard object such as a wall.' How did their minds work?" asked Justice Gratiaen.

"Professor Paul tells us there was that bruise behind. It could have been caused against any hard object. It could not be the kitchen floor because there was no evidence of kitchen dirt on the back of this woman's garment, therefore we will take her upstairs and find a bedroom floor where she could have been strangled on the floor receiving no stains on the back of her saree!"

Analysing the bruise on the back of Mrs. Sathasivam further, Justice Gratiaen remarked, "You must remember another thing regarding that particular bruise, which was 4 and a 1/4 inches x 3 inches. Half that injury, with the external abrasion and with the top of the internal abrasion, was within the most protected area of the whole human body, between the shoulder blades. The other half was in the unprotected area above the shoulder blades, which seemed a remarkable phenomenon."

"All the doctors had to concede that both the protected and the unprotected halves were subjected to the identical reaction from the same abrading object."

"It was as if one of two things had happened. Professor Paul's theory was and so was Professor Peiris's inclined to be, that if the strangulation was on the floor, the way that whole injury could have been caused would have been if in some way or another, the protecting shoulder blades withdrew their protection so that the unprotected and previously protected areas were subjected to the same treatment by the external agency. That is one theory."

"In that view of the matter a theory had to be formed as to how that protection of the shoulder blades could have been withdrawn."

"The other view, of course, presents far fewer complications, but that does not mean that it does not require as much or more important consideration."

Justice Gratiaen explained that the other view was that the person was being put against some hard object, which was so situated, that being narrower than the width of the space between the shoulder blades, and it had applied its external pressure equally to the protected and unprotected areas.

"Sir Sydney Smith says that if you are only considering that agency, leaving out the soot on the foot and the drag marks, he could not exclude the floor, provided that you placed on the floor a suitable object like a brick, which would fit in between the shoulder blades, and extend to the unprotected area so that you will get the same degree of treatment and identical treatment of the area by that object, as one complete entity."

"Sir Sydney Smith tells us on oath, with a sense of responsibility, that he looked for and found 3 feet and 10 inches from the ground - we are dealing with a lady just over 4 feet 10 inches - just what fitted in perfectly. The only criticism of that, although you can get the internal abrasion, as he suggests, that you would naturally expect some different form of abrasion from those that were described by Professor de Saram."

"Sir Sydney Smith says no, that is what I would expect and it is perfectly consistent with the woman being pushed against that door-jamb and being manhandled and strangled as I think she was."

"Gentlemen, it would have been so helpful, would it not, if these doctors told us 'Now that we have seen the door-jamb we admit the internal injury but we are not quite convinced about the external injury.' I was agreeably astonished to find that in the course of Professor Peiris's evidence, I myself asked, in my layman's innocence, whether a projection sticking out of the wall would not possibly explain this injury."

"You see Professor Peiris was saying 'You could do it against an ordinary wall or you could do it against a door-jamb just as you do it against a wall, but I prefer the floor to a wall, because I would have expected a certain amount of plaster to come out, and I also would have been inclined to exclude a door-jamb for certain other technical reasons', and then I blundered into a particular question, and this is what I said."

"I said, 'Take the strangling from in front with either the right hand grip, as you suggest or the left hand grip as suggested by Dr. Taylor, if the strangler was unaidd, had no accessory, could injury number 10 have been caused, not by forcing the victim on to the ground, but by pushing the victim against some projection in the room where the strangling took place?' and his answer was 'Yes'."

"And I asked, 'Similarly by banging the head, could injury number 10 have been caused?' And his answer was, 'Yes, you will have to have a horizontal projection'."

'Well, in due course Sir Sydney Smith arrived and saw a projection. Now Professor Peiris thought about it. He had given an answer 'Yes' when I asked him on that occasion, but he was not so categorical when I asked him or one of us asked him the same question on another day."

Justice Gratiaen said the question was 'In answering me, with regard to those injuries on the back of Mrs. Sathasivam you did make this concession'."

"And then I quoted the question and the categorical answer 'Yes'. Then I said 'and similarly by banging the head, could injury number 10 have been caused? And your answer was 'Yes, you will have to have a horizontal projection'. I went on 'Now at that stage you perfectly frankly did concede an alternative possible explanation to injuries 11, 18 on the back and 10 on the side of the head. Do you still concede that possibility doctor?' "

"His answer was 'Yes, with one reservation only, that the multiple abrasions in injury number 18 are not explained'."

Question: "You mean they cannot be explained in that way?"

Answer: "They cannot."

Question: "Then should not your answer have been 'No' and not 'Yes'."

Answer: "I feel myself that the implication of those abrasions would exclude that."

Question: "Do you put it on a question of degrees of probability, or would you suggest that the alternative suggestion that injury number 18 was caused while the lady was on her feet is an impossibility?"

Answer: "Yes, impossible."

Justice Gratiaen remarked at this stage, "Gentlemen, taking half a minute as eternity, can it take an eternity to get from the categorical 'Yes' to the impossible?"

Justice Gratiaen said his next question was "In other words you cannot possibly visualize a woman who was being strangled on her feet receiving that external injury number 18 by coming in contact with any object in the room?"

Answer: "I will put it in another way which I think would answer Your Lordship's question fairly. If the strangler forced the victim against the wall and kept the victim there all the time you would have substantially the same conditions as on the floor. If the person was forced against the wall and that person was struggling to resist, you have substantially the same effect as struggling on the floor."

Question: "And that you concede as an equally reasonable explanation?"

Answer: "Yes, I considered that point before coming into Court. What one felt about that was that if you do that, you would have some marks, such as of the plaster, on the back, but it depends on the wall."

Justice Gratiaen remarked, "You see, gentlemen, it depends on the wall but you must never look at the wall."

Question: "Mr. Thiedeman did not take you there and show you the wall?"

Answer: "No."

"Gentlemen, would it be wrong to enquire whether the preference for the theory of the strangling on the floor does not involve an explaining away of the injuries, rather than as Professor Paul suggests, preferring the wall because of the injuries."

"His explanation, gentlemen, was that because it was a classic case of asphyxia there must have been a violent struggle wherever it took place. He then conceded, and then agreed quite logically that if there was a violent struggle, the shoulder blades which protect that area are raised by the woman trying her utmost to release the grip and to get up, tearing away at the hands and at the same time trying to lift herself."

" I then asked him whether if there was such a violent struggle by a woman trying to tear away the hands he would not expect some injuries on the hands and he said 'Yes, that is so'. He had conceded that there was some indication against a violent struggle. But he said, 'Well, leave out the struggle, you know there are always convulsions'."

"So that we came to convulsions. In the course of these convulsions which I understand are semi-purposive, he says that one's natural instinct would be to try to get up so that the particular area of 4 inches x 3 inches is exposed for the abrasion and the internal injury."

"Then we came to the question of what kind of floor it must have been. He said it could be explained by the clothes of this woman producing friction while she was being pushed up against a rough floor during strangulation – clothes and a rough floor. Then he was told that it was a smooth, well-polished floor with fine sand. Then he said, 'Did you say sand? Then sand is the abrading agency.' Those were his words. The clothes were unnecessary; it was the sand."

"On that point, what did Sir Sidney Smith say? He said, 'You cannot with fine sand explain that large bruise'. That is his explanation."

"Then with regard to these semi-purposive movements of a person trying to free herself, I remember I finally asked Professor Paul on this issue the following questions. I said, 'You have now more or less agreed that there could not have been a violent struggle but you say that there must have been semi-purposive movements of somebody trying to release herself?'"

He said, 'Yes'. I said, "Would you or would you not expect a semi-purposive reaction of a woman fighting semi-purposively for her life to clutch at the hands and at the face of the strangler nearest her, or would you say that she would rather semi-purposively bypass the strangler and get at the person who was holding the legs from behind?' and Professor Paul told me on the last date of his evidence, I remember his words, 'Your Lordship has started a new train of thought in my mind'. And so in that perplexed state, chasing this new train of thought, he left us with the permission of Court to attend the Coronation!"

"Gentlemen, with regard to those changes of opinion, in regard to that one particular issue, I have expressed more strongly than a presiding judge would normally do, my opinion of the theories of one particular doctor. He has, be it said to his eternal credit and most commendable frankness, changed his views and he had the honesty almost to show us how his mind was working. Now that is frankness to a degree which we would all commend, but how much happier all of us would be gentlemen, if one goes through all these intellectual conflicts before the case starts?"

"Heaven knows that I had no desire to start a new train of thought in Professor Paul's mind just as he was leaving the witness-box. Having pursued it, what does he think now? I do not know. So much for the projection except this, that Professor Peiris did say 'All I can say is that it was a hard object, not necessarily the floor. I cannot rule out strangling against a wall'. Well, are you convinced by that, in that particular department so to speak of the evidence, that there was a strangling against the floor, because both doctors told us this, that the external injury number 18 was in their opinion the most vital pointer to the floor as against the kitchen."

Continuing Justice Gratiaen said there was another bit of 'real evidence', which he would take the jury to.

"There was this controversy about a footprint on a mortar. Professor de Saram, rightly or wrongly, saw a mark that afternoon which struck him as a significant and important clue. He said, 'I saw a bare footprint with toes stretched out, particularly the big toe'. That is a fairly graphic account of something that he saw."

"Mr. Chanmugam saw it too! He says, 'It had the size and order of the outline of a footprint in light brown mud. When I saw it, it was clear'. Professor de Saram wanted it photographed. Mr. Thalaisingham, the footprint expert, who be it said in fairness to him gentlemen that in our country, most investigations in regard to footprints left by suspects are bare footprints, and finger prints where one looks for ridges and so on, said, he looked for ridges and found none."

"He put a chalk round it but he did not put his initials because he said 'If I put my initials a photograph is taken'. He says he did not see any ridges which were identifiable, which I think we will accept as correct, but he says in his opinion he could not say whether it was a footmark or a shoe-mark or a mark of either kind of foot at all."

"Now gentlemen, what a pity it was not photographed there and then. If Thiedeman is speaking the truth, Thalaisingham's final inspection was under electric light after 6 p.m. It was for the Police and not for Professor de Saram to decide, but he said, 'I saw it. To me it looked clearly the mark of a bare foot; particularly the big toe was stretched out'. It was photographed in due course – 11 days after."

Thalaisingham did not get it photographed. It went off to the Criminal Investigation Department (CID) Office and in due course some CID officer said, 'Well, let's photograph the thing for what it is worth', and we asked Mr. Thalaisingham whether he could give us any help now on this point and he said truthfully, 'It is not the same now'."

"It is because these marks are not the same 18 or 20 months later that one wants photographs taken at the time, as Professor de Saram gets Mr. Webster to take photographs to assist us in due course when the trial comes along," Justice Gratiaen said.

"Gentlemen, it is there left in the air. If it was a shoe, if some expert greater than Thalaisingham could have flown out and looked at the photograph showing something which is not the same now, he might have told us it was not a bare foot as Professor de Saram thought, in spite of the apparent stretching of the toes, particularly of the big toe, but that there was a clear heel mark of the shoe, shall we say a crepe sole, that would have been a point against Mr. Sathasivam."

"But if it was clearly in the eyes of a person looking at it under a microscope and if it was a foot mark left by a bare foot and some measurement could have been taken. And it was found that it was not Sathasivam's shod foot, but the heel or whatever part it was, corresponded satisfactorily to somebody else's foot mark, we would have been a lot happier, would we not have been, one way or the other? That is the difficulty, one of the difficulties which we have to face up to," remarked justice Gratiaen.

When the summing up resumed next day, on 25th June, Justice Gratiaen made a statement regarding a newspaper report.

"Mr. Solicitor, before I continue my charge, I think it is proper that I should state that a newspaper which I read this morning seems to have, possibly due to unsatisfactory acoustics, got a wrong impression of a comment I made yesterday."

"The newspaper report gives the impression that I had insinuated that the Attorney-General's Department was in some way responsible for the law's delays of which I complained. I think you will recall that what I did, in fact, say was precisely the opposite."

"I am very well aware of the difficult conditions under which everybody in the Attorney-General's Department is working. Nobody knows better than myself that the Attorney-General has done everything within his power, as the Judges have done, to remedy a state of affairs, which really can only be remedied through another source. I think it is fair I should state that."

Continuing the summing up, Justice Gratiaen said, "Gentlemen, I was discussing with you last evening some aspects of the 'real evidence' which should give you some assistance in your deliberations. I think I was touching on the controversy regarding the mark on the mortar. Before I go on to another item of 'real evidence' it is necessary that I should remind you, as the Solicitor-General has already pointed out, that the impression gained by Mr. Chanmugam, who himself claimed to have seen something resembling a mark left by a bare foot, was that there was a light brown mud impression on the mortar."

"Well, obviously if that mud had itself been placed there by either a shoe or a foot, one would imagine that that would rather tend to exclude a foot print made either by a man's shoe or by his bare foot. On the other hand, if the light brown mud was already there and a foot or a shoe was stamped upon it, different considerations would arise. Well, as a result of the failure to take a photograph, as requested by Professor de Saram, at the proper time, leaves you and me in no position to judge one way or the other. That is, as I have said, another unhappy feature, even though perhaps not a particularly important feature in this case. So that we shall just remember that and pass on."

"Perhaps a controversy of some kind can be conducted between Professor de Saram and Mr. Thalaisingham and Mr. Chanmugam and they can decide whether it was some other impression. You will remember people claimed to have seen the foot prints of a snow-man up Mount Everest!"

"There is also another piece of evidence which Sir Sydney Smith invites you to pay special regard to. That is the pearl under the rocking-horse. You will remember, about 12 days after the tragedy, the Police found under the rocking-horse, a few feet a way from the head, in fact on the left side of the head of where Mrs. Sathasivam's corpse was, a pearl, which had been dislodged from the ear-ring which the photograph shows on her left ear."

"Professor de Saram also claims, and states positively, both on oath in the witness box and in his post-mortem report, that there was, apart from the circumstance that clearly some external object had slightly bent the ear-ring itself, so as to loosen the pearl, and there was an ante-mortem abrasion on her left ear. Now, the first question is, 'Was it an ante-mortem injury or not?' The Crown it was, that arranged that Professor de Saram, whose competence is well acknowledged, should conduct the post-mortem examination."

"Mr. Sathasivam was not at all consulted in the matter and he had no power to appoint anybody else to carry out that work. Well, it therefore is a matter, which the Crown is in a sense, bound by as far as any question of fact spoken to by Professor de Saram is concerned. But I agree that the question whether a particular injury is a post-mortem injury or an ante-mortem injury is what one might call, a mixed question of fact and opinion."

"The Crown does not accept any opinion expressed by Professor de Saram, except those, of course, which suit the Crown. That is perfectly proper and legitimate. But Sir Sydney Smith says that, although Professor Paul expressed doubt as to what kind of an injury it was, and even though Professor Peiris conceded that it is not for him to question the finding of a competent pathologist like Professor de Saram, it would be quite impertinent for him, or anybody else, to take the view that it could have been possibly a post-mortem injury."

"As it happened, it is rather an important issue. You will remember that I gave permission to the Crown to cross-examine Professor de Saram on any question relating to opinion."

"Professor Paul had said, 'I am not convinced, but on the other hand, I know Professor de Saram. I have respect for the quality of his work but I would not accept his bare statement on that point unless I know the reasons'. It is quite true that in a well known text book written by Professor Keith Simpson, who is the Consultant Pathologist in Scotland Yard, there is a passage in which the author says that in the case of some injuries, not all, which were inflicted, as this particular injury was inflicted, very shortly before death, it may be impossible, not it is impossible, to decide one way or the other whether the injury was inflicted before or after death. He does not say that it was always impossible."

"Well, all I can say on that issue is that Professor de Saram was cross-examined by the Crown and, subject to correction by the Crown lawyers, not one single question was put to him in cross-examination for the purpose of testing the validity of his opinion with regard to that particular injury."

"What follows then? Obviously there is no evidence that it was a post-mortem injury, and there is the unchallenged evidence, as far as the cross-examination goes, of a competent pathologist that it was not. I do not see, gentlemen, therefore how, as judges of fact, you can take any other view than that Professor de Saram must be presumed to be correct."

"Now, let me explain the importance of that issue. You see, if there is any blow which caused an injury on Mrs. Sathasivam's ear before death, and also damaged the ear-ring at the same time, one would naturally expect that the pearl, which was loosened, was dislodged somewhere near the spot where the injury was caused."

"The pearl was found, as a result of somewhat delayed diligence of the investigators, two feet or so from the left ear where the ear-ring was damaged, prima facie therefore, one would expect that ante-mortem injury to have been caused in the garage," said Justice Gratiaen.

"The important part on that point is this. Every doctor called by either side has told you that one thing is certain. If in fact Mrs. Sathasivam was strangled upstairs in the bedroom, she was dead, in the fullest sense of the term, by the time she was dumped in the garage. In that event, prima facie one would expect the pearl to have fallen off where the ante-mortem injury was caused, namely, upstairs."

"Sir Sydney Smith therefore expresses his opinion that, apart from the tell-tale injury, as he would describe it, on the back of the woman, which, in his submission, strongly point to a strangling in the kitchen, there is also the circumstance that the pearl was found after the ante-mortem injury was caused in the garage, because all the doctors also agreed that if the strangling took place as suggested by Sir Sydney Smith, I wish to leave Professor de Saram's opinions out as far as possible, if it can be so avoided, and I shall tell you why, then, according to that theory, Mrs. Sathasivam could well have been still alive, breathing her last, 'vital' in the medical sense of the term, when she was carried across to the garage and put down where she was found."

"Gentlemen, there is only one counter suggestion which the Crown can offer to meet that position," said Justice Gratiaen.

"They suggest that it is possible, and I do not think they can hope to suggest that it is certain, that if the woman was strangled upstairs, which was the only place where she could have sustained any injury before death, then with Mr. Sathasivam carrying her head and shoulders and William carrying her feet, one should imagine by accident, but the suspicious Crown say by design because it was a planned murder, he may well have had his left shoulder protecting the loosened pearl which remained so protected and in fact all the way it was jolted down the staircase, carried through the dining room, through the two kitchens, taken down and then placed there."

"And indeed, to complete that suggested alternate theory, it remained there until a mortar had been placed across in a position which no one has been able to help us about. It was suggested that as the mortar was placed so as to come across her left ear, the pearl, which had been already loosened might have been dislodged. Well, there was a demonstration, which Sir Sydney Smith was asked to consider. He said he for one rejected that theory."

"But he said, 'Well, if it survived the jolting downstairs when the mortar was removed by Podihamy, it is just possible it rolled off then.' It is for you to use your common sense, assuming that it is an ante-mortem injury or whether Dr. Sydney Smith's theory is more acceptable."

Justice Gratiaen said that Dr. Colvin R. de Silva has also asked the jury to pay some consideration to the fact that if the mortar was placed in such a position as would protect the loosened pearl until Podihamy took it away, that it is unlikely that Podihamy would have carried this enormous mortar across the body and placed it on the other side of the body.

"That is a point that you are as capable of judging as anybody else."

"Now we come to another item of 'real evidence', namely the urine stains on the petticoat. We have been told by everyone that an unfortunate victim of manual strangulation almost invariably is in addition, during the final stages before her death, the victim of an involuntary act of urination."

"It is really a matter for the exercise of common sense, rather than of the advice of experts like all these doctors, to visualize what would be the normal passage of urine, if Mrs. Sathasivam was lying flat on her back, as opposed to the position if during that final act just before she died she urinated while on her feet, while the strangler had her against the wall."

"The description of the stains have been given to you by Mr. Chanmugam, the Government Analyst. He says, there were extensive stains both behind and in front, and he says there was a particularly large patch behind which was tapering down to within three inches of the hem of the garment."

"Counsel for the defence held it out and gave a somewhat graphic description of that particular stain as resembling the map of South America! Use your common sense and ask yourselves, whether an act of urination with Mrs. Sathasivam lying flat on her back, could produce anything resembling the map of South America down to within three inches of the hem of the garment. There were also patches in front."

"That particularly large patch behind was 30 inches long. We have to consider the opinion of Mr. Chanmugam himself, whether he gave it as a technical man or as a man of ordinary common sense, he tells us that those patches were different patches to what one would expect to find if Mrs. Sathasivam was urinating while she lay on the ground."

"He also said categorically that on the other hand, those patches, which he examined, were consistent with an act of urination by the victim while she was standing up. This is a matter for you to decide."

"The Crown, gentlemen, relies on the discovery of the mirror in the garage. The Crown invites you as men of common sense to draw from that item of circumstantial evidence the necessary inference, that it had been taken there by the strangler for the purpose of satisfying himself that Mrs. Sathasivam was in fact dead; that he presumably went upstairs and brought it down and held it to see if she was still breathing."

"Having done that, mark you, after having strangled her so effectively as the doctors all admit, having stamped with the shod foot on her neck, and then having dumped her in the garage, and then having placed the mortar which somebody saw Mr. Sathasivam pick up before the mirror was brought on the scene, he still had, what lawyers call, a reasonable doubt as to whether she was alive or not. So with the mortar across her neck he went upstairs and brought the mirror down and left it there."

"There again, it is entirely for you to judge whether you as men of common sense would find yourselves impelled to accept that theory as a necessary inference, not the possible inference, because a possible inference from circumstantial evidence is not a necessary inference."

"It would certainly have been a nice little point to have been taken by Counsel appearing for the defence of William fighting for his life. It is for you to decide whether it is as effective an argument coming from the Crown claiming to establish the guilt of someone other than William beyond reasonable doubt," commented Justice Gratiaen.

"We do know this, that Podihamy told Thiedeman, though she denies it now, that this was the particular mirror which the little children were in the habit of playing about with. Well, of course, she said 'Never downstairs'. Well, when the laundryman arrived, they were playing very naturally downstairs. You see, their mother was not there to stop them. She was dead and the mirror was in the garage. Can one conclude anything either way? You must decide that matter for yourselves."

"I think it might be convenient now if you consider the effect of Mr. Sathasivam's version in regard to this whole matter as stated in his deposition given on oath, tested by cross-examination by William's counsel, tested by cross-examination by the Legal Adviser attached to the Police Department."

"There is a little difference between our procedure in certain matters and the English procedure. In England, the position is that a policeman when he arrests a man with the intention of charging him with the commission of any crime, cautions him and says, 'You are not bound to say anything to me now. This is the charge for which I am arresting you. If you wish to say anything it will be taken down and it may be given in evidence at your trial.' In England, they do not say 'It may be given in evidence against you.' The words 'against you' are deliberately omitted, because there is in England an invitation to a man arrested on the suspicion that he has committed a grave crime, to tell his version there and then at the first opportunity, and invariably according to the great traditions of British justice that statement made voluntarily after caution, is invariably placed in evidence before the jury, whether the statement is favourable to the accused or not."

"Well, late in the 19th century our Evidence Ordinance was enacted as a code. It was brought over, copied practically verbatim from India where it had been taken over embodying substantially the English rules of evidence, but with certain marked and important differences."

"There was a suspicion in those days that Asiatic policemen could not be trusted to record confessional statements from accused persons. So any confessional statement is absolutely prohibited as an item of evidence in a case against an accused person. I believe the theory was, I don't know whether it was based on temperature or on national characteristics, that the policeman of those days would otherwise be tempted as someone said to rub chillies into an accused person's eyes and extract a statement and go about in the heat of the sun looking for evidence."

"However, the stigma still remains, and we know now that there are suspicions and counter suspicions in high circles still about the Police Officer. However, we have not got such a procedure, as I understand it. So that when Mr. Sathasivam was arrested, whatever he said voluntarily or otherwise to a Police Officer certainly in his favour could not be placed before you, but if he later gave evidence on oath any contradictions, any discrepancies, between what he said to a

Court of law and what he had previously said to a Police Officer could be placed against him for the purpose of discrediting him."

"So that the first opportunity which an accused man has in our country to say what he has to say in order that it might be placed before the jury, is in the Magistrate's Court itself."

"After the evidence for the prosecution has been led the accused is told, 'Do you want to say anything? Anything you say will be taken down in writing and led in evidence at your trial against you'. He is also told in so many words, 'You can make a statutory statement from the witness box, but if you make a statutory statement from the dock you will be in the happy position of not being subjected to cross-examination, but any statement which you make on oath will be tested by cross-examination.' Then there is another section of our code, as I understand it, in accordance with my ruling, which says that any statement, which a man makes at that stage in the Magistrate's Court, whether sworn or unsworn, shall be placed before the jury at the trial."

"That is how Mr. Sathasivam's deposition given on oath, his own version of what he knew of this unhappy affair, together with all the answers he made in cross-examination and in answer to questions in two cross-examinations are all before you."

"They are not part of the case for the Crown," emphasized Justice Gratiaen.

"The Crown is not bound by that, but it is evidence according to the English Ordinance when it comes before you, and according to my conception of law it must come before you, and it is evidence both for the prisoner and against the prisoner as any other evidence."

"But, of course, it is a matter for you to decide what weight is to be given to the whole statement or parts of the statement. You know Mr. Sathasivam's statement. Every part of it, on which the Defence relies, has been read to you by Dr. de Silva. The parts on which the Crown relies as evidence against him, have been placed before you by the Crown."

"Consider shortly what is the effect of that statement if true. He starts by admitting categorically and unambiguously that he was in the house till 10.30. That is a strong admission, if it fits in with some other acceptable portion of the case for the Crown, which he has voluntarily made, but he proceeds to say 'But Mrs. Sathasivam was alive; I saw her alive and I never went back to that house again'. That, if it carries any weight with you, is a point in his favour. So in a sense he relied on an alibi."

"Now, gentlemen, if a man at the end of a trial suddenly decides to give evidence of an alibi in his own favour, judges warn juries that, that evidence so belatedly given is evidence which they must view with suspicion for an obvious reason, because that statement of an alibi, such as 'I did not commit this crime. I was in Jaffna at the time' is given at a time when the Police with all their machinery have no opportunity of testing beforehand," explained Justice Gratiaen.

"Now here be it said to his credit that true or false, Mr. Sathasivam at the very first opportunity did in fact say what was the root of his case and he persisted in it true or false. Anything that he said which was found to be false was said at a time when the Prosecution had the fairest opportunity, after further investigations, to disapprove it."

"So that is a point in his favour. Please also remember this, not as evidence of the truth of what he said, but as evidence of his conduct, evidence at least, true or false, from which he never swerved. He never swerved from one line of defence."

"When he was arrested on the lawn of his friend Haniffa on the evening of the murder - the precise time is not known - but for the present purpose it is quite sufficient for me to tell you that as soon as he was arrested on the evening of the murder, he immediately or within a few minutes, protesting or pretending his innocence is another matter, said to Mr. Nadarajah in the presence of two Police Officers – suspect or not, but certainly not co-conspirators, that is clear – 'I do not know what all this is about, she was alive when I went out of the house this morning'. Mr Nadarajah took the opportunity of exercising his gifts as a cross-examiner in the presence of the Police."

"Possibly his cross-examination was so effective that for some time very soon afterwards he was retained as Counsel for the defence!"

"He said, 'You know you have not got a motor car. How did you go?' Mr. Sathasivam said 'I went in a 'Quickshaws'. Mr. Nadarajah, another helpful investigator, turned to the Police Officers and said,

'You can check up on that. Find out if he is speaking the truth'. Now they do check up, and not a particularly bright Inspector but an honest one, thank God, was sent by Attygalle who was attending to all the other investigations to find out from the 'Quickshaws' Department whether in fact there was a 'Quickshaws' cab which had taken Sathasivam from St. Alban's Place, and if so at what time."

"Then we know what happened. There was the checking of the records, the note of a '10.30 booking'; then they looked at another record and found out the name of the 'Quickshaws' driver and then M.L.A. Perera goes on. He was just accounting for all his collections of the day and he was immediately told, 'Come with us to St. Alban's Place'. Well, Perera's evidence is another point. That is something, which cannot be left out as a point in favour of Mr. Sathasivam that there and then he made a statement, which still represents his defence."

Justice Gratiaen observed, "The principles of criminal law are so much concerned to see that the prosecution proves its case and that the accused does not have the obligation of disproving it, that the attitude has always been that an accused, without giving evidence on oath and without – unless he wishes to – making an unsworn statement, which is of less value, while he remains in the dock protected from cross-examination."

Justice Gratiaen said that the accused is entitled to sit back and say, 'I am not guilty. Prove my guilt.'

"One knows on the other hand, that human beings serving on a jury are never happy unless they know what the accused has to say about it. But our law in its wisdom has expressly prohibited the prosecution from ever inviting a jury to draw adverse inference against an accused, on the ground that he did not give evidence."

"A judge, for some reason, presumed to be wiser, may in certain special circumstances comment on it," said Justice Gratiaen.

"Gentlemen, fortunately I have got before me the guidance of a very recent judgment of the Privy Council on that very point. A Judge in Jamaica who presided at a murder trial had commented on the fact strongly: 'If the accused was innocent, why did he not face the ordeal of being cross-examined on oath as to his version?' Now there too the evidence presented to the jury was that as soon as the man was arrested — their law is different to ours and their policemen are less suspect than ours - he said 'This is what happened and then his friends and relations came and asked him what he had to say for himself and he said, this is what happened' and it is in evidence, not on oath, that from the beginning to the end he persisted in the same defence which he had disclosed to the prosecution and to other members of the public."

"And the Judge presiding at the trial said to the jury, 'Well, that is all very well, but if he was innocent why did he not give evidence?' Mark you gentlemen, whether the same judge would have said it in a country where it apparently takes nearly two years to bring a man to trial I very much doubt. For 20 long months, a man is in the special agony of a lonely incarceration waiting for his trial on a count of murder."

"Be that as it may — in Jamaica trials take a very much shorter time — the Privy Council quashed the conviction because the Judge had unjustly criticized the accused for not getting into the witness-box."

"This is what Lord Oakney said with regard to the matter. 'In such a state of the evidence, namely, that the accused had given his version from the very commencement and persisted in it throughout, the Judge's repeated comments on the failure of the accused to give evidence, may well have led the jury to think that no innocent man could have taken such a course. The question whether a prisoner is to be called as a witness in such circumstances and on a murder charge is always one of the greatest anxieties for the prisoner's legal advisers. But in the present case, their Lordships think that the prisoner's counsel was fully justified in not calling the prisoner'."

"Gentlemen, if those words were appropriate to a case where a man had made merely an unsworn statement to the Police at the time of his arrest, how much more do they apply in the case of a man who has not only made the statement at the commencement, but at the very first opportunity he had of giving version to a Court of law, he did so on oath, rejecting the more agreeable alternative of saying without being cross-examined, without the oath, what his version was while he stood in the dock. That does not mean, gentlemen, that what he said is true. You must test it like any other evidence, but it is a point which you will pay due regard to."

"Now there is one particular comment – a criticism which was made against Mr. Sathasivam which you must certainly pay consideration to. It is the case for the Crown that Sathasivam with the sure and certain knowledge of his own guilt, went about the town with his drinking companions, pretending to behave as a normal man – well we know that his behaviour is consistent the other way equally – his continuing to drink as he always does with the same old companions."

"But was it all play-act? It is common ground that after they had drunk sufficient for the morning and afternoon, and before starting drinking again at the club that evening, they went home to Haniffa's. While Haniffa attended to the best of his ability in his capacity at the time to some business affairs of some urgency, Sathasivam went to bed and he was asleep."

"He says it was the sleep of the just and innocent. They say it was the sleep of a guilty man with so callous a nature, with even knowledge of the guilt of that horrid transaction and the certain knowledge that as he had not decided like William, his accessory, to run away and escape from arrest, he stayed in his address, at the proper address perhaps to which he had gone to receive the summons."

"One thing is strange," Justice Gratiaen said. "Of course, we do not know ourselves how people behave after committing a murder. On the other hand, different people behave differently, but I suppose it certainly must be a great advantage to a man that in such a state of guilty knowledge he can nevertheless, when there is the opportunity of sleep, he can take his mind away from his guilt and sleep. It is like the British Prime Minister, apparently who when he has got half an hour he sleeps. Well Mr. Sathasivam slept soundly until he was roused by Haniffa, with the information that there was a telephone call."

"Now we come to a controversial matter. At least, it has not been very fully probed. Mr. Sathasivam said that as far as he was concerned, he was first roused with the information that his mother wanted him and then he says the telephone conversation was about some matter quite unconnected with the death."

"Then he says he returned to his bed and slept again when Haniffa woke him up a second time and said that somebody else wanted him. That somebody else we know is Mr. Ramanathan, who says – and everybody gives his own impression as to time – that he had heard some news that Mrs. Sathasivam was dead and he knew where Sathasivam was to be found, so he rang up Haniffa."

"He put a few questions to Sathasivam as to whether she was ill or not – words to that effect. Eventually Sathasivam says, 'I rang my home and I told this man, you come to St. Alban's Place and pick me up there. We will go on from there to the Tamil Union Club.' All brilliant play-acting by a man, who knew that his wife was dead in the garage."

"He said he rang upstairs where his wife's telephone was and there was no reply. So he said 'I rang downstairs and a lady answered the phone' and we are told now she was Mrs. K.C. Nadarajah. And then we are told she called her husband up."

"Then you have got the rest of the story from lips of Mr. K.C. Nadarajah. Further play-acting says the Crown. 'I am K.C. Nadarajah.' Sathasivam said, 'What the devil are you doing in my house? I am coming there now.' K.C. Nadarajah replied, "Don't be a fool. I will come there,' and then the Policemen went with Nadarajah and arrested him," Justice Gratiaen said.

"One little point strikes me gentlemen - whether it is true or not - that K.C. Nadarajah was able to use the telephone, which earlier was padlocked according to Mr. Thiedeman and Mrs. Foenander."

"On the vital question as to whether it is true that Mr. Sathasivam rang downstairs to his mother's telephone and received a reply, it would not be proper at all for you to take the view that that cannot be true because of the padlocked telephone."

"I will tell you why. Mr. Sathasivam's mother's telephone was not disconnected till the 20th of October. She had inserted a padlock on the 8th of October to prevent dialling and trying to get somebody else on the phone when you are away."

"Try it yourselves. You can padlock your telephone to prevent the servant or anybody else talking to their friends, but as long as the department has not disconnected the line, you can receive every telephone call, which somebody else chooses to make. That is the point."

"Haniffa, - after many further months of leading a life, which as far as we know has not altered - he gave evidence 16 or 18 months after the incident, and he tells us on oath, whereas the accused seated in the Magistrate's Court, that he did receive one telephone call from his mother, and a later one from Ramanathan, that it was after the mother's call that Mr. Sathasivam said, 'A terrible thing has happened. My wife is dead,' and therefore says the prosecution, if it is true, that is a legitimate criticism, why was he dawdling all that time, if he heard from his own mother's lips that his wife was dead?"

"The Crown points out that Mr. Sathasivam's mother had, according to the recollection of the step-brother K. Sathasivam, received the information shortly after 3 o'clock. Pathmanathan says that he received the news shortly after 3 o'clock."

"Gentlemen, those people were giving their impressions as to time. Mrs. Foenander, who was the first person to telephone anyone about this tragedy when she contacted the Bambalapitiya Police, had telephoned the Police at 3.15 – that is the only fixed time – Pathmanathan corrected himself and he ultimately conceded that as his wife telephoned him some time afterwards – when, we do not know precisely."

"The eldest daughter presumably had time to get over her distress sufficiently to ring up her grandmother and her aunt Mrs. Pathmanathan. Mrs. Pathmanathan rang up Pathmanathan her husband in the Fort. Pathmanathan says that, it normally takes him 10 minutes to come to his own home. Then he picked up his wife and it took another 5 minutes to get to this house of death."

"He then says, as one would expect, that they were all very excited and so on. Then he says, that it was half an hour later that he phoned Mr. K. Sathasivam - so many minutes after 3.15 - (10 minutes to come to his house, 5 minutes to come to No. 7, St. Alban's Place, and half an hour his estimate of the time that elapsed between his arrival at No. 7 and his telephoning Mr. K. Sathasivam). Therefore, it could not have been till 4.15 that he rang up Mr. K. Sathasivam. And Mr.

K. Sathasivam, what did he do when he heard this terrible news? He rang up his sister, and the sister came immediately after him in a motor car and then they went to No. 7, St. Alban's Place."

"Is it, in a criminal case, safe therefore to presume that Haniffa's later recollection is right, that it was the mother who gave the news, when we find that Haniffa himself, when he was making a statement that very night to Thiedeman, had said, as Sathasivam says, that it was Ramanathan who actually telephoned and gave the news that Mrs. Sathasivam was dead?"

"He admits, 'Well, I have forgotten. It really made no special impression on me. What I have said earlier must be the truth and I accept'. Is Haniffa's recollection, after the innumerable drinks which he must have had during these 18 months, sufficiently reliable to draw an adverse inference against Mr. Sathasivam?" Justice Gratiaen asked the jury.

"I think it will now be the time for me to take on, as shortly as is proper, the medical evidence concentrating on the real controversies between the Prosecution and the Defence, leaving out, so far as decency permits, any, if I may use the term, domestic controversies between the Crown and the Government Pathologist, or the Consultant Pathologist, in regard to matters with which the Defence is not concerned."

"You see, it is my great desire that, whatever happens at the end of this case, some public officers at least will be able to say, 'My reputation was unscathed in the Sathasivam case'. If it has to be attacked, certainly it had to be attacked."

"Whether or not this doctor was right in saying that he likes to use the eye test as a rough guide for estimating the time of death, and which he did not put forward before, whether or not he was justified in suggesting that you could not exclude the possibility that Mrs. Sathasivam had nutritional anaemia which, it is suggested, is a monstrous suggestion to make without removing the marrow from this already mutilated corpse and carrying out certain other tests, whether or not Professor de Saram was right in various other matters, let us stick to the main medical controversies in the case."

"On questions of fact, regarding the condition of the body,

regarding the injuries sustained by her, regarding the injuries found on William, regarding the very important absence of any injuries on Mr. Sathasivam, on all those matters, Professor de Saram's evidence has been unchallenged, uncontradicted."

"Nobody else can dare to contradict; nobody had the opportunity of seeing what he saw before that little woman was buried. Professor de Saram is a distinguished pathologist who, no one will dispute, enjoyed, until the Sathasivam case, the completest confidence of the Crown, lawyers, defence lawyers and Judges on all matters concerned with Forensic Medicine."

"More than one man has gone to the gallows justly on the unchallengeable evidence of Professor de Saram who, after Dr. Sinnadurai died, was appointed as Judicial Medical Officer of Ceylon, having first been sent out for special qualifications in a branch of medicine in which he had previously taken a special interest. He was sent as a pupil under Sir Sydney Smith. He was sent for a long course in Egypt to an institution, which had been established by Dr. Sydney Smith. He had worked under Kieth Simpson, the author of that famous book."

"Why was he sent to Egypt in particular? Because, you know, the summer of Egypt, according to Sir Sydney Smith, is very much like all our hot months in Ceylon, but that does not mean that Professor de Saram's opinion, or as a matter of that of any other doctor, is infallible on that point. We must agree on all matters of opinion expressed by these distinguished doctors. It is the reasons given, tested and then further cross-examined by us that really count," said Justice Gratiaen.

"Then we have doctors Paul and Peiris. Those two doctors are two most eminent surgeons. On matters within their special spheres their views no one will challenge. On other matters, too, one must assume that any views they express are responsible views."

"Then we have the distinguished Dr. Taylor who gave evidence in the Magistrate's Court and unhappily died and we have his deposition. We have Dr. Welikala, who at least stuck to his special province and resisted every temptation, even the particularly attractive ways of Dr. de Silva as a cross-examiner, who said, 'Can't you tell us even a little of the alimentary canal? and he said, 'Oh, no, I have nothing to do with the alimentary canal!'. A man who can resist a man like Dr. de Silva is worthy of special regard."

"Then we had the distinguished Sir Sydney Smith, an acknowledged world figure, in the field of Forensic Medicine. In regard to all these gentlemen, their professional skill and their integrity no one can dispute, no one should dispute and I hope no one does dispute. In some matters some of them enjoy advantages, which others lack. Professor de Saram in this instance has a special advantage which we hope he has not abused, of having seen the corpse and having seen the house where the murder occurred."

"Sir Sydney Smith shares the advantage of having seen the house, but neither he nor the other doctors had the initial advantage of having seen the corpse. Some of the disadvantages were of their own seeking. With regard to the cause of death, it is essential that we should realize that everybody agrees that this was a classic case of manual strangulation, which nobody can deny."

"Let us refuse to get involved in this subsidiary controversy whether something called a 'carotid sinus' operated or not. Apparently, there is some particularly sensitive part in the neck where if a person suddenly received pressure there he could die without there being a struggle at all. Nobody suggests, and it would be quite improper for Professor de Saram to suggest, that Mrs. Sathasivam died of anything other than manual strangulation."

"The question of the operation of the 'carotid sinus' has only slight relevancy as to whether death supervened as a result of the operation of the 'carotid sinus' supervening at an earlier stage or not. It has some slight relevancy to the question as to whether Mrs. Sathasivam at any probable time, even if she had the strength or the capacity to do so, put up any kind of struggle sufficiently violent to result in her temperature going up. That is all that matters, and we will deal with that when we come to that question."

"I have discussed with you quite fully already the controversy as to whether strangulation took place against the upstair floor or against the kitchen wall. On that point the Defence relies on the stains, the back injury, the dark marks, the position in which the pearl was found and various other matters."

"The Crown relies on the opinions of Professors Paul and Peiris and of Dr. Taylor. I have pointed out that the Crown, having regard to the cumulative effect of their evidence cannot, as I see it, but you must judge, exclude the possibility of strangulation against any hard object such as a wall."

"Whether the Crown can claim to exclude strangling against a wall, which had in addition a particular projection which only Professor Smith saw, we really do not know, because we have not had the benefit of a single witness for the Crown who did see that particular projection. They do admit that there may be some kind of projection sticking out of some kind of wall, which may explain the injury. Professor Paul said that it depends on the wall, which he had not seen, and the kind of projection, which he had not seen."

"The back injury is the main plank on which both sides take their places. As to whether she was lying or standing up when she was strangled, it is common ground that there was no brick on the floor, which in Sir Sydney Smith's opinion is the only kind of object to cause the back injury, which would be consistent with strangling on the floor."

"Then there is the controversy with regard to this extensive head injury, leaving no external mark but a deep bruise underneath, a very long deep bruise."

"Now let us examine the opinion of the Crown experts with regard to that injury. Both of them expressed this opinion in the Magistrate's Court, that it may have been caused by the head being banged on the floor, but the theory of the bed nobody had heard."

Justice Gratiaen reminded the jury that when William gave evidence, he said that Mrs. Sathasivam was flung away from the bed and put on the floor.

Continuing he said, "Professors Paul and Peiris at that point of time had been the victims of unexpressed unhappiness regarding the sworn explanation given to the Magistrate, evidence which, please note, is very important for the purpose of deciding whether one man or two men should be placed on trial in connection with the charge of murder."

"While they were never very happy about it, and were all discussing it, they heard that a bed had had something to do with the events immediately preceding the strangling.

And Professor Paul told his friend Professor Peiris, 'You know it might be that bed.' I have no doubt, gentlemen, that was his honest opinion, but Professor Peiris was skeptical."

"He said, 'Well, it may be the bed; well you really can't be sure about these matters.' That was one of the points of controversy between the two doctors."

"According to one of them, when they came together there was an interesting debate about whether some injury could have been caused by a bed which neither had seen."

"Then they gave their evidence, first Professor Paul. He said, 'I am sure it was bed. William has confirmed me on that.' Very good."

"He then under cross-examination did admit one little difficulty in his mind. He said, 'You now tell me that according to William, Mr. Sathasivam caught the woman's neck with the right hand, gripped her hair with the left hand and flung her across like this and brought her down heavily on the floor.' He said, 'There is one difficulty there which we must face up to. If William's story is true I really find it very difficult to understand how the back of Sathasivam's hand could have avoided some little injury at least as a result of contact with the foot of the bed and further, as a result of contact with the floor when it came down'. He was worried about that and when a doctor expresses difficulty we should be grateful to him."

"So that with regard to this injury, which he admitted could have been caused by contact with some hard object as he had sworn in the lower court, he left the witness box rather thinking that Professor Peiris had won the first round of their earlier debate."

"Professor Peiris then gave evidence. He had previously doubted the bed, and he said, 'Do you know I have come to the conclusion, having seen the bed, that really the first round was won by Professor Paul.' Gentlemen, if that was right, I really must claim a little credit for strengthening and confirming in Peiris's mind the theory, which Paul had expressed but later doubted."

Justice Gratiaen said that these surgeons were on a high theoretical plain and they rejected his hints that they should go and look at what were the geographical features of the house.

"Ultimately, when we really came to the question of the bed, one of the doctors who refused to go to St. Alban's Place was compelled by me to look at the bed here. He would not go to St. Alban's Place, so I brought the bed here for them. That is the only thing, of all the objects in this unfortunate house of death, which either of these surgeons had seen."

"Peiris looked at the bed. He said, 'It fits perfectly. Let me measure it,' and it fitted perfectly. He said, 'Even though Paul thinks there must be injuries on the back of the strangler's hands if William's story is true, I do not see any such necessity at all.' So there is still a little unresolved conflict between them each fighting from the other's end of the ring."

"Now, what is Sir Sydney Smith's submission on this point? Mark you, neither of the doctors excluded the possibility that it might have been either that piece of firewood or some piece of firewood like it that was brought down flat across the right side of that unfortunate woman's head and produced this injury, but they said, this particular piece of firewood is rough and they would have expected an abrasion and there is no abrasion."

"That is a difficulty which must be faced up to. Sir Sydney Smith tells you that in his opinion the whole matter is somewhat inconclusive. He really does not know. You will remember that his opinion is that when you get these strangling cases, it is really quite impossible for any skilled professional man to explain every injury, which has been caused in the course of such a transaction."

"He said the head could have come down flat on the side of a kitchen table. If there was a bed, it could have come against the bed. The injury could have been caused by a piece of firewood, and he does say this about the abrasion, 'I nevertheless agree that unless the whole of that part where the injury was, was covered by hair, and covered by hair does not mean growing hair but it also includes the arrangement of the hair, there would have been an abrasion'. Well we have seen these pictures."

Justice Gratiaen at this stage requested the jury to look at the photograph of the face of Mrs. Sathasivam and said, "If the injury was on the left side of the head, a little bit near the eye does not have any hair covering. But I challenge any one of you to show me one part of the right side of the head, which sustained the injury which is not covered by hair."

"But there is a more important matter and that is this. In the opinion of Sir Sydney Smith, which you must not completely disregard, because he is an eminent man, he says the same objection in regard to the abrasion, also applies to the edge of the bed, as it would to a piece of firewood."

"You know, it was a pity perhaps that when that bed was brought here, I did not give Professor Peiris a complete picture of the only object which he has ever seen, because the mattress was not brought and when one sees a bed without a mattress, even the foot of the bed seems pretty high."

"But if the mattress was on, and the woman's head was brought down, the top of that ledge would not have been sticking so high up."

Referring to a photograph of the bed, Justice Gratiaen said that there seems to be only a few inches of the foot of the bed projecting above the mattress.

"Now, try and visualise for yourselves a strangler getting the grip described by William, bringing that woman down to the floor in such a way that the head comes down just on that tiny bit of projection, which we find at the foot of that bed."

"Anyone is competent to work it out for himself, but I do respectfully suggest this, that if one could bring that woman's head down to that precise projection she would be lying practically flat on that bed and about which Sir Sydney Smith says, 'Why bother about the floor? Why soil your beautiful pair of flannel trousers? Here is a perfect bed for strangling the woman. You have got her down, why not strangle her if that is your plan?'"

"Now gentlemen, we come to the controversy about the stamping of the foot causing a deep-seated injury below the throat, external abrasions, more or less parallel lines, above that area, the little bruise underneath the jaw, some part of it with black material which Sir

Sidney says it is a pity that was not analysed, but one will assure that that was some sort of dirt from the floor with a bit of coconut fluff adhering to it, so much so that Professor de Saram had to use his nails to pinch it out."

"You got an idea of those two marks in this photograph yourselves. You see the dark substance under the chin and you see the dark substance over the chin. Now everybody had his own theories originally as to how those injuries were caused."

"But when William became a pardoned witness he talked about the stamping of a foot. But he was in the best position to know. It is not the kind of thing which an eye-witness would introduce if it had not happened in that way."

"An accomplice, if really a guilty man himself or a comparatively innocent man, so he says he was, would naturally tend to describe substantially what happened in regard to graphic incidents of that nature, but with the tendency perhaps – that is another matter for you to consider – to substitute somebody else's foot for his own."

"Well, as I see it, Paul, Peiris and Smith are all satisfied that it must have been a foot and they describe it. Now whose foot was it? Was it the bare foot of a villager who never wears shoes and therefore was rough, hard, projecting heels and soles, or was it the shod foot of Sathasivam?" asked Justice Gratiaen.

"One thing is clear in this connection; those injuries particularly that deep bruise below the throat, were caused when the woman was fully alive, whether she was conscious or not. All that extravasation of blood proves that she was fully 'vital', as the doctors say, at that time."

"So gentlemen, it must have been either a shod foot or some kind of foot, upstairs if that is where the strangling took place, or a foot downstairs in the garage provided that she was still alive, which involves necessarily that it must have been a strangling in the kitchen, because she was too completely dead to be capable of sustaining a bruise of that nature if she had been dumped in the garage after the strangling upstairs. Everybody agrees on that."

"Well now, where do we go from there? Whose foot? Professor Smith tells us that in the best-regulated medico-forensic circles one gets hold of the shoe of one suspect and one examines the bare foot of the other. I do not know and I do not care whose fault it is, but you are gravely handicapped in that respect."

"You see gentlemen, whether it was a bare foot or a shod foot, the sole which caused those black marks to be left behind must have had some tell-tale marks of a similar description on the foot."

"If it was taken to the Police Station, an Inspector of Police was vigilant enough and sufficiently awake at that to have a look at those shoes and say, 'Yes, I remember his shoes; they were a pair of crepe sole shoes; brown suede shoes with crepe soles'. Never did it occur to anybody to take that pair of shoes, give it to the Government Analyst and say, 'Have a look at this sole; is there any evidence that this pair of shoes walked across the kitchen and collected some dirt?' Then it might be suggested: 'Oh yes, that was the pair of shoes he was wearing that night; how do we know which shoes he was wearing on that morning?' Well, did anybody look in his bedroom in Haniffa's house? Did they search for any shoes, which he might have left behind at No. 7, St. Alban's Place? 'Oh no, that is not the way we carry out our investigations. You see, if we investigators do carry it out in such a way it would make it rather too easy for jurors.' Gentlemen, for all you know, that pair of shoes, whatever it was, if analysed, might have conclusively helped to point the finger of guilt at Sathasivam."

"Might it not, if different results were achieved have conclusively proved his innocence, having regard to the fact that everybody now admits that at least these three injuries were caused by somebody's foot, which must have had some tell-tale stains if he walked through the kitchen?"

"Then Sir Sidney Smith says: 'Did anybody examine the soles of William's feet to find out if his bare foot was capable of forming these injuries?' As I said in the course of the evidence of one of those professional witnesses, I said really we are not concerned with the general controversy as to whether the injury was caused by a bare foot or by any old pair of shoes. All we wanted to know in this case is whether these injuries were caused by a particular foot or caused by a particular shoe worn by a particular murderer."

"We have had interesting discussions as to whether it may have been caused by the leather sole of somebody's foot. If that is conclusively proved and Professor Peiris thinks that that is most probably the kind of foot which would explain those injuries, well then on William's evidence we have an alibi confronting us, because not only does Thiedeman say that Sathasivam was wearing crepe-soled shoes at the time of his arrest, but William in the presence of Thiedeman in open court, walked up to Sathasivam who was in the dock, looked at the pair of crepe sole shows which he was wearing and he says, 'This is what he was wearing at that moment.'"

"Now could a crepe sole shoe in fact, leaving out those difficulties created by the absence of meticulous and scrupulous investigation, could they have caused those injuries? Professor Peiris was asked and all he says is he thinks that a shod foot is more likely to have caused them than a bare foot and that a hard leather sole was more likely to have caused them than a crepe sole. Less likely was the crepe sole."

"Sir Sydney Smith says, 'Well, if I have to give an opinion handicapped as I am, in my opinion I think that a rough sole of a bare foot is much more likely to have caused it than any shod foot,' and the reason he gives is for your consideration."

"He says, 'If you have a shoe I do not see how it can fit into that particular injury under the jaw.' He says if it were a shod foot slipping, it would miss that out altogether. I think a bare foot could easily work itself in, and you see also you have the dark stains and the coconut fluff, and he says, 'I do not see how they could have worked in if they were adhering first to a shoe', and he too agrees with Professor Peiris that in his opinion that a crepe sole shoe is very unlikely, but he agrees to this extent with Professor Peiris, if it was a leather sole with nails on it, the nails could easily have caused those abrasions."

"Then he is asked how he explained them and he says, 'I tried a little experiment on my own skin.' At least we have somebody's skin which is easily bruised in this case, and then Sir Sydney Smith says 'Never mind the dead lady.' He says he wanted to look at the 'thalikody' and he had a good look at it and he noticed a pendant on it and he got someone to wear it, and he said, if you put it like that you get just those parallel lines. He says in the present state of the available facts that is his belief and he cannot help us more."

"You have to consider all this but do not forget this, that if Sathasivam murdered his wife upstairs, he could not have brought down any kind of foot on her to cause those injuries in the garage because she was dead, and says Professor Paul, that by a strange coincidence the position in which this unfortunate woman's head is lying to the right in the garage was assuming that she was still alive, which was only possible if the strangling commenced in the kitchen, the ideal position for somebody to produce those injuries 9 and 3."

"It may be a pure coincidence, a pure fluke, but if somebody carried her out of the kitchen alive and put her down, and brought his foot down with the appropriate kind of sole, which is a matter of doubt, he said you could get just those injuries. That is a strange coincidence, is it not?"

"Now, that gentlemen is the real evidence in the case and I do not think there is any more, except one controversy which will not take me more than a few minutes to discuss with you, and that is the almost unending discussion as to whether the nail marks on the right side of this woman's neck were caused by the right hand or by a left hand."

"Dr. Taylor before he died said it was the left hand and Professor Paul, be it said to his credit, has never budged an inch. He said it was the right thumb, which was fixed to her face while the neck moved about causing seven separate nail marks. But the main controversy was whether the concavities came inwards at the bottom or outwards, and after days and days of quarrelling over this, Sir Sydney Smith said, 'Does it really matter?' And he then demonstrated to all of us with his right hand that he could bring it down firmly on the left forearm and produce all kinds of concavities going in all directions."

"He similarly did it with his left hand and showed it to you. Does it matter if, as he says, that it was the lower concavities that were pointing outwards? He said it is quite likely, as Professor de Saram says, it is quite possible, that if Mrs. Sathasivam, before she went unconscious, unsuccessfully tried to remove the strangler's grip, her own nails came in contact with this particular part of her own neck. Gentlemen, then if that was so why were no nail marks found on her hands? We do not know."

"There were no nail marks on William's hands. Even if there were not, is it not reasonable to say that the process of trying to take somebody's hands away is quite different from the process of strangling? Well, there is stricture about the right-handed grip and the left-handed grip. Does it matter?"

"If you have the opportunity again, work out for yourselves whether you prefer Sir Sydney Smith and Professor de Saram, with whom Dr. Taylor agreed, or whether you prefer the right hand of the other two doctors. Whichever conclusion you come to, does it not all boil down to this? Was Mrs. Sathasivam strangled on the floor upstairs or strangled standing against the kitchen door downstairs? Neither the right hand nor the left gave anybody any alibi in this case."

Justice Gratiaen then analysed the evidence presented to determine the time of death of Mrs. Sathasivam.

"I am now going to discuss with you perhaps the most important aspect of the medical controversy, the time Mrs. Sathasivam died. Whichever formula is used, I think that we should always have before us what Sir Sydney Smith said one day in this Court."

"He said that there are so many variable factors that you really cannot, with a biological formula, reduce it to a mathematical formula. Keith Simpson in his book made a statement with which everybody agreed, including Professor Paul, but which he subsequently slightly withdrew from, that the best and most reliable index of the lapse of time during the first 18 hours or so after death – it may be shorter in Ceylon – is the rate of cooling."

"Apparently, it is one of the natural laws of science that when a body dies, it automatically proceeds to lose its temperature until it reaches the temperature of the room or the locality where the corpse is lying. At the early stages, the tendency is for the temperature to be reduced comparatively rapidly, and during the final stages, when there is not such difference between the two temperatures, the rate of cooling is proportionately reduced."

"Gentlemen, there are other propositions which are fundamental, such as, the proposition that a sparse body, not well covered, is far more likely and would naturally retain its heat for a shorter period of time than a well covered corpse."

"Text books have also said that in certain causes of death, such as asphyxia, there is a tendency for the body to retain the heat for longer period. But we have all got the explanation why it is not some biological factor which is inherently connected with the asphyxial death which brings about that phenomena."

"The fact is that a body of a person who has been strangled to death may, not necessarily must, according to Sir Sydney Smith and Keith Simpson, be in such a state that, as a result of the intense muscular activity, which is frequently associated with an attempt to resist strangulation, there is a tendency for the body before death to increase its temperature beyond the normal temperature of that particular body."

"It depends, please note, on the extent or the duration of that additional muscular activity. In this case, we have the positive evidence of the effect of an intense muscular activity in two medical students, who at the request of Professor Paul, agreed to wrestle with one another in an attempt to get at each other's throat. What do we know with regard to those two particular cases? He says they did it so effectively that although he had insisted on a struggle for five minutes, he thought it more than enough after two minutes."

"In the case of one of them, the temperature at the end of two minutes' struggle rose by half a degree, and in the case of the other it rose by 0.3 of a degree. It so happened that the initial temperature which was recorded before the struggle commenced was unusually high in each case, but that does not matter."

Justice Gratiaen said in the two well-built men, from a known initial rectal temperature, after two minutes of violent exercise, the temperature went up half a degree in one and by 0.3 of a degree in the other.

"Professor Paul says, 'In my opinion, Mrs. Sathasivam, even if she might well have been unconscious within half minute, must have taken part in a far more violent and intense struggle than those two lads had,' and therefore, he gave her a higher initial rectal temperature."

"He was then asked, 'Well, would you make any other allowance for the other factors such as convulsions, involuntary muscular spasms and so on?' He said, 'I do not think it would be fair to add anything further'. So, on that basis, starting with the assumption that Mrs. Sathasivam's temperature, before the struggling commenced must have been half a degree higher than the assumed normal mouth temperature of 98.4 degrees, and you would get 98.9 degrees. Then he said, 'I add something and bring it up as a result of the struggle to 100.1 degrees'."

"Professor Peiris himself made a similar assessment and said that he thought it was safe to assume, making an allowance firstly for the difference between the mouth and the rectal temperatures of any human being, and a further allowance of one degree for the struggle which must necessarily have occurred. He said, 'I will start with 98.9 degrees'. Dr Taylor said it would come up at least one degree. If one works out his method, it looks as if he started with 98 degrees."

"The first matter for consideration is this," continued Justice Gratiaen.

"Is it safe in this particular asphyxial death to assume and postulate with confidence that there was an increase of temperature due to an inevitable struggle? It is fair to Professor Paul to say that he ultimately conceded that having regard to the admitted fact that the head injury must have dazed the woman before the struggle commenced and she was unlikely to have been able to put up very much of a struggle."

"So very unlikely, indeed, that the scratch marks on William's face and arms could safely be attributed, not to the natural reactions of a conscious woman struggling for her life, but rather to the semi-purposeful reactions of a semi-conscious woman just groping about."

"Professor Sydney Smith says, and I think Professor Paul does not agree, that the muscular activity, the semi-purposeful activity is not the kind of muscular activity which causes the temperature of the body to increase."

"Professor Paul considered that it was not safe to postulate any kind of effective struggle at all owing to the other factors in the case, and he said there are always convulsions. Though I said it would not be fair to add anything for the convulsions, if there was any initial struggle, I say that the convulsions must have produced just the same increased muscular activity to which Sir Sydney Smith refers. He says, 'I don't concede that convulsions are invariable accompaniments of an asphyxial death. They may happen, they may not'. You must judge between those two views."

"The question is this. Is it safe to assume that there were convulsions in this particular case? All one can say to the Crown is, 'You have a witness (William) who says he was there. He talks nothing about any movement which one can approximate to convulsions'."

"Professor Peiris says that he accepts the proposition that convulsions are not an invariable accompaniment, but he says in any event even if there are no external manifestations of convulsions, nevertheless there are invariably involuntary muscular spasms which would tend to increase the temperature."

"Smith and de Saram say it is not safe to assume any struggle or any convulsions, particularly having regard to the fact that, to use the words of Sir Sydney Smith, 'That little lady was incapable of putting up any kind of a struggle, particularly if she was first dazed and then strangled subsequently'. Well you have the two views," said Justice Gratiaen.

"Gentlemen, on any issue which is vital to a question relating to a charge of murder probabilities and possibilities are not enough. You must have the moral certainty that Mrs. Sathasivam's temperature did go up substantially as a result of the strangulation. That is an issue on which you yourselves must judge. Is it safe to assume that if there was any sort of a struggle or any kind of convulsion which William does not say he saw, or any kind of involuntary muscular spasms?" queried Justice Gratiaen.

"In any of those alternative positions, is it safe to assume that the temperature of that little lady increased and must have increased to any greater extent that was produced in the case of those two healthy medical students, struggling voluntarily with one another in an equal combat, which was an excellent demonstration of a pretended attempt of one to strangle the other? Those are matters for your consideration."

"Then there is another question. Both doctors Smith and Paul refused to recognise it as a necessary fact that the rectal temperature of Mrs. Sathasivam before the struggle commenced, was more than 98.4. They did not dispute that the rectal temperature would tend to be higher, by say half a degree, than the mouth temperature. Well, says the prosecution and the other doctors, 98.4 is the average normal mouth temperature and if you add half a degree to that, surely no one can pretend that the initial rectal temperature could possibly have been less than 98.9."

"Gentlemen, there is something to be said for that argument. It must be considered, but I do beg of you to appreciate that we are not concerned with averages. We are concerned with what is safe to assume as the temperature of a given individual and a given corpse."

"You will remember that Professor Paul took the rectal temperature of 12 ladies in the General Hospital. He said they ranged from 98.8 to 99 point something and he gave the average as 98.9 - it does not matter what the figure was. I think he therefore gave Mrs. Sathasivam as an initial temperature before the strangling commenced the average of those 12 ladies. If one woman can have – a normal woman can have – a temperature of 98.8, why not another? Now accepting half a degree as the difference between the mouth temperature and the rectal temperature, we have it from Professor Peiris himself that the normal mouth temperature of a human being in this country ranges from 97.8 to 98.6. Adding half a degree it would appear that the normal rectal temperature of people ranges between 98.3 and 99.1."

"What does it mean gentlemen? It means that to a particular individual 98.3 is his normal rectal temperature. At the other end 99.1 is the other person's normal rectal temperature. Nobody goes to a patient and says, 'You are normal you know, but you are a little below the average'. I mean these averages have nothing to do with the question at all. If somebody can have a normal temperature of less than 98.4, should you say, 'Well really we will have to promote you from the normal to the average for the purpose of assessing the time of your death?' It does not seem right gentlemen to try and transfer a normal person to the category of an average person. Everyone's temperature within that range is normal."

"No one would say to the 98.3 ladies 'You are below normal'. You might say 'You are below average', but that is an interesting fact, which has nothing to do with the state of health of the body."

"Why, asks Professor de Saram, is 98.4 unsafe to take as the rectal temperature if other normal, persons can have the same? If you can point to me any special features in Mrs. Sathasivam's case, then I must account for it. In other words, if someone can tell us, if some doctor who attended on Mrs. Sathasivam over a certain period of time can tell us, that he knows for a fact that her normal temperature was something other than 98.4, that is the proper starting point."

Referring to Sir Sydney's opinion, Justice Gratiaen said, "Sir Sydney Smith says, in any case, Mrs. Sathasivam is not the kind of woman – according to the description of her – whom one would expect necessarily to run a temperature higher than 98.4 degrees. He says, 'Speculate as much as you like, but I refuse to be drawn into the region of speculation'. Well, that is the controversy so far as it goes."

"Is it safe to assume that Mrs. Sathasivam had a temperature above 98.4 before she was strangled and is it safe to assume that a woman of her capacity to struggle who was not able, according to the Crown, to produce any more effective marks in a struggle than a semi-purposive scratching of a person, who was squatting behind the strangler, would have had a temperature above 98.4? How much would her initial temperature have been?

"Professor Smith says, 'I do not think it is safe'. If you gentlemen take a different view you must work it out for yourselves because I cannot help you any more on that particular issue," said Justice Gratiaen.

"Then we have got to get the rate of cooling, the rate at which a body lost temperature until it reached the temperature of the garage. The two surgeons did not profess, until very shortly before they gave their evidence, to have conducted any experiments of their own. Such experiments as they have spoken to do seem to indicate that in the first two hours after death, it is pretty safe to assume that a body loses at least one degree per hour, in Ceylon. They have not carried out experiments to work out the later rate of cooling after the first two or three hours."

"We do know also that - just as one would expect – if a person starts with a temperature above 98.4, the original early drop would be more than after the temperature had gone below normal."

"Those are the bodies following the normal rules of science. With regard to the question of variable factors the Solicitor-General himself has pointed out to you that the first executed prisoner spoken to by Professor de Saram, seems to have lost temperature at a faster rate than the other two men, although, having regard to the actual temperature of the room, you might and should have expected a slower rate of cooling."

"But where I do not necessarily agree is this gentlemen. It does not necessarily mean that the body was not running true to form. It means that there must have been some special features in that particular corpse, such as that he might have been more muscular than the other two, which as Dr. Smith says, involved another law, namely that the well covered body loses heat less rapidly than a sparse body."

"Now, Professors Paul and Peiris in this court accept 0.7, as I understand it, as a reasonable rate over the period with which we are specially concerned."

Justice Gratiaen reminded the jury that in the Magistrate's Court, Dr. Taylor took 0.6, 0.7 and 0.8 as the likely rates of fall of temperature for no other reason than that he accepted the wider experience in this field in Ceylon, which was claimed by Professor de Saram for himself.

"Peiris likewise followed, and in the result Taylor said that Mrs. Sathasivam, applying the rate of cooling, might have died at any time between 5.30 in the morning and 10 a.m. Paul, taking the initial assumed temperature of a 100.1, fixes the time of death at somewhere between 7.25 and 10.19 in the morning."

"Peiris was a little more generous to the defence. He said first that she would have died anywhere between 7.42 a.m. and 10.35 a.m. and then later he said, 'Well, I cannot exclude 11.30 either.' So his range is 7.42 a.m to 11.30 a.m."

"Gentlemen, if you accept their pronouncements for the reasons they have given that Mrs. Sathasivam must have had a higher temperature than 98.4, ranging somewhere between 99.4 and 100.1, and if you accept their acceptance of Professor de Saram's rate of cooling, even then, assuming that you confidently reject the contrary views of Smith and de Saram, where do you come to?"

"Merely this, that the earlier points of time spoken to by all three doctors is demonstrably not in conformity with the facts, because she was reading the 'Ceylon Daily News', not having had her morning meal, at 8.15 a.m. Therefore, relating their views to the facts, in their opinion she must have died between 8.15 a.m. - and taking Professor Peiris' range - he is a Crown witness- and 11.30 a.m. Anywhere between 8.15 a.m. and 11.30 a.m."

"All I say is this gentlemen. Therefore, not one of those doctors does postulate that the woman must have died before 9.30. It only proves that if their opinions are right, she may have died before 9.30."

"When you come to the question of corroboration, the effect of the medical views on which the Crown relies in regard to the time of death, do not constitute independent evidence, which implicates Mr. Sathasivam. It only goes so far as to say that in their opinion, William's story and Sanmugam's story are not inconsistent with the possibility of this woman having been dead before 9.30. It goes no higher than that."

"That is not corroboration but it is circumstantial evidence which does not exclude the possibility of William's story and Sanmugam's story being true."

"But I have one criticism to suggest with regard to the calculations of these two doctors," Justice Gratiaen said.

"Gentlemen, if 0.7 is a reasonable rate to accept for the cooling of a body from the normal 98.4, until it reaches the region of the ground temperature, they have all agreed that if the temperature started from above 98.4, the initial drop to 98.4 at least is very much more rapid than the later rate."

"Professor Paul admits that, and everybody admits that, and with great respect, I would suggest to you that the Solicitor-General in his very able address fell into the same error when he said, 'Well, even if it was one degree more than 98.4, making some allowance, which was inevitable for the difference between rectal and mouth temperature, and making a little allowance for some slight increase of temperature as a result of the asphyxial death, we then have demonstrably proved that Smith's calculations would be wrong because if he said the time of death would be 11 a.m., starting with 98.4 he must give, say one and a half hours for the other one degree."

"Gentlemen, that is just not right, because it does not fit in. Even Professor Paul says one degree at least in the first two hours and Professor Paul's own experiments show that in the case of the woman who started with an initial temperature of 99.9, she dropped something like 2.7 degrees altogether in three hours, a rapid drop in the first two hours and then down."

Justice Gratiaen then referred to the experiments Professor de Saram carried out on executed prisoners.

"But in this controversy let us examine what assistance we can get from the experiments on those three unfortunate executed prisoners, which Professor Smith had arranged and requested Professor de Saram in Colombo to carry out."

"Now he gave directions to Professor de Saram that as far as was humanly possible, he should be able to test the drop in temperature in three given bodies lying in conditions as closely as his ingenuity could arrange for, conditions approximating to the garage, as it was on the 9th of October."

"He has told us the almost astounding details which he insisted on. Somebody had told him that the Dover stove kitchen had a fire working on the morning of the death. So he said 'I will get a Bunsen burner with 20 lights and try to introduce something corresponding to that additional heat.'"

"The only relevancy of this dispute as to whether the rice was boiling in one kitchen or the other is that fortunately for the value of these experiments Professor de Saram did try to introduce those conditions, because what do we find here?"

"Three bodies draped, those poor corpses, in women's sarees and petticoats in a room where he tried to eliminate, as far as he could possibly, air currents, and the reason for this was to attain in his laboratory on those three given dates, conditions corresponding to the conditions in the garage."

"That is what Professor de Saram was able to achieve of the garage temperature, and the garage temperature at 7 p.m. was 81.5 degrees.

In three given cases, and this is the first and the last time that I am going to mention averages, the average room temperature was 81.5. It ranged in fact between 83 and 80.1. There is not much of a difference there, is there?"

"And, is there any reason to suppose that just as obviously there is a curve with the temperature in a room throughout the day, it comes down and goes up according to the hour of the day, is there any reason to assume that an enclosed garage or enclosed room, having practically identical temperatures at 7 p.m., would show marked variations of temperature at 3 p.m. or any other time? Just ask yourselves."

"It is true that Professor de Saram was quite unable to get three strangled women to experiment on - fortunately for us these strangling cases are rare -, but he got three healthy men wearing the same clothes and the difference in regard to those particular corpses and Mrs. Sathasivam's corpse is that she was a sparse woman whose body was likely to lose heat faster than a well-built man."

"As for an asphyxial death, first I will suggest for your consideration, it does not matter a bit, because asphyxia does not alter the rate of cooling."

"Well gentlemen, the defence relies as one part of its argument in regard to the executed prisoners, 1, 2 and 3, that each of those particular bodies, where death we know had occurred at 8 o'clock, reached a temperature approximating Mrs. Sathasivam's known temperature of 93.2 at a point of time between 7 and 8 hours approximately."

Justice Gratiaen said that he agreed that this argument is subject to very reasonable criticism.

"As the temperature of a room varies with the time of the day, you cannot without making the necessary allowance, approximate the cooling of the body where death had occurred at 8 a.m. to the cooling of a body where death had admittedly taken place after 8 o'clock."

"I suggest to you that we come to a more satisfactory comparison if we work out the known loss of temperature of these three bodies under reasonably similar conditions between 11 o'clock which Dr. Sydney Smith fixes, and 7 p.m."

Justice Gratiaen explained how in the three unfortunate prisoners the temperature had dropped. He said that in the first prisoner, there was a drop of 6.5 degrees in 8 hours, or a rate higher than 0.81 of a degree. In the second case, the drop in 8 hours was 6.4 degrees, giving the actual rate of cooling of 0.8 of a degree per hour. In the third case a drop in 8 hours of 6.1 degrees, or 0 .75 of a degree per hour as the rate of cooling."

Justice Gratiaen argued that Mrs. Sathasivam who was a thin woman, whose rate of cooling would normally be increased, that is more rapid than in the case of these men, or if she approximated to the first executed prisoner, starting backwards from 93.2, she would have had a temperature of 99.7 at 11 o'clock.

"This is somewhere around, is it not, the assumed temperature of doctors Paul and Peiris?" queried Justice Gratiaen.

"We get 99.6 in the second case and 99.3 if we apply the third case. Then remember, that in the first two hours, if Mrs. Sathasivam's temperature started at 99.7 or more than 99, there would have been a drop in the temperature necessarily more than the average drop, if the body's temperature had fallen well below normal."

"So the question is this. Sir Sydney Smith gives, as his considered opinion, that the assessment he has given leaves plenty of room for an unjustifiably assumed increase of temperature as a result of asphyxia. He says, 'Still in my opinion my 7 hours does in fact make plenty of allowance for all that. Therefore I am convinced'. As a responsible man whom both sides admit, has all the skill and integrity required to assist us in this matter, he says, 'I am satisfied that this lady did not die before 10.30 and I am also satisfied therefore, a fortiore she could not have been dead before 9.30'. He did say at the end, gentlemen, when I pointed out these figures that it did look as if one would be justified in accepting for Ceylon, 0.7 degrees as a reasonable rate of cooling over a long period like 20 hours, but not over a shorter period. Indeed gentlemen, this is what we find in this case."

Justice Gratiaen said it did not matter what was the assumed initial temperature of the executed prisoners.

"It is safer, for our calculations, to go from the known points of time. We find that in the first 20 hours, after the initial two hours between 8 and 10 a.m. when the rate of fall must have been very considerably more than at the final stages, even then between the 2nd and 22nd hour after death the rate of cooling over that enormously long period is 6 ½."

"Now, we come gentlemen to the other method - rigor test. One thing that everybody is agreed upon in the medical profession is that the rigor test is unreliable except for the purpose of a check, but this unreliable test can only have a special value in this case because some of the doctors, including Professor de Saram, bring the assumed point of death, on an unreliable method, between 8 and 10 a.m. It has no other value except that it does help the Crown in this case," Justice Gratiaen remarked.

"Gentlemen, if you are going to apply the rigor test, all that I ask you is carry away with you, when you retire to consider your verdict, the contemptuous or justifiably contemptuous reference to the rigor test that Professor Peiris gave us the benefit of. He says that rigor tests are bad enough; eye tests are worse. Well, eye tests are fantastic. How much value would a jury apply to a rigor test which is bad enough?" asked Justice Gratiaen.

"Professor Smith says that the conditions in Egypt are similar. His view is, though the rigor test is less satisfactory, he would not think, in the case of this sparse woman, having regard to the fact that 8 – 12 hours is the normal rate for full rigor to set in, having regard to the fact that after 7 hours at 6 p.m., she was in such a state that full rigor had not quite set in and that it did set in at 7 p.m., that she would have died before 11 o' clock. He says, 'Applying the rigor test, which I think is not quite satisfactory, I do not think this woman could have died before 11 o'clock.'"

"In this connection, I may say Professor de Saram differs from Professor Paul. He might be right; he might be wrong. But why quarrel over apparently an admittedly unreliable method in assessing the time of murder in this case?"

"There is only one bit of criticism which I have to offer in the case of Professor de Saram in his otherwise admittedly extremely thorough job of the post-mortem, and that is this."

"Nobody realised at that time how important the time of death would turn out to be. You know Professor de Saram went in there just before 6 o'clock and took the temperature of the deceased just before

7. Learned Solicitor-General asked him quite correctly, 'Would it not have been better if you had taken the temperature at 6 o'clock instead of 7 o'clock?' My criticism goes further. How helpful would it have been if he had taken the temperature at 6 o'clock, at 6.30 and then at 7? You would then, at any rate, know what was the actual drop in the temperature between those two points of time in the given body with which we are concerned," remarked Justice Gratiaen.

"Then we have only one other combined test, gentlemen the stomach contents and the alimentary canal test. Whichever of those alternative matters is concerned with the digestive process, we are here attempting, in a murder case, to assess, if you think it will help us, the number of hours or minutes which divide an unknown point of time from another unknown point of time."

"Having got it by the most perfect mathematical formula, if that is possible, having got the proposition beyond reasonable doubt to the stage of mathematical certainty, what is then the answer? She died so many hours or so many minutes after she ate her string-hoppers, but we really do not know at what time she ate her string-hoppers and therefore, $x + 1$ amounts to how much?"

"We all know the Crown points to the habits of our women folk. Nobody, after getting string-hoppers from a boutique, which is a proof of poverty, because that is where I get them whenever I have them, waits, but you eat them at once, otherwise they get cold," said Justice Gratiaen.

"I was wondering what would have been the position if we had identical contents in the stomach and the alimentary canal, if this deliberate murderer had condescended to let Mrs. Sathasivam have a string-hopper lunch before attempting to strangle her."

"Nobody told us at what time Mrs. Sathasivam had a lunch, and if you had been asked you would have said somewhere between 12 and 1, or somewhere between 12 and 1.30 p.m. Then you would have worked it out and from that safely assumed the initial point of time and you would have said so and so's alibi fails and so and so's alibi succeeds, and then you would have been told by Podihamy that Mrs. Sathasivam never had her lunch before 3 p.m."

Justice Gratiaen informed the jury that this only helped to show the danger of assuming when a person has her meal.

"With regard to the stomach contents, the modest Dr. Welikala has told us and proved to us that in the average normal case, a woman who has had so many string-hoppers and so many cups of tea regains her ordinary empty stomach somewhere in two and a half hours to three hours and he could tell us what proportion of the meal you can assume will be in the stomach after so many hours or so many minutes."

"Where do we get from there? We know that at the time of the post-mortem there was found in the stomach 10 ounces containing fluid gastric juices and undigested string-hoppers. After one hour, when kept in some special receptacle the floating string-hoppers soaked in fluid came to one third of the total. What proportion of the meal was that?"

"Professor de Saram states that if it had occurred to him as vital he would have worked out what was the weight of the solid. He would have carried out some more elaborate processes, because what he found there was not all solid, but there was liquid mixed up with it. We do not know, therefore, what was the quantity of string hoppers in the stomach when the lady died, and if we knew that we would not still know what proportion that was of the meal she had."

"The doctors on whom the Crown relies for the assumption of the time of death, except Dr. Taylor, who said, 'I do not know anything about string-hoppers, except for having eaten with 'sambol' at the Peradeniya Rest House', were perfectly content to rely on the stomach contents without any regard to the alimentary canal! They thought that was the obvious method, leaving out the rate of cooling and the state of rigor."

"In the long interval of time which attends our administration of justice, I do not know exactly when, but it was after they had both given evidence, we were told the obvious solution which hits you in the face but they forgot, namely that right through the small intestines there were found particles of partly digested string hoppers."

"Then they said, 'The only thing that is more remarkable than that is that this remarkable thing never struck us before!' That is what it comes to. They said, and that I think we will all accept as true, 'We are sure' they said, 'that several times in the course of our rounds in our surgical wards we have been cutting up abdomens and small intestines, but never in our experience have we come across such a phenomenon. Therefore it must be the case that there was a very quick digestion in Mrs. Sathasivam's case. We think what happened is that the fluid which leaves the stomach and leaves it faster than the solids, had rushed away with these partly digested particles'."

"Professor de Saram, who has gone into a number of cases does not regard it as a strange phenomenon at all, not in dead bodies."

"Well I hope we will be able to believe both of them. I am sure we can. One possible explanation suggests itself to us and that is, that one does not know how many cases which come to these distinguished surgeons involve the cutting up of the small intestines, but we do know that except for accident cases the bodies of the living are prepared for operation. How many cases have been handled by these two surgeons, where that particular part of the alimentary canal had to be out we don't know. Where do we go from there? When did she take the liquid which rushed the food through the alimentary canal into the small intestines?"

Justice Gratiaen reminded the jury that Dr. Welikala did say that it occurred to him, having regard to the quantity of solids and liquids in Mrs. Sathasivam's body, even if she had a mixed meal with cups of tea and string-hoppers, she might have drunk something else as well at some unknown point of time. This was because there was still a lot of fluid to be accounted for.

"That is all the help I am able to give you on the time of death. What results from these assessments? If you are convinced that Sir Sydney Smith's assessment of time is reliable, then obviously the evidence of William and the evidence of Sanmugam and the evidence of the other witnesses for the Crown go by the board," Justice Gratiaen said.

"There is an alibi for Mr. Sathasivam from St. Alban's Place at the moment of killing. Therefore, there is an alibi for William from 37, High Street, Wellawatta right up to 11 o'clock. That is if you are convinced that he is reliable."

"In order to convict, you must be convinced that Sathasivam's evidence is so unreliable that you certainly reject it, that you can safely reject it."

Justice Gratiaen then referred to the Sydney Fox case referred to in the cross-examination of Sir Sydney Smith by the Solicitor-General, Mr. T. S. Fernando.

"To my mind, gentlemen, the only significance of the Sydney Fox case is the very brilliant speech made by defending counsel when he said in regard to the conflict of opinion between the distinguished Sir Bernard Spilsbury on the one hand, and a group of other distinguished, but not so distinguished doctors at that time - he said, in regard to Sir Bernard Spilsbury's reputation, in so many words that he prayed that the time would never come when Sir Spilsbury's ipse dixit would automatically be accepted by juries."

"That proposition equally applies to Sir Sydney Smith. We know that everybody agrees that he is competent, that he is brilliant, that he is cautious; that he is not the kind of person who would, one should imagine and one hopes, deliberately mislead a jury."

"Nevertheless, we must be careful," Justice Gratiaen warned the jury. "We must not be overawed by the reputation of Sir Sydney Smith. Examine his reasons."

"Ask yourselves then, 'Are we so convinced by the evidence of the other doctors on whom the Crown relies, that we can say to ourselves in this murder case, that we can safely reject his considered opinion; that whereas the Crown says the murder took place before 9.30, we are satisfied, Sir Sydney Smith is satisfied that she was well and alive at 11 o'clock at least?' None of the other doctors I have said go so far as to postulate that death must have taken place before 9, but they say it may have. They say it may be. And that therefore does not demonstrably disprove William and Sanmugam. It does not go any further than that."

"Then there is de Saram's opinion. Gentlemen, the reason why I have left out some of the controversies in which Professor de Saram was concerned is that when you get a man of his integrity and ability, one would like, if it were possible, to avoid any criticism of him in any matter which is not fundamental to the case."

"The reason is this. He was a Crown witness on facts and he was nobody's witness on questions of opinion! Before a man's medical evidence is contemptuously rejected as unreliable in matters of medical opinion, I would prefer, unless I was compelled, to say I would like to have him re-examined by his own counsel before I destroy his reputation. He had no such benefit. The defence claims the benefit of opinions which a man of his eminence has expressed," said Justice Gratiaen.

"So, gentlemen, in regard to points and major points at issue where does Professor de Saram stand? He said the time of death is between 10 and 11.30. Professor Peiris now brings it up to the point of not being able to exclude 9 to 11.30. He is satisfied or claims to be satisfied that the strangling was in the kitchen against the kitchen wall.

"And those are two vital issues in the case. Where did the strangling take place and when did it take place?"

"In regard to those matters this professional man whom nobody claims completely as his own witness, expressed an opinion which substantially corresponded with the defence witness Sir Sydney Smith. Professor de Saram was a pupil of Sir Sydney Smith. So in this case, let Professor de Saram, the pupil allows his reputation on those major issues to stand or fall by the opinion of his master," said Justice Gratiaen.

"Well now the next point which I am going to come to gentlemen, you will remember that on the question regarding that hand mirror, I had said that there was evidence that the laundryman had seen the two children playing in the kitchen. Apparently I was wrong. They were seen in the kitchen but whether they were playing or not, there is no evidence."

After discussing and painstakingly analysing the medical evidence, Justice Gratiaen proceeded to evaluate the evidence of key lay witnesses.

"Gentlemen, it remains for me to direct your attention to the oral evidence of the witnesses who testified before you for one side or the other. In the case of every witness who speaks to relevant facts, when you have to ascertain and judge for yourselves whether they are speaking the truth or not, you apply the normal common sense tests which would obviously be applicable when you are coming to a conclusion on any important issue."

Justice Gratiaen informed the jury that those tests would include,
(a) the impression that they formed of them in the witness-box,
(b) their antecedents,
(c) the possibility of their having any motives for saying what is not true,
(d) the inherent probability or inherent improbability of their story,
(e) the question of consistency, and,
(f) all those innumerable indefinable matters by which we judge each other when the necessity arises.

"Before I turn to the evidence of William and Sanmugam, I propose to commence by discussing with you the evidence of the three defence witnesses, M.L.A. Perera, Mack and Mendis," he said.

"My reason for doing so is this. In the ultimate stages you will have to ask yourselves conscientiously, whether you are convinced that William and Sanmugam are speaking the truth."

"One of the matters which must receive your consideration in that connection gentlemen must necessarily be, has the evidence of this group of three people, Perera, Mack and Mendis, or the evidence of any one of them made a sufficient impression on your minds to enable you to say, 'I am convinced that those three men or one of them, is speaking the truth or at least that their evidence is of a kind and a quality, which leads me sincerely and honestly to doubt whether any person who testifies to facts entirely inconsistent with what they say can confidently be accepted.' Leaving questions of social strata apart, I suggest to you that the evidence of the 'Quickshaws' driver M.L.A. Perera is the most important evidence coming from that particular group, because the other two ask you to rely on the test of the ear."

"M. L. A. Perera asks you to accept the test of his own eyes. Well he was a man, who as far as the evidence indicates had no special reason for loyalty to Mr. Sathasivam to such a degree, as to induce him to perjure himself on behalf of a man, who certainly on that day, was being branded as a loathsome murderer by everybody in that locality!"

"In fact, Mr. Sathasivam is here today to ask your verdict as to whether that preconceived theory is, or is not justified. We know that there is a suggestion that some Police Officers, for some unspecified reason, are alleged to have been concerning themselves to assist Sathasivam but without his knowledge and connivance."

"Was there anytime for any Police Officers to get at M. L. A. Perera by the very evening of the murder? I have told you the circumstances in which he was sent for by Attygalle from St. Alban's Place. There were a number of police officers there each carrying out his part of the investigation. If you believe K. C. Nadarajah, immediately after the arrest of Sathasivam and immediately after he was taken to the Fort Police station, he brought the two senior officers Silva and Attygalle back to the house."

"Shortly after 8 o'clock this man M. L. A. Perera was sent for arrived, and he made this statement saying 'All I can tell you about this case is that when I arrived with the 'Quickshaws' cab at 10.30, or few minutes after that, I saw Mrs. Sathasivam standing by the doorway as we were leaving'. He had a very short time within which to recognize her. He had an exceptionally short time within which to attempt to take a mental picture of what she was wearing."

"But one thing is this. Was he wrong or was he not, when he swears that he saw a lady standing there. If he was lying on that point, that is the end of that. Secondly, was he lying or not, when he said that the lady whom he did see was in fact Mrs. Sathasivam? You must here pause to consider whether or not he had the opportunity within that brief space of time to be able to claim to say who it was that he saw."

"On that point, you must remember that he says - and no one has challenged - that he had, before joining the service of the 'Quickshaws' company, he had been employed by young Dr. Lucien Gunasekara, a well known young doctor of this town, the son of the better known and most distinguished professional man, Sir Frank Gunasekara."

"He says, that during a certain period when he was employed by young Dr. Gunasekara, he was required in the ordinary scope of his duties as a chauffeur to take Dr. Gunasekara to the house of Sathasivam senior who was seriously ill. He says, the father and son were both in medical attendance on Sathasivam senior, and he asks you to believe him, when he says that on many occasions he had seen this young deceased lady and had come to know her and recognize her."

"He also tells you that after he left private employment and went into the service of his present employers who still, whether he drinks or not, still presumably consider him sufficiently trustworthy and efficient a chauffeur to work in their service, he says, that he has had occasion himself to take Mrs. Sathasivam as one of his customers in a 'Quickshaws'."

"Well, gentlemen, if that is true, one would imagine that if he was disposed to speak only to matters which he could truthfully speak to that a fraction of a second would be ample time for him to recognize Mrs. Sathasivam's face. He knew the house and he went there."

"It seems to me that is a far more important method of testing his ability to identify the woman, than by the test of what she was wearing. If a stranger to Mrs. Sathasivam saw her for a fraction of a second, without any necessity arising for him to claim to recognise her thereafter said, 'I can tell you that woman whom I saw in a fraction of a second was wearing such and such a pattern on it,' I should very much be inclined to disbelieve him."

"If two years later or there about, someone showed him, not a saree as it was draped round the woman's body, but a saree placed on the top of a table and he said, 'This is the saree,' I would myself hesitate to believe him. But if he said, 'I knew her face and that is the lady,' that seems to me a question on which he is either deliberately lying or obviously speaking the truth."

"There is I suppose the remote possibility, it is for you to decide how remote it is, that it is true he saw a lady but she was only a lady like Mrs. Sathasivam, when it was somebody else. If so, who was this courageous woman who had placed herself at the disposal of the murderer and was willing to go into that house and help him to build up an alibi for himself?"

"I think the only precedent that I have come across for this part of the plot of the murderers who stained the feet of their victims and who produced others to come and pretend to be the living woman, while in fact she is the murderess is in the tragedy of Macbeth!"

"There, Lady Macbeth told her husband when she found her husband was preparing to murder, she said, 'We will daub the sleeping guards with blood so that it seem their guilt.' Well, here the murderer on that theory was Macbeth."

"It is not suggested that there was a Lady Macbeth at No. 9, St. Alban's Place or, was their indeed a Lady Macbeth who helped to daub the feet, helped to feign the voice over the telephone and then arrive at the door looking like Mrs. Sathasivam. Well, if M. L. A. Perera convinces you, that is the end of the case!"

Justice Gratiaen then referred to evidence of Mr. Mendis, the Manager of 'Quickshaws' cab company.

"He asked you to accept his own confidence in his ability to recognize a voice. Well, he is, and has been for quite some years a responsible Traffic Manager with an exceptionally well run establishment where the methods employed are the model methods of impressing a customer. This 'Quickshaws' service has become a new feature of Colombo's activities. Well he speaks to it that he had learnt by long experience to know the voice of Mrs. Sathasivam and to associate it with requests, often at the same time of the day that a 'Quickshaws' cab could be sent to a particular address, at which we all know she resided."

"He says sometimes he would write 'Sathasivam' and sometimes 'Mrs. Sathasivam' and the books he has produced, if reliable, do show that the words "Sathasivam" had been indiscriminately used at a time when there was no Mr. Sathasivam at the house or in Ceylon."

"He tells you on the very morning of the murder, Thiedeman came round, having known what M. L. A. Perera said, and checked up the books and asked certain questions. He says, it is a matter on which you must think deeply, he says, Thiedeman went through the list of calls and found it was 'Sathasivam' and he asked him, 'Why did you not write Mrs. Sathasivam?' and he said, 'I honestly cannot exactly say.' You do find, if you look at the book, that there are a number of pencil marks down the line wherever the name 'Mr. or Mrs. Sathasivam' was written, that 'Mr. or Mrs.' appear."

"Thiedeman's recollection, which is backed by that initial entry he made in his own note book, is not so much a difference of words, but a complete difference of meaning," remarked Justice Gratiaen.

"He says what he wrote down and we know that was what he wrote down. What he wrote down was that this man Mendis, who was merely the assistant, could not exactly say who booked that call," said Justice Gratiaen.

"Well, there is a vital point of difference between them. It is not a question at this stage whether Mendis is speaking the truth when he says Mrs. Sathasivam phoned, but it is a question to decide whether he did in fact claim at that time to have received a call at 10.30 from Mrs. Sathasivam. Now, the answer to that is, in the submission of the defence, to be found in the two statements Mendis made to Thiedeman himself."

"The first minute was made on the 13th of October, not after a further conversation with Mendis, but in connection with a discovery which he had made in the bedroom of No. 7, St. Alban's Place, this telephone chit. He writes down there the possibility that it might be Mrs. Sathasivam who had booked the call but to make sure he went back to the 'Quickshaws' office on the 14th, interrogated both the 'Quickshaws' driver and Mendis in considerable detail, checked up everything each of them said in the book, made crosschecks and then he writes down, 'I have found the following facts' - meaning what he believed the facts to be - at that point of time; nothing more."

"There he says that Mrs. Sathasivam telephoned the 'Quickshaws' office and booked a 'Quickshaws' at 10.30 a.m. That, he says was a minute made after his second interrogation of Mendis."

"Gentlemen, I asked him, 'Well, if your interpretation of the first interrogation is correct, then there is a glaring inconsistency between what Mendis appears to have stated on the first occasion and what he had stated on the second occasion. Did you not ask him how it was, when he could not exactly say who phoned on the first occasion, that he was able to exactly say who had phoned four days later?"

"His answer is, 'Quite frankly to tell you the truth, at that time it did not occur to me that there had been an inconsistency at all'. Well, does that fit in with the interpretation of Mendis of what he had discussed on the first day or not?"

"Mendis was somewhat dramatically supported by a witness who came into this Court to call upon an advocate whom he had retained in a case. He heard this conversation and he said, 'Good gracious, I remember him telling me about it'. Then he swears that it was certainly before the 13th that he was told this, but that on checks and cross checks, to the best of his ability, he was able to state, as his honest opinion, that the conversation took place on the 10th of October. Well, there it is."

"Then you have Mendis claiming that he had developed this astonishing gift which, I have no doubt, if it does exist, is of splendid public value, and gives great comfort to the customers who do like their voices to be recognised. And he tells you that he pulled Thiedeman's leg one day just about this time. You remember the evidence. Someone said, 'I want to talk to Mr. Mendis' and he said, 'Good morning Mr. Thiedeman. Are you now satisfied that I am capable of identifying voices of people when I am familiar with them?' - and he says there was no reply. Well, was that true or not?" queried Justice Gratiaen.

Justice Gratiaen then discussed the evidence of the third witness, Proctor Mack.

"Mack's position, very shortly summarised, is this - that he had a telephone conversation between 10.25 and 12 with a lady, who did not give her name, but in circumstances in which he assumed that the voice was the voice of lady with whom he had previous professional discussions on the telephone, and that he believed that lady to be Mrs. Sathasivam."

"In this Court - and I think in the course of a later interrogation also - he said that the lady asked, 'Has the divorce case summons been served?' and the only lady who could probably have asked the information in that connection was Mrs. Sathasivam, because she was the only client at that time in a divorce case."

"He says that if he had any doubt he would have asked who she was but he had no doubt on the point. In the evening, he went round to the Golf Club and he heard this news that Mrs. Sathasivam had been 'battered to death.' He told you rather graphically how he reacted when he heard the information."

Justice Gratiaen, who was six foot four inches tall and weighing over 113 kilogrammes said, "Well, I suppose gentlemen - I must confess - I am particularly disqualified to be vicious about the size and shape of other people to ask the seven of you, who do not possess this qualification, to try and visualise what he says did happen. You can picture for yourselves what must have happened - this rounded figure flopping back on the lounge saying, 'Good Heavens, I was talking to her this morning' but no."

"A typist in a CID office, took down, to the dictation of a CID officer a sentence, which was not signed by Mr. Mack, in which Mr. Mack is supposed to have enacted that particularly extremely realistic drama to Mr. Koelmeyer in these words, 'He flopped back and said, Good Heavens oh! Her mother telephoned me this morning.' Why on earth he should have mentioned the name of a person whom he had never met and never spoken to, is difficult to imagine. He says, 'If you say it is down there I cannot deny it, but I do say it is extremely unlikely that I said it'."

"It would be quite wrong to assume that that was a deliberately incorrect record, but I will merely say this. Although the Criminal Procedure Code does prohibit the obtaining of signatures by Police Officers interrogating witnesses in the course of their official investigations, it is frequently done."

"I am sure it is very desirable that it should be done, but would be very desirable, would it not, that that practice today should only be confined as far as one can judge, from the statements we have come across to the obtaining of signature from people who cannot read English, the language in which the statements are recorded or who cannot sign in that language at all?"

"Whereas to a man who can read English and is not a dishonest man, the opportunity of reading the statement and saying, 'Yes that is correct. I will sign' is not necessary. One would like to know what questions were put to Mack specifically."

"If the question was, 'Do you think it was Mrs. Sathasivam? Are you sure it was not her mother?' He would probably have said 'I am not sure as I never saw her' and in the meantime, he may also have said that she was dead long before I had the telephone conversation with her and doubts growing in my mind."

"In matters of that sort, where an admittedly honest witness is confronted by an apparent contradiction or an obvious contradiction, it would be more proper if the question and answer were recorded separately. However, there is the record of a contradiction taken by a most efficient Police Officer, Mr. Koelmeyer. You will also remember that it is not in dispute that in the course of the two earlier interrogations the name of Mrs. Rajendra (Mrs. Sathasivam's mother) as the possible telephone caller did not arise, but it arose on the third."

After the analysis of the evidence of these three key defence witnesses, Justice Gratiaen asked the jury to consider whether they were truthful or not.

"Are those three gentlemen lying? If they are not deliberately lying, are you certain that there must have been an honest mistake in the case of all three witnesses of that group? Otherwise, there must be doubts in your mind. On the question of probability and possibility assuming that they are speaking the truth, one saw Mrs. Sathasivam and two others heard her voice on matters affecting her private affairs. One doubt the only divorce case which she was concerned and the only divorce case for a lady with which the Macks were concerned, and the other about sending a 'Quickshaws' cab to No. 7, St. Alban's Place where she was either alive or dead in the garage having, I do not know how many degrees of rectal temperature."

"There is a point which you must consider, the possibility of a conspiracy, that some woman conspired to imitate Mrs. Sathasivam when Perera turned up, and to imitate her voice during the two telephone conversations. Then never forget that there is found the next day a pad near her telephone, an admittedly genuine document except for the last two numbers, except for which it would be a perfect corroboration of all three witnesses."

"In a murder case, the fact that all three witnesses have given evidence of such a quality that you can confidently reject them as completely unreliable for one reason or another, is quite essential to the case. Just as it is essential to the case for the prosecution that you should with confidence reject Sir Sydney Smith's professional opinion, because he himself says or claims to say with confidence that

Mrs. Sathasivam must have been alive at 10.30 a.m."

"I have mentioned this witness because you must weigh him against the evidence of William and Sanmugam. As I see it, gentlemen, you must be convinced that Sir Sydney Smith's evidence is unreliable and that the evidence of both Sanmugam and William is reliable to seven sensible men."

Justice Gratiaen then dealt with evidence of William, the key prosecution witness.

"William must be approached in a slightly different way. But to begin with, although he is a tainted witness for the reason I shall explain, the question whether you should look for corroboration of what he says to the extent which I shall shortly indicate, only arises if and when you approach his testimony on the assumption that it is not tainted, and he appears to be a witness of truth in your eyes. That is the law."

Justice Gratiaen asked the jury to approach his evidence as if he was an honest witness, a prima facie honest witness until gaps or some flaws are found in it.

"Has he been consistent in what he said? How did his story progress as it developed? What did he then tell Police Officer de Saram in the Matara Police Station?"

"He said that he was turned out of the house for not washing the bathroom, given a few rupees and turned out. Then the Police techniques were brought into operation by confronting him by known or pretended inaccuracies. They said, 'You are not speaking the truth. Tell us what happened?' He says, 'As a matter of fact I heard a *dadibidi* noise upstairs' indicating that there was a scuffle between the man and his wife."

"He had told somebody else that the master had come down and given him some jewellery. He was asked about the scratch marks and he said, 'Oh, I worked in a *padda* boat and I got scratched. I am only talking of non-controversial matters now. What were the two final statements which he in fact made to Superintendent Albert de Silva at Matara, when that Senior Officer took over the interrogation?"

"We have William's recorded admissions to Sir Richard Aluvihare of what he did say. He admits having confessed to Mr. Albert de

Silva that he and he alone committed the murder. He admits that he had previously made an exculpatory statement to Mr. Albert de Silva that the master had given him 80 rupees and told him to get out of the house."

"But in fairness to him, he told Sir Richard Aluvihare that he made that final confession to Mr. Albert de Silva because he was induced by the offer of employment to do so. He says that there was a further offer of a bribe of 1000 rupees but he tells us now that second bribe was not offered at all!"

"Well, one can understand a young man who had foolishly accepted a first bribe to help in the killing of a woman going about the village and telling Police Officers a lot of lies through the temptation to remove himself as much as possible from the scene. That is not commendable but that is a feature or a manifestation of human nature which we can understand."

"But, gentlemen, what do you say of a man who says, 'I confessed to a murder which I did not commit because a Police Officer offered me the benefits and privileges of domestic service in his establishment'? Mark you, his version here is that the offer was made but that he refused to say anything."

"He says that when Sir Richard Aluvihare interrogated him he asked him whether he had made such a confessional statement and he said, 'No, that is what I was asked to say but I did not say it'. Well, if you believe Sir Richard Aluvihare, the words and the details of the confession were words which came from William."

Justice Gratiaen said William must have been very tired that day. Detailing William's movements he said, "William had been running about escaping the Police, escaping from Police custody for days on end. He was finally arrested in the early hours of the morning. He was driven to Tangalle. He was then driven to Matara. He was interrogated for many long hours with all the familiar police techniques, but Mr. de Saram says he gave different versions on different occasions."

"He was then badgered again by different techniques by a new group of Police Officers. He was taken to a lavatory for a few minutes and coached to say something in some detail. He was taken back, he is badgered again and he makes a confession in the dead of night. He is driven again to Panadura where he points out the places where the jewellery or some of the jewellery had been sold. He is then rushed off to a Legal Adviser's bungalow."

"He says there again he was asked to repeat the words which he refused to do and the poor little man was not taken even to the proper Police Station Bambalapitiya. He was taken further miles away to Modera. The next morning the Police began working on him again. He made a detailed statement for many hours to Mr. Koelmeyer where he says he told the truth. Then he is taken to Sir Richard Aluvihare and this lad who had not slept still, remembered the details of a prompt statement which he was invited to make some 36 hours later or 30 hours later."

"I would like shortly to refer to a complaint against Albert de Silva, in connection with this confession. That the confession was made there can be no question if you believe that William admitted making that confession to the Head of the Police, but quite correctly the complaint has been made that Mr. Albert de Silva did wrong, from a departmental point of view, in not recording that confession there and then."

"If Thiedeman is right, the technique of recording suspects' statements after long interrogation is to lead them on, see if they can correct their statement and then to take down the final version. If that was done, the only statement that would have been recorded was the final confession William admittedly made."

Referring to the alleged statement William made to Albert de Silva, Justice Gratiaen said, "Gentlemen, if that statement was recorded, it would have been of no avail in a Court of law against William because Section 25 of our Evidence Ordinance says that no confession made to a Police Officer shall be led in evidence against him."

"Gentlemen, whom was Albert de Silva trying to help when he failed to record a confession? It is only necessary to consider the particular suggestion that he was trying to help Sathasivam. All I can tell you gentlemen is that, as I understand the law of evidence applicable to Ceylon, that statement, if recorded by Albert de Silva, would have been a valuable piece of evidence which Sathasivam could have relied on in his defence."

"Any complaint made on that score should have been Sathasivam's complaint. Well, departmentally Albert de Silva erred. Was he dishonest in his decision? What did he choose instead to do?"

"Here was a boy who had made a number of incorrect statements. Finally, it is not suggested that Albert de Silva knew of the alleged bribe in the alleged lavatory. He had then one of two decisions to make immediately; either to spend some time in recording the confession or to rush the lad to the nearest place where the jewellery had been sold, and that is what was done and the stuff was recovered."

"Then gentlemen, assuming that Albert de Silva was an honest policemen he had evidence which he could lead in a trial against William, because the Evidence Ordinance which governs our courts definitely says that though a confession to a Police Officer is not evidence against him, any statement which leads to the discovery of any incriminating production, any confession leading to the discovery can be led in evidence."

"This man de Silva, gentlemen, according to the evidence, retired from the Police force after what we must assume to be an honourable career of 28 years police service. If he made an administrative blunder, well, that is regrettable. He is not here before us to justify his actions, but I am only concerned to ask you to consider whether that item of evidence is something, which affects the innocence or guilt of Mr. Sathasivam in the dock."

"Upon those matters, the honesty or the dishonesty of policemen is not our concern. I hope that in fairness to an important Public Service insinuations like that will, if possible, be avoided in the interests of the whole State, except before tribunals where they can defend themselves against the insinuations, and not leave it to people troubled by their own murder charges to defend in addition Police Officers with whom they have no concern at all," Justice Gratiaen informed the jury.

Analysing William's evidence further Justice Gratiaen said, "William's evidence is that of a self-confessed accomplice, and the Crown accepts the position, that having regard to the character of that evidence, you should, if prima facie the evidence of the accomplice appears to you to be truthful, nevertheless refuse to act upon it unless there is independent evidence coming from an unpolluted source which implicates Mr. Sathasivam in regard to this crime."

"It must not necessarily implicate him on every detail, because then you need not bother about William at all. Why does the law require judges to warn jurors against acting on uncorroborated evidence of this class of witness?"

Justice Gratiaen said there are two obvious reasons for this.

He said, "The first is that a man of that quality, apart from his having admittedly committed a crime in as much as he knows in fact all the details of what actually took place, is always faced with the understandable temptation either of giving a true version of what happened by substituting some other person in his place in the transaction, or which is an equally tempting situation, that the man knowing the truth, knowing exactly what happened, should slightly twist the truth in regard to what he knows did happen and substitute slightly altered incidents, which in the altered version would tend further to exculpate himself."

"Take this very case. It is for you to decide, but there is the temptation and it is for you to decide whether William fell to that temptation or not. If the truth is that the murder took place in the kitchen, then in order to keep himself away from the murder as much as possible, there would be the temptation to take the crime upstairs so that he would be dragged upstairs to watch the crime, instead of taking part in it where he works."

"There is another temptation and that is this gentlemen. You see, if you are unwary you would say to yourselves, 'Well now, if he was not speaking the truth how does he know about the mortar; how does he know that there was just 3 rupees in the bag and some coins in addition? How does he know about the stamping of the foot?"

"You must be cautious gentlemen," warned Justice Gratiaen. "You must be convinced in your minds in this case that he does not speak to those details because he knows the facts better than anybody else because it was his foot that stamped, it was his hand that removed the jewellery."

"You must be convinced that it was not his hand that took the money from the bag which lay in the almirah. Unfortunately, again one little test, which might have helped you in your deliberations on that little point has been withheld from us."

"That almirah, which somebody opened in order to take out the bag was the best polished article of furniture in the whole house. It was an almirah that made even Mr. Thalaisingham smack his lips with pleasure at the excellent medium that it presented for the reception of finger prints. But unfortunately nobody thought of looking for finger prints there until many days after when the sea spray had done its work."

"So that you must be sure, must you not, as against Mr. Sathasivam that if the finger prints were taken on that very day on that perfect medium - the almirah - that there would not have been one single tell-tale finger print left by William because William never touched the almirah; it was somebody else who opened the almirah, took out the bag and gave him the money. Don't forget that."

"In addition, there is a final warning note that must be struck in regard to the acceptance of William's evidence as against Mr. Sathasivam's, and that is this."

"It does not often fall to the lot of a man who has helped in a murder for pecuniary gain, that he should receive a conditional pardon from those who act in the name of the Crown. All that is relevant on that matter is this. That a man who receives a pardon on condition that he speaks the truth does not realise that the Attorney-General intends to impose dignifying and proper conditions which affect the validity of the duration of the pardon."

"A man like William would admittedly interpret the transaction as a different kind of bargain, viz. you give evidence against Mr. Sathasivam, and if he is hanged you go free! If you fail to convince the jury on that matter, then we have the evidence that even on your own confession you must inevitably be found guilty of an act of abetment for which the punishment is also death. That is how he understood the pardon. How else could he have understood it?"

"So those are, shall we say two special danger signals which confront seven jurors as it were on the public highway in search of the truth and when the red light goes up William comes and says, 'If you are looking for the truth I will show you the way'. The red light goes up because he is an accomplice, the second light goes up because of his interpretation of the conditions attaching to the pardon."

Justice Gratiaen then explained to the jury why William was pardoned.

"May I say this with regard to this conditional pardon in fairness to the Attorney-General? If a certain view of a case is decided upon on the expert advice available to the law officers of the Crown, it sometimes happens that because of the insufficiency of evidence in the case, the person who in that view is regarded as the principal offender might go off scot-free, unless the person who is supposed to be a minor accessory can be induced to give evidence to bring the real murderer to book."

"Well, if William's case goes out, how can you say that there is circumstantial evidence sufficient by itself without William's evidence to convict Mr. Sathasivam?" asked Justice Gratiaen.

"With great respect, I should have thought that the answer to that submission is the fact that a conditional pardon was granted to a man who on his own assessment of his own character is surely a thoroughly despicable fellow. If it was possible to place before you this body of circumstantial evidence against Mr. Sathasivam without slightly tainting the ground, with the temporary association of a person of William's character, why pardon William? Why not have both convicted?"

"There is then the other witness Sanmugam. Well, you saw Sanmugam for yourselves and it is for you to decide whether he is a person on whose evidence you would act with confidence, unsupported on the only important aspect of the case, viz. the time of arrival of William. Unsupported perhaps is the wrong word - supported by one - the man called Edmund, who is conceded to be an incalculable liar."

"There again you must consider the conduct of a man, who saw in the papers that a Tamil lady had been dead, who says he remembered seeing the boy coming to Edmund's boutique dressed, as it subsequently transpired, in exactly or substantially the same kind of garments answering to the description in the Police message, and he says that he talked to Edmund about it and they decided to check up the description and they got hold of Sirisena, who admitted the sale of the 'thali'."

"He heard that on the 13th of October. Then he says, 'When I knew it was a *'thalikody'*, though I am a sick man, although I am too old and feeble to be troubled with giving evidence in a Court of law, then I decided to give this evidence at the risk of my life.' Dramatic and stirring words, if true."

"How did he decide to risk his life? He did nothing till the 16th on which day the newspapers announced that the Police were offering a reward of 1000 rupees to anybody, who gave information, which would successfully lead to the whereabouts of William."

"How did he react to that? Here was a man, who Sanmugam was now convinced in his mind, had taken part in the murder and had sold the 'thalikody', which has special significance to people of the religion and race to which Mr. Sanmugam belongs."

"He did nothing about it then, and on the 17th, he tells you it was a pure coincidence, he read a paper saying that a Buddhist priest had gone up to the Police and said some information which may be forthcoming. So half an hour later, he decided to write a letter and this is the man who had decided to risk his life, and he writes a letter, in which he says 'Edmund tells me that he saw a boy who wanted to sell an article of jewellery. Edmund tells me that he answers the description so and so, which in fact corresponds to the police description. Edmund says that he had nothing to do with the matter himself'. That is the gist of it."

"But all he said was, 'There is Sirisena's boutique, go to him, and now Sirisena admits that the transaction took place. I am writing this for your information. Edmund is frightened of Sirisena. Please keep my name out of it. Please keep Edmund's name out of it.' That was the 17th and he telephoned. One Albert de Silva of the Crimes Police arrived in answer to a telephone request at 10 o'clock in the night and took the letter from him."

"What did he say to Albert de Silva in connection with his knowledge of the transaction? He says, he told Albert de Silva in so many words, 'I know nothing about it. This is what Edmund told me.'"

"Well, Albert de Silva, Superintendent of Police, who was by now hot on the trail of William himself, who in fact went down in the early hours of the morning and was there at Matara in time to continue the interrogation, who was able to take William to a particular place where some jewellery had been sold, is criticised - we are in the field of departmental fix - and it is suggested that he should have recorded the statement of this gentleman that very night."

"What would that statement have contained if it had been recorded? 'I know nothing. Edmund knows everything.' There again the complaint, if any, against Albert de Silva should be the complaint of Mr. Sathasivam," Justice Gratiaen remarked.

The whole of the 18th everybody is busy. Albert de Silva receives this letter asking that Sanmugam's name should be treated in confidence and he respects that confidence, and in fact, within 24 hours, Albert de Silva is bounced out of the investigation himself and is functus officio as far as the Sathasivam case is concerned."

"Then comes the 19th. The Police raid Sirisena's boutique and get further evidence confirming William's confession that he had sold some stuff to somebody in that locality. So they send for Edmund, and they send for Edmund only. That is important. Edmund is a little timid about going unless the witness Sanmugam comes too and this evidence, of course, as to the sale is interesting. Sanmugam was sent for by Edmund and not by the Police and he went."

"Gentlemen, at that time it is common ground between the prosecution and the defence that Edmund, Sirisena and Dharmasena had planned to tell an entirely untrue story about the sale of this stuff. They had planned to say that the sale had taken place not in Edmund's boutique, where it was supposed to have taken place, but in Sirisena's boutique and that the purchaser was not Sirisena but Dharmasena, his brother, the unmarried brother, who was prepared to take the blame."

"Well, they are told, 'If you get some evidence about Edmund please go and check that up and come back to me.' Then on the 20th Sanmugam wrote and for the first time says, 'As a matter of fact I saw the boy'. Well gentlemen, I asked him, 'Why didn't you tell Attygalle on the 19th when you went of your own free will?' He first admitted that he had not said it; then he said that he probably said it and then finally said, to use his words, 'As a matter of fact to some people I said, 'I did not see the boy because I wanted to stick to the letters,' and then he says, 'At the wrong time I have stuck to my letters.' So there you are."

Justice Gratiaen said Sanmugam had three separate opportunities of telling the truth, at the risk of his life, but he failed to do so.

"So there is the letter that he wrote. Nobody had bothered to take any notice of his information because it turned unnecessary and did not lead to any information, which would bring reward, but he says, 'I gave you the information, valuable information.' What was the value of the information? 1000 rupees. But he says, 'I would have given that to the deaf and dumb school'. That is his evidence."

"Taken generally - and here again I must fight on behalf of a public officer - it has been suggested that Dr. Handy was not speaking quite the truth when he said that this witness Sanmugam is ill. Really gentlemen, as I said before let a few public officers emerge whole at the end of this case. Suffice it for us to say that Sanmugam being ill, is given the privilege of being cross-examined under the conditions most conducive to the continuation for his health, and that I am very glad that he survived the experience in the Durdans Hospital, and I may say that I am also very glad that we all survived it too!"

"Sanmugam is a somewhat evasive person perhaps. He says, 'Well the truth is that Premawathie (the patient he admitted to the General Hospital) is in fact the niece of my wife, but I finally decided to make a statement to one Police Officer who was willing to record my statement and I described the niece of my wife as a servant of one of my tenant's.' Why? He was apparently, it is suggested, ashamed of having married to someone beneath his status. If he had decided at long last to give his wife his name and to further privileges of legitimacy of his seven children, why call his niece a servant gentleman?"

"When he made a genuine mistake he stuck to it. He was asked, 'How did William look like when you saw him in Court?' He said, 'Oh good heavens, that boy had grown out of all recognition; he was such a little fine fellow; he was frail when I saw him' - too frail apparently to get involved in any effective strangulation. When he was pointed out that it was only months after he had seen the boy, he said, 'I made a mistake'. Well, we will pass on to the next question."

"He said, 'I stick to that statement. He went to his village and he ate food that he was accustomed to and had jamborees in the jungle and naturally he would have changed his stature."

"One way of testing a man, who has said he never saw the boy and then said he had, and then claims to give evidence on vital times, who saw that boy for a brief moment of time when his mind was concerned with the health of a servant girl who was in truth his niece, is to say, let him identify him at an identification parade. Let us put him amongst a number of others."

"But that was not possible because before anybody could arrange an identification parade this witness Sanmugam, at the risk of his life went to the Colombo South Court with Edmund because he was anxious, as he told Koelmeyer, to see the boy."

"After that advantage which he had obtained, an identification parade would have been useless. I do not think I can help you there much more. I have emphasised these points because I thought it my duty to do so because of the many difficulties which strike me as difficulties, which you may not lightly brush aside."

"If as conscientious men, knowing the extent of your responsibilities, you feel, as the sole judges of fact that there is a sure and certain answer to each of these difficulties consistent with the guilt of Mr. Sathasivam, then only can you convict. You must be sure and you must be always sure that he is the only man who strangled Mrs. Sathasivam," Justice Gratiaen said.

"I have, as I conceive it to be my duty made these points with emphasis in the interests of the defence. But I have also done so, I assure you, in the interests of the Crown because the Crown is the symbol of Justice to which the whole Commonwealth dedicated itself afresh, and the Crown, we have been told is only concerned that the truth should be known and not concerned that any particular person should necessarily be convicted."

"If you are sure of Mr. Sathasivam's guilt, I can think of no case in which any jury would hesitate for a moment to bring in a verdict against him, because it is murder or nothing, a diabolical murder or nothing."

"Learned Counsel for the defence has invited you, I think, to bring in a rider stating, if that is your view, not merely that Mr. Sathasivam is not guilty, but that he is innocent. It is not for judges to presume to suggest to any jury whether or not they should bring in a rider, but may I say this? If you are convinced that he is innocent, even then, I beg of you, in the interests of justice, not to bring such a rider, and I will tell you why. Because that rider would necessarily involve the preconceived conviction of the man William, who is not on trial in this case, whose Counsel you have never heard. And that is not my conception of justice," emphasized Justice Gratiaen.

Continuing he said, "However agreeable it may be to one man we must be just to all potential people who will be brought into dock. I do not like verdicts that necessarily involve someone not in the dock as having committed the murder. It is worse than these suggestions against Police Officers, which have not been substantiated."

"If you are not convinced of Mr. Sathasivam's guilt, still more, if you are convinced of his innocence, the verdict is, 'Not guilty.' In which event it will be your duty, and I am sure your pleasure to bring back a verdict, which will set Mr. Sathasivam free after so long a period of incarceration."

"Let us hope that at any rate if your verdict is in his favour, that his long lonely hours have helped him to realise that the folly of his ways has led to so much unhappiness to so many others, and let him remember his obligation to the dead and to the children who for twenty months have had neither a father nor a mother. But if he is guilty that is the end of the case. Will you please retire and consider your verdict?" concluded Justice Gratiaen.

The jury then deliberated for 64 minutes (from 3.26 pm to 4.30 pm) and brought a unanimous verdict of 'Not guilty'.

Addressing Mr. Sathasivam, Justice Gratiaen said, "On the verdict brought by the jury you have been found not guilty. You are now free."

Mr. Mahadeva Sathasivam then walked out of the dock a free man, after spending twenty months in the remand prisons, for a crime he did not commit.

At the conclusion of the trial, while the jury was deliberating, Justice Gratiaen called on four prosecution witnesses, Edmund, Dharmasena, and Sirisena and the prisoner Piyadasa, and asked them if they had any cause to show as to why they should not be dealt with for contempt of court, by giving false evidence.

Justice Gratiaen said that it was common ground in this case that they had given "Palpably false evidence on a matter of vital importance affecting the guilt or otherwise of the accused."

All four witnesses begged for pardon on the ground that they had never been to Court before and had given false evidence through ignorance.

Justice Gratiaen sentenced P.A. Edmund, and the jewellers at Wellawatte, Dharmasena and Sirisena, to two months rigorous imprisonment each, and discharged Piyadasa, the remand prisoner with a severe warning.

Mr. Sathasivam and his counsel Dr. Colvin R. de Silva were mobbed by the large crowd which burst into applause as they entered the car to drive to No. 7, St. Alban's Place, the residence of Mr. Sathasivam where his mother and four children awaited him. This was the house he left at 10.30 a.m., 20 months ago! (See Figure 23. Page 479)

Interviewed by a 'Ceylon Daily News' reporter at his residence, Mr. Sathasivam said that he would be the happiest man to see the murderer of his wife brought to justice.

"My immediate concern is to see to the welfare and education of my children. I would once again turn my attention to cricket," said Mr. Sathasivam.

It was a strange coincidence that John Reginald Haliday Christie, a self-confessed strangler of seven women, was sentenced to death in Old Bailey Central Criminal Court, London, on the same day Mr. Sathasivam was acquitted. The jury of nine men and three women took one hour and twenty one minutes to reach their verdict. They had rejected his plea of insanity.

CHAPTER 16

IN SEARCH OF WILLIAM - AGAIN

After studying all the available documents on the tragic murder of Mrs. Sathasivam, I was interested in meeting the only person who is alive today who can speak about what happened at No. 7, St. Alban's Place, on that fateful day in October 1951.

I inquired from several prison officials regarding William and some of them told me that he was rearrested subsequent to the Sathasivam murder case for sexual offences and was in prison again. Some said he was released after a while and then he had died.

Then I inquired from a colleague working with me in the University who hails from down south. She said she would ask a lawyer from Matara about William and let me know.

A few days later, I was delighted to hear from this lawyer that William is still alive and living in his own village, and that through a Buddhist Priest in the area he will be able to contact William.

The Buddhist Priest had contacted William and told him to be present in his temple around 1.00 o'clock in the afternoon on full moon day (poya).

In 2003, on a somewhat dark rainy day that reminded me of Glasgow, where I had an opportunity to work in the University, my colleague, the lawyer, the Buddhist Priest and I went to meet William in his own village temple.

We arrived at Angunabadulla, a village in the Thihagoda area after travelling 160 kilometres from Colombo to Matara and a further 8 kilometres down the Matara-Hakmana road towards the interior of the country. A dilapidated tarred road spreading through scenic green paddy fields lead us to Angunabadulla.

As we turned our vehicle to the gravel road leading to the temple, an old man dressed in a white shirt and sarong and carrying an umbrella smiled with the Buddhist Priest.

"That is William," the priest said. (See Figure 24 Page 479)

We sat down in the front room of the Priest's residence and the Priest introduced my colleagues and me to William.

"This doctor is from the University of Colombo and he wants to speak to you about the case you were involved in sometime ago," said the Buddhist Priest.

I told William that I was from the same department as Professor de Saram. Then I explained to him that I had read his evidence in the Sathasivam case and all the other relevant documents and I was quite keen to find out from him what he had to say now.

Without any hesitation William started talking about the murder that happened 52 years ago.

William said he was staying with his elder sister in Colpetty, the town next to Bambalapitiya at that time and his elder brother hit him for coming home late after watching a movie. He left the house and slept one night on the pavement and then he met a lady called Dosihamy who found him the job at Mrs. Sathasivam's. William said he spent about 4 to 5 months in Colombo before this employment.

On the day of the incident William said Mr. Sathasivam came to the kitchen when he was scraping the coconut. He told William that he should agree to what he was going to say and that he will look after him well. Then he held William by the hand and took him upstairs after closing the front door.

William then repeated what he has said in his statements to the Police, the Magistrate's Court and the Supreme Court, that he was an accessory to the murder committed by Mr. Sathasivam.

William said the murder took place between 9.00 and 9.30 a.m. He said he went to buy drumsticks by 9.00 o'clock and about 5 minutes after that Mr. Sathasivam came to the kitchen.

William said Mrs. Sathasivam scratched his face and later his forearm.

"First time when I held Mrs. Sathasivam she kicked me and I fell down! Then I got up and held her legs tightly," he said.

His story about the act of murder was the same as what he said in Court.

"After the body of Mrs. Sathasivam was kept in the garage, Mr. Sathasivam asked me to go to the Fort station and stay there. I agreed. But I quickly went out of the house. On the way I told the children touching their heads that I am going because I felt sorry for the children," William said.

He said he got into the first bus that came to the halt.

The gold chain (thalikodi), that was worth about 1000 rupees at that time had to be sold for 100 rupees because the jeweller told William it was not worth more than that.

I asked William about the presence of dirt on the feet of Mrs. Sathasivam and he said one foot of Mrs. Sathasivam was dragged across the kitchen.

William said he was arrested at about 7.00 a.m. on 19th October by Police Officers who were in civil as well as in uniform.

"The story that he was responsible for killing Mrs. Sathasivam was created extremely well by some Police Officers," William said.

He could still remember the names of the Police Officers who came to arrest him.

"They wanted to save Mr. Sathasivam," William said. "Inspector Wickramarathna told me near the lavatory at the Police Superintendent's office at Matara, that I should say that I killed her and not Mr. Sathasivam. I agreed. Then Mr. Albert de Silva asked Inspector Wickramarathna 'Is everything OK?' and Mr. Wickramarathna replied 'Yes, Sir'" William explained.

William said his statement was recorded in Matara but his signature was not taken. Then he described how he was taken to Colombo via Panadura.

"When we were passing the Bo Tree at Kalutara temple, Mr. Wickramarathna gave me 50 cents to put as a donation for me to get a pardon in the murder case," William said.

William was brought to Modera Police Station around 1.00 o'clock in the morning and he refused to sign the statement he has made earlier. He was kept in custody and he spoke to the reserve Police Officer guarding him, who gave him food to eat and a cup of tea.

The reserve Police Officer asked William whether he was the person who killed Mrs. Sathasivam because that is what he read in William's statement. William told him that he was asked to say that by the Inspector who arrested him.

William said, "Then I told the reserve Police Officer the truth. This officer after getting an assurance that I will not tell anyone, told me that I would be taken before the Inspector-General of Police (IGP) to make a statement and asked me not to say what I have told in the statement."

William said he refused to sign the original statement and in front of the IGP he told him what happened at the Matara Police Station.

"Whenever Mr. Haniffa, a friend of Mr. Sathasivam, came to the house he told me to be obedient to Mr. Sathasivam. I could not understand this earlier but later I thought what Mr. Haniffa hinted at was that I was to help him to murder Mrs. Sathasivam," said William.

William said Mr. Pathmanathan's driver, Ragel, had told him about the behaviour of Mr. Sathasivam and that he was having an affair with an English lady.

William said Mr. Sathasivam had also told him just before the murder that his wife has filed a case against him and that he was having an affair with an English lady.

Referring to the evidence given in the trial, William said that the 'Quickshaws' cab driver lied in court regarding seeing Mrs. Sathasivam at the door when Mr. Sathasivam left.

I asked him about the statement Piyadasa, his fellow prisoner, made stating that he (William) had confessed to the murder in the prison. He said Piyadasa was a suspect in a bombing case at the Wellawatta Spinning and Weaving Mills and his lawyer was Mr. K. C. Nadarajah, a friend of Mr. Sathasivam.

"Mr. Nadarajah was responsible for Piyadasa's statement implicating me in the case," complained William.

After the case William came to his village in 1953 and worked as a cleaner of a lorry for sometime. In 1960, he got married and became a father in 1961. He had seven children and one son died a few years ago after being attacked by a crocodile in the river, when he was picking sand from the riverbed.

I asked William about the story that he spent sometime in prison for certain offences after the Sathasivam murder case.

He said a man calling himself 'William' and stating that he was the person who was involved in the Sathasivam murder case, committed some offences in Padaviya, a village in the North Central Province. The CID issued a statement for the arrest of this 'William' and the Police again visited him at his village!

He was not arrested but he was asked to come to the CID Office in Colombo. He came to Colombo and stayed with his sister and brother. Then he went to the 4th floor of the CID Office. The Police Station in his village (Kamburupitiya) had also sent a report to the CID that William had been living in the village for a long time and never left it.

After the CID recorded his statement, William was released.

He was asked to come again the following day. On that day, the CID had arrested the other 'William'.

To check who was the correct 'William', the arrested man was asked where Mr. Sathasivam's house was and he had said that it was in Wellawatte. Then he was asked how many children they had. He answered 'only one'. Both answers were wrong!

"Then the arrested man was assaulted by the Police," said William. The CID then gave William a railway warrant to travel back to his village.

William said about two years after the case he went to see Mrs. Sathasivam's elder sister. William told her that he was sorry that he could not do anything when Mr. Sathasivam got him to assist him in the murder of her sister.

Finally, I asked William how the Police traced him in 1951.

William said the learned 'guru' priest of the present priest of the village temple, Reverend Wellethota Pannadassi, had given information about him after reading the details of the murder case in the newspapers. William said that the reward of 1000 rupees was paid to the priest (500 rupees) and two other men (250 rupees each). One of them also became a Buddhist priest. Later he became famous as the chief incumbent priest of the Dimbulagala Temple, Reverend Kithalagama Seelalankara.

It is regrettable that the elder priest of the village temple, Reverend Pannadassi, who was involved in social service and non-partisan political activities, was killed by the activists of the Marxist-oriented Peoples' Liberation Front (Janatha Vimukthi Peramuna) in 1989. The much loved and respected Dimbulagala priest, who was similarly active in social service, was killed by the Liberation Tigers of Tamil Eelam (LTTE) in 1996.

CHAPTER 17

POSTSCRIPT

After spending 625 days in the remand prison, Mr. Mahadeva Sathasivam became a free man again on June 25th 1953.

Two months after his release, Mr. Sathasivam went to England. There he married his lover, 35-year-old Dutch-born Yvonne Sacha Kinzler (Stevenson) in August 1953, at the Kensington Registry in London.

Only one Ceylonese, an army officer, was present at the Registry. There were five others, including Yvonne's parents. After the ceremony, the couple and the guests celebrated with a drink at a nearby pub.

Mr. Sathasivam and Yvonne returned to Ceylon thereafter. They were blessed with three children and Mr. Sathasivam's all seven children grew up together in Ceylon.

Mr. Sathasivam played cricket on and off in England, as well as in Ceylon.

Keith Miller, one of the best all-rounders produced by Australia, and a test captain visited Ceylon with Don Bradman's 'Invincibles' in 1948 and became friendly with Sathasivam. When Lindsay Hasset's Australian test team was travelling to England with Keith Miller they visited Ceylon again in 1953. Mahadeva Sathasivam was such a popular cricketer, Keith Miller went to the remand prison on 30th March to see him.

It was rumoured that Frank Worrell, a former West Indian cricket captain and later Sir Frank Worrell, had sent a cable to Mr. Sathasivam to hire the best lawyers for his case and he would pay the fees.

In 1953, Mr. Sathasivam scored 153 not out for a Ceylonese team against the Indian Gymkhana Club in England. His best and the last century in the Island was in 1955, when he scored 206 not out for the 'Rest' team against the Government Services team in a tournament at the Nondescript Cricket Club (NCC) grounds in Colombo.

Mr. Sathasivam migrated to Malaysia in 1958. In 1959, the legendary 'Satha', as he was affectionately known, had the unique distinction of captaining two countries in cricket.

He captained Malaysia, when an All-Malaysian team played against the legendary Don Bradman's Australians in Singapore. This was the first and perhaps the only occasion that any cricketer has led two countries at cricket. Even in Malaysia, playing for Selangor, Mr. Sathasivam scored 106 runs.

In 1971, Sathasivam was made an Honorary Member of the Marylebone Cricket Club (MCC) for his unstinted services and devotion to cricket. This is a crowning glory for any international cricketer.

Ceylon, now Sri Lanka, continued to produce excellent cricketers like Sathasivam. It was joy, happiness and euphoria for all Sri Lankans wherever they lived when they won the Cricket World Cup in 1996.

They have come a long way since 1948, when the Lion Flag was hoisted over the Island. When the great Don Bradman's Australian team played in Ceylon, the pitch was found to be embarrassingly some two feet short! It was a big laugh for the Australians.

In the final of the World Cup on that memorable night of 17th March 1996 at Lahore, it was the Australians that Sri Lanka trounced by 7 wickets!

Mahadeva Sathasivam, one of the finest cricketers ever produced by Ceylon, passed away in July 1977, after suffering a heart attack, at the age of 61 years.

"A glorious innings declared closed," reported the Ceylon Daily News.

I had an opportunity to meet the only daughter of the Mr. and Mrs. Sathasivam living in Sri Lanka. She told me that all family members firmly believed that Mr. Sathasivam did not kill her mother.

"He was a gentle person. He could not have killed anyone. He did not do it," she assured me.

Sir Sydney Smith, CBE, Emeritus Professor of Forensic Medicine and Rector of the University of Edinburgh from 1954 to 1957 died on 8th May 1969 at the age of 85. He served the General Medical Council of the United Kingdom, the authoritative body that regulates the medical profession and maintains high standards for doctors, from 1931 to 1956.

Sir Sydney's well-known textbook "Forensic Medicine" passed through many editions by his own pen between 1925 and 1960. He also edited the two volumes of the classic textbook, "Taylor's Principles and Practice of Forensic Medicine", between 1928 to 1956.

Professor Keith Simpson, the then Professor of Forensic Medicine at Guy's Hospital, London, writing the obituary of Sir Sydney said, "He enjoyed an international reputation as a medico-legal expert, and as a writer and editor of standard treatises on medical jurisprudence."

"The remarkable galaxy of forensic figures in the Scottish firmament has never had a brighter star than Sydney Smith. He was a man who had a breadth of vision, remarkable talents and the industry that endears anyone to the Scots. He had two fundamental assets in personal relationships that undoubtedly carried him far - the first was obvious sincerity and a hearty dislike of humbug; the other a plain desire to achieve some accord with his colleagues that meant skill in negotiation."

"Sydney Smith's fire and determination may have stemmed from New Zealand fibre," Professor Simpson wrote. "His relatively short period of service with the Egyptian Government as its principal medico-legal examiner showed him to have the skill, perceptive eye and honesty of purpose that could not fail to make their mark in the forensic field. In a few short years he had become the figure that Edinburgh took him to be capable of, when inviting him to take the Chair in Medical Jurisprudence. Any one who has either read his memoirs, "Mostly Murder" or seen his Cairo Museum will accord him this early repute. He was a good observer, wrote well and timed his comments; overburdened with administration at which he excelled, he had little time for original work, but thought and taught with clarity."

The Crown called Sir Sydney many times to assist murder investigations. One important case was, the killing of the wife and a young nursemaid by Dr. Buck Ruxton, who then dismembered them and dispersed the remains. Some of which were found in a ravine. Professor Keith Simpson in his obituary mentioned the other important cases Sir Sydney was associated with.

"Scotland had never enough medico-legal work for a man of his appetite, and it needed cases like Fox, opposition like Roche Lynch in the Hearn arsenic case, the stimulus of a Birkett or a public wrangle like that in the Sathasivam case in Ceylon to bring out the best in this colourful actor. It was fatal to underestimate him for though an opportunist, he was sound and had courage under forensic fire. Opposition did not cow him; he thrived on it. He was not made a great public figure as Spilsbury was; his repute was greater, for it lay with his colleagues."

Professor G.S.W. de Saram, OBE, MBBS (London), MRCS (England) LRCP (London), LMS (Ceylon), became famous in Ceylon, and perhaps among the forensic fraternity all over the world, because of the Sathasivam case.

As this case to a great extent rested on determining the time of death of Mrs. Sathasivam, and particularly whether this event occurred before or after 10.30 a.m. on 9th October 1951, Professor de Saram performed experiments on executed prisoners on the advice of Professor Sydney Smith.

His experiments were published in reputed international forensic journals and received worldwide attention. His articles were quoted in almost all forensic textbooks published subsequently. As a Sri Lankan, it is extremely heartening to me to hear experts at international forensic meetings and educational courses mention Professor de Saram's name whenever the complex problem of the determination of the time of death is discussed.

On 2nd June, the Coronation Day in Great Britain, Professor de Saram sent the following letter to Professor Sydney Smith, expressing his appreciation for the assistance and advice given to him. He also indicated his displeasure about the events surrounding the case.

"Coronation Day 1953

My dear Sir Sydney,

This is to thank you for all your interest in our laboratory and the very good advice you have given us. Webster in particular has been very heartened by your good opinion of the work he has done for the Department of Forensic Medicine.

May I also say how encouraged I have been by the opinion you have given in Court of the various aspects of the Sathasivam case? That you with your experience should have corroborated so much of my evidence has greatly heartened me. But that you did come out to Ceylon has greatly impressed me.

For I had begun to feel depressed at the way the case had been conducted from the very start; and I had begun to feel that my effort would never be sufficient to establish all that democratic justice stands for.

I shall, therefore, look forward with no small interest to your promised visit to this country later in the year.

We have all been listening in to the coronation service and cannot but realise the great traditions of Equity and Justice the British Crown stands for.

We do hope you had an uneventful journey back. Please remember me to Lady Smith, the Fiddes and Kaye.

Yours very sincerely,

G.S.W. de Saram"

"P.S. Since writing the above, I have heard that the post of Judicial Medical Officer (J.M.O.) Colombo is to be filled and that applications from members of the Ceylon Medical Department have been called for. I have no doubt that Dr. Fernando who is training under you has had intimation of this. The post, which was vacated by me in 1951, has been held by an acting officer up to now. He had worked as Sinnadurai's assistant and had acted as J.M.O. while I was under training. You will remember him as one of those who were assisting the Crown in the

Sathasivam Case and I understand was present in Court during your evidence."

In fact Professor de Saram's reason for depression is quite clear. According to the records kept in the Department of Forensic Medicine, University of Colombo, after joining as the first Professor of Forensic Medicine, he did his first autopsy on 23rd March 1951.

Mrs. Sathasivam's autopsy, performed on 9th October, was his tenth. He did three more autopsies till 22nd November 1951. After that, he was not requested to perform any autopsies by the Police until 3rd March 1953!

'Dr. Fernando', mentioned in Professor de Saram's letter above, was Dr. W.D.L. Fernando who was appointed as the Judicial Medical Officer, Colombo, in 1953.

Dr. Fernando was a popular and distinguished medical professional. He, like Professors Paul and Peiris, later elected to the post of the President of Sri Lanka Medical Association.

Dr. Fernando served the office of the Judicial Medical Officer with distinction, honesty and integrity and retired in 1971. He passed away in 1978.

Forensic pathologists are almost always advised and reminded not to be concerned about the outcome of a case where he gives evidence or expresses an opinion. It is sometimes difficult. There was no doubt that Professor de Saram might have been happy that the jury accepted his opinion and acquitted Mr. Sathasivam.

The letter he wrote to Professor Sydney Smith on 26th June, the day after the 'Not guilty' verdict was given in the Sathasivam murder trial is quoted below for you to form your own opinion about Professor de Saram's feelings.

"My dear Sir Sydney,

Your letter of the 22nd instant has just reached me. I shall certainly make inquiries about a suitable place for you to stay at while you are in Colombo. I shall let you know in due course so that you could make your choice of such places that we consider will be suitable and convenient to you. I believe you that you would be here for about 6-9 months.

I am so sorry to hear that Fiddes is not to succeed you, but I am sure the future holds much for him.

The Sathasivam case ended last evening with a unanimous acquittal. An appeal by the defence that the jury should bring in a rider, if the jury found the accused 'Not guilty', to the effect that the accused was innocent, was turned down by the judge, who said that 'Even if they were convinced of the innocence of the accused, in the interests of justice they should refrain from doing so, for a rider of that nature involved a preconceived conviction of William who was not on trial, nor represented by counsel.'

Four of the prosecution witnesses - the jewellers who had participated in the purchase of the jewellery etc. - were called up by the Judge later as they had 'Palpably given false evidence on a matter of vital importance (the time of the transaction) affecting the guilt or otherwise of the accused'. All four witnesses begged for pardon on the grounds that they had never been to court before and had given false evidence through ignorance. Three of them were sentenced to 2 months rigorous imprisonment each and one was discharged with a warning.

I understand the judge made scathing criticisms of the methods adopted by the Police. And he gave every weight to your evidence.

I am so glad it is all over. And the result will, I'm sure, give you every satisfaction in view of the great inconveniences you underwent to get here and back in so short a time especially with the busy time you had ahead of you with the coronation.

I reiterate my own gratitude and as I say look forward with eagerness to your arrival here in September.

I shall now make tentative arrangements for your visit to the ruined cities of Ceylon and to our National Game Parks. We also hope that you will spend Christmas with us up in the hills in the house which now is being built and should be complete by then.

You have not mentioned Lady Smith at all. I presume, therefore, that she will not be accompanying you. She will, of course, be very welcome if she intends accompanying you."

This letter showed how relieved and perhaps happy Professor de Saram was after the acquittal of Mr. Sathasivam.

In 1957, Professor de Saram published an article in the Journal of Forensic Medicine, a prestigious international forensic medicine journal on the Sathasivam murder case, titled, "The Medical Aspects of a Case of Manual Strangulation". I quote below a paragraph from this article.

"Estimation of Time of Death from All the Factors: Of the medical opinion called by the Prosecution, Dr. Taylor (who gave evidence in the lower court) was of the opinion that death would have taken place between 5.30 a.m. and 10 a.m. One of the surgeons placed it between 7.25 a.m. and 10.19 a.m. and the other between 7.42 a.m. and 11.30 a.m. The deceased, however, was reading the morning papers, not having had her morning meal, at 8.15 a.m. Therefore, as was stated by the trial judge, relating these views to the facts, the opinion of these medical men was that death may have taken place any time between 8.15 a.m. and 11.30 a.m. None of them, however, stated that it must have taken place before 9.30 a.m."

Some aspects of the personality of Professor de Saram could be understood from the answers he gave Mr. T.S. Fernando, the Acting Solicitor-General during the cross-examination on his experiments on the time of death and passage of food in cases of the victims of judicial hangings.

Mr. Fernando asked, "You may have been present at a judicial hanging?"

"No, I have never been and I don't want to be," replied Professor de Saram.

"Up to this you don't know what happens?"

"I don't want to be there."

"As Professor of Forensic Medicine you say you don't want to know?"

"What I mean is I don't want to be there. I don't want to see these people being hanged," replied Professor de Saram.

Clearly, Professor de Saram did not want to be a witness to the gruesome events of judicial hangings where an asphyxiating person has terminal convulsions. Perhaps he was against judicial hanging as a form of punishment.

It is relevant to mention that four years later, Hon. S. W. R. D. Bandaranaike, who was elected the Prime Minister (in 1956), abolished the death penalty temporarily in the Island. It is strange that after the assassination of Mr. Bandaranaike in 1959, the new government re-enacted the death penalty in Sri Lanka and the assassin of the Prime Minister was executed by hanging!

Although the law is still in the statute book, no person was hanged since 1976. The new leader elected at the 1977 General Elections, Mr. J. R. Jayewardena, and all Presidents elected thereafter, continued to give Presidential pardons to those who were to be executed, and commuted the death sentence to life imprisonment.

If Mr. Mahadeva Sathasivam was convicted for his wife's murder he would have been executed.

Professor de Saram continued the study he started with executed prisoners even after the Sathasivam murder case was concluded.

In 1957, he published an excellent scientific article titled "Estimation of the Time of Death by Medical Criteria" in the Journal of Forensic Medicine where he documented experiments on the bodies of 41 condemned prisoners, who were judicially executed.

Professor de Saram retired from the University of Colombo in 1958. Dr. Sextus Corea writing in "The Colombo Centenary 1870 - 1970" said, "Though Professor de Saram inspired awe among the students, he was capable of putting their subject across with great clarity and ease."

Professor de Saram's junior colleague, Dr. H.V.J. Fernando, who had his training with the world renowned forensic pathologist Professor Keith Simpson at the prestigious Guy's Hospital, London, succeeded him in 1958.

This book would not have been written if Professor H.V.J. Fernando had not selected me as a lecturer in his Department in 1977, and arranged my postgraduate training at the same Guy's Hospital with Professor Keith Mant, another forensic pathologist of international repute, who succeeded Professor Keith Simpson.

The two eminent surgeons who gave evidence, Professor Milroy Paul and Professor M.V.P. Peiris were giants who bestrode in the medical profession in Ceylon. As mentioned earlier, both served as Professors of Surgery in one of the oldest medical schools in Australasia, the present Faculty of Medicine of the University of

Colombo, established in 1870.

Both have been Presidents of the Ceylon Medical Association (CMA), the oldest professional medical association in Australasia. The CMA was started in 1887 as a branch of the British Medical Association and is now known as the Sri Lanka Medical Association (SLMA). This is the apex professional body of all the doctors in Sri Lanka.

Professor Paul was also elected as a President of the Medico-Legal Society.

Professor Peiris was appointed to the Senate and held the post of a cabinet minister for a short period. Later he served as the Ambassador to the Soviet Union.

The Judge who heard the Sathasivam case, Edward Frederick Noel Gratiaen, a King's Counsel, was born on 30th December 1904.

He was an outgoing, towering six foot four inch, 113 kilo gramme (250-pound) rugby player who represented the Ceylonese Rugby and Football Club (CR & FC), a popular club started in 1922, and All Ceylon. Mr. C. V. Wickramanayake, in an article published in the "Island" newspaper commented, "In the forward line, he stood out, not merely because of his size, but because of his prowess. The tiny little rugger ball, tucked under his arm, he would bulldoze his way to the touchline."

He had a Bachelor of Arts degree from the Oxford University. He enjoyed a large practice at the Bar and was conferred the dignity of silk in 1946.

In 1948 when Ceylon received Independence from the British, he was nominated as an Appointed Member to Parliament, representing his community, the Burghers.

Since they were appointed by the government in power, Appointed Members are usually expected to toe the Government line.

But not Noel Gratiaen. He was honest and spoke out fearlessly whenever the occasion demanded. It is said that the government at the time found that he was a thorn in their side!

They could not remove him from Parliament simply for that reason.

So Gratiaen was elevated to the Supreme Court Bench!

In 1952, he received the honour of being made a Companion of the Order of St. Michael and St. George (CMG).

His friend and relation, Aubrey Collette, the finest cartoonist Ceylon had produced, drew a cartoon depicting a classroom with the teacher, Prime Minister Hon. D. S. Senanayake, telling a big fat boy "Get on the Bench". In the cartoon the fat boy with Gratiaen's face, grinning like a Cheshire cat, was seen climbing his chair to stand on his desk. This cartoon, in the original, later adorned the Chambers of Justice Gratiaen in Hulftsdorp.

On May 2nd 1956, he relinquished his office as a Puisne Justice to accept his appointment as the Attorney-General of the new Government led by his friend, Prime Minister Hon. S.W.R.D. Bandaranaike. After two years, he left the country to practise before the Privy Council in London with huge success until he died in 1971.

Hon. Lakshman Kadirgamar, the former Foreign Minister of Sri Lanka, was a private secretary to Justice Gratiaen. He has said that Justice Gratiaen's judgments were lucid, elegant and masterly in every branch of law, and justice was safe in his hands.

Mr. Wickramanayake says in his article that, "Apart from his skill as an advocate, his Solomon – like wisdom as a Judge of the Supreme Court, and his immense popularity with everyone with whom he came in contact, Gratiaen made an even greater contribution to his motherland, when he headed the Gratiaen Commission on prison reform. Pity we do not have men of his calibre today."

When Mr. H. N. G. Fernando was sworn in as the new Chief Justice in 1966, he referred to what he had learnt from Justice Gratiaen about the art of judging.

"An attentive and receptive ear, a mind open to conviction, a readiness to acknowledge error and a will resolved to do justice regardless of personal motives or prejudices."

The Acting Solicitor-General Mr T.S. Fernando obtained a Bachelor of Laws degree from University College London and was called to the Bar from Lincoln's Inn in 1931. He joined the Attorney-General's Department as a Crown Counsel in 1936 and was appointed Solicitor-General in 1953. In 1954, when Mr. H.H. Basnayake replaced Sir Alan Rose as Chief Justice, he succeeded Mr. Basnayake as the Acting Attorney-General.

He took 'silk' in 1953. In 1955, Her Majesty the Queen conferred on him the rank of Commander of the Order of the British Empire (CBE).

On 2nd May 1956, the day after Justice Gratiaen became the Attorney-General, Mr. Fernando was appointed a Judge of the Supreme Court. He acted as Chief Justice on several occasions. He retired in 1968, but was recalled from retirement in 1971 to be the President of the short-lived Court of Appeal, which was established as the highest Court of Appeal after the abolition of appeals to the Privy Council.

After his retirement from the bench, Mr Fernando served as President of the International Commission of Jurists and as High Commissioner for Sri Lanka in Australia.

Colvin Reginald de Silva, the versatile defence counsel, was born in Balapitiya, a town in southern Sri Lanka. (See Figure 25. Page 479)

Young Colvin entered the University College in Colombo and obtained his Bachelor of Arts degree as an external student of the University of London. He then proceeded to King's College, London, where he was adjudged the best student of the academic year 1927-28. He was an outstanding scholar and his treatise "Ceylon Under the British Occupation 1795 – 1833" yet remains one of the best accounts of the political and economic development of that period.

Dr. de Silva returned to Ceylon in 1932 having obtained the degrees of Bachelor of Arts and Doctor of Philosophy from the University of London and after having been called to the Bar by Lincoln's Inn in 1931.

He enrolled as an Advocate of the Supreme Court in1932 and since then he appeared in practically every primary court, whether civil or criminal, in the country. He had a penetrating and analytical mind and it is not an exaggeration to say that many an accused was saved from the hangman's noose as a result of his formidable skills as a tactician.

Dr. de Silva played a major role in the country's politics in the days of the struggle for national independence from the British in 1930s and 1940s, representing a Marxist political party.

The British rulers were after him and other party activists. His arrest and detention did not come to him as a surprise, although it came to him at an unexpected time and place. He was arrested in Court just after he concluded a case!

While saving many a suspect accused of murder from ultimate punishment, his interest in politics continued and he eventually became a member of the cabinet in 1970.

Dr. de Silva is considered the "father" of the First Republican Constitution. As the Minister of Constitutional Affairs, Dr. de Silva drafted this Constitution, which changed the name of the country from 'Ceylon' to 'Sri Lanka', in 1972.

In the mid-eighties I had an opportunity to discuss the Sathasivam murder case with Dr. de Silva just after he delivered an interesting lecture on 'Circumstantial evidence' for the Medico-Legal Society of Sri Lanka, at the Anatomy Lecture Theatre of the Faculty of Medicine, Colombo.

He was convinced that Mr. Sathasivam did not strangle his wife. In his inimitable style, Dr. de Silva demonstrated to me how William described in Court the way he held Mrs. Sathasivam, while her husband was strangling and how William said he got his injuries on his face and forearm.

"It was not possible to get those injuries on William from the way he described how Mrs. Sathasivam was strangled," he said emphatically.

Dr. Colvin R. de Silva was an outstanding statesman and a great lawyer the country produced. He passed away on 27th February 1989.

FIGURES

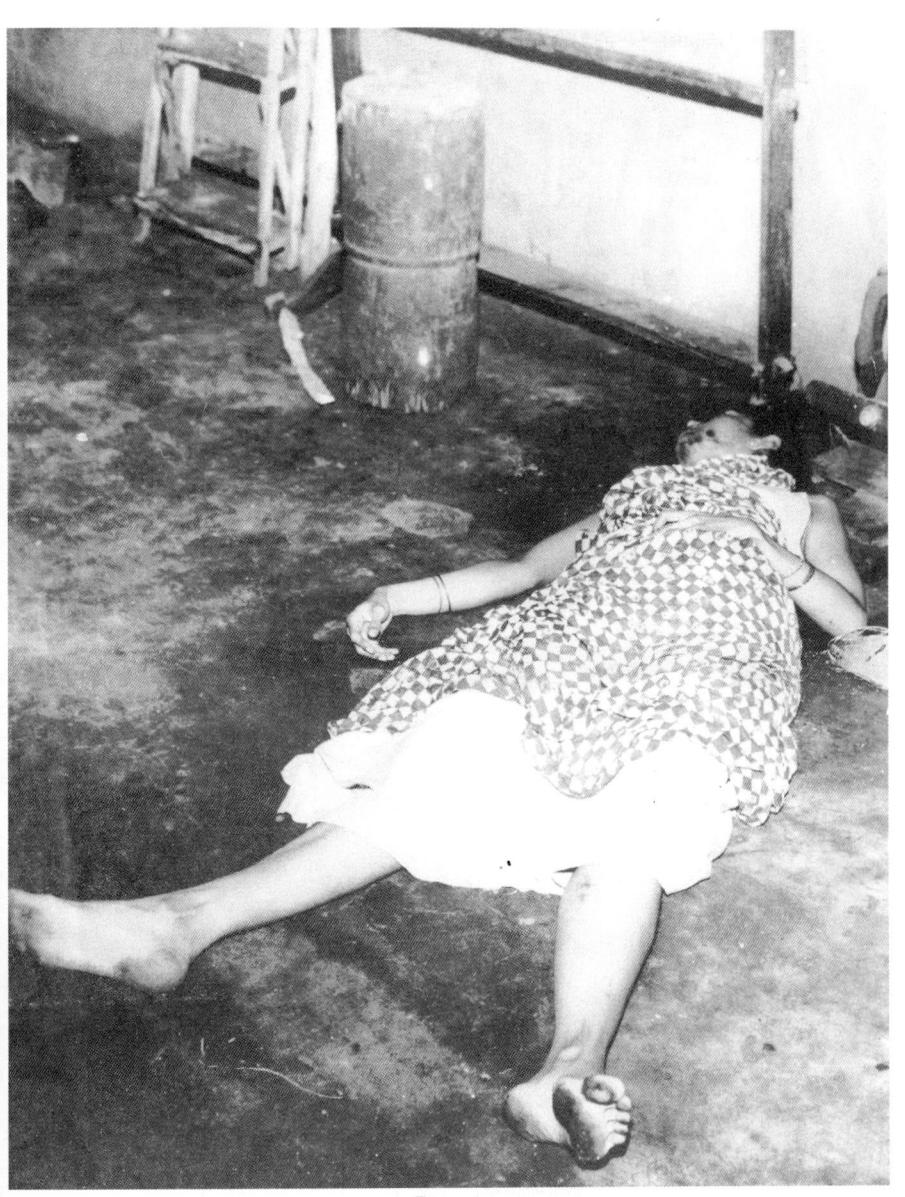

Figure 1
The scene of Mrs. Sathasivam's death. The mortar and the billet of firewood are seen to the right of the body

Figure 2
Miss Yvonne Stevenson

Figure 3
Professor G.S.W. de Saram

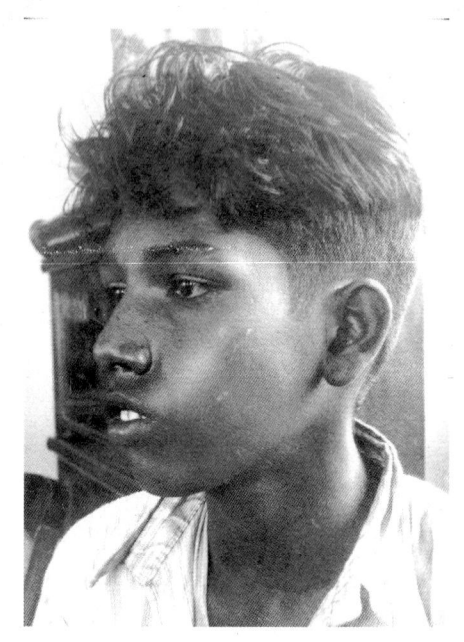

Figure 4
William's face showing healing injuries

Figure 5
Justice E. F. N. Gratiaen

Figure 6
Mr. T. S. Fernando

Figure 7
Coconut scraper.
Reproduced from
Professor G.S.W.
de Saram's article
titled "Medical
Aspects of a
Case of Manual
Strangulation",
published in
the "Journal of
Forensic Science"
in 1957

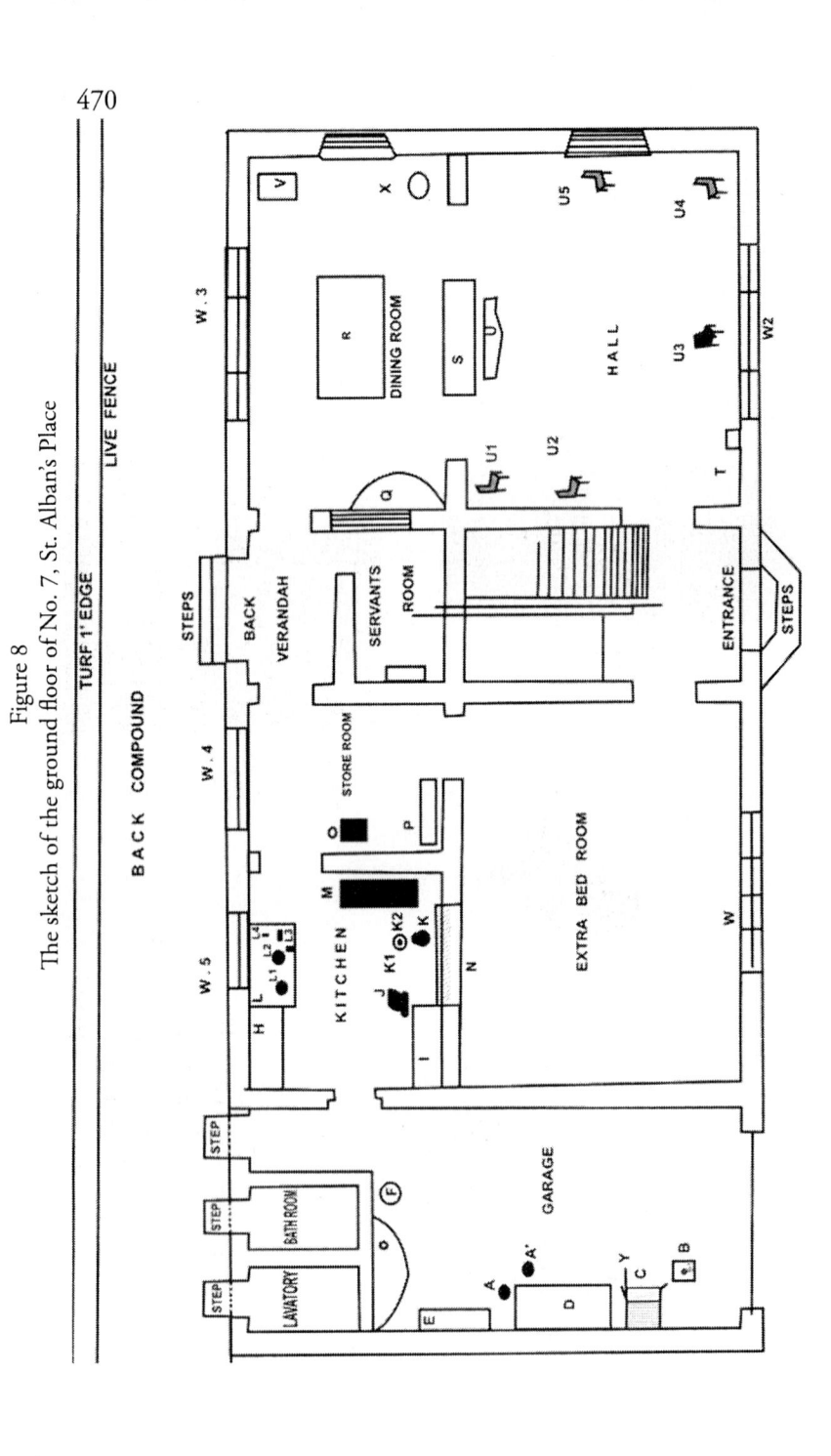

Figure 8
The sketch of the ground floor of No. 7, St. Alban's Place

A- Position of head of Mrs. Sathasivam's body and legs pointing west.
A1- Position of Mortar found across neck of Mrs. Sathasivam.
B- Stool with hand mirror said to belong to Mrs. Sathasivam.
C- Wooden step ladder.
D- Old clothes horse.
E- Old rocking horse.
F- Broken chair.
G- Half table under which were stacked coconut husks.
H- Kitchen sink.
I- Small table for plates etc.
J- Grinding stone and roller.
K- Coconut scraper
K1- Chatty under scraper.
K2- Half coconut just scraped once.

L- Kitchen table proper.
L1- Chatty with cut ash plantain.
L2- Chatty with cut drumsticks.
L3- Dextrosol tin with curry stuff.
L4- Kichen knife.
M- Dover stove with water tank.
N- Kitchen cupboard with doors.
O- Gas stove.
P- Cupboard
Q- Half table.
R- Dining table.
S- Whatnot.
T- Telephone of Mr. Sathasivam's mother.
U- Settee with chairs U1-U5.
V- Refrigerator.
W- Windows.
X- Circular table.
Y- Fire wood.

Figure 9
The scene of Mrs. Sathasivam's death. The mortar is seen on her right and the coconut husks are on her left. The entrance to the garage is seen on the right hand corner.

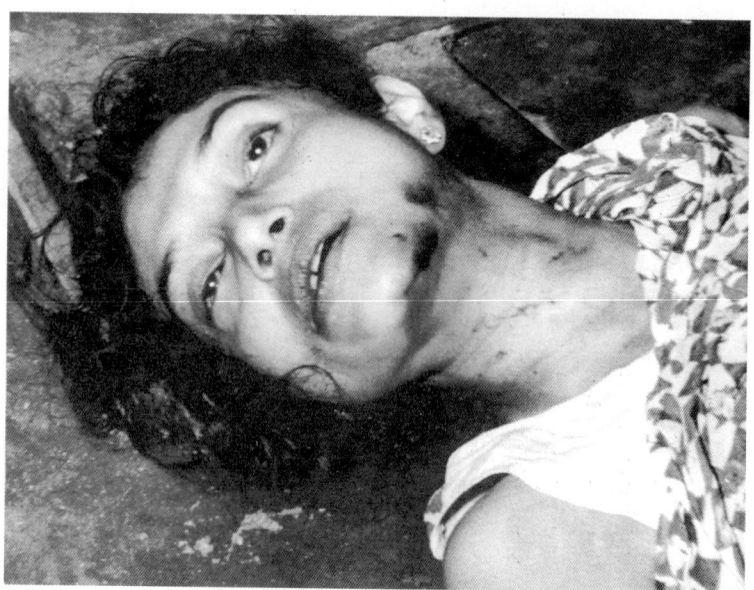

Figure 10
The face and neck of Mrs. Sathasivam showing injuries

473

Figure 11
Neck injuries (nail marks) on Mrs. Sathasivam. Reproduced from an original drawing of Professor G.S.W. de Saram

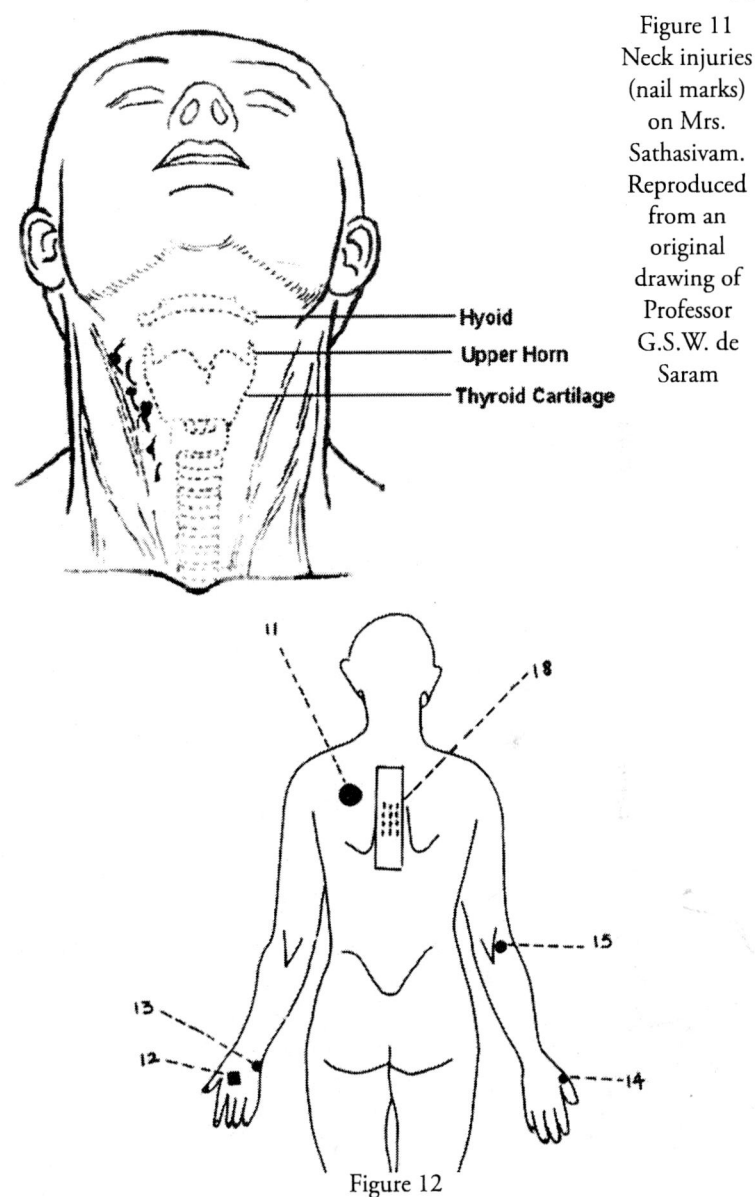

Figure 12
Diagram of the injuries on Mrs. Sathasivam's back. Reproduced from an original drawing by Professor G.S.W. de Saram

474

Figure 13
Diagram of the injuries on right leg of Mrs. Sathasivam. Reproduced from an original drawing by Professor G.S.W. de Saram

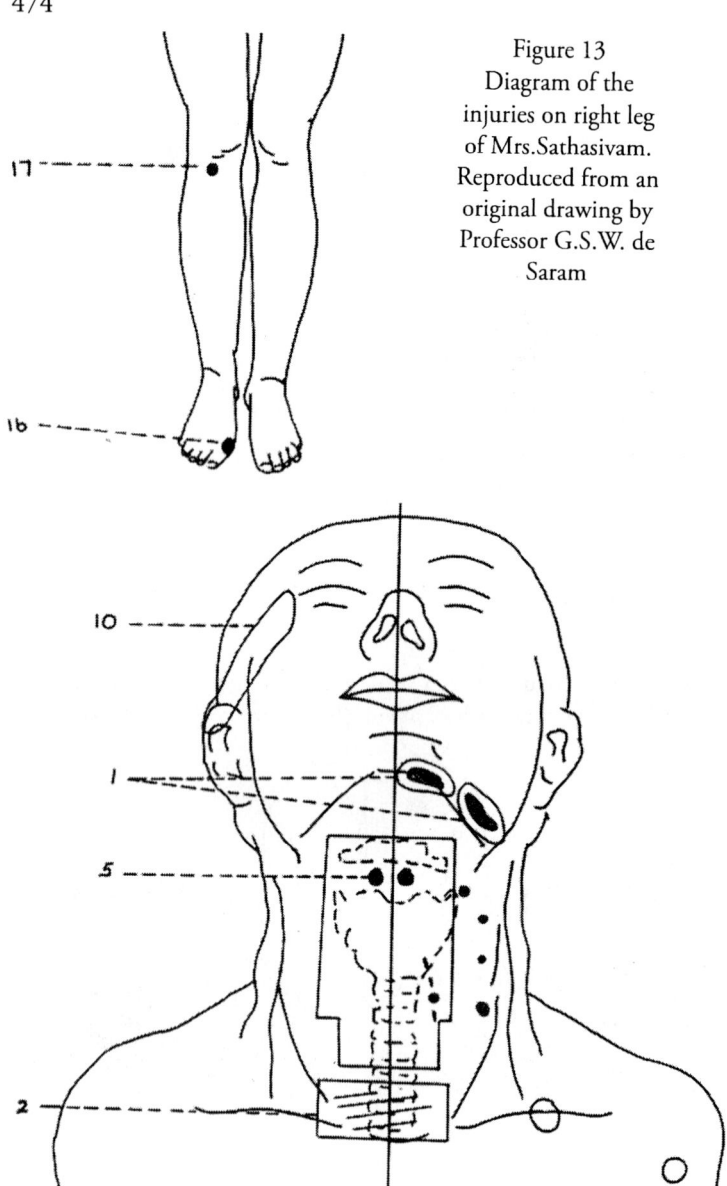

Figure 14
Internal injuries of Mrs. Sathasivam, reproduced from a diagram drawn by Professor G. S. W. de Saram

TONGUE

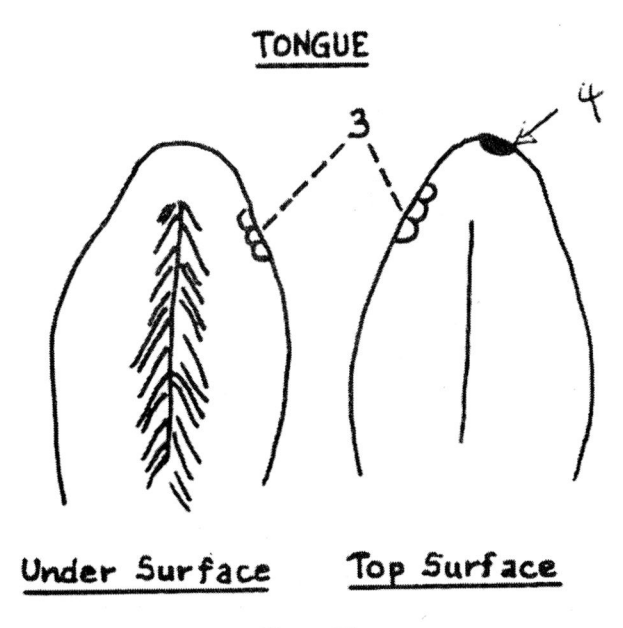

Under Surface   Top Surface

Figure 15
Diagram of the tongue of Mrs. Sathasivam showing injuries No. 3 and 4.
Reproduced from an original drawing of Professor G.S.W. de Saram

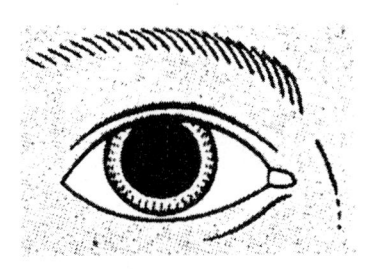

Figure 16
Diagram of a human eye with dilated pupil

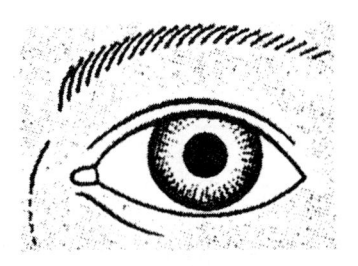

Figure 17
Diagram of a human eye with normal pupil

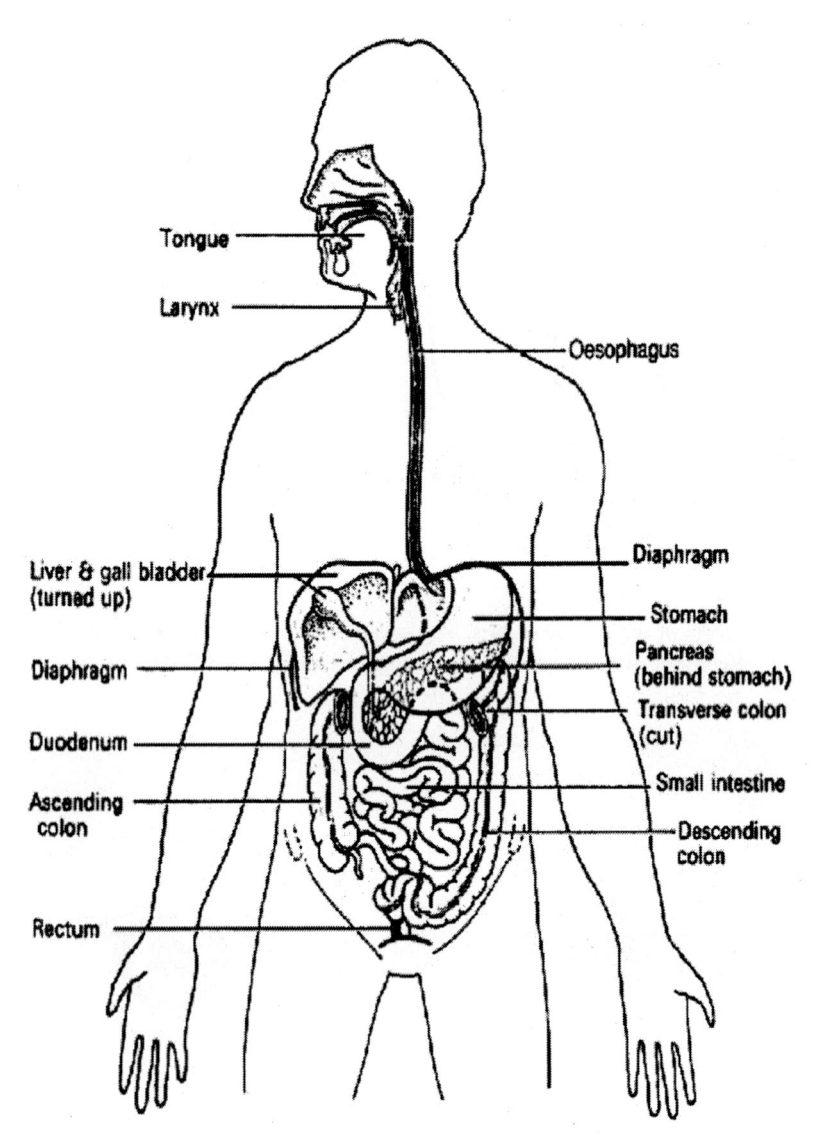

Figure 18
Diagram of the gastrointestinal tract

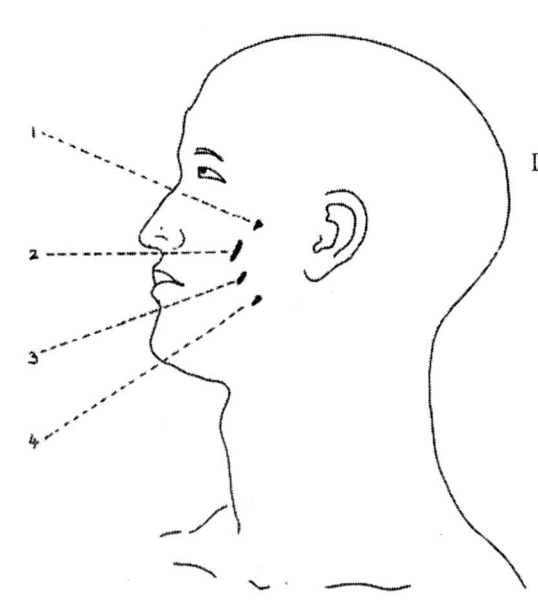

Figure 19
Diagram of the injuries on William's face. Reproduced from a diagram drawn by Professor G.S.W. de Saram

Figure 20
Diagram of the injuries on William's hand. Reproduced from a diagram drawn by Professor G.S.W. de Saram

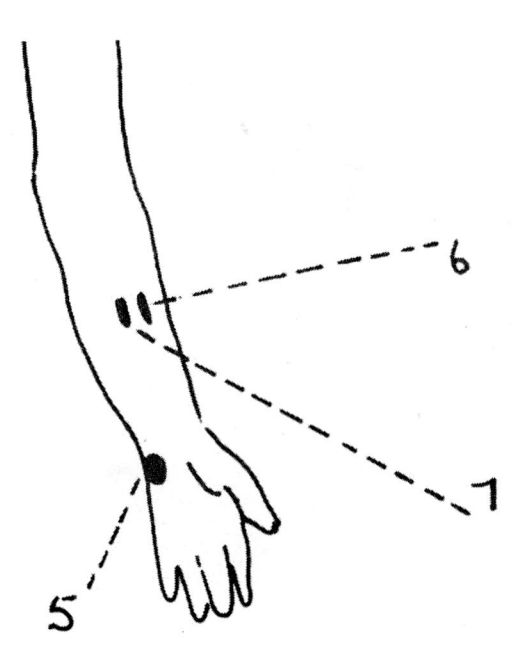

Figure 21.
Professor G.S.W. de Saram's opinion as to how William strangled Mrs. Sathasivam. Reproduced from Prof. G.S.W. de Saram's article titled "Medical Aspects of a Case of Manual Strangulation", published in the "Journal of Forensic Science" in 1957.

Figure 22
Sir Sydney Smith on his arrival in Colombo with Dr. Colvin R. de Silva's daughter, Miss Manouri de Silva (Mrs. Muttetuwegama) and Advocate Mr. K. C. Nadarajah

479

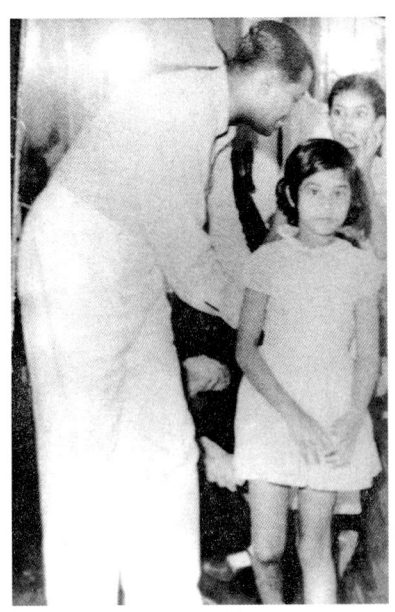

Figure 23
Mr. Sathasivam reunited with his children after spending 625 days in remand prison.

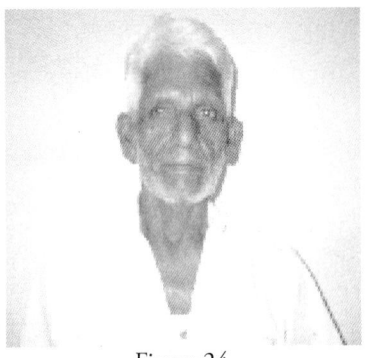

Figure 24
Photograph of William taken in 2003

Figure 25
Mr. Sathasivam (in white suit), with his counsel Dr. Colvin R de Silva on his left and Mr. T.W. Rajaratnam on his right, after the verdict.

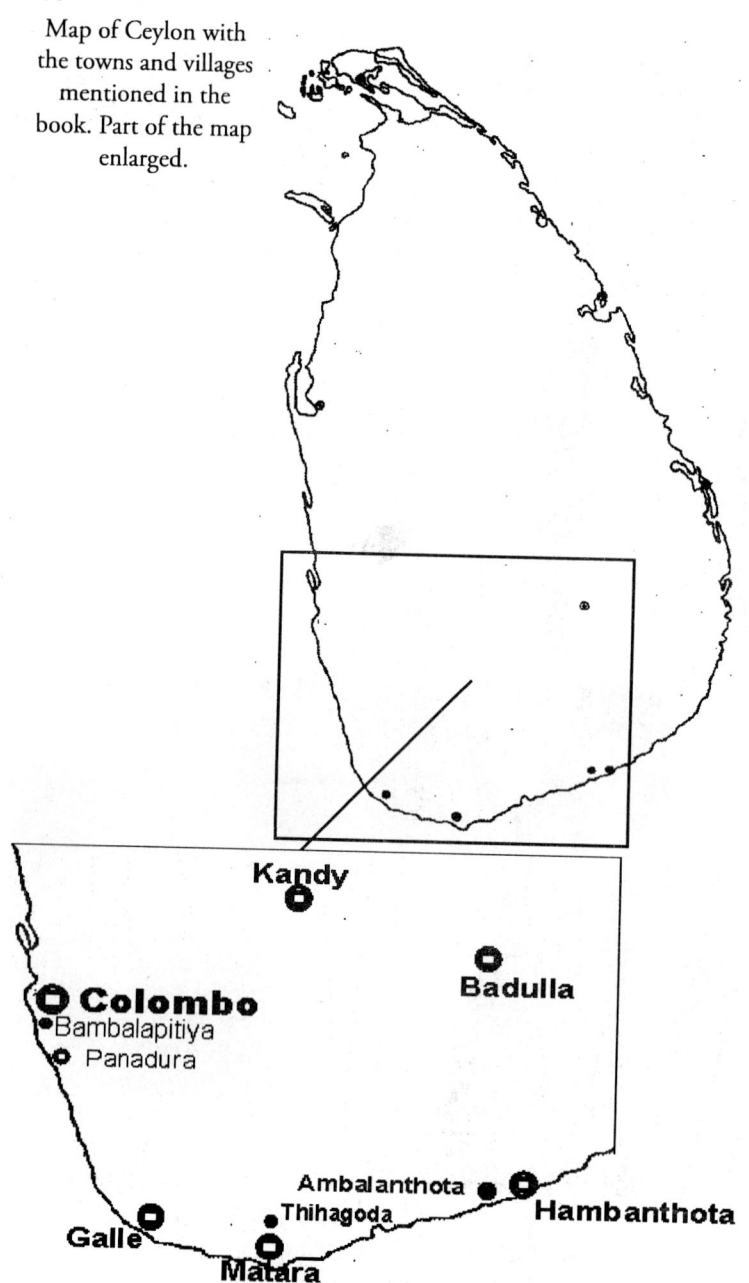

Map of Ceylon with the towns and villages mentioned in the book. Part of the map enlarged.

Kandy

Colombo
Bambalapitiya
Panadura

Badulla

Ambalanthota
Thihagoda
Hambanthota
Galle
Matara